Domesticating
Brown

ANIMA: Critical Race Studies Otherwise
A series edited by Mel Y. Chen, Ezekiel J. Dixon-Román, and Jasbir K. Puar

Domesticating Brown

*Movements of
Racial Imagination*

CHRISTOPHER B.
PATTERSON

Duke University Press *Durham and London* 2026

Project Editor: Bird Williams
Designed by Courtney Leigh Richardson
Typeset in Garamond Premier Pro by
Westchester Publishing Services

Library of Congress Cataloging-in-Publication Data
Names: Patterson, Christopher B. author
Title: Domesticating Brown : movements of racial imagination /
Christopher B. Patterson.
Other titles: ANIMA (Duke University Press)
Description: Durham : Duke University Press, 2026. | Series:
Anima: critical race studies otherwise | Includes bibliographical
references and index.
Identifiers: LCCN 2025028351 (print)
LCCN 2025028352 (ebook)
ISBN 9781478032892 paperback
ISBN 9781478029465 hardcover
ISBN 9781478061656 ebook
Subjects: LCSH: Race discrimination—Southeast Asia—
History | Human skin color—Social aspects—Southeast Asia
| Race—Economic aspects | Colorism—Southeast Asia |
Imperialism | Capitalism—Social aspects | Southeast Asia—
Race relations—History | Southeast Asia—Colonization
Classification: LCC DS523.3 .P388 2026 (print) |
LCC DS523.3 (ebook) | DDC 305.80095—dcundefined
LC record available at https://lccn.loc.gov/2025028351
LC ebook record available at https://lccn.loc.gov/2025028352

Cover art: Members of the author's family pictured in
Luis V. Teodoro, ed., *Out of This Struggle* (1981). Painting
overlay courtesy Adobe stock/tofutyklein.

TURN:

Deadication

This book is ac/knowledge/ment

                    dedications to the dead

moving through   worlds

                of mothers, lovers, and friends

Contents

Acknowledgments

I am writing this on May 9, 2024, from the Professors for Palestine tent at the People's University for Gaza encampment within the University of British Columbia, my current home institution. Currently, a genocidal bombing campaign led by the state of Israel and supported by the United States and its allies has ended the lives of over 34,900 people in Gaza and injured over 78,000 others. I write from a university occupation, aware that every major university in Gaza has been decimated by bombs. I eat from the people's kitchen, knowing that all humanitarian aid has been cut off at the Rafah-Egypt border, intensifying the starvation and famine of over two million people.

I am writing this on day eleven of this encampment, which I have been present at and active within since day one. I am writing this while receiving constant phone *bings* from fellow organizers, letter writers, and safety rangers. I am writing this just after editing text for a teach-in, the third I plan to give here. I write this on an iPhone notepad titled "Kent State," the moniker I use to camouflage notes on direct actions and teach-in programming, a name that reminds me of the students who were massacred by the US military while speaking against the secret aerial bombing of a neutral country—Cambodia—which resulted in the deaths of thousands and a genocide that would kill millions.

"What would our world be like," I asked the students on day six of this encampment, "had the world listened to the students at Kent State, rather than murdered them?" Five years of aerial bombing preceded the deaths of those protesters, followed by five years of genocide. A university that refuses to acknowledge the ethical knowledge of student protest is a university that can only produce "knowledge."

This book, *Domesticating Brown*, began as a travel log of the colonial race-making I saw while traveling through the Banana Pancake Trail of mainland

Southeast Asia in 2008. It later resurfaced through collections of notes written alongside the camp city of the Occupy movement in Seattle's downtown, then solidified within the art galleries and domestic worker alliances of Occupy Hong Kong in 2014. Now I write its final edits within a Palestine solidarity encampment. As such, this book connects entangled contexts; it modulates alongside the traffic of American war munitions. Here we remain exposed and overseen, we who refuse the demarcations separating the university and the camps of refugees, of migrant laborers, of open-air prisons, of those massified populations slated for exposure, debilitation, and death. The campus encampment: an intrusion of the inhumane into the space where humanity itself is produced.

An acknowledgments section often consists of many lists of names, giving space to individuals and communities that helped produce the book. In the Palestine solidarity encampment, we have no names. Some inhabitants I know now only by their camp names: Babes, Eggplant, Lilac, Meteor, Mothera, Solid, Hummous, Salmon, and Not-a-Name. As a colleague commented, "All these names make me feel like I've entered a science fiction novel." The encampment of administrative resistance is a speculative space because it is one created by the colonized, the brown worlds becoming undomesticated. We attend camp rallies and meetings in poly-queer disguise, with glossy pink sunglasses, netted kaffiyehs, and black COVID-19 masks. In this encampment I have seen students struggling with depression, self-hate, and grief smile, laugh, dance, and create for the first time, in ways no classroom has ever invited them to do. Here the students call me "Sky," the protagonist of my first novel: a suicidal young man who, like them, might turn his anger and grief into radical political action in solidarity with the victims of our own empire.

For any book that centers our colonial histories and our brownness, a traditional acknowledgments section will appear redundant. You will find names all throughout this book. In every chapter you will find expressions of gratitude. In the endnotes you will find Easter eggs of appreciation. In the afterword you will find grief toward those our communities have lost. What is an acknowledgment that lacks names? What kind of knowledge can such an acknowledgment create?

In this encampment our lack of identities tethers us together, commits us to our politics, and sees our ethical and moral commitments, not our titles, as central to who we are. This is where the project around brownness for me began, and where it is coming to a close.

As I wrote this last sentence, another buzz on my phone: The long-feared and anticipated Israeli invasion of Rafah, the last refuge for civilians in Gaza, has now begun.

I have to finish writing this now. It is still May 9, 2024, less than an hour after I began. I am stopping here because my shift is beginning, where we may undergo new safety training that will prepare us for an escalation that might occur tonight, tomorrow, or not at all. I cannot explain it here before I leave, but this feeling for me is a feeling of brownness: It is a feeling of enthrallment, of facing the machines of war in solidarity with Gaza, with Rafah, with Papua New Guinea, with Kashmir, with Kānaka Maoli, with Sudan, with Haiti, with Uighurs, with all those whom the colonial war touches, with all those who believe the permanency of war is not permanent: It is a thing and, like all things, can be struck in its neck and left out to bleed. It is we, the brown domesticated masses, who hold the knife.

Whatever the next hour brings ~ thank you for reading this, and for acknowledging us.

Foreword

The body is the site of physical and social experience, and as such
cannot be denied the potential for generating knowledge.
—TERESIA K. TEAIWA, "bikinis and other s/pacific n/oceans"

Wherever invoked, brownness summons an archive of our embodied selves.
Like for most people in the world, brownness has shaped my own history of
deviations.

My mother's side of my family is descended, as far as we can tell, from a
mixture of Filipino (Ilocano) and Chinese (likely Gaoshan/高山 peoples from
Taiwan). Our certainty about this is paper-thin, as the primary patriarch from
whom we are descended—Basilio Agsalud—was not, in fact, our biological
kin. Debates thread through our annual gatherings about the racial background of his wife, my great-grandmother Luciana, who some say looks more
Chinese than Filipino, as well as the racial mixture of her first husband, my
biological great-grandfather, who disappeared from the archives and remains a
mystery in our talk-stories.

With our pasts a blur, my family has remained living on or connected to
the island of Oahu in the settler colony of Hawai'i for over a century, expanding family networks through intermarriage with people of Chinese, Japanese,
white, Black, Khmer, and Kānaka Maoli (Native Hawaiian) descent, many of
whom do not identify as Asian American or Filipino but as local or brown.
This transpacific and oceanic sense of brown has nurtured particular affective
affiliations within my extended family, yet has also shifted dramatically for my
mother and siblings, who ended up in Portland, Oregon, where we became the
only brown people on our block besides our Laotian neighbors.

My own sense of brown took root in Portland in relation to my white father; my Ilocana mother; my twin brother; my Black, Indigenous, and Filipina sister; and her half-white son. It grew with frequent visits to Hawai'i, where I was the lightest skinned of my family, and in Las Vegas, where my family moved when I was thirteen, a place where brownness was conceived as primarily Latino, or sometimes Filipino, but was always tied to minimum-wage service employment. The sense of brown that I experienced in Las Vegas was worlds apart from that of family belonging in Oahu or of hypervisibility in Portland. In Las Vegas I felt brownness mostly through the invisibility of brown labor, as I took jobs alongside other browned coworkers in movie theaters, warehouses, and sales floors. My sense of brown has shifted many times since. From Las Vegas I moved to Seattle, Washington, where brownness was often subsumed into Asianness; then to Gimhae, South Korea, where I was often grouped with Filipino entertainers; then to Nanjing, China, where I found brief community among South and Southeast Asian and Arab migrants; then to Hong Kong, where brownness most often signified migrant construction workers, criminalized exiles and refugees, and live-in domestic workers from Indonesia and the Philippines. Today I live in Vancouver, Canada, where brownness is usually imagined through colonized histories and diasporic generations of South Asians, who represent some of the most vulnerable populations within the city.[1]

In each instance of brownness I've experienced, my knowledge of what it meant to be brown fractured, bit by bit, eventually shattering my sense of how the world viewed me, and how I imagined myself. Whenever brownness emerged, it just as quickly slipped away, outside of any verifiable lineage, characteristics, or nation. Even now, as I remain in place, my brownness continues to shift, depending on who I am encountering, where they are, and what time of year it is (or how harsh the lighting). My body will read differently to different people. To some, I am white, white-passing. To others, I am East Asian. To others, South Asian, Southeast Asian, Latino, Middle Eastern. My brownness also changes depending on the season, as my skin is significantly darker in summer and lighter in winter. It depends too on my clothing style, on whether or not I am wearing glasses, on the way I walk, on the way I talk, on the type of people I surround myself with. These moving contextual elements that help dictate how others see me are entirely absent in most diversity languages and protocols, which tend to mark me and other brown peoples as passing or not passing as white, as being a visible minority or a non–visible minority, or as being mixed race. Despite institutionalized (mis)recognitions, these flexible racial encodings carry a privilege that many racialized people do not have. I do not take this for granted. Being visually ambiguous—being brown or browned—can be both a blessing and a curse, a cage and a key.

~

Wherever it is invoked, brownness makes trouble. When racial categories become comfortable, brownness reveals contradictions. When lineage and tradition feel like the solid ground holding us up, brownness turns history into vapor. When we desire to protect our homes or our homelands, brownness enters as contamination, as virus. When our political allegiances feel sacrosanct, brownness turns our gaze to the desecrated, the unseen, the earth, the dirt.

~

Whenever brownness is invoked to mean a single people, a single history, I think of the many forms of brownness in my family and loved ones, peoples who are variously—and often seen as mixtures of—Filipino, Indigenous, Black, Japanese, Khmer, Chinese, Turkish, Arab, Korean, Latino, Laotian, South Asian, white. Who, among us, is more brown than anyone else? Then I think of my own body and its history of brown movement. When and where was I the most brown, and when the least brown? Was I brown when, returning to my white grandmother's house after a jog, a neighbor called the police, describing me as "a Black man in a hoodie"? Was I brown when, in the dead of a Canadian winter, a colleague told me that I shouldn't study race because "everyone will look at you and only see a white person"? Was there ever a perfect, Goldilocks middle ground, where I was most purely, definitively, brown? Or can we imagine that all of these experiences, and all of these people in my family circles, could be called *brown*, with no hierarchy among them, only the constant movement of a sliding, straying racial form?

~

Domesticating Brown seeks to understand not brown people as racialized subjects but rather the possibilities that the uprooting movements of brownness open for imagining race otherwise. I begin with my own storied articulation to understand how brownness alters from person to person, modifies its surroundings, and creates a multitude of brown meanings and ways of being. The futility of brownness as a singular, coherent racial form directs us to theories not of brownness but of brown movements, and to the scholarly and creative practices that emerge from its eruptive, disruptive paths.

If brownness cannot be separated from the desire to know brownness itself—or in the academic sense, to understand what brownness *is*—then brownness is not an object or an agent but a metaphor for an ecosystem of racial imaginings. Brownness, like all racial constructs, is not a thing, not matter than can be followed or defined without exposing the contradictions of our own desires to follow and define it. But as Logan Smilges writes of their own crip and queer experiences, "some differences seem to matter more, and the differential mattering of those differences matters."[2] Though brownness might not be matter itself, our embodiments of brownness, even a single shade, matter, and create matter too.

Brownness frustrates in its movability, in its change and transition. It is also the metaphorical change of a musical composition, the "movement" that may pattern other forms but can also let go of deterministic definitions. Brown movement is the moment of political, social, and artistic movements, which claim an era only to shift away. It is also the material and putrid sense of "having a movement," as in to defecate, to take a shit (usually brown in color). Likewise, brown movement is the matter that remains with us, the critical and creative practices that end up sticking to our bodies, to our butts, as we continue to move through the world. Brown movement is thus akin to what Sandra Ruiz and Hypatia Vourloumis describe as the "momentum" that "undoes linear temporal and spatial orders," that's "already there and we need to attune our ears to hear it."[3]

To move with brownness is to follow the matter we are left with, to understand how it was needed, desired, discarded, made waste, and made anew. What are the problems of our world, our empire, our capitalist systems, our communities, that brownness, often imperfectly, becomes needed, desired, and discarded to solve?

~

Domesticating Brown attempts to manifest a poetic imaginary of a brown world. Édouard Glissant saw "the imaginary" as "all the ways a culture has of perceiving and conceiving of the world."[4] Multiple imaginaries intersect, activate, and change through encountering "the Other." For Glissant, these imaginaries are shaped by colonial forms of history and race-making meant to produce an "imagined transparency of relation," where racial histories and identities are taken as authentic and real, making the powers that structure them both legitimate and necessary.[5] Yet even these totalizing imaginaries can embark toward poetic relations with others, new creative imaginaries that do not reflect reality but refigure it, projecting imagination into reality. In doing so, as Paul Ricoeur wrote, a form of "productive imagination" emerges that can free itself "from the rule of the original, then provides a new aspect, a new dimension to reality."[6]

Following Glissant, this book's attempt to relate realms of knowledge across space and time cannot be categorized "as either a discipline or a science but, rather, as an imaginary construct of reality," one that can trace the imaginary's networks of culture, power, and language, without the "abusive generalization" produced by empire's singular and totalizing view of itself.[7] Following Ricoeur, this book's melding of creative and analytical forms attempts to manifest a brown imaginary that can open "new ontological possibilities that were blocked by the already existing."[8] Wherever brownness emerges as an imaginary site for the ungovernable, untraceable, and unpredictable mass, it becomes marked for domestication through scientific categorizations and strategies of colonial containment.

~

The chapters of *Domesticating Brown* trace imagined domestications by following the overlapping racial formations of colonial Asia and Oceania, focusing on narratives of brown bodies and peoples, as well as the forms of creative imagination that reframe brownness. Specifically, I read across narratives of the brown body in Southeast Asia, southern China, the Philippines, and the Pacific Islands, focusing on the ways that brownness has been shaped by colonial travel narratives as well as Indigenous and Southeast Asian local narratives to reveal forms of creative and imaginative domestication that are characteristic of liberal empire. Each chapter of *Domesticating Brown* seeks to understand how colonial subjects and other marginalized peoples have strategized ways of resisting and reversing dominating notions of brownness through art, curation, and epistemological difference—in alternative imaginings, in sliding among shades of brown.

Since brownness does not move in a straight line, the chapters of this book too sway in a series of turns that Kandice Chuh might call "deliberately promiscuous," less an interweaving of disciplinary methods and more an interlacing of academic categories—of knowledge, of identity—with the messy forms of creative and speculative writing.[9] These chapters turn toward historical events and academic discourses to just as easily turn away from them, toward forms of fiction, poetry, and creative prose. By deviating from given genres, each chapter attempts to flow alongside brownness; by tethering storytelling to academic research, each chapter is a storied manifest of my own travels through brownness as I have experienced it. These chapters thus see brownness from its margins, untethered to a particular racial form or genealogy, a turn to the way that nonbrown peoples become brown, and the way brown peoples inhabit particular shades of brown. Thus, the "turns and turning" in these chapters follow the "inherent incoherence" of transpacific studies, where, as Tina Chen writes, ideas and methods are in constant "rotation, revolution, repression, relation, and recursivity."[10]

The introduction begins by tracing a very brief history of transpacific brownness, focusing on efforts to transform meanings of race during the colonial projects in the Philippines, in Hawai'i, and during the Vietnam War. The second half reimagines brownness not through a deep archival dive but through the movement of a theoretical triptych that skims along the surface of brownness, moving from brownness as (1) a site for the ungovernable "brown mass," to (2) peoples marked for domestication through strategies of colonial containment, and to (3) the complex "shades" that reveal troubling genealogies and shameful intimacies.

Chapter 1 turns toward the academic and popular histories that express the tensions of yellowness and brownness in the mythos of the Mongol Empire. I present my short story "Crossing the Caucasus," as well as my own creative, academic, and racial relationship with the Mongols to explore histories and feelings of yellowness (as Mongolian or Mongoloid) in ways that presage and reframe the histories and feelings of brownness (as Arabic, as Indian, and as non-Mongolian Asians). Chapter 2 turns to the historical formations of brownness in my own migratory lineages within the Philippines and Hawai'i, and attempts to reframe migration as *motility*, where any individual or group migration has crucial effects on the systemic movements of the whole. Chapter 3 then turns toward the contemporary figure of the Filipina domestic worker in global cities known for cosmopolitan attitudes and sexual difference (Bahrain, Hong Kong, Honolulu, Las Vegas), focusing on literature, documentary film, and erotic performance. Chapter 4, cowritten with Y-Dang Troeung, turns to forms of Chinese brownness, focusing on films and video games about Hong Kong before and after the 1997 handover. We consider how these texts produce "organic Chineseness" as a brown form of Chineseness whose dynamic complexity invites domestication by Western empires through global capitalist labor stratifications and hybrid cultural expressions. Finally, the fifth chapter turns toward aesthetic expressions of brownness that have pushed against Western creative writing industries. It examines the critical conversation around master of fine arts (MFA) programs, as well as my own creative and academic responses to MFA-style writing to reflect on my own "brown crafts" and to offer a new brown creative praxis. The afterword provides a final storied manifest of this book's travels, noting the people, places, and collaborations that made this line of thought possible. Particularly, I dwell on this project's debt to my deceased partner, Y-Dang Troeung, whose imagination and intellect formed the brown world we shared together.

Between chapters, I have placed a "turn," a brief poem or story that attempts to defamiliarize our relationship to brownness and to embark toward a new shade of brown through differing contexts and archives (from history to family talk-story to anecdote to literature to film to video games). At the beginning of every chapter, there is a charting of each chapter's travels, from its origin in thought, to the places it was presented as a talk or dialogue, to the hybrid forms and arguments it undertook, to the journals where it was published or rejected, to its revision for this book. Through these formal expressions of movement, the context of these chapters—and my own positionalities while writing them—helps form every shade of brown.

~

Domesticating Brown is the last book in a "transpacific empire" trilogy that began with my first academic book, *Transitive Cultures: Anglophone Literature of the Transpacific* (2018), and continued with *Open World Empire: Race, Erotics, and the Global Rise of Video Games* (2020). Both books navigated the ways that racial formations have manifested across the transpacific, from colonial history to today: *Transitive Cultures* explored narratives of Southeast Asian migration, mixture, and transition among given racial identities; *Open World Empire* focused on the forms of racial hybridities and "Asiatic" spaces that emerge in new media forms. This trilogy's main aim has been to engage transpacific frameworks to investigate the imperial forms of racial capitalism as they have manifested through art (literature, digital media), history (colonialism in Southeast Asia, information technology manufacture), and discursive encounters concerning migration, war, and the promises of imperial inclusion.

Domesticating Brown is the third in this trilogy of transpacific empire but also belongs to a different writing trajectory of creative poetry and prose, which includes my novels *Stamped: an anti-travel novel* (2018) and *All Flowers Bloom* (2020) and my prose-poetry work *Nimrods: a fake-punk self-hurt anti-memoir* (2023). All these works were written and published under my matrilineal name, Kawika Guillermo, my mother's maiden name and the name she had intended for me. While all my publications have, thus far, kept my "academic" and "creative" works and identities separate, *Domesticating Brown* disrupts this demarcation to seek more creative, speculative, and poetic methods that reveal how our own writing, as brown peoples, has remained situated within processes of domestication.

~

Domesticating Brown was not written in log cabins, during vacations, or within any secluded environment. I have yet to take a sabbatical, nor have I been on a writing retreat, nor have I ever won a major state-funded grant. This book, like many books of brown authorship, was written within the commonplace norms of hardship, the daily struggles to survive, the knowledge that writing might also mean sacrifice. As I expand on in chapter 5, brown creative works are often publicized as a response to an exceptional crisis. Yet there is a danger in seeing our own writing as exceptional, as a way of pushing through our struggle, rather than a habitual practice of recuperation, reflection, and community. We do not merely write to survive our lives; we write for life itself. This is the writing of care-takers who poem while children nap, of service workers who edge out stories between smiles, of educators who struggle to find an hour free from attending to students, administrators, bosses, and banks. The depiction of a clear-headed writer within a quiet and reflective rural setting does not reflect the forms of writing that commonly come from marginalized peoples. Even the presumed need for a writer to have "a room of one's own" can mark writing practices as impossible from within the norms of poverty, debilitation, and crisis.

Domesticating Brown was written during multiple deaths and tragedies in my family: the deaths of three grandparents, my son's seizures, my nephew's drug addiction, my cousin's suicide, the sudden death of a treasured mentor. But, more than any other crisis, I faced the diagnosis of my wife Y-Dang Troeung with pancreatic cancer, which took her life only a year later. To write this proj-ect within these moments was not merely a sense of rising above or dealing with the pain of these events. As Sandra Ruiz writes, brownness opens the possibility for "a type of liberatory mourning," "a practice of engagement for harboring loss and its possibility for more abundant ways of living."[11] In much of brown life, our work is for the living and the dead, because tragedy is our norm. And writing is just one of our daily, communal acts that imagine our norm otherwise.

~

This book's chapters parse through the colonial violences that have produced the imaginary malaise of brownness through a mode of writing that is both episodic and exilic, a mode that the historian Vicente Rafael once called "a re-move from any single public or place" that remains "the product of the aleatory conditions" as well as "a signpost for future projects."[12] The exilic meander-ing of *Domesticating Brown* moves within the form of a spiral, one that flows alongside the elusive and universalist modes of the human and the relational frame of racial formations. The spiral moves through various contexts and con-cepts that illuminate the imaginaries of brownness, ultimately reaching toward its darkest, coldest gravities—that is, the colonial conditions of emergence and the imperial violences of each turn. As Glissant writes, imagination it-self works "in a spiral: from one circularity to the next" that "encounters new spaces and does not transform them into either depths or conquests."[13] The brown imaginary's spiral cannot be confined to the binaries of race-making present within any particular time and place but rather "creates a network and constitutes volume."[14]

Domesticating Brown's trust in the spiral as a generative structural form is also deeply personal: It is the form my late wife Y-Dang Troeung used in her final book, *Landbridge [life in fragments]*, a spiral text that moves through context and concept, as well as through prose, image, documentation, and anecdotes. The book's rush of movement perforates linear timelines to seek out the gravity at its center: bombs, genocide, refuge, illness, and death. The feeling of this movement, as Y-Dang wrote, reveals "a rhyming [that] happens at different points in time, [when] the personal chaos within can match the spiral of violence without."[15] Written alongside the intimate writing and editing of *Landbridge*, *Domesticating Brown* too uses the spiral form to trace violences that are both personal and historical, experiential and social, within and without. To trace violence in this way, as Y-Dang affirmed, is not necessarily to lose yourself in it, to accept its mad incoherence. This chaotic, violent spiral "doesn't always have to drag you down. . . . It can generate new things."

~

We are a family gifted at the art of movement, of straying and sliding and striving.
—Y-DANG TROEUNG, *Landbridge*

The chapters of this book work recursively, in a spiral, beginning and ending with a foreword and afterword that reflect on the ways we encounter brownness, how we latch on to it in endearing and intimate ways. Traditionally, forewords and afterwords are not written by the book's author but by a distant supporter—or in some cases, a corrective critic. This is true for this book as well. From the introduction to chapter 5, this book was written in Y-Dang's presence, and it absorbed all the care and wisdom she had to give. Its foreword and afterword were written after her presence, by a changed and estranged author who could never write the same again.

This book is dedicated to Y-Dang, who showed me how brownness moves differently, how it contains lifeworlds that can be shared from place to place, person to person. On the day we met, Y-Dang and I merged these lifeworlds together. We joked about our curves; we compared our skin color; we shared clothing; we brushed hair. Our momentum grew as we learned more about each other's backgrounds, histories, families, and writings. Our brown worlds formed when we shared our fantasies, our ideas, and our love. Our worlds changed when we began to imagine a future together. After her death we continue to move, to stray, to slide, and to strive.

if   every word
          may   be
               your   last
        let   every word   be
        beings for
                                  life

Introduction

Dawn comes rapidly in the Peninsula, up to a certain point, though the sun takes time to arise from under its bed-clothes of white cloud. One moment all is dark as the Bottomless Pit; another, and a new sense is given to the watcher—or so it seems—the sense of form. A minute or two more, and the power to distinguish colour comes almost as a surprise— the faint, dim green of the grass, the yellow of a pebble, the brown of a faded leaf, each one a new quality in a familiar object, hitherto unnoticed and unsuspected. —HUGH CLIFFORD, *Studies in Brown Humanity*, 1898

The above excerpt is from *Studies in Brown Humanity*, a mixture of story, travelogue, and "study" written by the British colonial administrator Hugh Clifford. Meant to interpret "things which have actually occurred in the Malay Peninsula," Clifford's stories frequently deploy the term *brown* to characterize people understood within an amalgam of races and classes, and whose destinies were under the charge of the British.[1] Describing brown as skin color and as landscape ("the surface of a muddy puddle"), Clifford also, as in the excerpt above, conceives of brownness through language strewn in the muddiness of metaphor, and against other races.[2] Upon arrival to the jungle valley, the watcher first sees a "white cloud" and the darkness of a "Bottomless Pit."[3] But given time, he begins to sense other forms of color: "dim green," "yellow," and "brown." Mentioned last, brownness appears within the colonial gaze only in relation to others, an unspecified, indefinable mixture that comes "hitherto unnoticed and unsuspected."[4]

Published in 1898, Clifford's *Studies in Brown Humanity* gave metaphor to brownness at a crucial moment of imperial expansion. British, French,

Dutch, and Spanish empires would be joined in Asia by the Americans, who in 1898 presumed power over the Philippines and Guam following the Spanish-American War and in that same year colonized and annexed the independent state of Hawai'i. But before the Americans' arrival in Asia, brownness had been conceived in the eighteenth century as a term of race analysis, mostly credited to the German racial scientist Johann Friedrich Blumenbach, who also popularized the term Caucasian to mean the white race. Blumenbach became one of the first to insist on the term *brown* as a means of classifying Malays, Polynesians, and others in Southeast Asia and Oceania. As with Clifford's metaphorical description, for Blumenbach, brownness only arrived as an afterthought, an addendum written twenty years after his original 1775 taxonomy that included white (Caucasian and Arab), yellow (East Asian), red (Native American), and Black (sub-Saharan African). Despite its late arrival, brownness became visible as a conceivable threat to white purity. White races, Blumenbach argued, had a tendency to "degenerate into brown."[5]

The racial scientific discourse of brownness gave legitimacy to a term that is used quite differently in North America today. *Brown* in the contemporary United States, as Nitasha Sharma has argued, signifies racial groups who hail from the Global South but who do not fall under the signs of Black or Arab: mainly Latino/a/xs and South Asians.[6] Yet even in the United States, races seen as yellow or white were once conceived of as brown (Japanese, Koreans, Italians), and brownness has been a significant marker within communities of color (brown African Americans, brown Indigenous peoples, brown Arabic peoples, brown Hawaiian locals). Once we broach the confines of America and into Asia, other senses of brown play important roles in imperial design. As Eng-Beng Lim has argued, the colonial discourses in Asia—whether British or American—were regulated by an age-old orientalist dyadic formation: "The colonial is a white man and the 'native' is a brown woman."[7] That the "native" was cast through the "ethno-visual" marker of brownness produced an ambiguous and fantasy-driven colonial subject, where brownness was always othered within binaries of "white/brown, man/boy, rational/exotic, clean/dirty, First World/Third World."[8] Turn-of-the-century traveling writers like Jack London wrote of Japanese as brown-skinned farmworkers, as "the little brown man" who, unlike "yellow" people, could not constitute a "brown peril" because his achievements were borrowed from the West.[9] In the same era, the mixed Chinese Canadian author Edith Maude Eaton/Sui Sin Far traveled to Jamaica and wrote in solidarity with the colonized populations that she was "of the brown peoples of the earth," invoking brownness to refuse "the anti-black construction of Asians as the colonial handmaidens of whiteness."[10] Later studies by postcolonial authors, like *Brown Heritage: Essays on Philippine Cultural Tradition and Literature* in 1967, deployed brownness to express the multiple (and sometimes unwieldy) standpoints produced within colonial subjugation.[11]

Domesticating Brown: Movements of Racial Imagination interrogates the slippery senses that brownness has manifested and follows its transitions among transpacific colonial encounters. *Domesticating Brown* conceptually rethinks a universalist (and widely North American) idea of race to consider the constant movements in racial contexts, meanings, and practices that brownness reveals. From this transpacific framing, *Domesticating Brown* tracks a storied manifest for brown theory limited in scope to the author's own brown lifeworld—in this case, focused on Southeast Asia, the Philippines, Oceania, and the American West Coast—in the hopes that other theories of brownness will follow, each concerning their authors' own brown worlds. By activating the transpacific both as the imperial relations among Asia, Oceania, and America and as an epistemological paradigm that navigates the disciplinary logics produced through these encounters, I will attempt to untangle a story of how some people in Asia went from resembling a wild and uncontainable threat to representing a form of brownness that became necessary for the reproduction of the Global North.

As I hope to show throughout this book's chapters, the story brownness tells is about how some people in Asia and Oceania became shaped as domesticatable—as in, were offered the gifts of inclusion within a global community but only as its necessary handmaidens. This shift was not uniform and, in fact, depended on racial tropes of wildness allotted to previous generations to legitimize the process of domestication and to presume its potentiality. Untethered to a particular racial identity, this story interrogates the slippery roles that brownness has played within histories and spaces of colonial encounter. As the last color term to be used by racial scientists, brownness has delineated racial hierarchies in between Blackness and whiteness that, to Western colonial powers, have emphasized the possible degradation of whiteness, or, to the colonized, have promised future induction into whiteness. These are the movements of brownness: its constant reemergence within new mixtures of racial constructs, identities, and bodies, which reveal the colonial histories and the imperial designs of each context.

The movements of brownness across the transpacific chronicle multiple colonial formations within the ongoing present of racial capitalism, where "the loss, disposability, and unequal differentiation" required of capitalism are enshrined by race and racism.[12] My first academic book, *Transitive Cultures: Anglophone Literature of the Transpacific*, sought to expand on this framework by seeing contemporary modes of empire as operating through a "pluralist governmentality" that expects individuals to "visibly express their difference...and in doing so, to represent imperial state power as neutral, universal, or benevolent."[13] As I argued in that book, pluralist governmentality was tested in the colonies of Southeast Asia and Oceania to differentiate forms of brownness into separable capitalist labor forces. *Domesticating Brown* builds on this previous work by attempting to explicate how the ongoing violences of racial capitalism exploit and reshape worlds of brown, whose horizon of progress is *meant to be and to remain* colonial whiteness. Connected through colonial whiteness, these brown worlds are by no means restricted to Asia and Oceania but have been reiterated in colonial empires across the globe. During the United States' colonial acquisitions of the Philippines, Hawai'i, and Puerto Rico, brownness came to address the contradictions of US colonialism with its anti-imperial legacies of throwing off its own colonizer.[14] In such an iteration, the domesticatable brown subject was a crucial form of colonial race-making that helped shape the US empire, according to Faye Caronan, as "not a conqueror but a liberator," "not a colonizer but a teacher," and to mark overseas US territories as "first and foremost a burden, not a benefit."[15]

Brownness draws attention to the forms of disciplinary as well as creative and imaginary ways of reframing the colonized body. Following queer women of color feminists like Teresia Teaiwa, Andrea Canaan, Maile Arvin, Gloria Anzaldúa, and others, this manifest reads across narratives of the brown body in Southeast Asia and Oceania, focusing on the ways that brownness has been shaped by colonial encounter and reshaped by creative narratives of brown embodiment. As brown movements can only be traced through specific attention to bodies, families, and communities, brownness elides universalizing forms of "Theory" that can hide, neutralize, and universalize the experiences of being within a visibly white body. These theorists of the flesh have cultivated a form of embodied knowledge that does not "emerge to the sight of institutional knowledge management, [but] escapes its notice," and have seen their authors' bodies and histories as sites "for apprehending generic colonial technologies of marginalization and erasure."[16] My own experience with brownness as both a racialized labor category and a sense of affective belonging resonates with Andrea Canaan's 1981 essay in *This Bridge Called My Back*, "Brownness," where she writes that to be brown—in Canaan's case, light skinned and Black—is to be swayed by both material and personal conflicts of interest that carry the affective charge of steadily reaching out toward whiteness.[17] For Canaan, brown peoples are pushed to play "a diabolical self-destructive game" where some get the role of the "superhero image" of the brown woman or the "super-stud image of the brown man," but in so doing, many unwittingly transmit racist presumptions onto the mass of brown people who cannot measure up.[18]

These narratives of the body bridge the analytical divide between material and affective experiences. Rather than see these analyses as separable, brownness tethers them together, revealing their interdependency within our research as well as their tangled impacts on our present. As brown embodiments are radically plural, their seemingly incoherent histories remain uncontainable within a multiculturalist racial order of things. Yet these histories and various experiences of brownness resonate on the level of affect, attunement, and sense, as they reappear within networks of shared stories of colonial encounter and domestication. For José Esteban Muñoz, this "sense of brown" describes a world that "is already here"; "is vast, present, and vital"; and belongs to the "majority of those who exist, strive, and flourish within the vast trajectory of multiple and intersecting regimes of colonial violence."[19] Colonial violence past and present is definitive of a sense of brownness, a racial form that emerges and transforms through and against imperial conquest. But colonial violence perpetrated by whom? Muñoz need not say, and neither must we articulate a particular perpetrator here, except to express that it is, in remaining unnamed, also necessarily plural; it cannot be merely attributed to whiteness, but also yellowness; not merely yellowness, but also lighter shades of brown; not merely lighter shades, but a brownness of colonized futurity.

Muñoz's own theoretical manifest on brownness began during the continual HIV/AIDS crises in the 1990s, which were delimited by queer-of-color communities who suffered in greater numbers but were far outside state and media narratives. His understanding of brown shifted from "feeling" to "commons" and "sense" alongside the growing xenophobia during the war on terror against "brown terrorists" and the influential performances of latinidad artists. Muñoz's meditations on brownness, alongside other theoretical frames, allow us to trace a nascent yet unarticulated field of brown theory by broadening our gaze to the brown transpacific, the site of the first articulations of brownness, but also one of the most elusive forms of brownness today. If Muñoz came to understand brownness as "a sense" rather than "a feeling," as he initially conceived of it, then, like any sense, brownness must be interpreted through particular genealogies of colonialism before it can be sufficiently understood within the realm of embodiment and sensory articulation, that is, of feeling and affect.

This introduction attempts to move alongside transpacific movements of brownness by venturing on two diverging paths. First, it traces a brief history of the structure and ideology of transpacific brownness, focusing on efforts to transform meanings of race during the colonial projects in the Philippines and

Hawaiʻi and during the Vietnam War. To trace brownness in this way challenges "limited understanding[s] of transnationality as only manifest when multiple locales are addressed," as it attends to the ways that borders themselves participate in reproducing brownness.[20] As these varied contexts show, the slippery formations of brownness showcase the impossibility of its own capture. Following this brief history, I attempt to conceive of brownness not through a deep archival dive but through the movement of a theoretical triptych that skims along the surface of brownness, feels for its textures, and offers ways that we—the always present *we*—might relate. Specifically, I move from brownness as (1) a site for the ungovernable *mass*, to (2) peoples marked for *domestication* through strategies of colonial containment, and to (3) the complex *shades* that reveal troubling genealogies and shameful intimacies. Rather than reveal a bounded identity, brownness arrives as a concept that cannot be grasped or produced into knowledge. For Muñoz, brown was most often the body rendered as Latino/a/x or latinidad when approached from the confining and conflating prism of North American pluralist governmentality. For others, brownness signifies South Asian peoples, North African and Middle Eastern peoples, Oceanic peoples, or what some have called "Filipinx hispanidad."[21] Brownness, in its ceaseless reimagining, will always look askew when approached from different spaces, times, and positions. As one's point of view moves, so too does brownness stray.

Brown Transpacifics: Malayness in the Philippines, Hawaiʻi, Vietnam

One way to begin a storied manifest of brown theory is to trace brownness not from south to north but from east to west, that is, as a sense of brown based in transpacific migration patterns, triangulating among East and Southeast Asia, Oceania, and North America. These geographies of brownness deviate from the casual ways that *brownness* is used and often universalized within North American ethnic studies scholarship to mean either Latino/a/x or South Asian. The brown transpacific decenters the US as the figurative space where brownness is most relevant, to see other forms of brownness in relation to nonwhite (but often lighter-coded) majorities: the Middle East, where over 60 percent of Filipino overseas workers reside; East and Southeast Asia, where brownness is often compared to yellow forms of East Asianness; the shared sense of south-to-north brownness in the Philippines via Spanish colonial history; the forms of brownness that instantiate forms of Blackness untethered to the continent of Africa (Filipino "Negritos," Melanesians, Sri Lankans, dark(er) Indians, Indigenous groups in Papua New Guinea). As the brown transpacific has remained at the margins of brownness, it can detach us from the American prism of pluralist governmentality to help us understand how others have also become brown.

In unsettling historically separated regional boundaries, a transpacific sense of brown motions toward an archipelagic and oceanic understanding of those who have been colonized by both the West and the East, by both state and capital. Brownness becomes more visible when we sharpen onto the spaces of Southeast Asia and the South Pacific, whose peoples have historically been presumed to have no traces of modernity within their precolonial societies, with few, if any, "modern structures" of bureaucracy, education, or impersonal government. While precolonial India, China, and Japan have consistently been held up as examples of precolonial modernity, brown peoples in Southeast Asia and Oceania have been seen as better positioned for domestication within a Western empire's provinces than those from larger state bureaucracies who had little aspiration and felt little need to adapt to Western colonial powers (Qing dynasty China, Joseon dynasty Korea, Edo period Japan).[22] From this point of view, brownness remains a signifier for nomadism, for weak or even anarchic state forms, and for nonbelonging within ethno-states. Inheriting traits of nomadism within our modern world, brownness is so often perceived as a bug in the system of nation-state belonging, or perhaps a virus. Whereas Blackness has been recently theorized to form the negation within a modern racial episteme, and yellowness has been typified as the alien diasporic, brownness has remained implicit as an incalculable mass of colonial leftovers seeking rescue, refuge, and privilege.

If brownness is tied to coloniality, it can look tricky from the viewpoint of Asia, where not all colonization has been Western. Yet as brown theory keeps visible the limits of its author—in this case, me, the Philippine American Anglophone—we can hereon consider how Western colonization in Southeast Asia and Oceania solidified a particular form of brownness both as a wild threat and as adaptable "brown boys" adopted into the "benevolent assimilation" of Western colonial power. As we saw in Hugh Clifford's *Studies in Brown Humanity*, brownness in Southeast Asia and Oceania has often taken the racial marker of Malay racial origin. In the Philippines, Spanish colonial scholarship "regarded in large measure the Filipinos as Malay," so that Filipino Malayness widely operated as a form of transnational racial belonging.[23] Throughout the late nineteenth and early twentieth centuries, Malayness was known to racial scientists and anthropologists as "the Malay Problem," which the famed anthropologist Louis Sullivan, in his 1919 book on racial types in the Philippines, saw as *the* sustained racial conundrum of Southeast Asia and much of Oceania. For anthropologists like Sullivan, Malayness represented neither tribe nor culture nor race, and its peoples were often of such mixed backgrounds that any assigned racial categories could only be tentative. These variations of brownness were a problem in that they resulted in "an apparent stratification of the population" but also could not "be definitely solved from anthropometric data," forcing Sullivan and other anthropologists to categorize populations less through categories of racial heredity and more through religion (Christian, Muslim, Pagan) and geography (coastal, jungle, mountainous, islandic).[24] Today Malayness continues to remain a murky construct that can be domesticated into national belonging (Malaysia), Indigeneity (bumiputera), Islamic religious beliefs, and sharia law. Malayness has thus remained "slippery as an object of analysis" and has fluctuated within the space of the "not Chinese," the "not white," and the "not Indian/black."[25] Within this brown mosaic, Malayness has been claimed by Malaysians, Indonesians, Polynesians, and Filipinos, yet a more expansive form of Malayness has been downplayed, suppressed, or simply ignored, in fear that an unrestrained view might dilute the accuracy of Malayness as a racial category.

During the anthropological era of the "Malay Problem," two important figures sought to adopt discourses of Malayness to create a new anti-imperial and transnational racial imaginary. The first was Dr. José Rizal, the Filipino-Chinese Hispanic mestizo associated with laying much of the groundwork for Filipino nationalism. Not long before his execution in 1896, Rizal found intellectual grounding in Malayness that would later be utilized for anticolonial organizing against the Spanish. Though Rizal mainly believed in reforming Spanish colonialism, his influence has represented both "an anticolonial striving for political and intellectual self-determination in the face of Spanish malfeasance and debilitation" and the views of "a Philippine mestizaje that integrated and replicated colonial rehabilitation."[26] Before his death Rizal tried to persuade mestizos and ilustrados (educated leaders like Rizal himself) to see their collective futures outside of Spanish colonialism and within a "Malayo-Tagalo" race that had connections to the "ancient kingdoms and ruins" of Sumatra and Japan.[27] Asserting Malayness, as Nicole CuUnjieng Aboitiz argues, was a way for Rizal and other ilustrados "to counter the argument of Europeans who described the archipelago as overrun by an anarchy of tribes and races."[28] According to an early biography, Rizal's formation of the Indian Bravos in Paris was secretively pledged to the liberation of "the Malay people" as a whole, imagining Philippine independence as a first step toward liberating Malay peoples in Borneo, Indonesia, Malaya, and elsewhere.[29] For Rizal, ever the linguist, the term *Malay* also invited aspirations of revolution, as it was stunningly close to the Tagalog term *malaya*, meaning "free" and "independent." However, in using evidence found in European scholarship to create these inter-Asian racial relations, Rizal and other ilustrados also depicted Malayness within a racial hierarchy, as superior to and separate from others lost to colonization or barbarism. "The Filipino race," Rizal wrote, "like all the Malayans, does not succumb to the foreigner as do the aborigines of Australia, the Polynesians, and Indians of the New World. . . . The Filipinos accept civilization and maintain contact with all peoples, and can live in all climates."[30]

Similar notions of Malayness as a hybrid racial form grounded in an Asian-centered anticolonialism emerged within the same historical period in the islands of Hawai'i, where King Kawika Kalākaua—Hawai'i's last sovereign king and the first monarch ever to circumnavigate the globe—was drawn to forms of Polynesian racial brownness that descended from the Malay race. As Maile Arvin has argued, settler colonialism in Hawai'i was and continues to be "fueled by a logic of possession through whiteness," where Kānaka Maoli (Hawaiian natives) are "repeatedly positioned as almost white (even literally as descendants of the Aryan race), in a way that allows white settlers to claim Indigeneity in Polynesia."[31] As with the Philippines, the brownness of Hawaiian natives had for decades disrupted anthropological divisions of racial types due to their mixtures and absences of subjects with verifiable purity. Brownness in both Hawai'i and the Philippines was formed within a colonial racial imagination structured by anti-Blackness, by an alien and alienated form of yellowness, and by a wild(er) form of Native Americanness. Ethnographic divisions within Oceania as a whole, as early as 1879, relied on separating Polynesians and Filipinos as brown stock rather than yellow, red, or black stock, or as Negrito-Polynesian and Malayo-Polynesian populations, where the Malayness of Malayo signified a brownness contrasting the yellowness of the Chinese, as well as the Blackness of the "Negrito," the Melanesian, or the Indonesian.[32] In Hawai'i, anthropologists began to see Kānaka Maoli as emerging from a "Maylay" stock, notably deemed "less inferior" due to their physical prowess, their navigation skills, and the beauty of native women.[33] Polynesian—and by extension Malay—brownness thus signified an exceptionalism where the colonized "savage" could become noble rather than wild and was therefore governable.

As US sugar barons and diplomats descended on Hawai'i, ultimately annexing the kingdom as a US territory, King Kalākaua sought to invoke colonial racial theories of brownness to imagine cross-oceanic solidarities among colonized peoples. His 1881 World Tour visits to Siam, Singapore, Johor, Malaya, and Penang were ostensibly to import labor into Hawai'i's sugarcane fields—a role that would eventually fall to Japanese, Chinese, and then Filipinos—yet this tour also compelled Kalākaua to see Polynesians as sharing racial kinship with Malays, as his visits with state officials led him to conclude that Malays and Polynesians were "long-lost brothers."[34] For Kalākaua as well as Rizal, Malayness represented an anticolonial racial form that could unify colonized peoples into a familial solidarity against white oppressors by cultivating a racial background that was more hybrid and worldly than those who supposedly remained in the darkness of racial stagnation.[35] While Kalākaua's writings often appeared to be "steeped in the ways of white imperialism" (by, for example, seeking primarily to import workers from Asia rather than Black workers from the racially segregated United States), Rizal's writings on a new Filipino "enlightened" populace (implicitly mestizo/a) were, according to Sony Coráñez Bolton, "structured and enabled by the unfreedom of Black peoples in the epoch following the emancipations of slaveholding nations across the world."[36] This sense of brownness as a hybrid racial form, signified through a transpacific sense of Malay belonging, became a space of conditional possibility for the dispossessed as well as a means of enshrining some colonial racial hierarchies, and it would help frame national liberation struggles across Southeast Asia and Oceania.

Both Rizal and Kalākaua sought to use brownness to jockey for control within given colonial structures by reimagining imperial subjectivities into forms of inter-Asian solidarity. Both their leaderships ended in tragedy: Rizal was executed by the Spanish; Kalākaua was pressured to sign the Bayonet Constitution, which stripped the Hawaiian monarchy of its sovereignty. Subsequently, their efforts at inter-Asian racial blurring left brownness to be reshaped within a context of US colonial violence. In Hawai'i, shortly after Kalākaua signed the Bayonet Constitution, the 1893 Chicago World's Columbian Exposition reclassified brownness in Oceania and Southeast Asia on a two-mile strip, placing the races of the world "along a smooth linear progression from dark anachronistic primitivism to enlightened white modernity" and situating Kānaka Maoli between the "American Indian Show" and "Algeria and Tunisia" and before the wide array of more civilized races "of the Mohammedan world, West Asia, and East Asia."[37] Kalākaua's attempt to bring Indigenous Hawaiians within closer proximity to Malayness by inhabiting a Malayo-Polynesian brownness represented a shift in racial discourses from when Polynesians were once made similar to Caucasians.[38] Similarly, after the Philippine-American War, the skin color symbolizing beauty and might began to shift from brown Malay skin (moreno or kayumanggi) to fair (maputi) or mestizo/a mixed skin, while American colonial forces began to dismantle the solidarities of both Malay and Filipino by emphasizing cross-ethnic hatreds and hierarchies.[39] President William Howard Taft, then American governor-general of the Philippines, was the first to call Filipinos "our little brown brothers" to reemphasize their proximity to both savagery and domestication, while also denying forms of white, Black, and red racialization of Filipinos that had been prevalent before and during the war. These common racial comparisons shifted when the Philippines became a colony to govern rather than a war to win or a space to settle, and American anthropologists went to great lengths to typify Filipinos as brown brothers deserving of "white love."[40] Further brown racializations manifested through the distribution and cataloging of a colonial census (1903–5) and the zoo-like voyeurism of the 1904 St. Louis World's Fair, which, like Native Hawaiians at the 1893 Chicago World's Fair before it, staged visual representations that placed Filipinos into a hierarchical amalgam of brown races.[41] As newly colonized people, Filipinos were placed within internal stratifications of brownness, from "civilized" mixed mestizo/as to "savage" Igorots to darker-skinned Negritos. These delineated racial categories saw Filipino colonial subjects as fluctuating between wildness and civility, while also subsuming differences so that all Filipinos—wild, civil, Christian, Muslim—remained contained within a Malay brown color code.

The transpacific colonial genealogy of Malayness in the nineteenth century provides wider historical context for how the contemporary use of *brown* as a term of endearment to potentiate collective agency was later part of a broader sea change in racial terminology throughout the twentieth century. In the United States, rulings in the 1920s against Japanese and South Asian individuals attempting US naturalization—*Ozawa v. United States* and *Thind v. United States*—codified brownness as distinctly and legalistically nonwhite, drawing brown away from a discourse of whiteness or civility and closer to a discourse of Blackness that had been emerging among Black authors and artists. In 1906 W. E. B. Du Bois opposed the eugenicist racial science of brown and black taxonomies by using the term *brown* as a "commonsense judgment on color" that showed "the diversity and mutability of racial characteristics," writing that "black" was "really a series of browns varying between black and yellow."[42] During the Harlem Renaissance, *brown* was a key trope used among Black women poets to signal mixed heritage, beauty, and eroticism, traits that often challenged the New Negro image of modern African American women "increasingly rooted in urban, middle-class values."[43] In 1928 Zora Neale Hurston wrote that leaving Eatonville—one of the first all-Black towns in the United States—for Jacksonville made her "a fast brown," "a brown bag of miscellany . . . against a wall in company with other bags, white, red and yellow."[44] In these creative racial imaginaries, brownness was used to express self-determination with the knowledge that the term itself was not autonomously defined and was a product of movement itself.[45]

The American war in Vietnam presented another shifting racial imaginary of brownness that fluctuated through military violence and anti-imperial political mobilization. The new context of militarized empire in Vietnam would deploy familiar anthropological taxonomies of Malay, Malayo-Tagalog, and Malayo-Polynesian, less as a positivistic language of scientific race-making and more as a signifier for colonial subjugation tethered to US colonial projects in the Philippines (as well as Cuba, Puerto Rico, and Hawaiʻi).[46] In the 1950s the newly formed Central Intelligence Agency (CIA) took advantage of an increasingly slippery sense of brown through military propaganda campaigns like Operation Brotherhood, where operatives attempted to "befriend and win the trust of the Vietnamese" by exporting Filipino doctors and nurses to South Vietnam so they could "explain, as one brownskin to another, what the real purpose of American assistance is."[47] As Yến Lê Espiritu argues, American imperialists in Vietnam relied heavily on the "widespread claim of the unique success of the American colonial project of the Philippines to reshape backward people."[48] The narrative of Americans venturing to Asia to civilize Vietnam formed through America's previous depictions of Filipinos as "little brown brothers," as well as through French orientalist depictions of Vietnamese men as "effeminate 'boys' who were indistinguishable from women."[49] For Vietnamese as well as for Filipinos and Japanese before them, brownness emphasized the ability to adapt and display hybrid senses of culture and knowledge—talents that also made the colonized brown people suspects of wildness, hypersexuality, and organized resistance. These tendencies became recoded into a pathological state of brownness: *running amok*, a phrase borrowed from the British in colonial Malaya, since its entry into the English language has become "a means of typecasting entire cultures and peoples, especially Malays, Indians, and Filipinxs, as essentially cruel, violent, and volatile."[50]

Within the US anti-imperial protests of the 1960s and 1970s, organizers and artists reimagined imperial notions of brownness from wild and resistant colonial subjects to radicalized political movements of various racial constructs, identities, and heritages. The Chicano-based Brown Power and Brown Berets movements helped form the basis for an anti-imperial sense of brown alongside Black Power, while the budding Asian American movements imagined forms of solidarity with Vietnamese victims of war, and the Delano grape strike (1965–70) brought together Filipino and Mexican farmworker unions to create a movement that, for the historian John Gregory Dunne, "would inaugurate 'brownness' as a mode of thinking."[51] Meanwhile, popular figures like Muhammad Ali formed affiliations with Vietnamese people through the color brown: "Why," Ali stated in 1967, "should they ask me to put on a uniform and go 10,000 miles from home and drop bombs and bullets on brown people in Vietnam while so-called Negro people in Louisville are treated like dogs and denied simple human rights?"[52] To insist on a Vietnamese brownness during the Vietnam War was to call attention to a much longer colonial subjectivity, where under French colonialism Vietnamese subjects were forced to depict themselves within a hygienic regime of "clean and fair, rather than dark and dirty."[53] When left in the hands of artists, writers, and activists, brownness has carried the potential to slide across nations, oceans, and languages, representing a wild, messy ambivalence that reflects empire's own ambiguity as a dominating entity offering both freedom and violence.[54]

A Brown Triptych

Here is the drama within the color brown: it is itself a mixture of yellow, red, and black—the iridescent reminder that we are in brownness and of brownness, here and now.
—JOSHUA JAVIER GUZMÁN, "Brown"

The discourses of transpacific brownness in racial science and anthropology, and among anti-imperial leaders and communities, trace and help undo the amalgamations of brownness as a mere means of inclusion into whiteness or as a separation from colonial wildness, toward a brownness that is always plural and present, whose categories and characteristics can only proliferate. Indeed, this very brief history alludes to sharper instances of brownness that move alongside discursive history but cannot be explained by its thematic flow—the more granular moments of resistance, reinvention, recasting, and rearticulation. These moments evade critical genealogical methods as they are often camouflaged through what I previously called *transitive culture*, or what the artist Kiam Marcelo Junio has called *dazzle*: "when an animal or print will move so quickly that it confuses a predator's visual field."[55] Here I will attempt to approach the dazzling impressions of brownness through a triptych format, where, as Gilles Deleuze writes, "rhythm takes on an extraordinary amplitude in a *forced movement* which gives it an autonomy, and produces in us the impression of time."[56] One could perhaps call this "impression of time" an impression of transition among nonbinary forms, the "trip" our mind takes as our eyes wander the triptych. When we read for movement, we can't help but see the brownness of ourselves not as a source of stability or settlement, but as a force of movement that "emphasizes the dynamics of the encounter and the ever-shifting possibilities for generating knowledge through diffuse strategies of embodiment."[57] Brownness thus never appears as a whole mirror reflecting our selves, but as a blurred and broken prism, what Muñoz called "shards of a larger and continuous world."[58]

This section turns from a genealogical critique of transpacific brownness and toward ways of impressing brownness through three shards of power and position, which I will invoke throughout this book:

Brown Mass / Domesticating Brown \ Shades of Brown

The syntax of these shards tells us how we can perceive brownness outside of a familiar colonial grammar book. In the first, *brown mass* is the noun—it remains present yet does not approach a claim to existence (no definite article *the* that would imply an *is*); in the second, an unnamed actor we can only distinguish as nonbrown has agency and attempts to domesticate the brown object, to do the work of domesticating said object; in the third, a plural complement, *shades*, indicates an opening that reveals the noun as a structure unto itself wherein more nouns and adjectives are presumed to coexist. In the way brownness once exposed the limits of anthropological race-making in the nineteenth and early twentieth centuries, these shards too can disrupt traditional, disciplined studies of race and history in our present, as they make little attempt to discover elisions in historical narratives, or to dissolve binaries. Rather, the triptych as method joins theorists such as Amit Rai and Jasbir Puar in seeking to intensify and proliferate race by attuning to "the perpetual differentiation of variation to variation, of difference within rather than between, and the multiplicity of affirmative becomings: the becoming otherwise of difference."[59]

Shard: Brown Mass

But who among us would know our way back, could climb over that mess again?
—SOUVANKHAM THAMMAVONGSA, *Cluster*

Brown mass names the "unhuddled" and "unwashed" masses on the move; organic populations that expand ever outward. In news media, brown masses are explicitly characterized not by race but by infrastructure: migrant caravans, boat people, wetbacks, island hoppers, slum dogs. Brown masses conjure brownness within a logic of pure mixture, which, in an order of pluralist governmentality, can only recall illegible blurred forms of human beings often presumed backward or developmentally forestalled by their own cultural mores: their often Catholic or Muslim religiosity, their poverty in respect to nations within the Global North, their histories of colonization and war that are somehow untethered to the imperial violences committed by the Global North. Within national discourses, brown mass is conceived as an outside threat—in covert wars and coups in Vietnam and Central and South America, often called *dirty wars*; and in the ways that terms like *migrant, undocumented,* and *illegals* will not name an official racial identity but will imply darker skin.

As a term, *brown mass* conjures Hortense Spillers's notion of Black female bodies as "that zero degree of social conceptualization," or as bare flesh; as well as Anne Anlin Cheng's notion of yellow female racial form as "ornamental/surface/portable."[60] These theories of embodiment are not mutually exclusive but express focused alchemies of racialization that allow us to reinhabit and disidentify with interlocking forms of personhood. In turn, brownness coheres not as a hypervisible and vestibular flesh, nor as an ornament or decorative surface, but rather as an organic and omnivorous mass whose main affective production is the incitement of an outside capable of unsettling (only to reaffirm) the boundaries of national sovereignty. As shown in the cases of Rizal, Kalākaua, and others, such affective limits can be reframed to incite anti-imperial political mobilization, to reanimate conceptions of brown mass into transnational solidarity movements against nonbrown colonial powers.[61]

Care must be taken with notions of embodiment, which can sometimes imply bodily difference as an originator or indicator of a particular type of cognition (to reiterate a colonial mind/body dualism). Rather, the ever-shifting embodiment of brownness can trace what Coráñez Bolton calls a "colonial bodymind" structured by the violence of colonial disablement that is "anchored and thus rendered the benchmark attesting to Filipino success or failure."[62] The colonial bodymind (what I will simply call *brown embodiment*) traces how race, queerness, gender, and disability (or hierarchies of capacity and intellect) are formed through particular bodily signs and functions in ways that subjected peoples who embody these traits are constantly subjected to, made aware of (through their own difference), and can thus react to (or reenact). It is thus within an ambivalent form of perihumanity that brown mass operates as an uncontainable threat to the (white) nation, as a human flow needing to be dammed or redirected. Brownness thus produces the limns of the nation: healthy population versus diseased mass; timeless borders versus growth and movement; national multiculturalism versus indistinguishable mixture; secular humanism versus spiritualism; civilization versus barbarism.

As a racialized referent to infrastructure as much as population, brown mass has manifested in the contemporary period through the media image complex of wide (often aerial) views that circulate and curate visual experience, producing not just images but the seen and the scene itself.[63] Images of brown mass are often accompanied by a spectacle of statistics that understand brown peoples only as stateless populations, numbering in the millions and always growing.

These inconceivably high numbers are dramatized as mass, so that brown-ness becomes coeval with scale itself, producing a *trypophobic* image complex of clusters and porous surfaces. Brown mass is not the swarm of yellow peril led by a villainous mastermind but a trypophobic sensescape of clumped-up, tangled, and stomped-upon organisms still somehow plodding forward. These are the visual scenes of slums, refugee camps, migrant caravans, or domestic workers huddled on cardboard mats. In films they are the indistinguishable crowd whom the hero must propel above and grapple over; in video games they are the zombielike enemies who run straight into death, desiring only flesh. These images are trypophobic because they produce a phobia of the voids (trŷpa) that swallow the pristine order of civilization. Coined in 2005 to mean a "fear of clustered holes," *trypophobia* elicits disgust as much as fear, and can be associated with objects meant to produce cleanliness, like sponges and soap bubbles, but is most often triggered by detailed images of organic matter: skin swelling, goosebumps, seedpods, the skin patterns of poisonous snakes and oc-topuses.[64] The disgust conjured from these images can be easily overlaid with images of undifferentiated brown masses. As Sara Ahmed writes, the affect of disgust slips from objects to bodies where they "stick," so that being disgusted by a thing or an event—the lack of food and water in a refugee camp, the het-eropatriarchal norms of a culture or nation, or the 9/11 attacks—eventually transfers to the bodies of peoples who are associated with such acts. The speech act of disgust, as Ahmed writes, thus translates from "It's disgusting!" to "They are disgusting" to "We are disgusted by them."[65] The *we* and the *they* here draw clear distance between the disgusted and the disgusting that recalls the ele-vated gaze of an aerial view, so that "through the disgust reaction, 'belowness' and 'beneathness' become properties of [the others'] bodies."[66]

The trypophobic conjoining of fear and disgust characterizes the image com-plex of brown peoples as a disordered mass. Its visual power reinstates viewers within a national body vulnerable to contamination. Abstract design and digi-tal media see "mass" as ordered and algorithmic: the artwork of Victor Vasarely, digitized pixel art, smartphone apps, GIS mapping systems, contact-tracing systems made visible by COVID-19. Brown mass intercedes within this visual sensescape as a return of organic decay, as the perforation of smooth digitized surfaces. The digital artist Scott Eaton's 2019 video *Entangled II* expresses the digital anxieties of brown bodily decay by applying algorithmic neural networks to an archive of over twenty-five thousand photographs of human bodies (figure I.1). Though each photograph features "carefully lit and staged human figures," the digital output of the project's artificial intelligence inter-prets this mass data as brown mass, a spill of fleshy mounds with barely discernible arms and legs whose color fluctuates from dark to light brown.[67] In Eaton's similar 2019 work *Humanity (Fall of the Damned)*, Eaton applies his neural network AI to an archive of a hundred thousand nude photographs, which are used to shape the texture, color, and appearance of a thousand hand-drawn human bodies (figure I.2). Though *Humanity* is a digitally enhanced painting rather than a video, it too captures the fear of bodily (and brown) mobility in its tumbling, coiled brown masses on the move. Both artworks, one of entanglement and one of "the Damned," play on the anxieties of digital realms that could become "impure" through brown anarchy, thus illustrating the racializing processes that form brown people into an unruly mass. The bodies in these artworks meld, mix, and threaten to pour out of the screen (or out of their secured digital demarcations within the World Wide Web). So too the images' brown bodies resemble forms of inhumanity—the stretching and concaving of their organs and limbs seem to cause no pain but are merely part of their material, monstrous forms.

For human rights practitioners, the response to the trypophobic image complex that renders brown people inhuman has been to individualize, to pluck out figures from the entangled spill of bodies. The mass of refugees from a burning Vietnamese village is cropped out to focus on a single nude child, Kim Phuc; the brown mass of Syrian refugees retreating across the Mediterranean gains the empathy of a mass movement though the circulated image of a single deceased child, Alan Kurdi. While these images later become the most memorable pictorial responses to brown death, the typical colonial response to the brown mass is to exercise a form of control that blurs the biopolitical with the zoological, which consists of creating new infrastructural surveillance that transforms the brown mass from distortion into distinction. The trypophobic image complex thus operationalizes large-scale tactics in response to the supposed scale of brown mass: During and after his 2016 presidential run, President Donald Trump's answer to southern border migration was to build a border wall 1,300 miles long costing $45 billion, even though nearly half of undocumented immigrants arrived by plane. Similar high-scale responses can be found in the growth of drone technologies and satellite surveillance; the vast network of over eight hundred US military bases; mass aerial bombing in Vietnam, Cambodia, and Laos; and the global mobilizations of permanent war itself.

Efforts to depict both the scale of war and the subsequent movement of wayward populations from an aerial view need not always be seen as villainous, or as Caren Kaplan writes, as an "opposition between powerful panopticism and subterranean resistance," but can rather trouble the "conventional divide between power and resistance."[68] We see this in the work of the artist and film-maker Ai Weiwei, whose works have attempted to depict large-scale death,

FIGURE 1.1. Video still from Scott Eaton, *Entangled II*, 2019. From Eaton's website, https://www.scott-eaton.com/2020/entangled-ii.

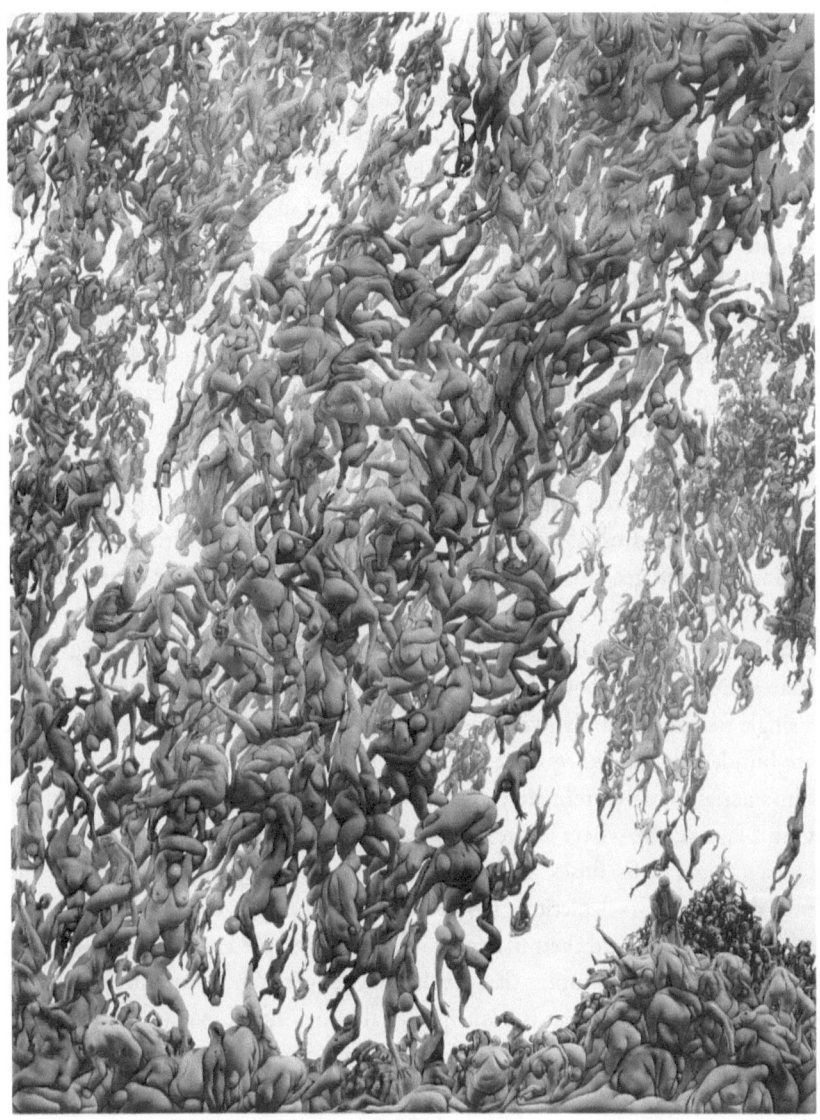

FIGURE 1.2. Scott Eaton, *Humanity (Fall of the Damned)*, 2019. From Eaton's website, https://www.scott-eaton.com/2019/humanity-fall-of-the-damned.

mourning, and displacement. His 2009 work *Remembering* sought to represent the tragedy of the 2008 Sichuan earthquake and to criticize the Chinese government's low construction quality (as well as its efforts to silence survivors) through an art piece of nine thousand school backpacks that spelled the words of one victim's mother in Mandarin: "She lived happily for seven years in this world." As Hentyle Yapp has written, Ai's work on the global stage "grapples with race as a fracturing force in the world, rather than something to be included, considered, remedied, or made whole," by exploring "what it means to be seen as a faceless mass and horde—those repeated as objects of history."[69] Rather than individualize the people out of the mass, Ai's work dwells within the perceived networks of capitalist, state, and imperial violences that conditioned its emergence.

Ai's attempts to represent the scale of masses of peoples outside of a trypophobic (or merely static) image complex returned in his 2017 film, *Human Flow*, which depicted refugees across the world through aerial footage from nonmilitarized drones, while also showing interactions with the cameras themselves: refugee children playing with the aerial machine, Ai's own use of selfie sticks, the camera crews creating the footage, the border guards who arbitrarily sought to limit its range, the documentation required by each respective state entity. We the viewer feel the camera's gaze in profile shots that linger on a single person or family; we notice its shakes when walking with refugees; we are blinded by sandstorms; we hear the gusts of wind and feel its push. The film's aerial views of refugee camps—similar, as Ai says, to the northeastern China labor camp where he grew up—pace slowly over tin and tarpaulin roofs, tents, inflated boats, buses, life jackets, warehouse dorms, miles-long fences, and mud dwellings. Ai's depiction of forced movement shifts focus away from masses of peoples and toward their material and left-behind presences, challenging the trypophobic image complex that sees brown people as infrastructure by revealing the infrastructure that is built specifically to control, manage, slow down, expose, debilitate, and exclude brown peoples (figures I.3 and I.4). The film's aerial views thus defamiliarize images of refugees away from trypophobic affects of fear or disgust by consistently "alerting us to the fact that what we are witnessing is not only an ongoing humanitarian crisis but also the *production* of crisis itself."[70] The aerial views of *Human Flow* avoid the voyeuristic desires to know and surveil brown masses, and rather call attention to the dehumanizing regimes of such a gaze, one that is taken on by border guards, administrators, and state representatives.[71] Rather than clarity, the aerial views of masses of peoples in *Human Flow* create what Kaplan calls a "world-making propensity" that demands viewers take an active role in imagining the views and experiences of those relegated to the below.[72]

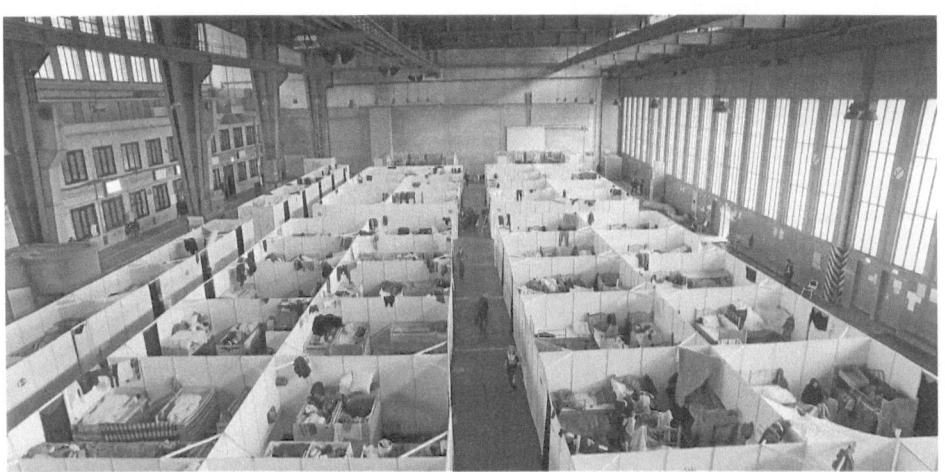

FIGURE 1.3. Ai Weiwei, "Airport Tempelhof Camp, Berlin, Germany. 2016/02/09," from *Human Flow*, 2017. http://www.humanflow.com.

FIGURE 1.4. Ai Weiwei, "Nizip Camp, Gaziantep, Turkey. 2016/03/27," from *Human Flow*, 2017. http://www.humanflow.com.

Shard: Domesticating Brown

The animal is always linked to the story of mass and individual dispossession. —JOSÉ ESTEBAN MUÑOZ, *The Sense of Brown*

Depictions of wild and uncontainable brown mass present a sense of a brown world to come that brings anxiety to those invested in the present order of things. For them, brownness is only a coming deluge that demands every nation nail up its windows. The arrival of the brown mass on the borders of nation, city, or screen reiterates the promise and purities of nation-state sovereignty, while disavowing the nation-state's historical and continual role as an imperial power that has caused the very dispossession, colonization, and extraction that produced the stateless figures of the brown mass itself. Rather than invoke the injustices of war and exploitation, the brown mass resembles the unfinished work of colonization. The shard of brown mass cannot bridge what Nikhil Pal Singh has called the congruous but often separated "inner wars" of racial conflict and the "outer wars" against brown people.[73] Instead, its imaginary work is to invigorate a process that transforms brownness from an indistinguishable mass into incorporable but servile populations who presage a safer, postracial future where "we are all brown." This process we can call *domestication*.

Domesticating delineates a process whose completion is always deferred into a postracial future, the operational *-ing* of the gerund. Domesticating is not to be confused with the process of assimilating, that is, the process through which the new arrival transforms from a *migrant* (eluding the state, stateless, rightless, targeted by police, and subjected to carceral enclosure and exploitation) to an *immigrant* (subject to rehabilitation, cure, conversion, national belonging). I use the term *domestication* not to name a real process of assimilation but to illustrate the colonial logics of an imagined process toward an imagined state of progress. *Domesticating brown* thus names a colonial logic similar to the logics of elimination that Patrick Wolfe uses to frame the long violences against Indigenous peoples in Australia, and the logics of possession that Maile Arvin uses to frame the long violences against and incorporations of Polynesian peoples in Oceania.[74] Like these, domesticating brown is a logic of slow, slow violence, which understands racial difference through forms of animality and organicism—in this case, through the domestication of dogs, horses, and flora. In undergoing generations of domestication, such nonhuman beings construct a symbiotic relationship with the humans who come to depend on and even identify themselves with the domesticated.[75] Domesticating brown accounts for the self-fulfilling logics that colonial powers have used to blur the colonized subject with the domesticated animal in order to orient brownness toward a future in which later generations will have normalized and interiorized the violences that the previous generations once fought against. Domestication is about long (often generations-long) processes where seemingly temporary states of colonial violence become habituated and routine until future generations only recall past normalcies as myth and legend. These long processes can seem nonviolent, benevolent even. The slow drip of domestication allows one to forget that what one is witnessing, feeling, and experiencing is injustice; when the building of walls over time means future generations will grow up inside those walls, never seeing their neighbors except through iron sights.

The shard "domesticating brown" illuminates the threat that brownness represents as an infiltration of racial purity, a threat that Louis Sullivan and other anthropologists once found so jarring that it made biological categories of race seem "meaningless and indefensible."[76] This is brownness as it has appeared in many scholarly studies: as a glitch in the multicultural system defined by the problems of "shadism," "colorism," "mixed race," or "passing." This private and invisible asylum of relational intimacy rouses erotic ways of seeing and feeling, but it must contend with the uneasy genealogies of mixture tattooed onto the brown body, which signify the unrestrained and ongoing transgression of sexual taboos: the exotic, the erotic, and the often wayward forms of proliferation. Such fears of brown sexuality are tethered and reproduced through imperial imaginaries of nonhuman domestication, where the term *husbandry* refers to both the domestication of nonhuman animals and the controlled monogamous patriarchy of the colonial family unit, and often requires forms of selective breeding: fixing, neutering, and other forms of producing biological limits on reproduction and managing the unpredictability of sexual desire.[77] Brownness thus invokes incarnate pleasures; as Amber Musser writes, "In contrast to an ecstasy that imagines transcending corporeality, brown jouissance is a reveling in fleshiness, its sensuous materiality that brings together pleasure and pain."[78] For Hiram Pérez, in encounters with (queer) white desire, the brown body often acts "as a repository for the disowned, projected desires of a cosmopolitan subject[;] it is alternately (or simultaneously) primitive, exotic, savage, pansexual, and abject."[79] In this erotic sense, brownness is recursive—it is both reviled *and* desired because of its exoticness, its wildness, its reproductive danger. Brownness resembles a form of libidinal sexuality that cannot be contained yet must always *be in the process of being* contained.

Brown sex holds not the transcendence of procreation but the fleshiness of proliferation. For some, this can elicit "brown jouissance"; for others, it is a thing to be controlled or culled. To be brown is thus to be within the orbit of domestication, to be ever moving, ever evading, ever developing, because one can never be fully domesticated, even if one wanted to, even if one chose to stand still. Domesticating brown thus goes beyond sexual policing to perceive the erotic disciplining that concerns how the brown body is expected to experience life itself: how one works, plays, speaks, and moves. The excesses of pleasure that brown people—particularly brown women—experience threaten the world as affective auras, as the "brown jouissance" that must be domesticated within the future-oriented promise of colonial belonging.[80] Put simply, one should not gain erotic pleasure from domestic work, caretaking, construction, entertainment, service, or even sex work but should undertake such service with the duty and gratitude of being granted a brighter (and more domesticated) future.

Domesticating brown thus references the brown figure as a feminized subjectivity—a woman to be domesticated into the house rather than left to roam, love, and be. Discursively situated within what Alys Weinbaum calls "the race/reproduction bind," the procedural logic of domestication reframes the sexual, effervescent energy of brown women into recognizable labor power.[81] Its main representational figure across the globe is the migrant brown female affective laborer, whose dark(er) skin can signify either the maternal duty of the domestic worker in the Global North or the erotic improprieties of the sex worker who inhabits the peripheries of extraction zones, military bases, and tourist sites. Indeed, brown women from Southeast Asia and Oceania have become globally recognized examples of a brown femininity feared to fluctuate between these seemingly opposed types, which compel brown women to perform acts of affective self-sacrifice that, as Neferti Tadiar puts it, reroute "libidinal energies" into markers for a migrant laborer's "capacities for suffering, for relieving suffering for others, [and] for using their selves as the instruments of others' relief."[82] Domestication thus points to the gendered and queer differences of brown embodiments, where, in order to bolster the cognitive and bodily abilities of brown men, the "cultivated mestizo mind needs an undomesticated one," whose presence as willful, promiscuous, or even insane women showcases the limits to colonial mixture.[83] As Coráñez Bolton notes, in Hispanicized spaces like the Philippines where mixed brown men can appear as leaders of a new nation or as marginalized identities within the nation, brown women are often named national/cultural possessions whose bodies are subject to colonial dispossession through sexual acts, resulting in the "mestizaje's domestication of the colonial bodymind."[84] To return to Sara Ahmed, these logics of domestication react to the affects of fear and disgust elicited from the brown mass, for as the brown mass feels closer to and comes into proximity with the national citizen-subject, intimate and unrestrained knowledge of the brown subject becomes imperative. As Ahmed writes, "The others who are the objects of our disgust must be penetrated or uncovered. We must 'get to them' to 'get away from them.'"[85]

Though the logic of domesticating brown is imagined, like brown mass, on a large scale, its everyday practices involve a system of tutelage that individualizes brown subjects by bringing them into the domestic space of the (lighter-skinned) national family. For Wendy Hui Kyong Chun, Grace Kyung-won Hong, and Lisa Nakamura, the exploitation of yellow working bodies in North America was often conditioned on their depiction as "hyper-productive automatons, exceptionally suited for the repetitive and inhuman pace of industrial labor."[86] In contrast, the exploitations of brown domestic and service work in the twentieth century have been ascribed by forms of sentiment toward white womanhood, whose tutelage over domestic subjects reinforced their own moral superiority, their "powers of sympathy," and codified the "affective structure of the proper bourgeois subject epitomized by white womanhood."[87] White domestic womanhood in particular was called on to temper the exploitation by white men, shaping the domestic worker as a brown woman of excessive feeling whose racial capacities of affective maternal care would only need to be harnessed by white womanhood to benefit the white(r) family. Rather than operating through the "racist hate" of anti-Asian discourses, tutelage toward brown workers has often taken the form of a "racist love" that promises full belonging and advancement up the ladder of brown shades, *eventually*.[88] As Chun, Hong, and Nakamura point out, this "eventually" never comes; "it is always a suspended and vestibular temporality that simply binds agency and humanity to whiteness."[89]

Hollywood films featuring brown protagonists express logics of white tutelage of brown subjects through the repeated trope of the brown orphan boy: Mogli from *The Jungle Book*, Aladdin the "street-rat," Jamal Malik from *Slumdog Millionaire*, Saroo Brierley from *Lion*, "Pi" Patel from *Life of Pi*. For brown women, this trope appears in representations of domestic workers like in Alfonso Cuarón's 2018 award-winning film, *Roma*, which, despite its many accolades, was critiqued widely for its main character, Cleodegaria "Cleo" Gutiérrez, who is given almost no backstory nor a family life of her own free from that of her bourgeois light(er)-skinned employers. Similarly, the 2016 Singaporean film *Ilo Ilo* sees the Filipina migrant worker as coming from an untraceable brown mass to affectively rescue the alienated Chinese family.[90] The film's title, *Ilo Ilo*, names the city that the migrant Teresa is pulled out of, yet the film never features images of the city, nor does Teresa discuss her own upbringing. We see the same type of "plucked out of the herd" brown domestic character in Marta Cabrera of the 2019 film *Knives Out*, whose original country is so forgettable that nobody can recall which country it is, and whose purity is so extreme that telling a lie literally makes her vomit.[91] Presumed religious and pure, the brown domestic characters of Cleo, Teresa, and Marta must reject their own origins, communities, and sexual desires to be individuated from an unknowable and irrelevant brown mass. Their domesticated station precludes lives that are not given value by communities or lovers, nor by clients or markets, but by the nationalist form of the bourgeois family (whether white, yellow, or lighter-skinned brown), upheld by the security apparatus of the state.

While the fear and disgust toward brown mass(es) can be resolved through large-scale operations like charity or war, the function of domesticating brownness is performed through individual or family-based tutelage. Yet both responses remain within a pluralist structure of patronage whose long-term aim is colonial domestication. Indeed, the term *domestication* itself comes from *domus*, the Latin term for "a type of house occupied by the wealthier classes," suggesting that the non-domesticated may be characterized less by not having a home than by coming from a home of ruin and poverty.[92] Narratives centering on brown people orphaned and rescued from the brown mass highlight the desire to domesticate the brown individual as a means of protecting them from themselves—their communities, their histories, their traditions, their own pleasures/desires—thus rerouting diverse cultural practices toward unified forms of domestic (national and household) maintenance. Logics of domestication thus see the individualized brown person's community and history either as irrelevant or as perpetually dangerous, elevating the home of the light(er)-skinned national family as a cocoon of protection, and the nation itself as a space of refuge for those orphaned from the brown mass. For such brown and migrant peoples, this domesticating narrative of home within a host family or nation, as Anna Lowenhaupt Tsing writes, "too often sugarcoats captivity."[93]

Shard: Shades of Brown

"Hey mom, you want milk in your coffee?"
"Yeah, make it as brown as your skin."
—a conversation with my mother

If the previous two shards can be situated within theoretical discourses of embodied personhood (as with brown mass) or of colonial logics (as with domesticating brown), the third shard, *shades of brown*, emerges not through discursive theorization so much as through sites of culture, art, literature, and the conversations that shape brown intimacy. They are in the unmeasurable, messy, and sometimes contradictory lives of brown peoples and in those who study brownness for whom "the failure to domesticate and tame the unpredictable queer migrant is itself a way out of the strictures of oppressive evaluative frames."[94] Shades of brown is thus less about forming judgments through discourses of brownness and more about making reparative worlds through the playful experimentation and reimagining that the sense of brown affords. Put simply, shades of brown emerges not when brown people are making a speech or teaching a class, but in the complex and ambiguous spaces alongside given and found families, when we feel no need to represent ourselves as an identity. Put crudely, it is the way we abuse given languages of race in queer and intimate spaces by operationalizing them for laughs or for the smallest possible gestures, to "make my coffee as brown as your skin."

Queer theorists of color have often attempted to account for brown shades through conceptions of value. Eng-Beng Lim, Lisa Marie Cacho, and José Esteban Muñoz have argued that brownness remains a site of devaluation and surplus labor, remaining easily (even untenably) reproducible, mere surplus. This method of understanding shades of brown accounts well for the contextual (but still colonial) distinctions of brownness tied to value. Where brown reproduction seems to need no protective mechanism, a language of value and devalue can capture the slippery capacity of brownness by reinstating class, caste, and colorist distinctions evident within local contexts. Here brownness represents not a race or a minority identity but a "commons" for those who remain browner than their immediate communities, or are otherwise browned by colonial and imperial subjugation.[95] This constant reinscription of darker shades of brown informs the "ideological codes used for deciding which human lives are valuable and which ones are worthless."[96] And yet to articulate shades of brown as a shard—as elusive and straying movement—means only tentatively invoking concepts like value and devalue, colonizer and colonized, marginalized and privileged. To think in shades is not, as one might suggest, politically sound, as its discursive traffic moves through terms that carry the seemingly infinite adjectival meanings of the transitive form. Shades cannot be approached fully through a materialist language of value, as even in precise contexts the very term *value* replicates, as Jodi Melamed argues, a universal rationalization that can insist on the same racial capitalist structures "for social forces as a whole everywhere."[97] Shades of brown signals value within subjective limitations, as brownness is not approached as such but is peppered through erotic and playful lexicons of *bronze, tan, ashen, tawny, fulvous, dusky,* and *dark.* Who could name the value of such terms? Who could posit patterns in their use, or name their misuse?

Perhaps a more palpable way to think with shades of brown is through the shame that we—brown academics invested in social justice—might have when facing our own family's racisms, or with the way we ourselves have capitulated and allied with power even through languages of decolonization, antiracism, intersectionality, community belonging, and so on. For my own family in Oahu, the tension between the terms *local* and *settler* often manifests in an unease that brings shame to our family gatherings, where I have witnessed and partaken in talk-stories of family histories that blur the boundaries of Indigenous (Kānaka Maoli) and Asian settler through our unknown genealogies, our cross-racial intimacies, our openness to familial adoption, and our affective ties to Hawai'i. Within our shared senses of brown, our family gatherings are beset by undeniable inequalities that expose the importance of these critical designations: Most of the Kānaka Maoli members of my family live in poorer historical plantation areas like Waipahu and Wahiawa and work in service, retail, fishing, or various forms of caretaking and affective/eroticized labor, while the more broadly local-identified live in wealthier areas of Kailua and Honolulu, or in the mainland United States. Much of the tension in my family is tied to the way the term *local* emerged in the early twentieth century through solidarity labor movements within diverse and stratified Hawaiian plantations but has also been invoked to flatten Indigenous peoples with Asian migrants through a presumptive reference to colonial whiteness. As Haunani-Kay Trask famously argued, the reductive effects of *local* can allow Asian settlers to "claim Hawai'i as their own, denying indigenous history, their long collaboration in our continued dispossession, and the benefits therefrom."[98] At the same time, *Asian settlers* and *settlers of color* have also carried an unease among Asians in Hawai'i who feel their positionality being conflated with that of white colonial power.

The discursive shift of *local* and *settler* illuminates the task of brown theory to trouble binaries that remain dependent on a reference to colonial whiteness, to instead centralize the complex relations within the relative incoherence of brownness and its vacillating plurality of colonial subjectivities. As Dean Saranillio argues, the critical distinctions of the term *Asian settler* are too often forgotten to instead reinscribe binary relations of "oppressed or oppressive."[99] Likewise, the anxieties of *local* and *settler* capture a brown feeling of fluctuating between binaries, a sense of being both oppressor and oppressed. To think within shades of brown thus undertakes the difficult and crucial work of dismantling not merely binaries but also relational modes of racial thinking, where brownness is seen in relation to nonbrown peoples within a North American racial formation. Rather, shades of brown conjures methods of self-referencing and interreferencing, as it parses through various forms and power relations of brownness that are also never exclusively brown. The shift from *local* to *settler* accounts for the disproportionate colonial effects on Indigenous peoples and the way localism has widely been crucial to the curtailment of Native Hawaiian sovereignty. Shades of brown frames this shift not as a reinscription of a new oppressor/oppressed binary, nor as a racial relation between two distinct types (since the boundaries between native and settler, as in my family, are never uniform or clear), but as the very axis of coalition for differently brown groups.

Thinking through shades of brown compels us to see terms like *Asian settler* as discursively practicing a similar coalition-building work that the term *local* once performed, except not through the rhetorics of sameness but through a critical assessment of the differences of our various brown genealogies and their historical relations to colonial power. Shades of brown thus does not take the point of view of "marginalized people" but that of brown people who talk-story among other brown people within a brown world. It sees logics of domestication as neglecting the view of brown people who have "chosen" domestication, who perhaps see themselves engaging in acts of manipulating, adopting, repurposing, even flourishing in an ambivalent but intimate relationship with state and capitalist power, a symbiosis that could be interpreted as parasitic as easily as exploitative, but could also be reframed as doing good for marginalized people because it reinforces power's dependency on the peripheral brown ethnic. Thus, thinking in shades can get pretty shady. Through it, we can throw shade at ourselves, and we can help understand the shame we experience when racist and colonial ways of thinking emerge not from white perpetrators but from Indigenous, Black, brown, and yellow people within our intimate circles. Such shades are difficult to write about within academic languages because they can dispel the cultural logics of marginalization that condition the very livelihoods of brown people, where trauma and oppression often signify a capacity to give wisdom or to create art. To think in shades is to consider how shared oppression does not necessarily make us better, wiser, or more morally sound people, nor does it help sharpen our critique, but can merely press us down into silence, self-absorption, debilitation, and contradiction. Our shades often bring us shame. Their danger is in revealing, as Olúfẹ́mi Táíwò puts it, that our "oppression is not a prep school."[100]

Ever Eve Kosofsky Sedgwick's student, José Esteban Muñoz expanded on his mentor's notion of queer shame through his own story of brown shame as a Cuban American whose community was characterized by an "ultraconservative dominance."[101] Similarly, my own shame comes from my brown communities who sometimes ally with anti-Black, anti-Indigenous, anti-Asian, and antibrown interests while denying their own historical circumstances. To see shame as shades is also to see the spirit shades of our past, the apparitions without bodies who sit beside us as we comprehend our own embodiment. These shades are also the ever-present histories of our disturbing relations—the genocide and eradication of Indigenous communities, colonial complicity, rape, and all the acts of forgetting that occur when we reduce ourselves to narratives of grievance. Indeed, these shades of brown sit with me as I write this; they disrupt my own political position (and, by extension, Muñoz's) because they force me to account for myself as light(er)-skinned, American, academic-educated, worldly, English-speaking, gendered as masculine, and a professor who, like the members of family and community I examine here, has also partaken in questionable alliances in order to survive in academia, holding on to the notion that I am producing *radical* pedagogy, scholarship, and art. Thus, to think in shades is not just about value or position but also about the hidden forms of language, performance, and affect that emerge when brown people of many shades dwell alongside each other in what Muñoz called a "commons of the incommensurate" that "goes beyond a politics of equivalence."[102] Our "being-in-common-in-difference" reveals a storied manifest of intimacies that have taken place among those we call servants and masters, colonized and colonizer. As shame descends on us, we are reminded that our very being-in-the-world was made possible by troubling forms of affection, which are ever present within relationships that future generations might consider merely exploitative or opportunistic. Shades of brown disturbs the presentist political visions of our pasts and futures, laying at our feet not merely the act of intimate encounter (the mixed-race subject) but the ways that we brown people have dwelled uncomfortably within our own worlds.

Brown Theory

This world is white no longer, and it will never be white again. —JAMES BALDWIN, *Notes of a Native Son*

The brown triptych has moved us to a considerably different place than where we began. We are no longer within a theory of marginalization or minority subjectivity or even, at its core, race. Brownness reminds us that the nonwhite gaze describes the vast, vast majority of the world, and so too brown theory proceeds with brownness as already the way of the world. It seeks not to draft grand theoretical axioms but to reinvigorate bodies with the histories and perspectives of our brown world, to move through the multitude of transitions that form brown personhood, among the indistinguishable and the categorizable, the plastic and the fungible, the queer and the queered, the people who wave flags and the people who dazzle in shards. In this way, brown theory attempts to trace what Sony Coráñez Bolton and Ryanson Alessandro Ku have called the "subterranean nature of empire—its quality of being everywhere at the same time always absconding from sight."[103] Brown theory does not ask,

"What if we centered marginalization rather than whiteness?" but "What if our theory did not only reflect our world but moved with our world?" Brown theory tends to dissolve rather than solve, problematizing the roots of the questions themselves. What does it mean "to call," and why do we feel that one name, one position, one coherent self, could possibly account for our many selves, souls, and roles?

The refusal to remain consistent with a single term (*brown mass / domesticating brown \ shades of brown*) embraces the messiness of multiple terms, of indefinitive definition, and provides a flexible method for flowing alongside the fluctuations of brownness in various contexts. Through this triptych form, we can also return to the artworks of Scott Eaton to see how the multiple shards of brown theory can transform an art object. "Domesticating brown" asks us to reread the interwoven, monstrous "brown mass" of *Entangled II* and *Humanity of the Damned* as expressing the anxieties of the para-human object reaching out to intoxicate the viewer, a being in need of saving, of being put to use, of being individualized, incorporated, domesticated. "Shades of brown" ponders how these brown objects themselves refuse their own objectification by refusing stillness itself. The movements of brown theory are thus the movements of constant rereading: We reread the images of brown peoples as a mass caught (and damned) through their own tangles and knots, as domesticatable subjects whom viewers are tempted to pluck out of the wriggling and writhing populace, as proliferating shades of threshing, floundering movement, whose brown bodies are the very slippery surface of flesh needed to remain mobile. All these analyses intersect to interpret a work of art that is, in every description by the artist and critics, not about brownness or race at all but about systems of thought that primarily concern "the human" (in this case, the progression of AI and the aesthetics of human bodies within digital archives). To the white world, as in Blumenbach's initial formulation, brownness appears only as a nuisance, an afterthought, a stray idea that misses the larger point. For the rest of us, it is the story of colonialism, of power, and of ourselves. And so long as colonial relations remain, brownness will flow through every instance of human expression.

Throughout this book, *brown mass \ domesticating brown / shades of brown* will reappear and guide us along the wayward movements of brownness within a spiral of diverging discourses and representations. In chapter 1 they help trace the historicity of the Mongol Empire in our ever-imperial present, where brownness arrives in contemporary and popular revisions of Mongolian imperial histories as the mass of intolerant, anticapitalist imperial subjects (peoples inhabiting the modern-day Middle East) as well as the subjects who benefit historically from imperial domestication (collaborators who were, according to these narratives, granted multiculturalist capitalism), and as the many shades of brown that encompass living within the Mongol Empire (those who created everyday means of sustaining beliefs, cultures, and forms of survival). In chapter 2, which considers my own lineage of Ilocano migrants and plantation workers (sakadas) in Hawai'i, the brown triptych follows the figure of the sakada through various narratives of brown mass, as seemingly infinite migrants; of domestication, as collaborative enforcers and exploitable labor; and of shades of brown, in relation to Indigenous and other browned migrants in Hawai'i. Similarly, the subsequent chapters use the brown triptych to trace movements of brownness through the personal, media, literary, and academic representations of domestic workers (chapter 3); the various imaginings of "brown Chineseness" in politicized representations of Hong Kong (chapter 4); and the discourses of ethnic authorship within life writing and autotheory (chapter 5). Each chapter's movement also explores my own sense of brown, relying on the methods of the brown triptych not to theorize or universalize *me* but to enact ways to feel, be with, refuse, and survive all the contexts that uniquely brown *us*.[104]

The movement of theory is also the story of a movement, with each author taking on a new role. Like brownness itself, brown theory cannot be separated from the gaze of the author(ity). As we attempt to account for brownness as being-in-process, as the mass to be domesticated, as the shards of color and the shades of history dwelling beside us, brown theory must remain enmeshed with the lifeworld of its author, whose sense of brown will always beg to differ. This book will inevitably privilege some understandings of brownness and marginalize others. Sometimes I will give particular reasons for doing so. Because brown theory can never be universalized, it is not merely theory but antitheory; because it cannot be made distinct from its author, it is not merely antitheory but autotheory. Thus, brown theory must be manifest rather than manifesto. We cannot attempt to create something that already exists; we can only graph its movements along the tide. Brown theory does not produce knowledge but rather, as Saidiya Hartman writes, a "storied articulation of ideas."[105] Through the storied manifest, brown theory has the potential to be just as relevant on a large scale as in one's living room, around one's (queer) family table. When political racial identities might flicker off, brownness continues to move.

In a gallery hangs a painting gazed on by a small but exclusive audience. Centered in this painting is the hypervisible Black body of exoticized bare flesh. The land around her is pristine, untouched, just as the land where the art space stands was once said to be. The crowd—pleasant and dull, of course—is dressed in the yellow woman, who is present not in body but in object and ornamentation. But for us, we wonder just where within the halls of this fleshy sensorium does brownness lie? This is a trick question, for so long as we conceive of the painting as original and "of its time," brownness cannot be sensed or seen. Yet it is there: within the frame, outside our frame. It is the mass emerging over time, the last color anticipating our future. It is in the weathering, oxidization, humidity, and microbacteria brought by patrons who fill the gallery halls. It is in these ever-present threats, yet it is also in the value given to the painting that stands tall against it, and in the workers who preserve its colorful oils against the inevitable tide of brown decay. The more that brownness is controlled, the more prestige is granted to the space of art itself. In weathering the wears and tears of time, the painting, too, is remade.

I

Crossing the Caucasus

DOMESTICATING HISTORIES OF YELLOW
AND BROWN IN THE MONGOL EMPIRE

2012
I wrote the story "Crossing the Caucasus" for an open mic night.
Afterward, I began an academic essay about Mongol history.

2012–17
revision, research, rejections

2018
I merged the story and academic essay together for a special
issue of an academic journal.

2018–20
rejections, revisions, and more rejections

2021–25
revised for *Domesticating Brown*

If Germany, thanks to Hitler and his successors, were to enslave the European nations and destroy most of the treasures of their past, future historians would certainly pronounce that she had civilized Europe. —SIMONE WEIL, *Selected Essays*, 1940

Some histories can only be written by imagination. The first human to carve a bow and arrow. The first time explosive powder was used not just to scare ghosts but to make holes in a human body.

One such imagined history is how the horse became domesticated. On this we can only speculate, with estimated dates thousands of years apart (4000 BCE–1000 BCE). Certainly, the process of domestication was slow, consisting of multiple stages: First, the horse was caged for meat and eventually milk; then it was tamed to draw chariots and carts; finally, the animal was bred into a new species with a backbone strong enough to carry a rider's weight into battle.[1] While the dates of the horse's domestication must remain conjectural, historical consensus has emerged on the region where it occurred: the Eurasian Steppes, a supposedly inhospitable and treeless blanket of pasture-heavy grasslands that reach over a hundred thousand square miles.[2] In what's routinely referred to as the Middle Ages, the warriors of the Steppes—the Huns, the Kipchaks, the Seljuks, the Uighurs, the Mongols—harnessed the horse into the greatest weapon yet known to humankind. They would train their children to begin riding at the age of three, and once they got hold of a horned bow and a stirrup, their archers could shoot arrows while retreating from an enemy, firing at the exact moment when their horses' pace carried all four hooves off the ground.

The horses of the steppe nomads were the envy of the ancient states. In 104 BCE the Han dynasty emperor Wu waged a brutal three-year war with an eastern steppe people, the Dayuan, to capture and breed their renowned "celestial horses" (天马). The War of the Heavenly Horses would result in tens of thousands of deaths and only a dozen breedable horses for the Han emperor.[3] Yet the war would historically be known as a crucial event for the founding of the new Silk Road, the largest and most expansive series of global arteries for both trade and military campaigns. For the next millennia, the steppe nomads inhabiting Silk Road routes were typed as militaristic barbarians on horseback, while the horses they domesticated would become proof of China's heavenly mandate: They who had captured the horses had also tamed the wild peoples and their lands. Today, as the anthropologist Natasha Fijn argues, the legendary and contrived wildness of the Mongolian horse (or Takhi) illustrates how terms of wildness and domestication depend less on the conditions and social hierarchy and more on the nonhuman animal's behavior and will (wild animals are often in captivity, in zoos, in protected national parks).[4] If, as Jack Halberstam and Tavia Nyong'o write, "wild is the will," then to be wild is to be indicted, pushed to the margins, walled off, enclosed.[5] Here, perhaps, is a lesson from the horse: Wildness need not be eliminated, not when it can be managed and controlled through a process of domestication.

How does domestication take place? One first weeds out the bad ones. Just as Alexander the Great was said to tame the untamable black horse Bucephalus, one's ability to domesticate demonstrates the rider's ability to bring others into submission. Over succeeding generations, a survival of the fittest takes place, an artificially imposed evolution where the animal does not survive the elements but the will of their captors. Yet domestication is a mutual process that works both ways; humans are not merely the active agent of change, the nonhuman merely passive and acted upon.[6] The domestication of the horse changed the society of steppe peoples, welding them together as a cross-species entity (*horse people*, they were once called). The horses' milk gave life and made alcoholic beverages. On long journeys, riders borrowed the horse's blood for sustenance. And it was through the horse that the Mongols, over fourteen hundred years after the founding of the Silk Road and the War of the Heavenly Horses, would create the largest continuous land empire that has existed to this day.[7]

But, as with any history of an ancient empire, it is difficult to determine how much of the Mongols' legacy and impact on our modern world was real and how much has been lost to time, only to reemerge as part of the imperial imaginations of our present. During the anti-war movements of the 1970s, Deleuze and Guattari theorized that the domesticated Mongolian horse held the potentials of a liberatory and nomadic "war machine," a paradigmatic example of nonstate power "to which the imperial centers were subordinate."[8] And yet such power, once wielded, was enforced upon other nomadic populations themselves, enacting, as Anna Lowenhaupt Tsing writes, a form of freedom as masculine fury, "a freedom opportunity mainly for men," that, contra Deleuze and Guattari, fully utilizes "the power of citizenship, the state, and capital."[9] Indeed, the conceptual opposition between the nomadic "war machine" and state apparatuses of war not only reinforces questionable depictions of Mongol imperialism (as anarchism, as nonstate actors, as Asian wildness), but also reveals our reliance on these depictions in imagining political radicalism against present-day imperial power. How, then, might we begin to understand the Mongols beyond given notions of wildness and domestication—that is, within the turns of brown movement—without idealizing their very form of wildness and mobility?

To move with the Mongols, this chapter follows my own experience of looping in and out of Mongol history over the past decade, since I first began writing the short story "Crossing the Caucasus," about a Cuman (Kipchak-Turk) forcibly enlisted within the Mongolian empire after being captured during a raid. The character is a survivor of empire: diasporic, integrated, hyphenated. After bearing witness to the massacre of the entire city of Merv, perhaps the most populous city of Central Asia at the time, our Cuman puts his guile to use for his adopted nation and helps bring their imperial war into further reaches, across the (not yet Caucasian) Caucasus. Originally written for a Chinese American open mic night in 2012, "Crossing the Caucasus," over the next decade, would become my most unpublishable short story, returning to me time and again like a wayward disciple, each time leading me to dive deeper into the histories of the Mongol Empire. With every rejection I carefully revisited Mongol history, revised the work, then sent it out again, only to be rejected some months later and repeat the process. This consistent dipping in and out of the history of the Mongols was, at first, brutal. Time and again I became absorbed in the collective slaughter of ancient Baghdad, Nishapur, and Merv. But after some years, revising the work became a ritual of entering a familiar zone of speculation. The violence of the Mongol raids took me from the modern world. Their atrocities minimized my own problems, rendering them merely tiresome. After more years of revisions, this zone of speculation turned to one of confrontation with such a violent and brutal empire. I began to wonder: What unintended benefits have come about from the Mongol conquest? How were the Mongol generals not mere brutes but, in fact, tolerant of other religions and races, and inclusive of anyone capable of hard work? How are we of the Pax Americana like those who lived within the Pax Mongolica?

As I dwelled with the Mongol Empire, I began to understand how my own fascination with them was placed within an unprecedented historical revisioning situated in the rise of the American academy. In the past twenty years, the histories of the Mongol Empire have become a zone of revisionist conflict. Historical battle lines have been drawn on many sides, but mostly between the traditionalists (those who understand Mongol history as violent, repressive, tragic) and the revisionists (those who celebrate the empire for its tolerance, free-trade capitalism, and globalizing infrastructure). Meanwhile, varied interests have plied these historical narratives with both money and support, from big publishing houses, to the Mongolian state itself, to the far descendants of the Mongols' victims, to Asian American organizations who have sought to resurrect the figure of the Mongol from common racist caricature and to transform Genghis Khan himself into a figure of heroic empowerment.

As with all histories, those of the Mongol Empire often reflect the values of the historians and the national and political ties they represent. Work on the Mongol Empire had almost entirely been relegated to university presses until the 2000s, when revisionist historians of the Mongols emerged to literary stardom, beginning with Jack Weatherford's *Genghis Khan and the Making of the Modern World*.[10] The two-season Netflix show *Marco Polo* highlighted Polo's supposed relationship with Kublai Khan, and the 2007 film *Mongol* traced Genghis Khan's rise to power.[11] In video games, the Mongol Empire has been a popular playable army from *Age of Empires II: Age of Kings* (1999) to *Mount & Blade II: Bannerlord* (2020). These popular revisionings of the Mongol Empire have accompanied similar revisionings within Mongolia itself. As Orhon Myadar has argued, the figure of Genghis Khan has been revised by the Mongolian state through "countless symbolic and material grand-scale state expressions" that appropriate Khan "to reconfigure and invigorate Mongolia's national identity and use[] his carefully appropriated persona to rally the public and galvanize a new national identity detached from the Soviet era . . . toward a single goal of legitimizing the state and its power."[12] Such historical revisionings have promoted a new way to see Mongol imperialism as a form comparable to what Jeanne Morefield has called an "empire without imperialism"—a familiar phrase for researchers of American empire.[13] Similar to modern "civilizing nations," the depictions of brutal Mongolian colonial campaigns are replaced by a version of the Mongol Empire "as active promoters of cross-cultural connections," a focus that has recently been "enthusiastically embraced by world history textbooks."[14]

The fog of history reveals our own fantasies of what lurks beyond the pale. But history is not just fog: It is the blur of motion, the movement of historical imagination. In the case of the Mongols, the rush of historical revisioning follows our own (Western, imperial) desires either to escape the problems of race that frame the history of American empire (colonial conquest, slavery, Indigenous genocide) or to find empowering heroes that put us (the "Asian diasporic" us) on the same competitive level as these histories. While dwelling, time and again, with the Mongols, I was led to question my own desires while dwelling within American empire: How do histories of the Mongol Empire render the limits of colonial critique? How might they demonstrate a smokescreen for Western vanity by discovering a different, non-European history that lets one admire the "benefits" of colonial conquest—a fetish that can no longer, in institutions professing social justice, be placed onto white colonial histories? What are our responsibilities as subjects that reside in settler military empires that are structured by the hard-won yet ultimately vacuous democratic pluralism in whose name such seemingly progressivist historiographies advance? How is the desire to revise conquerors like Genghis Khan into marginalized heroes made possible through antiracist discourses that remain attached to neoliberal fantasies in which free-market capitalism and minoritarian criticism circulate? How does the admiration for an Asian medieval empire of free-trade zones and religious/racial tolerance minimize the intense, unfathomable, and *unimaginable* violence of empire itself, then and now, theirs and ours?[15]

When I first wrote the story "Crossing the Caucasus" for a Chinese American open mic night, I had only read the popular revisionist histories giving admiration to the Mongols, and as a descendent of Chinese lineage (through Taiwan and Ilocos Norte), I felt an inescapable and unfamiliar sense of pride. Given the popular discourses of Asian American narratives of empowerment at the time, I saw the revisioning of the Mongol Empire as a much-needed reclamation and sought to add to the cause through my own storytelling. Over the next decade, I struggled with delving in and out of Mongol history while trying to think through my own interests in learning and retelling that history. Once written and revised, the story never seemed to fit in any conceivable venue and was rejected wholesale from popular literary journals like *JMWW* to Asia-centered journals like *Cha: An Asian Literary Journal*. When I attempted to muscle all the historical research I had done for the story into an essay for an academic journal, again I—or perhaps it is better to say, my version of the Mongols—was rejected. I would have harbored some resentment for all this, except that when I considered including the short story in an early draft of my own queer speculative historical fiction novel *All Flowers Bloom*, I too rejected the piece.

As "Crossing the Caucasus" continued to get rejected and revised, I also happened to receive my PhD in literature and move to Nanjing, China, to teach as an assistant professor at New York Institute of Technology, the first American university to open a campus offering full degrees in China (which would later be followed by Duke University in Kunshan, New York University in Shanghai, and others). I arrived in Nanjing in January 2014, only months after Xi Jinping had announced the One Belt, One Road Initiative, and banners riddled Nanjing's city sidewalks proclaiming "中国梦我的梦" (China dream, my dream).[16] Within this emerging empire, which had already instituted state-led industries in Africa and had a long history of forcing provinces like Xinjiang and Tibet to their knees, I arrived, pulled out of the crowd: the descendant of Asian colonizers (Chinese) and American colonial subjects

(Filipinos) who could provide an authentic American education to those who would one day become fully active participants within this new empire. My training at a top research university in America, coupled with my own travels and knowledge of Mandarin, made me an ideal aspirant for this new type of imperial belonging.

I include my story in this chapter, as well as the story of my story, as a storied manifest of my own creative, academic, and racial relationship with the Mongolian empire to understand forms of domestication within affects of racial and imperial belonging—or, more specifically, as a way to flow alongside histories and feelings of yellowness (as Mongolian) in ways that presage and reframe the histories and feelings of brownness (as non-Mongolian Asians). Being an Asian American educator in China meant living within dual and often contrasting nationalist interests that helped me understand the ways my own position related to an empire many centuries past. Indeed, this experience provided a view of Mongolian history that Edward Said might see as exilic, as an ability to imagine histories as ways of imagining our present—and our imperial fidelities within the present—otherwise. To express this exilic view, this chapter breaks from traditional genre forms of both academic and creative writing to follow Said's own casting of the intellectual "as exile and marginal, as amateur, and as the author of a language that tries to speak the truth to power."[17] I write of the Mongols not as historian, theorist, or novelist but as an amateur who writes within a "love for and unquenchable interest in the larger picture."[18]

To reimagine the larger picture of empire today, I could not help but spend time with the Mongols. In a single generation, their story has transformed from being one of the most merciless imperial regimes in world history to one that many Western historians now look on as an early, Asian-originated form of free-market capitalism within a liberal and progressive (read: American) empire. Like the Americans, this recent historical revisioning goes, the Mongols too collected wayward others; allocated them into subempires; dealt violence mainly to monocultural, bigoted, and antidemocratic others; and curated our contemporary moment as one of tolerance and globalization (as free-flowing market capitalism).[19] Like many imperial agents today, the Mongols are now being framed as freedom fighters for an empire of free commerce, of racial and religious toleration—an empire of underdogs, of humiliated and marginalized peoples who never killed out of wanton cruelty but for the purposes of bringing stability and peace. Saddled as we are beneath the weight of multiple empires, let us consider the Mongols.

Georgia

1222 BCE

Edging around the mountain's final pass, our caravan of warriors and diplomats stopped to gaze on the sea of soldiers waiting for us in the valley. Archers, cavalry, and pikemen were gathered in the thousands, trapping us on the wind-battered hills of the Caucasus. Our journey through the gorge had already been costly: We had lost our catapults, all but one mangonel. Our army—the Khan's army—had lost hundreds of men to the freeze. But none of us expected to find on the other side of the mountains six Kingdoms of the North, at war for their entire history, now allied to destroy us.

A scout reported an army of fifty thousand. Twice the size of our own. They were of the Northern tribes—the Lezghians, the Alans and the Cherkesses, the Volga and Khazar Kingdoms. But these soldiers meant little to our warriors, for none were known for their ferocity. Our true enemy stood in the white plain below: a large camp of Cumans in white wool armor, part of the kingdom stretching from Lake Balkhash to the Black Sea. Before the Khan's army took me in, I was once of their people.

Before nightfall, I joined the other emissaries to build camp, while our front-line warriors, led by General Subodai, charged forward to force open the pass. We saw them through the trees. They followed a fierce frontal attack with a volley of fire arrows. But with no room to maneuver, our boys had no choice but to press on, scrambling apart as the Cuman cavalry, led by bloodthirsty revenge, slaughtered them with spears of Siberian cedar. Forced to retreat, our survivors returned from the field, grunting and cursing. We, the captured, remained silent.

A strong wind dislodged a felt-covered tent, and I used my body to weigh it down.

Fantasies of Yellow and Brown

The immediate effects of Chingiz Khan's conquests, seen from the point of view of those who bore the brunt of them, were undeniably catastrophic, though this has not prevented some modern historians from arguing that the destruction and loss of life have been greatly exaggerated. . . . North China was subjected to a series of destructive campaigns over a period of 25 years. . . . To the west, Transoxania and more particularly eastern Persia had to endure something that must have seemed to approximate very nearly to attempted genocide. —DAVID MORGAN, *The Mongols*

This book begins following the movements of transpacific brownness with the Mongols, a people rarely referred to as *brown*. If brownness emerges from co-lonial relations, then the conquest of the Mongols and their historical legacy provides a locus of discourses that allow us to read the straying movements of brownness within our present. My concern throughout this chapter is twofold: to try and explain how these discourses are invested in our current moment of transpacific empire, and to understand where, within all these discordant historical narratives, the bodies remain—the living and the dead.

The Mongol conquest frames our inquiry into brownness in two ways. On one hand, the historicization of the Mongols itself is a shade of brown that represents a wildness and brutality that contrasts the more civilized forms of East Asian racialization. Films like Disney's *Mulan* (1998) and its 2020 live-action remake depict the Mongols (renamed as their ancestors, the Rouran) as a darker-skinned barbaric horde, while the bestselling video game *Ghost of Tsushima* (made by a game studio in Bellevue, Washington) reiterates these villainous depictions in depicting Mongol battles against Japanese samurai. Before the Mongol conquest, the Chinese inhabitants of the middle kingdom referred to the nomads on their northern border as "cooked" or "uncooked" peoples, where "the cooked ones were those who lived nearer to China and were more influenced by Chinese civilization," while the uncooked had yet to adopt Chinese values and customs.[20] The Mongols who remained in the Steppes were implicitly seen as inferior and barbaric yet, like in all colonial formations of brown, were placed on a route toward domestication that would inevitably separate the civilized cooked Mongols from the wild uncooked ones.

Recent historical revisions of the Mongols cast them not as uncooked brutes but as important innovators of an East Asian–originated multicultural empire who began a global and unending process of civilizing others that would, in the long term, result in capitalist pluralism. Very often revisionist historians frame this civilizing process within a dual act of racial justice: first, by revising the Mongol conquest from a campaign of looting and mass violence to revenge for the racial injustices of being historically abused and forgotten by neighboring states (particularly China); and, second, by centering the historian themselves as an enactor of racial justice by seeking to take a more objective look at the Mongol conquest, free from the racial prejudice against Mongoloids and other anti-Asian stereotypes.[21] In most European histories, the Mongols had over time signified a distinct historical memory of brutalism before the modern age, much like the so-called barbarians in studies of classical Greece and Rome. To revise Mongol history thus signifies an act of social justice itself in the revisioning of a racialized other from a barbaric peoples who have long lingered within anti-Asian racisms of yellow peril and pandemic to an organized, civilized, capitalist, and advanced people viewed through a "racist love" that depicts the Mongol Empire similar to other "yellow" East

Asian states.[22] And yet, even in this seemingly progressive historical revisioning, the very celebrated methods of Mongol innovation were dependent on unimaginable acts of violence, whose main victims were not the ancestors of white historians but those we see today as brown: the peoples living in the Middle East, South Asia, and the kingdoms of Southeast Asia.

The slippage among various histories of the Mongol Empire reveals the straying and sometimes contradictory movements of brownness and, in so doing, manifests the ongoing fidelity to the violences of American empire that scholars routinely reiterate and even promote through flattening and appropriating the language of racial justice. In Margo Hendricks's oft-cited opening lecture to the 2019 "Race and Periodization" symposium, she distinguishes a premodern critical race studies from studies of premodernity that treat race as a mere event based on particular biological and bodily markers, which are either excluded to villainize a particular culture or included to celebrate them (common in studies on William Shakespeare). For Hendricks, such studies of premodern texts treat race "as a structural event, rather than a structural process," one whose "deep connective tissue . . . reinforces the underlying belief systems inherent in White supremacy."[23] The "event" of race in the Mongol era, for revisionist historians, has been that of a racially tolerant empire, clearing the woods of Chinese bigotry, as well as Islamic monocultures of intolerant patriarchs. As Hendricks suggests, the tendency to study premodern race as "a multiethnic system of competing sovereignties" rather than an "intellectual, political, and public interrogation of capitalism's capacious erasure of the sovereignty of Indigenous peoples," shapes history into a teleological narrative leading to white-supremacist capitalist empire, the natural imperial sovereign chosen by history itself, a history aimed to land in antiracist unity (of which the Mongols are argued to be a heroic forerunner).[24] As Geraldine Heng contends, rather than be understood as a structural form of socioeconomic power, race as understood by most premodern historians relies so heavily on "scientific racism's account of race, with its entrenchment of high modernist racism as the template of all racisms . . . that properly racial logic and behavior must invoke biology and the body as their referent."[25]

To see premodern race as a process rather than an event takes into account the socioeconomic forms that utilize racial imaginaries in times of encounter—that is, colonial subjugation. Race transforms from a single somatic event about the origins of particular skin colors or types and extends beyond the rhetorical or pseudoscientific. Rather, premodern senses of race move alongside colonial fantasies that do not remain dominant nor consistent. As Dennis Austin Britton and Kimberly Anne Coles argue, to critically understand how race functioned in the distant past means also critically understanding its function in imperial projects in our immediate present, where race "functions as a fiction defined by fantasies of the body, however fraudulently composed," in order to supply "pseudoscientific contours to naturalize social hierarchies already in place."[26] To see race as fictions of the body or fantasies of imperial domination (what I call in this book *racial imaginaries*) does not read yellowness and brownness as originating with the Mongols, but rather understands such discourses of bodily difference as they function in tandem with colonial enterprise, as race does not exist on a single historical axis but rather "appears, goes underground, rises up again when occasion demands, when it becomes a useful tool for colonialism."[27] My own fascination with the history of the Mongol Empire was, I realized over a decade, really a fascination with the ways yellowness and brownness rose up both during the Mongol era of imperial violence and within American-produced attempts to retell their history, a history that like race itself can "rise up when occasion demands" and can thus reveal how race functions in our present. So too, perhaps, a premodern understanding of race can give us new imaginaries for our collective future.

Though they are by no means an originator of racial discourses, the Mongols are a crucial starting point in this transpacific genealogy of brownness, as they compel us to consider how brownness has functioned in Western racial imaginations in relation to yellowness and has at times "risen up" to contrast with and offer comparative difference from yellowness, while also providing notable difference in how entire populations are valued, as the Mongols themselves are revised historically—imaginatively domesticated—from a barbaric brown mass, distinct from yellow forms of state organization (as enemies of China, Korea, Japan), into a yellow empire, a proud lineage from which both European and Asian forms of tolerance and global capitalism originated. Indeed, all of these histories (as well as this very metahistory) are guilty of presentism in terms of race. As historians like Michael Keevak have pointed out, medieval racial types like the Mongols could never be called *yellow* during their own imperial era, as the term *yellow* rarely referred to skin color prior to the nineteenth century, and until the eighteenth century, Chinese and other East Asian groups were commonly seen by missionaries and travelers as having white or tawny skin, while the term *yellow* was often reserved for people from India (as in Immanuel Kant's 1775 work "On the Different Races of Man").[28] Over time, *yellow* emerged both as a cultural signifier of China (referring to the Yellow River and the imperial color of yellow) and later as a racial category developed in the work of racial scientists, like in Carl Linnaeus's *Systema naturae* (1735) and later in Johann Friedrich Blumenbach's taxonomy that separated such racial forms from both whiteness (as Caucasian) and brownness (as a degeneration from whiteness).[29] But before yellow, East Asians were not racialized through scientific certitude, nor were they lumped together under a single race, that is, until the late eighteenth century, under a moniker that was not *yellow* or *brown* but *Mongolian* or *Mongoloid*. And this term, *Mongolian*, stuck Mongolian imperial history to bodies, stamping pluralities of peoples with the ruthless brutality and invasive force of the Mongol Empire. At the peak of European imperialism in the nineteenth century, both *yellow* and *Mongolian* were "symbiotically linked to the cultural memory of a series of invasions from that part of the world: Attila the Hun, Genghis Khan, and Tamerlane, all of whom were now lumped together as 'Mongolian,'" or sometimes as Tartars, a confederation incorporated into the Mongol Empire.[30] Not yet yellow or brown, Mongolians were seen along a wide spectrum of skin color and could be termed as "brownish red and yellowish, yellow and olive, brownish yellow."[31] As Keevak argues, "The invention of a Mongolian (and later, Mongoloid) race" was the catalyst for other racial terminology and categorizations, from yellow to East Asian.

While the racial category of Mongolian developed by racial scientists did not signify mixture or degeneration, it did, like *brown*, often shift dramatically along racial hierarchies, with some seeing the Mongolians as akin to whites (as in Linnaeus's racial chart and Lorenz Oken's 1833–42 natural history), while others situated them alongside Black Africans as the racial opposite to whites (as in Christoph Meiners's 1785 "Outline of the History of Man" and in Blumenbach's 1793 chart, where brownness was first expressed). In medical science, the term *Mongoloid* has been a euphemism for Down syndrome, introduced in the late nineteenth century but still commonly known today, revealing how orientalism has been inextricable from global eugenic norms and notions of cognitive disability that often place yellowed peoples on a cognitive development scale, even when East Asian nations like China, Japan, and South Korea have demonstrated advanced modernity paralleling the United States and Europe. As Mel Chen has shown, "the Mongoloid" in medical science intuits racial realities where East Asians are situated "in relation to a presumably white standard, [and] may be depicted as 'neotenous', more 'like' white children, say, before the white children go on to develop more advanced features."[32] Indeed, the yellow dualism of an invasive horde versus a civilized state represents two codependent and reinforcing forms of an imperial and ableist orientalism that reiterates historically from "yellow peril" and "model minority" to notions of inorganic and organic forms of Asianness (as we discuss in chapter 4), none of which are restrictively yellow, and like all racial forms tend to overlap among different shades.

Brownness often emerges out of racial aporia, as a way to make sense of a senseless racial logic. Yet the contradictions, extremes, and slippages of yellow and brown within both modern and premodern racial forms have thus far been either marginal to or outside the frameworks of most racial theories, even that of racial capitalism—where capitalism is understood primarily within modern (capitalist) and American imperial horizons. Brown theory, as not reliant on still frames but on wayward movements, follows the intersections of multiple imperial contexts, the imaginaries of multifarious encounters, and the historiographies that make sense of them. The movements of brown theory trace race through various contexts as well as discourses—pseudoscientific, sociological, religious, travel, colonial—where race reappears as an opportunistic fiction, one that scavenges from these other discourses to validate and make truthful racial conceptions of others, re-creating racial fantasies by "stitch[ing] together what was already there."[33] Thus, brown theory's movements do not evade or leave behind the imperial context of racial capitalism in which it is written but sees, within these turns in brown and yellow, the desire to laud liberal development through the domestication of colonial histories where yellow and brown might reemerge to valorize some nonwhite populations, while seeing others as expendable, barbaric, mere mass. Understanding *Mongol* or *Mongoloid* through a recuperative frame that critiques scientific racism's definitions of these terms to hierarchize humanity into racial groupings ought not excuse the racist imperialism of the ruling elites (like Khan and his descendants), whom such terms emerged to characterize. The movements of racial imagination, from yellowness to brownness and perhaps back again, orient us to these comparative histories, and the ways they speak to the racial imaginaries of our imperial present.[34]

CROSSING THE CAUCASUS

Merv

1221 BCE

After a summer of trekking pastureland, our families settled within a sheltered river valley, whose needled grass prickled the ankles of children playing in the brush. Water from the Oxus cleansed the riverbanks. We had settled there in previous years, as it was not too far from Merv, where two of my brothers had gone to sell wool.

The heavens came on a chilly morning when snow dotted the earth with small slivers of ice. We were merely on their route. My father woke coughing from smoke. Outside, I joined my clansmen, gazing at a cloud billowing from the city beyond the hills. The Mongol army approached in a procession stretching past eyesight, clad in robes from the places they had plundered. An entire civilization, mounted, mobile,

their loot-filled wagons carving the earth. My mother began gathering shallots, wild
onions, and dried fish to welcome them. As they neared our huts, we saw our own
men guiding them: Cuman herders who knew our routes across the grassland.

The last time I saw my mother, someone had taken her across the plains and
slung her onto a horse, riding pillion.

Painting a Target Where the Arrow Landed

The way [some] historians have written history casts certain individuals in that role of historical arsonists for a good cause. "The world is stagnant, all these cultures are literally in rotting houses that just can't seem to stand on their own. And then Alexander the Great comes in, with gasoline." —DAN CARLIN, "The Wrath of the Khans," I

As we stare unblinking into history's haze, it is easy to become dispassionate observers, to lose the feeling of loss with each successive generation. Even the history of European colonization is fast becoming disassociated from the destruction of life and culture by those who would stack the achievements of colonialism against the number of bodies and cultures destroyed in its name. Bruce Gilley's controversial 2017 article "The Case for Colonialism" attempted such a task. In it, Gilley insisted that Western countries should create new (democratically elected) colonies as a means of third world uplift; or as Gilley puts it, because "the civilizing mission . . . led to improvements in living conditions for most Third World peoples during most episodes of Western colonialism," "Western and non-Western countries should reclaim the colonial toolkit and language as part of their commitment to effective governance and international order."[35] Academics and activists alike responded to "The Case for Colonialism" with petitions and open letters, stating that there was no "debate to be had on the merits of colonialism," leading to the article's retraction and the resignation of fifteen board members from the article's host journal, *Third World Quarterly*.[36]

Before it sparked controversy, "The Case for Colonialism" was originally submitted to *Third World Quarterly*'s special issue on imperialism, and according to the journal's editor-in-chief, Shahid Qadir, the article was meant to generate conversations and insights pertaining to how empire operates today.[37] Such insights can, as a matter of fact, be found within the article's otherwise banal argument that Western states should, with the consent of the governed, "hold power in specific governance areas." I call this banal because it is no new idea, nor is it unpracticed. The United States holds military power in and protects the borders of at least seventy different countries, while intrusion in Africa and South America has often been led economically by the Washington (and sometimes Beijing) consensus. The article's controversy does not emerge from such arguments (which are really overstated observations) but from the author's advice that postcolonial states should not "speak in euphemisms about 'shared sovereignty' or 'neo-trusteeship'" but rather call such actions "'colonialism' because it would embrace rather than evade the historical record."[38] While the writer's recommendations seem paltry compared to the reality of US permanent war, Gilley's desire to resurrect the term *colonialism* as a value threatens to revise the historical record from one of colonial brutality to instead see colonialism as a case of historical arson, wherein a past atrocity is later revised as a beneficial event that later brought historical progress and inevitably promoted democracy, human rights, and economic development, regardless of what the powers at the time intended.[39] Where culture remains stagnant (as Gilley supposes, "brutally patriarchal"), the only way forward is for some great power to clear out the world's dead wood.

Though "The Case for Colonialism" was quickly condemned publicly, the historical revisioning of the Mongol conquest has remained controversial only to academic historians, not to the general public. Within a matter of decades, one of the deadliest imperial forces ever recorded in human history was popularly reimagined as an empire of tolerance and growth (not to mention the unintended benefits of displacing Islamic supremacy to prepare the world for European rule). Until the 1960s historians had accepted the Mongol Empire as one of the greatest catastrophes imaginable, causing more deaths of humans by other humans than any war and inflicting "more suffering on the human race than any other event in the world's history."[40] None of this was lost on those who lived through it, nor on many of their descendants.[41] Though these histories had some role in visualizing the extreme violence of war and empire, they were, in a time of Japanese empire and the Cold War, more often put to use for the very purposes of war, as a way to demean Mongolians, Arabs, and East Asian communists. In 1903–4 Japanese scholar and cultural propaganda spokesman Okakura Tenshin was able to proclaim that "Asia is one" only by identifying Mongolians and other steppe peoples—particularly those who were also Islamic—as an "ancient menace to civilization," who had to be placed "completely outside of Asia."[42] Caught between imperial powers during the Cold War, Mongolia itself was vilified on both fronts: by the West as communists needing to be reclaimed by their subimperial ally and by the Soviet Union as possible instigators whose religious and Westernized elements had to be purged, resulting in the deaths of tens of thousands.[43] Since the fall of the Soviet Union and Mongolia's establishment of a democratic state, today, in yet another age of empire, revisionist historians have attempted to invert the anti-Mongolian racisms to instead downplay the deaths and suffering inflicted by the Mongol Empire. As an imagined form of antiracist revisionism, today's history of the Mongols, like Gilley's revised history of European colonialism, speaks to the values circulating within imperial discourses today, and the language used to rationalize, justify, and downplay the mass suffering of both our past and present.

The historian Bernard Lewis—Edward Said's orientalist par excellence—was one of the first major revisionists who sought to minimize the violence of the Mongol conquest, writing in 1993 that after living through World War II and seeing the European countries recover quickly, one could easily see that the Islamic world, Russia, and China should have recovered just as fast from the Mongol destruction but had failed to do so.[44] Senior historians such as David Morgan have thus far been unable to take this claim seriously, yet younger (and more popular press) historians would carry forth Lewis's narrative by further minimizing the damage of the Mongol conquest and implicitly casting blame on the victims for neither submitting to the Mongols (thereby warranting their massacre) nor recovering from Mongol destruction.[45] The revisionist historians who followed have continued to reframe Genghis Khan's empire as a prelude to European colonization, which itself precluded a form of globalization led by multicultural tolerance, neoliberal capital, and American domination.[46] Others have depicted the Mongols as "free, unconstrained by law and modern morality," making them targets of "the settled world," which "seem[ed] bent on destroying all vestiges of the nomadic way of life."[47]

Today the most successful Mongol revisionist is undoubtedly Jack Weatherford, an American scholar who traveled to Mongolia and began to self-identify as "an admirer of Genghis Khan and lover of all things Mongol."[48] His books, many of which have made *New York Times* bestseller lists, spotlight the Mongols' religious and racial tolerance (*Genghis Khan and the Quest for God*, 2016), the strength of its female rulers (*The Secret History of the Mongol Queens*, 2010), and their contribution to art and paper money. In his most popular work, *Genghis Khan and the Making of the Modern World* (2004), Weatherford claims that the Mongols' legacy of conquest and destruction of the Chinese and Islamic world also brought about the European Renaissance. In Weatherford's opinion, the sheer numbers of civilian deaths often credited to Mongol conquests are probably exaggerated "by a factor of about 10," and those who died were offered chances to submit and live: "Every city was offered the chance to surrender and be spared."[49] Other historians have offered polite responses by cataloging the amount of massacres, rapes, destruction of crucial farmland, and circulation of the Black Death to Europe, which together resulted in far more deaths than can be confined to even the thirteenth or fourteenth century.[50] Yet despite these historical disagreements, Weatherford's work remains the most popular version of Mongol history and receives glowing reviews in popular magazines and some academic journals.[51]

Perhaps the revisionist history of empire is inevitable. Eventually, more work like "The Case for Colonialism" will emerge, with less and less pushback. For those of us who live in the Global North, it is tempting to admire the arrow that brought us here, no matter where (or at whom) it was aimed. At the same time, so long as military and economic domination proceeds under a different name, there might still be those who will find no harm in merely using the old language of colonialism to describe and encourage contemporary regimes of violence and conquest. Encased as many of us are within colonial educational institutions, is it any surprise that we may one day convince ourselves that the historical exchange of cruelty for civilization was, in the end, a worthwhile gambit?

CROSSING THE CAUCASUS

Georgia

1222 BCE

We waited until nightfall to ride to the Cuman encampment. We took with us a small caravan of wagons stuffed with gold. Once inside their hastily built shack, I offered my brethren a meal typical of our ancestors, of boiled goat, bread, and clotted cream. The Cuman king's brother, Mstislav, met us along with the king's son, Prince Boksa. Both wore the light blue robes signaling royalty. Mstislav gasped when I spoke his language, while the younger Boksa crossed beside me, comparing my look with his own. Like two moons they orbited me, opposing each other, until they sat on opposite ends of the table.

"Sälâm," I said in our shared tongue.

"You speak for Subodai?" the king's brother said. "General of the Khan?"

"I am his emissary."

The two men glanced at each other, unnerved.

"Why?" the king's brother asked.

"The great Khan accepts all. No matter their origins."

The prince tossed the bowl of goat onto the splintered wooden boards beneath us, stomping his foot in a loud whomp. *His raspy voice parried, "The Khan slaughters our people!"*

"The Mongols are people of the Steppes, like us." I tore a piece of flatbread, still warm from the ovens. "Who are your people?" I asked. "Us, or those Caucasians you

have allied with? Those staid Christians? We are after the rich kingdoms, whom heaven has abandoned. The Khan, like us, despises luxury. Look at me. I eat the same food, and dress in the tatters of herdsmen."

The young prince vaulted, his sword out, but I dared not move—it was a Cuman test of fear. I stood frozen, blade at my throat. My own life flickered in its reflection; it meant so little even to myself. If I could convince them to submit, the Khan might grant them plots within his empire, give them a regiment, or, at the very least, turn them into peasant serfs.

"I was near Merv," I said softly, "when the heavens found us." Candlelight flickered off the blade. I let my tongue do its work: "The heavens decreed that the Mongols would conquer all the people of the world, even those whom they had not yet discovered. Do you know what that means for royalty, such as yourselves? Heaven forbids the Mongols to spill royal blood. So they find other ways."

The two moons faced each other, crestfallen.

"What can you offer?" the king's brother asked.

"Gold. And after the battle, we will share its spoils. As brothers."

Empires of Tolerance

Chenghis Khan took everything from the Tanghut people.
He gave their ruler Burkhan the name Shigurghu
and then executed him.
He ordered that the men and women of their cities be killed,
their children and grandchildren, saying:
"As long as I can eat food and still say,
'Make everyone who lives in their cities vanish,'
kill them all and destroy their homes.
As long as I am still alive
keep up the slaughter."
—*Secret History of the Mongols*, translated by
    Paul Khan and Francis Woodman Cleaves

In his last act before he died, Genghis Khan waged war on the Tanghut, a Chinese state and ethnic group, and on his deathbed ordered a final massacre, a slaughter that would continue "as long as I am still alive."[52] This and other atrocities are recorded in the *Secret History of the Mongols*, the oldest surviving literary work in the Mongolian language by a Mongolian scholar, an account that was written—as far as historians can tell—specifically for the Mongol royal family, not long after Genghis Khan's death. Given that the most reliable accounts from both the Mongols and their victims do not seem to blush at the measure of their atrocities, perhaps we, students of history living within our own empire, would discover more insight not in questioning the acts of the Mongols themselves but rather in asking why so many of us living in the Global North—writers, scholars, readers, audiences—find value in questioning and evaluating the viciousness of these acts, and why there appears to be such a heavy investment in resurrecting the figure of the man who can most be blamed for causing it.

Revisionists tend to focus on Genghis Khan himself, who has become a hero of sorts, or at the very least a cultural icon. Very little is known of Khan outside of the *Secret History of the Mongols*, but even so, revisionist narratives remain clutched on the glowing image of a man with a "perfect intelligence," who was "unflinchingly brave" and "cared for his friends."[53] Such historians routinely downplay Khan's imperial ambitions and dedication to conquest by referring to his modest dress, eating habits, and kindness to his soldiers, a leader who "looted fabulous riches and took innumerable slaves, but . . . gave them away to his followers."[54] Books that idealize Khan in these ways claim to do so because they are objective; as Anwarul Haque Haqqi writes, honoring Khan's achievements comes easily to the scholar who has "no prejudices and predilections."[55] For revisionists like Weatherford, resurrecting Genghis Khan as a self-made man who climbed the ladder from "degraded circumstances of hunger, humiliation, kidnapping, and slavery" is a commendable virtue in itself, despite Khan's merciless means of self-making. The massacre of Nishapur remains a stunning example of this renarration of wanton cruelty for the sake of self-making. A city of around 1.7 million people in modern-day Iran, Nishapur was destroyed by the Mongol army, nearly its entire population slaughtered, their skulls stacked in pyramids—all of this *after* it had surrendered. Haqqi writes of this slaughter that the city "was laid low" because "cruelty was a necessity for [Genghis Khan]. In the grim struggle for survival and then for power, he had undergone all kinds of vicissitudes, suffered humiliation, and pocketed insults."[56] Here unimaginable cruelty becomes a "necessity" given the struggle for dignity that all marginalized people share. Even massacres and genocides can be revised as a mode of empowerment and a signal of the entrepreneurial spirit of neoliberal man, as Weatherford commands: "Fate did not hand Genghis Khan his destiny; he made it for himself."[57]

The fact that Genghis Khan reads, to white scholars, as an Asian conqueror whose victims were almost entirely other Asian people renders visible dual forms of anti-Asian racism reminiscent of Cold War racial imaginings: first, that Asian imperial violence is empowering only when it ultimately benefits contemporary Western empires; and, second, that massive deaths of Asian peoples are acceptable forms of collateral damage when they ensure the growth of those empires, and thus the regional power of the West. Indeed, Jack Weatherford's deep interest in nonwhite cultures did not begin with the Mongols. His first books focused on Native American history and influence, beginning with *Tribes on the Hill* in 1985, *Indian Givers* in 1988, and *Native Roots* in 1992. Many of the subtitles of these books on Indigenous people in North America parallel the hyperbolic adulations of Weatherford's books on the Mongols: *How the Indians of the Americas Transformed the World* and *Genghis Khan and the Making of the Modern World*, or *How the Indians Enriched America* and *How the World's Greatest Conqueror Gave Us Religious Freedom*. Framing Genghis Khan as a marginalized and Indigenous warrior who brings pride to his people masks the project of imperial domination with the values of social justice, transposing the cultural conversations concerning victims of white European settlement to a context where white Europeans were all but entirely absent. Brazenly, Weatherford even writes that Genghis Khan's achievements are similar to if an African slave in early America had founded a new country and liberated it from foreign rule "by the sheer force of personality, charisma, and determination."[58]

The characteristics that Weatherford celebrates from Genghis Khan are positively neoliberal, as some of his praised achievements are in establishing "history's largest free-trade zone" and lowering or abolishing taxes. For such revisionists, to spotlight the benefits of the Mongol Empire resists forms of white supremacy today, where *Mongoloid* remains a racist epithet used to show "the inferiority of the Asian and American Indian populations."[59] The postcolonial historian Noreen Giffney, who argues that Mongol studies should better absorb queer theoretical ideas, writes that when historians like J. J. Saunders call the unprecedented amount of blood shed from the Mongol conquests "unforgivable," that is akin to a racist or Eurocentric statement (strange, since it was not Europeans whom Genghis Khan's army massacred).[60] While Genghis Khan becomes a self-made minority/Indigenous/slave/queer/antiracist hero, those who morally denounce the unimaginable imperial violence of his empire are recast as themselves racist and intolerant. Revisionists thus see the Mongol conquerors as embarking on a revenge narrative, as their oppression by the Chinese (who thought them uncooked) as well as future historians (who would see their actions as barbaric) can be reread within a superficial social justice narrative that reflects the struggles and self-making potentialities of Black, Asian, and Indigenous peoples. For such scholars, the act of revising histories of colonial violence to defend the greatness of an empire, while also leaving out its victims, pushes against the tides of racism and intolerance (and also makes bestsellers).

While historians debate over how antiracist Genghis Khan could have possibly been in a time where racial science and racial capitalism had yet to emerge, the imagined trait of Mongol tolerance can tell us about how racial difference functions within a global empire not through an explicit mandate of exclusion (though the Mongols did have such laws) nor in concepts of inferiority (which the Mongols did apply to populations in Southeast Asia) but through the incorporation of colonized subjects in projects of imperial administration.[61] The contemporary revisionists of the Mongol Empire say little about the ways race could have performed differently in the thirteenth century, and more about how Western histories of war and empire rely heavily on explicit racial exclusions and hierarchies to cast other peoples or cultures as detrimental or regressive rather than beneficial and progressive (read: civilized). In other words, the failures to account for the countless forms of murder, maiming, rape, and looting to instead shift the focus to how these acts were not, in fact, racist, speaks volumes about how racial discourses operate under American empire today: in ways that condition us not to see imperial violence as violence when it is done within a regime of toleration and freedom.

The historical revisioning of the Mongols shapes acts of imperial violence as readily forgiven or even necessary when done in the name of tolerance and the opening of lands to global capital—as Chandan Reddy puts it, violence can be "nuanced" from illegitimate to legitimate depending on the values and orientations of the state enacting that violence.[62] The domestication of histories of the Mongol Empire into an innocuous empire promoting cross-cultural connections is entrenched in a neoliberal logic of the free trade of goods as an inherent good, even when the goods flowing along such routes have the express purpose of killing and death, from weapons to military rations to even disease (the same trading routes the Mongols helped put in place were almost certainly the same that later brought the plague to Europe).[63] Though the Mongol army was primarily sustained by looting and pillaging, its historical defenders would emphasize their importance in opening land routes long out of reach to European traders, and thus completing the project of world trade that the European crusades had for centuries failed to enact. Of course, the "we" who inherits this legacy (white European descendants) troubles this protoglobalization narrative, as "we" easily forget that the world was well globalized in many ways before the Mongols, when trading routes throughout the Islamic kingdoms and China were well established. As historians have argued with little disagreement, the Mongol conquest in most of the world "profoundly arrested economic development" and helps explain why China, "despite its high levels of economic growth, was unable to make the transition to capitalism," while commercial networks and trading cites in Central Asia were "negatively affected, if not entirely destroyed."[64] The sense that "we owe a lot to the Mongols," a phrase repeated in various ways by revisionists, takes the "we" as those who ultimately have benefited from European colonialism, as the praise for Mongol-era advancement of the global economy recurs particularly in the dissemination of maps, paper and block printing, and gunpowder, which Europeans would use to manufacture cannons for seagoing vessels to colonize territories through similar advancement of global capitalist trade routes. If "the global economy of the modern age was thus born thanks to the Mongol legacy," then what does our celebration of this legacy of extreme violence say about the ongoing extractive and debilitating violence of global racial capitalism today?[65]

The Mongols offer even more insight into our current imperial age when revisionists depict them practicing forms of multicultural acceptance even when this was not necessarily done for ideological reasons, since the Mongols ruled mainly by terror of total war (the complete death and destruction of entire villages, towns, or peoples). For the Mongols, tolerance was less an ideological category and more a pragmatic one, as a means of administration and management; as Morgan writes, "[Genghis Khan] was wholly devoid of race prejudice; his ministers and commanders were recruited from twenty different nations, and there was a general pooling of military and administrative experience which enriched and strengthened his empire."[66] This decision to diversify at every level of governance might seem, from a presentist point of view, mightily progressive, but as Morgan reminds us, this imperial form of tolerance "was determined not so much by high-mindedness as by indifference."[67] Implied in this indifference is that Genghis Khan's incorporation of various "races" does not speak to his moral sensibility (for he ordered the massacre of thousands routinely) but rather to his imperial strategy. His indifference to racial background mirrored his indifference to murder, as he and other Mongols killed generally without cruelty and torture, but "as quickly and efficiently as possible."[68] Massacre and tolerance were thus part of the same pragmatic strategy to induce total obedience in colonized subjects worldwide and to create realms of such diversity that alliances and coups were near impossible to organize. In other words, tactics that we might read as reformations of diversity and multiculturalism did not stop mass violence but in fact enabled the empire of massacre and total war to run as smoothly and as quickly as possible. While our own imperial imagination asks us to see forms of tolerance as a sacrifice for the greater good, Genghis Khan's indifference to race can actually reveal the uses of tolerance in imperial projects today, as a highly effective strategy of imperial domination to ensure the strength of "the supreme universal monarchy" intended and protected by heaven.[69]

The revisionist tendency to historicize the Mongols as a multicultural military implicitly (and sometimes explicitly) names their enemies as monocultural others, glossing over the fact that the Islamist states massacred by the Mongol Empire were themselves multiethnic and made up of various languages and ways of life. One of Genghis Khan's well-known enemies and victims, the Khwarazmian Empire in modern-day Iran, was led by a Turkish shah and had incorporated nomadic peoples of both Turkish and Persian origin so that even their army was integrated with other steppe ethnicities like Kipchaks and Cumans.[70] Moreover, Genghis Khan's grandson, Hulagu, became known for his hatred of Islam and broke the terms of the surrender of Baghdad "to destroy the city as a deliberate act of terror," so as to "remove the spiritual center of Sunni Islam which he perceived as an intolerable threat."[71] At the time of the Mongol invasion, Baghdad was inhabited by both Christians and Muslims and was the center of culture and commerce, bringing in people of various backgrounds from the Middle East as well as modern-day China, Armenia, and India. Its decimation meant the death of hundreds of thousands of people; the complete destruction of mosques, madrassas, and libraries; and the incalculable cultural loss of a city that had been "the intellectual center of the Islamic world for four centuries."[72] Indeed, the famed tolerance of the Mongol Empire, like empires of tolerance today, did not stop it from decimating what was perhaps the most tolerant "global city" of its age, once the empire had deemed that city's very existence intolerable. Perhaps it is no coincidence that the American-made books about the Mongol Empire ally almost uniformly with the American-led coalitions of imperial violence in depicting Islamic peoples as monolithic, intolerant, and deserving of both massacre and scholastic/cultural death.

The revisionist histories of the Mongol Empire that claim to seek justice for racism tell us how race functions within our own imperial moment: as mere skin color, as a mere event to be tolerated, overseen, and domesticated, for the smooth running of imperial domination. And in this self-serving definition, historians praise the Mongol conquerors for creating an empire of tolerance, one vastly similar to empires of the present. Gone are concepts of race as violent colonial processes of organizing cultural, historical, and religious differences within intersections of class, nation, and gender. The historian David Morgan provides an instructive account of how the Mongol Empire developed its "tolerance":

The cold and deliberate genocide practised by the Mongols, which has no parallel save that of the ancient Assyrians and modern Nazis, perhaps arose from the mixed motives of military advantage and superstitious fears.... As nomads roaming the steppes, they despised the inhabitants of cities and felt constrained and imprisoned within their walls, and by terrorizing the people by massacres they might hasten the surrender of the next town and facilitate the rapid conquest of the region. Yet their material interest was never lost sight of. From the thousands of defenseless civilians who perished at their hands, they always selected a number of useful craftsmen, artisans and engineers who were deported into the heart of the empire and spared to work for their masters.[73]

Empires of tolerance proceed under the instructions unwittingly outlined above. First, the empire must learn to massacre, maim, or subject deliberately and pragmatically, rather than with cruelty, as if hacking leaves from a bush.[74] Second, the empire should remain racially and culturally inclusive, especially to those who remain useful—in this case, it should spare the "craftsmen, artisans and engineers," or otherwise risk rebellion.[75] Finally and most important, the empire should exploit a prejudice that cannot easily be called racial or religious: the prejudice against people in cities, against the elite, against immigrants, against those who despise the empire, whoever they may be. Even if these people *are* religiously or racially different, never make it *about* religion or race, or, otherwise, appreciate their religion and culture only *after* you have decimated their cities and burned their books (as we see with Genghis Khan's all-too-late appreciation of Islam).[76] Given these instructions, it seems then that revisionist historians have found the perfect model in Genghis Khan, living as he did before racial science and modern notions of race, nation, or ethnicity even existed: the perfect antiracist icon for imperial violence today.

American empire and its subimperial forces are not the only harbingers of imperial tolerance, nor have they been the only center of imperial revisionist histories. As a few scholars (and many media personalities) have pointed out, China's growing investments in Africa have also taken on an imperial role, shaping China as more tolerant, accepting, and caring than Africa's previous colonizers in the West. By distancing their own histories from that of the Mongols (of which modern China is indeed an inheritor), and stressing their own "century of humiliation" at the hands of the West, Chinese imperial growth has marked itself as also a project of justice, tolerance, and stewardship. In some African countries, Chinese propaganda highlights routes of investment and debt as part of a "promoted South–South solidarity."[77] Indeed, if one were to write a revisionist history of colonialism, or a defense of imperial violence today, they better not use the word *colonialism* or *empire* at all (as Gilley does) but merely call it "The Case for Global Tolerance." None would find it controversial.

Merv

1221 BCE

A vivid morning light hung over the snow-polished plains, scintillating on the cottonwood leaves. We men had been divided from our families, lined up in a row, pacing forward until we reached one of their wagons. Any man taller than the wagon's spike was beheaded, their skulls tossed into the wagon that measured them, their bodies dragged to a growing pile. In the line, I followed my brother's tracks in the grass and watched the bay horses graze.

It was not because of heaven's decree that I survived the slaughter, but my own tendency to babble. By chance, as I stood in that line of my countrymen, I overheard one of the Mongols complaining that there was no place to put our dead, for the Khan wanted to erase all Cumans from heaven's eyes.

"Well, just toss them into the lake," one of the rosy-cheeked Mongols said. "The fish will do away with them soon enough."

"It cannot be so," I jabbered in the Uighur tongue. "Heaven cannot see us dead. But in the lake, they will see our ripples."

Our captors faced me. "Ripples disappear," one of them intoned as he chewed chunks of tea leaves from a roasted spit. "Drop a stone in water. Where is that stone now?"

Scratching my beard, I gave reflection, and then retorted: "But, with enough stones, the lake will overflow, and its waters will spread the earth. Do you really believe that heaven would allow such a disturbance?"

My captors pondered this and argued in their own language, imbibing more tea, until they came to a decision: bury the Cuman corpses, then ride their horses rough over the ground until the earth was flattened, and none could tell a burial mound from a hoofprint.

When their decision came to pass, I was not among my family, beneath the horses' hooves. I had proven myself useful.

Brown Geographies

Almost immediately after the Mongol conquest of the Song dynasty in China was complete in 1276, the Mongol leadership of the new Yuan dynasty sought to conquer the regions of Southeast Asia. But the lands south and southwest of the contemporary Chinese border were famously difficult for the Mongols to invade.[78] In Myanmar contingents of warrior elephants caused the Mongols' horses—their greatest weapons in the Steppes—to panic and retreat. In Java the Mongol-led troops were manipulated by the king's son-in-law and after losing thousands of soldiers were again forced to retreat.[79] In every sector the Mongols met resistance, often in forms of guerrilla warfare, and their merciless method of total war often left too many dead on both sides for either to declare a victory, which, according to some historians, hastened the decline of many Southeast Asian kingdoms: the Pagan in Myanmar, the Khmer in Cambodia, the Champa in Vietnam, and Java in Indonesia.[80] The seemingly unstoppable force of the Mongols could not surmount the geographies, strategies, biomes, heat, disease, and animal life of South and Southeast Asia, whose lands would, in the march of history, be considered part of an untamable wild associated with damp jungles and noncentralized governments.[81]

It was within Southeast Asian landscapes that the phenomenal endurance of the Mongolian horses met its limits. Whereas a soldier on a horse could traverse six hundred miles in nine days, jungle terrains meant that soldiers had to hack their way through dense bush. As one historian suggests, the more serious problem for the horses was that their selective breeding had resulted in a heavy fur, resulting in an "inability of the breed to thrive in hot climates."[82] The domestication of the horse was of use to the empire only within certain boundaries, as heat, terrain, and lack of local grazing forced retreats throughout Southeast Asia and India, as cataloged in the 1221 Battle of the Indus River.[83] These peoples surrounded by mountains and jungles and incapable of domestication provided a foil to contrast the Mongols themselves, who by then had become cooked and domesticated into China's elite cultural mores. In historical imaginings, the peoples of South and Southeast Asia became discursive others synonymous with jungle and other impenetrable climates where the new Mongol imperial civilization could never reach. Over time, the response has not been to see these peoples as superior for deflecting Mongol attacks (which no other power, including Europe, had been able to demonstrate) but to transmit categories similar to "barbarian" and "savage" from Mongol leaders in China to the not-yet-browned others on China's periphery.

The battles and failed invasions in South and Southeast Asia detail many of the first encounters with brownness in Southeast Asia that would travel to Europe, both in rumor and in the tall tales of Marco Polo, who praised the Yuan dynasty leader Kublai Khan as a wise ruler who, in terms of territory and infrastructure, "surpasses every sovereign that has heretofore been or that now is in the world."[84] Polo's praise for the territorial management instituted by the Khans was contrasted with rumors of lands that had remained unconquerable. Yellowness had begun to form in the Western eyes of this period through the massive and terrifying horde of uncooked invaders, on one hand, and the pristine order and conduct of the cooked Asians on the other. Yet this yellowness (which we only tangentially call *yellow*, as racial color coding had yet to become part of classifications of peoples) was always seen in relation to its others, both the displaced victims and later collaborators of Mongol rule—the Muslims and other peoples in Eurasia—as well as the shades of brown that resembled the untamed, the wild, the impossible to domesticate. What we have in this historicization of brownness, then, are less characteristics and categories—for both the Mongols and their victims were placed in binaries of civilized and wild—but brownness as it emerged through distinctly colonial relationships that instantiated some populations as more domesticable through distinctions conditioned not by modern scientific definitions of race but by race as defined through geographies and biospheres. The revisionist histories of the Mongols thus provide one origin story of transpacific brownness as peoples who cannot be conquered when surrounded by their natural elements, that is, the geographic advantage of forests, mountains, islands, and tropical climates (what comedian Ali Wong called the "Jungle Asians").[85] For many Western historians today, the legacy of the Mongols has turned into a narrative less about the loss of life suffered by these populations coded as different shades of brown and more about the Western supremacy that was to grow out of the scorched earth: free-trade infrastructure that would lead the way to the European Renaissance, the age of European conquest and empire, and the supremacy of the white West.

And thus we here face another contemporaneous event that speaks to the desire for Mongol historical revisioning: that the Mongols had never entered Europe and that by and large their greatest cruelty was dealt out to Muslim peoples in Eurasia, who understandably saw them as demonic. The Mongols effectively cut off the heads of so many Muslim leaders that by 1258, after the notorious sacking of Baghdad wherein wholesale massacre and rape took place over a week's time, "never indeed had the fortunes of Islam stood at a lower level."[86] Saunders writes that as the Mongol armies rolled through the Islamic world, "Christians of every sect raised their heads and prepared to avenge themselves on their Muslim rivals and oppressors," so that "in the eyes of the Eastern Christians, the next stage of Mongol advance assumed the character of a Crusade."[87] While historians may debate on Genghis Khan's personal penchant for religious tolerance, in practice, the Mongol wars were an immense massacre of Islamic peoples on such a scale that many Christians defected to the Mongols' side in hopes that they "might deal the deathblow to Islam."[88]

Are we to take as mere coincidence, then, that the Mongol Empire, which today represents a tolerant, multicultural, and protocapitalist power, spent the vast majority of their warring tearing down Islamic cities and sometimes massacring entire Muslim populations in ways that today would undoubtedly be tantamount to genocide? Is it mere coincidence that the rise of Mongol revisionist histories has emerged simultaneously with the US war on terror? Since its beginnings with the work of Bernard Lewis, the revisionist history of the Mongol Empire has been, in scholarly practice, a way of putting brown people back in their place (i.e., the "waiting room of history"). Weatherford, to give due credit, does not deflect from such a comparison when he writes, "The Mongol army had accomplished in a mere two years what the European Crusaders from the West and the Seljuk Turks from the East had failed to do in two centuries of sustained effort. They had conquered the heart of the Arab world. No other non-Muslim troops would conquer Baghdad or Iraq again until the arrival of the American and British forces in 2003."[89] Like the American and British forces, the Mongols were also legitimated in their imperialism in Islamic lands through the victims' demonstrated disobedience to imperial power.[90] The fact that Genghis Khan died before he could conquer Christian Europe suggests that the distraction and submission of the Islamic world was not merely a failure in strategy or technology but an act of God, framing the rise of Europe within a teleological narrative that results in the Western inheritance of the world today.

While the revisionist Mongol conquest continues to conjure a brownness of Arabic peoples coded within a pre-Mongolian period of orientalist imagining and of peoples deserving of invasion and massacre, such revisions of the Mongols as harbingers of free-trade capitalism also provide a means of reimagining histories of modern racial capitalism. Whereas capitalism today is often traced back to the emergence of the East India companies as they converged into protectorates during an age of piracy that would eventually result in the white European domination of the slave trade and the accompanying racializations forming global anti-Blackness, the story of the Mongols tells a different origin, a story of dominating lands rather than waters, where free-market ideals (in competition over the silk trade) resulted in new forms of brownness as lands open to conquering, as peoples whose cultures and cities could simply be looted and pillaged, whose skill sets were mere attributes to be domesticated into a growing multiethnic military, and whose only locus of resistance was a retreat into jungles and mountains. So too this story of the origins of globalization, accepted at face value, not only shifts the historical focus of racial capitalism away from the East India Company as the origin point of imperial economics but, in so doing, resonates with a contemporary racial capitalist system that, similar to the Mongol system of warfare, "was always inherently unstable, since [the Mongols] neither traded nor produced, [but] lived by extracting a surplus from the conquered and so depended entirely on the toil of the vanquished."[91] The Mongol economic form of "nomadic pastoralism" during the growth of the Mongol Empire relied on a means of production of "herds rather than soil," and in order to generate more surplus to feed their army and integrate new members, the empire "had to therefore integrate—by conquest or consent—more and more productive units from which they could extract tribute."[92] Like the forms of global capitalism they might help usher in, the Mongol military could only survive through constant expansion and ever greater production, "a never-ending cycle of conquest, subjugation and exploitation."[93]

When claims on marginalization and oppression seem free-floating, historical revisionists (mostly white and American) have had no problem taking up the Mongol cause in the name of people of color (implicitly, Asians and Asian Americans), by turning the Mongols from figures of brutal cruelty into marginalized warriors whose histories are mostly of rural, illiterate, poor, and downtrodden peoples, who became self-made. Even within this contemporary moment of war and terror, the cruelties of the Mongols toward Islamic peoples are today recognized in popular histories, medias, and textbooks as a symptom of their mistreatment and their—perhaps misguided but understandable—desire for justice. The histories we tell about past empires will always reflect the stories we wish to tell about our own. We too are destined to provide religious and racial tolerance, meritocracy, and global capital; we too are merciless and pragmatic historical arsonists, whose enemies are possessed by religious *intol*erance; we too form empires that dole out immeasurable cruelty to entire cities, entire nations, and call it justice.

CROSSING THE CAUCASUS

Georgia

1222 BCE

During the battle I floated about the cantina with the other diplomats: Garin the Lezghian, Crork the Cherk, and Sonam the Khazar. All of us were orphaned by the Khans, our tribes either slain or integrated into their vast mobile military. Adept survivors were made commanders; those who were nimble became herders; and those like us—those whose tongues could strike like a whip—became diplomats.

In the high atmosphere, my jittery tongue overpowered me. "It was a perfectly sunny day," I told them. "The first day in weeks without rain." My fellow emissaries were reticent, perhaps, unable to hear me above the battle cries and clash of iron. "Merv's prince was inside a bag," I whispered. "Tied to a stampeding horse. I saw it myself."

I knew the smell. Not the stench of death, which I knew well, but the stench of massacre, an altogether different thing. I first knew it near Merv. Even miles from the city, my lungs had fought the smell, swamp-sunken. To breathe again, my throat metamorphosed. I learned to inhale color, material, foam.

Smoke coughed skyward from the Mongols' oil fires, used to disguise their formation. I silenced myself, busying my mouth with aruul curds. We heard the war drums signaling the lancers to charge. A blanket of smoke swept across the sky, bringing an early dawn. Voices below screamed in a wailing chorus of crickets.

History, Domesticated

The Mongols ordered that, apart from four hundred artisans whom they specified and selected from amongst the men and some children, girls and boys, whom they bore off into captivity, the whole population, including the women and children, should be killed, and no one, whether woman or man, be spared. The people of Merv were then distributed among the soldiers and levies and, in short, to each man was allotted the execution of three or four hundred persons. —ATA-MALIK JUVAINI (1226–83), *Genghis Khan*

Over the decade of its writing, my short story "Crossing the Caucasus" helped me whenever I felt the writings of history and academia had failed to capture the weight of an atrocity that none could remember, for which only scant records exist. The deaths of an atrocity are not merely in its event but in its virtuality—that is, its ability to be renarrated, turned on its head, transformed into a call for justice, a tale of heroism, an origin story for a nation, a parable for our own ideals. To rewrite the story over a decade, to continue trying to get it right, then to present it here alongside this chapter in vignettes—these are ways of practicing brown theory by resisting the genres of historical analysis, and by that I mean the imperial domestication of history itself.

Stories resist the dualisms that squeeze historical eras (the Mongol Empire) into good and evil, barbarian and civilized, racist and tolerant. For me, story is the only way I've been able to shake off the needless words, the lexicon, the stuffy compartments that keep scholars from finding other sources of knowledge. This chapter, revised over five years, came after a story I had revised over eight years. Both are revisionings of revisions; both are failed attempts to creatively express what could not be expressed otherwise. My time dwelling with the Mongols has been an attempt to live within the story, to understand the conceptual threads that curate our current moment, a moment submerged within imperial discourses that legitimate the violence of empire and hide its dead. The story is about domestication, which is ultimately about relationships of interdependency led and framed entirely by the lead subject—the rider, the actor, the empire builder. Domestication makes the "submit or die" mentality of empire seem organic. One does not see the oppressor and oppressed, victim and victimizer, but a complex and interdependent relationship formed over generations. If the will of the wild, as José Esteban Muñoz writes, is the "refusal of cohesion and insistence on scatteredness," then the domesticated object works for us, while we are also worked on by it.[94] We are no longer judging history but seeing ourselves within history's retelling.

Like the horse, history too can be domesticated to work for us but also works on us. Mongol history can only be domesticated by the West, who through no effort of its own escaped the Khanate empire thanks to the ill health and death of Genghis Khan and then his son Ögedei. If not for these turns of fortune, "Latin Christendom would have suffered the fate of China and Persia, and the wholesale destruction of life and culture would have rendered impossible the subsequent Renaissance of art and learning."[95] Instead, the greatest victims of the Mongols were Muslims, who today have again become alienated and villainized within the global war on terror, as well as within the persecution of Muslims in China's Xinjiang province, the Philippines' Mindanao, and Myanmar's Rohingya populations. Mongol history works on us by reflecting our selves in a twisted mirror: The Mongols' massacre of Baghdad that claimed over 200,000 lives in 1258 was a feat that would be repeated with the British-led Mesopotamian campaign (1914–19) and later the American-led second Iraq War (2003).

But just as the domesticated horse had brought the Mongols to imperial domination, so too the horse formed their limitations. The Mongols could not broach where the horse could not ride: the forests of Southeast Asia, the sharp and well-protected passes of northern India, the storm-infested waters of Japan, the unkept pastureland of Syria. The Mongol soldiers had become as dependent on the horse as the horse on them. And at any moment their greatest weapons could be used by others, even more cruel, seeking to mimic them (like the infamous ruler Tamerlane). Whereas domestication can take many generations and even millennia, a domesticated horse can become wild within a single generation. Wildness never ceases to remain a threat. Even while settling within a tolerant empire, one could still live in utter terror.

"Crossing the Caucasus" makes little attempt to re-revise history. Instead, it considers what domestication entails for those who are incorporated, who come to see the empire of their time as a reflection of their own values. What does it take for a person to become all too eager to erase the dead? How are we, scholars and writers, tempted to turn our works (and our selves) into symbols of social justice within institutions eager to reward us for it? To ponder this, I find myself agreeing with Simon Winchester of the *New York Times*, in his glowing review of Weatherford's work: "In a sense we are all Mongols; we are all one."[96]

CROSSING THE CAUCASUS

It was as heaven had dictated. Now nothing could hold back our march.

To celebrate their victory, the Mongols built a new dining hall, a yam made of thick wood from nearby fir trees. They welcomed me inside as their champion of guile. They invited me to pick first from their buffet of foods, each dish from another region of our growing empire: the hearty noodles of the Jin, the thin rice dishes of the Song, the panned bread of the Uighur, the stews of the Persians.

I received Turkish wine from a plump-faced Lezghian and heard the soft croaks of someone struggling to breathe. I took another step. Another loud groan. I lifted my foot and felt someone gasp for air. The swampy floorboards shifted beneath me.

One of the Mongols gave a firm stomp. Whomp! *The floor screamed. Below the cracking wood cracked bone.*

"Cuman!" one of the jovial Mongols jabbed at me. "Here are your countrymen, still waiting for their spoils!"

The hall erupted in laughter. Pats on my shoulders, prods on my arm. Near my right boot, a finger weakly protruded through one of the floorboard cracks. Beneath my left boot, a patch of flattened hair. The Mongols did not believe in spilling noble blood. So they built their victory hall on top of royal bodies, tied up, laid down, stacked, and compressed. And I, still standing, had my pick of the spoils.

Servants brought kabobs and more wine. I spent the night drinking, listening to my countrymen's moans. Their sobs dripped upward from the floor until one by one they went silent. When I returned to my tent, wine-drunk, I felt echoes of their breath below me, groaning slowly out of existence. I heard a whimper, like a child, or perhaps a prince. A cry, piled forever beneath my feet.

In the desert, a thousand cars idle in a line, waiting to cross into an assembled oasis. Headlights in the night reveal people on the playa, some dancing, some drumming, some making sand angels. They entice you to join their joy. Welcome home!

You've escaped your home. You've found yourself longing to travel somewhere unfamiliar. But now you worry about those on the sand, desperate for a home to accept them.

You remember the day when, during your people's month, someone asked you about pride, and you answered with habitual boredom. But in this place, where home slithers to clutch unclad ankles, you do feel pride. Because unlike them, you don't need it. Unlike them, you don't feel it. Unlike them, you welcome the desert's nothingness.

You wait, eager to watch their temple burn.

Ilocanos on the Run

A TALK-STORY

1887–94
Luciana Castro is born in Ilocos Norte in the late 1880s;
Basilio Agsalud is born in Urdaneta, Pangasinan, in the early 1890s.

1916
Basilio Agsalud arrives in Honolulu as a plantation worker. Two years later,
he enlists in World War I as a US Army private.

1920–28
Luciana Castro arrives in Honolulu. She gives birth to at least two children,
Deborah and Prisca, with an unknown man.

1928–35
Basilio and Luciana marry and have two children, Florita and Joshua.

1981
The University of Hawai'i Press publishes *Out of This Struggle*,
edited and partially written by Basilio and Luciana's son, Joshua Agsalud.
Joshua presents his autobiographical essay "My Perceptions of the
Plantation Experience" at a Philippine studies conference in Honolulu.

2021–25
Prisca Agsalud's grandson, Christopher Patterson, conducts research on Basilio and
Luciana's migration history for the book *Domesticating Brown*.

This book sees no discontinuity between the history of the Philippines and the history of overseas Filipinos, whether in Hawaii or elsewhere. Neither can the Filipino be divorced from the evolution of these islands. —DANILO E. PONCE, Foreword to Luis V. Teodoro, *Out of This Struggle*, 1981

So begins *Out of This Struggle*, the first book dedicated solely to the subject of Filipinos in Hawai'i. Published in 1981 on the seventy-fifth anniversary of the first Filipinos arriving in Oahu, *Out of This Struggle* was written collaboratively by sixteen authors across the Filipino diaspora and edited and published by the nineteen members of the Filipino seventy-fifth-anniversary commission. These writers range from government officials to journalists to novelists like Ninotchka Rosca to labor organizers and educators like my own granduncle, Joshua Agsalud.

As Joseph Agsalud's nephew and as a descendant of Filipino plantation workers myself, I cannot help but read *Out of This Struggle* as an early example of brown theory for its refusal of both state nationalist and ethnic nationalist historical narrations to instead embark on a nonlinear and dramatic approach to colonial history (see figure 2.1). As the editor, Luis V. Teodoro, writes in the book's opening preface, "This book does not intend to establish the Filipino identity in Hawaii. . . . [T]he Filipinos who came and stayed in Hawaii presumably knew who they were. And yet, being in a new place, relating to other ethnic groups, responding to novel situations, must have, in time, given them a sense that their 'identity' had changed 'several times since then.'"[1] And yet, even as this landmark text seeks to evade the trappings of identity and nationalist progression from alien to immigrant to citizen-settler, I cannot help but observe my own feelings of pride on reading it: how my people, the Ilocanos of yore, are captured in this book through their long histories of revolt; how they had joined the British in the eighteenth century to fight against Spanish forces in Manila; how their great leaders, like Gabriela Silang, who was half Itneg, were examples of Indigenous solidarities in leading Ilocanos against the Spanish; how Ilocanos, like Native Hawaiians, were known as peoples who lived off the sea, mainly as fishers, and were often despised and made outcasts within the emerging Filipino identity; how the rural Ilocano peasants, under the command of the revolutionary Andres Bonifacio, initiated armed struggle against the Spanish.[2]

The narratives of revolt and revolution in *Out of This Struggle* give me needed refuge from the shame I've carried with me as a mixed-race descendant whose experiences discussing my Filipino background have felt anything but resistant to the US imperial order of things. Shame comes when I remember

FIGURE 2.1. My 1981 copy of *Out of This Struggle*, found for $1 at a used bookseller in Kailua, Oahu.

that once, when my family was living in Las Vegas, we were approached by a group of Filipino tourists at a buffet who asked if our family was Filipino. My grandfather told them we were not and turned his back on them in an instant. My family, not wanting to expose my grandfather's ruse, silently watched them return to their tables. These moments of shame bubble up whenever I reach for memories of my Filipino grandfather, and all I recall are his words preaching at his pulpit, his church half full of military service members and their families, telling them that sometimes the destruction of entire cities in the Middle East was good in the eyes of God: that just as God had commanded the Israelites to kill nonbelievers, God too could command his American soldiers to slaughter terrorists without sparing a single soul, to "put to death men and women, children and infants, cattle and sheep, camels and donkeys."[3] While most preachers would try to hide the Bible's direct encouragement of genocidal violence, my grandfather shocked his flock of local Hawaiians and military personnel by delving unabashedly into its heavenly ordained atrocities.

I first read *Out of This Struggle*, similar to the monumental anthology *This Bridge Called My Back*, published in the same year, as a countertext to the literatures my teachers taught, as a refusal of the sermons my grandfather preached, as a way of releasing me from the shame of my family's own imperial collaborations. Like many historical texts, *Out of This Struggle* also provides release from the neoliberal self-optimization of daily life: to think that my people, the Filipinos of Hawai'i, were considered the lowest rung on the racial labor hierarchy, whose "struggle" must have been more difficult than those of many around them, thus making my own personal success feel heroic—the destined end of my great-grandparents' struggle. Feelings of shame often leave one starving for narratives of pride. In my career as an Asian American author, my own struggle has been to analyze these histories without giving way to the affective promises of either shame or pride. And yet.

I return now to *Out of This Struggle*, and to my great-grandparents, who came from the Philippines and whose family photographs are present within its pages. Four images stand out, offering the only shared photographs of my great-grandparents, who, I was told growing up, came from families of peasant fisherfolk. Perhaps they would have felt estrangement from the term *Filipino* as well. Perhaps they would have smiled on me, not because of any achievement, but because my life mirrored their desire for assimilation: a mixed-white American citizen, with a PhD and a family of my own, whose racial background was once so irrelevant that it took him until the age of thirteen to even ask his mother, "What race am I?"

"Shhh . . . Auntie is talking story."

This chapter is a storied manifest of my family lineage across histories, family narratives, and critical frameworks. Like the previous chapter, this storied manifest is not merely about a domestication of brown peoples themselves but about the historicizations where domestication has become a teleological framing, particularly when roles of labor and liberal economics remain primary units of analysis and can stifle historical narratives that are products of everyday creative expression. Whereas the previous chapter looked at scholarly and popular histories of the Mongol Empire that framed the Mongols within neoliberal and multicultural values of imperial progress (to legitimate our own imperial moment), here I focus on the domestications relevant to the history of transforming migrants into immigrants as a means of conceiving how subjects have become domesticated from an unruly mass into laboring subjects defined by their economic contributions to a multicultural state. This shift from wild people to domesticated laborers speaks to multiple interlocking systems of power: the imperial routes in Asia that deemed Southeast Asians a wild brown mass capable of "running amok"; the global racial capitalism that sought to replace Black slave labor with "free" contract labor from exploitable and do-mesticatable populations in Asia (more in chapter 4); and the settler colonial projects in North America and Oceania that entangled "the Indian" with any notion of wildness, thus permitting "racial and colonial nostalgias [to] imagine freedom beyond the domestications, cultivations, and laws of settlement."[4] Formed through these interlocking systems, I consider how the pride that I and others might feel in the struggle of our laboring ancestors can further settler colonial projects in Hawai'i by erasing Indigenous peoples, obfuscating the ways that settler animus and coloniality structure Filipino presence in Hawai'i, and demobilizing durable and meaningful Indigenous-Filipinx solidarities. These historical domestications occur not just in nationalist histories of marginalized peoples but within family narratives, which can carry an ambivalent relationship to historical knowledge through a perforation of uncertain family stories. This important and ambiguous historical practice occurs every time my family gathers in Hawai'i and one of my uncles or aunties says, "Hey, let's talk-story."

Talk-story is often characterized as an intimate, familial, and Indigenous form of place-based storytelling in Hawai'i that was frequently used by plantation workers and continues through various communities on the islands today. In academia, the term was made famous through Maxine Hong Kingston's *The Woman Warrior*, with the scholar King-Kok Cheung referring to the novel's mode of talk-story as a performance art commonly heard in the Hawaiian Islands that "blurs the distinction between straight facts and pure fiction" while accomplishing "two key objectives: to reclaim a past and, more decisively, to envision a different future."[5] Talk-story thus sees historical events as initiating future-building possibilities. Its story form makes worlds while wrestling with the present in which it is spoken. This gives talk-story an imaginative function that blends traditions while "incorporating elements of the supernatural, spirited dialogues in pidgin, and vivid adventures told from a child's viewpoint."[6]

As a method, talk-story or talking story has been used to guide researchers when interviewing Indigenous Hawaiians to "preserve" ideas and spiritualities, and has been used by the Hawaiian state to solicit comments and convince its constituents.[7] Indigenous activists have used talk-story (often translated from *ha'i mo'olelo*, as in "to tell a legend, history, or story") to connect with other activists and settlers, as well as with police and other opponents.[8] In all of these methods, talk-story is meant to invoke a plurality of voices that evades the formality of institutional investments to work together for a more collective future.

Talk-story carries many elisions, many opinions, many unspoken allegiances, and many silences. So too this chapter represents decades of longing for the untraceable. In the past year, as I have revisited my family's talk-stories, I too have faced silences: "No one talked about our heritage back then," my mother tells me. My great-uncles and aunties who might remember it, like my own grandparents on both sides of my family, suffer from Alzheimer's and dementia and are unable to provide the answers I'm seeking (two of them died not long after I was in conversation with them). Then, of course, there are the troubles of the archive. While my great-grandfather, Basilio Agsalud, can be identified on transport documents, his wife, and my great-grandmother, Luciana Castro, appears on no historical records except for her citizenship and death—not even a date for her marriage or the birth of her children.

Like in the previous chapter, I am less concerned here with the particular events that transpired on my great-grandparents' travels and more with the legacy they represent, and the brown worlds that form through these histories. The story begins with my great-grandparents, though little is known about their migrancy. My great-grandfather, Basilio, is not actually my biological kin, yet my family has held strong to his story as part of our lineage. We express my grandparents' lives in our talk-stories as a series of movements that continue to bind my family and community together, as we, living in the present, have also remained on the move, escaping tradition, gentrification, militarization, and exploitation, often by finding new homes in various locales (Las Vegas, Eugene, Vancouver, Minneapolis, San Antonio). The movements of brown studies make sense of my own elusive family history through what Ma Vang calls a "history on the run" that "suggests a mobility that has no fixed origin or referent (whether in a singular repository or nation-state) except as a way of knowing attached to fugitivity."[9] *Fugitivity* here reads across terms for peoples on the run who are both composed by and critical to narratives of the ethno-state, multiculturalism, and global diasporas. Fugitive ways of knowing, for Vang, are constitutive of "silences, refusals, and evasions—and imagine ways of being in but not of the nation-state and its official history."[10] Vang's context here is as the daughter of Hmong refugees writing about Hmong peoples, who offer a position that is both composed by and critical of "the violence of colonialism and war, state governance, and national belonging."[11]

This chapter explores how brown theory can trace the history of a differently composed people, those who migrated out of Ilocos Norte and Ilocos Sur and who are commonly referred to as *Ilocanos*. I look at my great-grandparents' migration through a collective, present-making form of storytelling. Like *Out of This Struggle*, I hesitate to tell this story within affects of subject-making or sentimentality but instead narrate it as an imaginary public discourse regarding the meaning we can make of their movements, and the historical lineages that seek neither certainty nor resolution nor state recognition. In other words, I take a brown theoretical standpoint elaborated on in the foreword that spirals through brown contexts as a means of gravitating toward the weight of their colonial histories, turning from one epistemic framework to another: from narratives of economic and diasporic migration to narratives of travel, to narratives of exiles, to narratives of settler colonialism, to narratives of critical Filipinx studies, to refugee narratives, to narratives of Filipino nationalism, and to narratives of fugitivity and being on the run. These movements are not meant to emphasize the separability of these narratives but to show their uneven flows as discursive projects, and to understand how all of these frameworks overlap, fuse, and function. This form mimics and is inspired by my own family's talk-story of our multiple migrations as seen from various standpoints: through my cousins' mixed Kānaka Maoli heritage; my sister's Black, Ilocano, and Indigenous mixture; the viewpoints of both my twin brother and me, who travel widely and have lived in South Korea, China, and Hong Kong; my cousins who are transracially (Chinese) adopted; partners whose heritage comes from Japan, South Korea, and Cambodia; and the views of our own descendants, who carry various visions of place, religion, and affective belonging.

Over the years, almost everyone in my family has lived on or returned to the island of Oahu, and some have moved permanently to the US mainland, Asia, or Canada. Our talk-stories come from our various racial and ideological positions, as well as from our exilic sensibilities that, as Edward Said wrote, can realize a "nomadic, decentered, contrapuntal" "plurality of vision" of multiple cultures, homelands, and futurities.[12] Expanding on Said's ideas to center less on exiles themselves and more on "exilic affects," Zahi Zalloua sees such affects as able to "unsettle the cultural script of rootedness and national belonging."[13] Similarly, Evyn Lê Espiritu sees exilic affects as generating pluralistic forms of home, of belonging, and charting "connections between the destabilized figures of native, refugee, and exile" that can work toward "conceptualizing coalitional politics between differentially racialized communities."[14] This movement across frameworks and standpoints thus reflects the ways brownness was never an isolated racial form but has always been a means of revealing racial relations, a movement toward or away from others who are sometimes also brown.

To practice this brown movement in writing, this chapter proceeds by resisting the pinning-down tendencies of language itself, which are often delineated as mere acts of consistency or legibility. During the many years of writing this chapter, I have struggled to express a storied manifest of my own family history of brownness that avoids, as Neferti Tadiar puts it, the tendency to "presume to know in advance the social groups for whom particular practices comprise certain 'cultures,' which subsequently serve to define such groups (in the current fashion of cultural racism)."[15] To challenge this, Tadiar advises scholars to consider the emergent social constitutions of infrasociality, the "levels of social constitution that operate below the threshold of current codings of social identity . . . for example, whether one identifies forms of sociality as Ilocanos, Filipino Americans, OFWs [overseas Filipino workers], or peasants."[16] Following Tadiar, I use terms of identity like *Filipinx American*, *Filipino*, and *Ilocano*, as Dylan Rodriguez might, as a "troubled placeholder rather than a normative category," as identities whose normative functions make them discussable as one of many stops in a continual movement.[17] My great-grandparents could perhaps be called *migrants* and *immigrants*, even though these terms remain ways of reiterating the power of the nation-state as a global form of recognition. The uses of such terms can now be tracked through metadata sites like Google Books Ngram Viewer, which shows the appearance of words like *migrant* and *immigrant* growing only in the late nineteenth century's concurrent growth of immigrant documentation during the coolie trade, when passports and immigration documentation were put in use, and technologies like the railroad and steamship were democratized. This chapter will use these terms as well as the terms *sakada*, *Filipino migrant*, *colonial subject*, *diasporic subject*, *traveler*, *exile*, *refugee*, *manong*, and others. This lack of consistency follows the inconsistencies of migratory movement, where even the name of a people can shift depending on which diasporic people we are considering (Ilocano versus Ilokano, Philippine versus Filipino versus Pilipino versus Filipinx).

The slippery movements of brownness often result in slippages among terms that reveal how brownness has been conjured not as a fixed identity or position but as possibilities that shift depending on the racial roles that are available within the colonial racial imaginary, and the ways that people within realms of brownness tend to play with and against these roles. These slippages, as Sony Coráñez Bolton writes, are necessary when understanding colonial race-making across contexts, where insisting on the same terms inevitably reinforces a comparative frame that dilutes one context within the parameters of another.[18] Talk-story slips among terms of identity to reveal a plurality of brownness that appears not merely in relation to other racial forms but as a form of interactive praxis that notes how race-making is not merely one-sided but responsive to specific contexts, structures, and vantage points. Rather than attempt to intellectualize our way into a settled consistency, the movement of brown theory compels us to insist on the unsettling motions of the incommensurable, presenting a praxial approach to race-making that sees the terms naming us and others as not only multidimensional, not only relational, but mobile, potent with potentiality, and as proliferating into unseen and unknowable realms beyond our own racial imagination. These terms, while not interchangeable, will be used in this chapter as they seem appropriate to the context as a direct refusal to pin down a dazzling, elusive movement.

The shifting frameworks, standpoints, and languages of this chapter are also a means of seeking out narratives through what Roderick Labrador calls *motility*, a biological term meaning "active and seemingly spontaneous movement" that "directs our attention on the gradients around which identity movements pivot."[19] Such gradients of identity can reveal the "multivocal conversation[s]" of contested realities in which "multiple definitions coexist and often challenge one another."[20] I see Labrador's theory here as a means of understanding historical figures not as mobile individuals but as integral to the generation of political and strategic movements. Unlike *mobility*, *motility* refuses the nation-state's centering of border crossings (ideologically coded as "arrivals") as identity-making iterations but rather highlights the spontaneous movements and transitions of peoples who move through multiple infrastructures that connect and create identities, communities, nations, races. In human anatomy, *motility* is most often used to refer to the gastrointestinal system, especially the digestive tract, to describe the movement of fluids in relation to all the other parts of the system: the enzymes produced by the pancreas to break down proteins; the movement of food from the mouth through the pharynx (throat), esophagus, stomach, and small and large intestines and out of the body. Motility thus offers the gastrointestinal system as a metaphor for the interconnected systems of movement, reframing the movement of peoples from domesticating practices of self-development to the necessary movements of global empire that also have the power to transform entire systems, where one difference in motility has multiple relations to those who are within the same system. Motility asks that we see movements of peoples and ideas alongside and as productive to other peoples and larger systems. In other words, we understand motility not through traveling figures themselves but through the indirect impacts of their movements on the systemic whole, by exploring the ways that movement produces new ways, new memories, new connections. Motility guides us to the challenges that movement presents to the people who moved, the peoples they visited and left behind, and those whose movements seek to travel across time rather than space, and who travel again through our talk-story.

> "Our Ohana came from Ilocos Norte, yeah?
> They were fishermen?"

Before there were refugees or diasporas, transpacific brown movement was conceived mostly as two types—nomads or exiles. Other races had armies, hordes, explorers, travelers, and conquerors, but there was something nominally brown about the nomad and the exile.

The Ilocanos of the northwestern coast of Luzon in the Philippines were known as nomadic peoples. They were often juxtaposed against the exiles: the political and intellectual elites, or *ilustrados*, who were mostly Tagalog and Spanish speaking, and often Chinese or Spanish mestizo. At the same time, Ilocano migrations encroached on the lands of other native peoples: Igorots, and later Native Hawaiians. Their migration was a displacement into destitution and permanent labor exploitation. As Vicente L. Rafael writes, American colonial census forms categorized the vast majority of Philippine colonial subjects as "M" for *moreno* (brown) on punch cards, and placed them on a scale from wild to civilized that was primarily informed by the subjects' relation to landscape, where a proximity to forms of geographic wildness (jungles, mountains, seas) noted a more domesticatable colonial subject who would likely not know Spanish and would be more receptive to Americanism (and Protestantism) than the "civilized" peoples within large cities like Manila.[21] By the late nineteenth century, Ilocanos were no longer "peoples of the bay" (the literal meaning of *Ilocano*) but had become "peoples of the plantation." Or, as they were often called, *sakadas*: a migratory term similar to *coolie* that was unique to Ilocanos and then to Filipino plantation workers in Hawai'i. The term *sakadas*, which literally translates to "their feet," defined Ilocano peoples by their ambulatory displacement from region to region, plantation to plantation, island to island.[22] As subjects of modern plantation agriculture, Ilocanos in the late nineteenth century came to represent a state in between the wild Indigenous "mountain people" and the civilized "city people." Their in-betweenness made them suitable candidates for extraction and exploitation; the first peoples of the Philippines plucked for American domestication.

My family has much debated the racial origins of my great-grandparents, Basi-lio and Luciana Agsalud, who are rumored in our talk-stories to have been many things: fishers, farmworkers, Indigenous Filipinos (mainly Igorot), Indigenous Taiwanese (Gaoshan), and mixed Chinese mestizos who, unlike other mestizo elites, had to hide their lineage due to persecution. While DNA evidence has revealed only the uncertain blurs of our brown lineage (as I discuss later), it is important to note that, as Richard Chu and Caroline Hau point out, Filipino family lineages in general are often far more transnational than domesticated nationalist projects have narrated, and that Chinese mixtures in the Philip-pines have been complicated by anti-Chinese state violence as well as a surface-level (as profitable) multicultural inclusion ("the massacre of the Chinese in 1603 and 1639; application of the Chinese Exclusion Act in the Philippines in 1902; the granting of mass naturalization in 1975").[23] It is thus probable that my great-grandparents had, on arrival to Hawai'i, sought to hide their Chinese heritage, considering that this was during the Chinese Exclusion Act, and that the still-in-process identity of the Filipino was seen as a form of mixture, one that was unique from other Asian groups in that it occupied "a form of Indige-nous rehabilitation and philosophical distance from depraved Chineseness."[24] By hiding any Chinese ancestry, perhaps my great-grandparents were escaping not only the anti-Chinese racism in the Philippines but also that within the United States, as well as the anti-Chinese sentiments among other Ilocano mi-grants. Within Filipino American scholarship, one must admit this has been an effective labor of history. Perhaps in a reminder of the need to domesti-cate forms of brownness, historians have often tended to see Chinese mestizos during the time of exclusion and American colonialism as within a particular privileged elite, not as part of a brown mass of mixture, thereby reinforcing colonial racial typologies that could only conceive of mixture as belonging to a hybrid mestizo/a class. To this day, historians of Filipino migrants continue to rigidly separate groups of "Filipino" and "Chinese" migrants, as if Ilocanos weren't themselves ever also Chinese or weren't under great duress to shape themselves as purely Ilocano/Filipino.[25] If my great-grandparents were indeed Chinese mestizo, it is not a narrative they or their children widely promoted but a family secret living only in rumor and sharp glances at my grandmother's face, eyeballing her hidden racial signs ("She looks just as much Chinese as Filipino," my uncle once told me).

To follow my family's brownness means privileging some movements over others. Let us then stick to the paths where our family talk-stories and the his-torical records overlap, and privilege the narrative that Basilio and Luciana Ag-salud were Ilocano, sakada, nomadic people displaced by war, colonization, and global capital. Basilio was born in Urdaneta, Pangasinan, in 1894 (according to a census record), or 1892 (according to his gravestone), or 1891 (according to his second draft registration card in 1942, which would have made him fifty years old and less eligible for service). Before coming to Hawai'i, Basilio was already part of the Ilocano diaspora, having migrated out of Ilocos Norte. His future wife, Luciana Castro, was born in Piddig, Ilocos Norte, though my family has long believed she was from Laoag, the capital of Ilocos Norte, a city known for casinos and gambling (an amusing origin story, since many of us ended up in Las Vegas). Like Basilio, Luciana would likely have grown up working on the plantations, a fieldhand with the rest of her family. They both likely worked on tobacco plantations across the northwestern coast of Luzon in the late nineteenth century, when tobacco was the Philippines' major export. It is also likely that the tobacco my great-grandparents picked was sold to the elites in Manila, both Spanish and elite Filipinos and mestizos, whose pockets were filled with the profits of their labor.[26] As Carlos Bulosan wrote in *America Is in the Heart*, the national independence movement had been in "the hands of powerful native leaders" who were "slowly but inevitably plunging the nation into a great economic catastrophe that tore the islands from their roots, and obfuscated the people's resurgence toward a broad national unity."[27] Bulosan, also an Ilocano and born in the same province as Basilio, was economically impoverished by the political elite during the American colonial period. Their peoples were not the landed gentry of Manila but those who, as Jody Blanco puts it, were "landless and destitute in a republic yet to be, uprooted by the violent oscillation between the demands of a backwards economy suddenly hitched to the train of preferential trade relations with the US, on the one hand, and the constant outbreak of mass revolt, on the other."[28] For Blanco, workers like Bulosan and other Ilocano migrants "saw starting over in the sugarcane fields of Hawai'i and Alaskan canneries as the only escape from a predetermined fate of poverty and the impunity of authority."[29] Indeed, Bulosan's memories of his hometown of Binalonan as a child must have been very similar to Basilio's, as Binalonan is a mere fifteen kilometers from Basilio's village of Urdaneta. Like many sakadas who were not from wealthy or privileged legacies, "family and community existed not in the past, but the future."[30]

After being subjected to the dispossession of land and usury by Spanish colonizers and elites, Ilocanos like Basilio and Luciano were on the move throughout the nineteenth century, seeking employment on plantation lands. As Adrian De Leon writes, "American financial institutions capitalized on Philippine racial structures put in place through the forced ruralization of Northern Luzon through nineteenth-century Spanish agricultural policy, which generated an inland Ilokano peasantry through dispossession, coercion, and hunger."[31] Indeed, by 1903, years before any Ilocanos would leave for Hawai'i, more than 290,000 Ilocanos had already migrated throughout the island of Luzon, over 36 percent of its self-identified population.[32] In Manila they were known as the uncivilized, the rural poor, the "people of the bay" who threatened to encumber the enlightened ilustrados; in the Cagayan and Cordillera valleys, they were known as settlers encroaching on traditional lands of other native peoples (namely, Igorot peoples).[33] As Sony Coráñez Bolton has argued in his study of the historical transition of the Philippines from a Spanish colony to US imperial territory in the early twentieth century, "Filipino mestizaje simultaneously becomes a marker of difference from the colonized indio and a vehicle evoking and evidencing their reform—the mestizo body then is the evidence, product, and agent of colonial rehabilitation."[34] As Ilocanos, my great-grandparents would have occupied the interstices between the modern urban mestizo/a subject and the savage native, a space of domesticable brownness even in relation to the colonial populace.

Once a common enemy during much of the Spanish colonial period, Ilocanos had spread widely throughout the islands by the Philippine Revolution. During the American colonial occupation, they were identified by the Americans as suitable "transplantable labor."[35] Young Ilocano men would assist the American military by joining the Scouts program initiated in 1899, a recontextualized copy of the Native Scouts programs that the US government used to create Indigenous collaborators to enforce Native dispossession.[36] By 1903 the Philippine Scouts numbered fifty companies, with the largest proportion of scouts coming from Macabebe and Ilocano origins. During the long war against the Philippine "insurrectos," Scouts were crucial to the US consolidation of colonial rule through "fomenting and attempting to direct race war between specific Philippine tribes."[37] Though they were instructed to fight in the long war against Filipino insurgents, they quickly "began to take the appearance of an outfit destined to remain an integral part of the colonial army in the Philippines."[38]

While some Ilocanos became American collaborators, others defied Spanish and American rule, redefining the accepted brown racialization of Filipinos by focusing on the Ilocano as a figure of unsettlement. During the lead-up to the Philippine Revolution, when most ilustrados sought to build on a definition of Filipinos as characteristically Tagalog speaking, mestizo, and part of the landed elite, the Ilocano (and perhaps Chinese mestizo) journalist Isabelo de los Reyes sought a broader imaginary of the Filipino subject. Today known as the patriarch of many fatherhoods ("Father of Philippine Folklore," "Father of the Philippine Labor Movement," "Father of Filipino Socialism"), de los Reyes came to prominence when he was asked by a Spanish priest "to collect Ilocano 'superstitions' as signs of backwardness" in his native Ilocos.[39] Instead, de los Reyes used his investigations into traditional Ilocano cultures to "cast his net over an immensity of Filipino creativity" and to defend non-Tagalog forms of cultural creativity, from superstitions to games and idioms.[40] His seminal text arguing this, *El folk-lore filipino*, was published the same year as José Rizal's *Noli Me Tángere*, and like Rizal's, it also helped make him an enemy of the state. *El folk-lore filipino* argued for a use of folklore not to separate out the races but to enable a "reconstruction of the indigenous past that was impossible in the Philippines by any other means."[41] De los Reyes's research attempted to prove shared traditions (and thus shared bloodlines) among Filipino races (notably Ilocano and Tagalog) whose supposed racial separations had been supported by hundreds of years of Spanish divide-and-conquer rule. At the time, for a non-Spaniard to lay claim to (and win an award for) work on traditions and customs in the Philippines, and to then claim a common origin for browned peoples across the archipelago, could itself be considered revolutionary activity.[42] In 1897 de los Reyes was imprisoned for his scholarly work, as well as his publications in the propagandic newspaper *La Solidaridad*. He was promptly deported to Spain and jailed until 1898. On returning to the Philippines in 1901, de los Reyes founded the country's first labor union and became a senator and active voice in speaking out against US colonization.[43]

In the lead-up to the Philippine Revolution, de los Reyes's sense of populism and his distance from the exiled Tagalog elite as well as those in Manila led him to "stretch[] the boundaries of the Filipino further than any of his expatriate counterparts" by redefining the Filipino "in ways that subverted hierarchies of urban and rural, elite and popular, and even Catholic and animist religious cultures."[44] The racial divisions of the early revolutionary period were most often pronounced by the Prague-born ethnologist Ferdinand Blumentritt, whose 1882 racial schema of the peoples of the Philippines isles as one of two types, Malay or Negrito, was widely accepted by the ilustrados, including Rizal and de los Reyes. Yet, rather than see these divisions as inherently separative and needing to be kept distinct, as Rizal did, de los Reyes found them less significant than his counterparts and instead stressed the connections among migratory groups in places like Indonesia and Malaya.[45] In so doing, de los Reyes sought to decenter Spanish colonization as the origin story for race-making and racial lineages.[46] Rather than see brotherhood in the brown and mixed-race elites in Europe and Asia, de los Reyes called himself, in the opening to the 1885 essay, an Ilocano who was "brother of the jungle dwellers, the Aeta, the Igorot and the Tinguian and born in this remote Spanish colony, where civilization shines but with a very faint light."[47] As Benedict Anderson observed, "No one else in Isabelo's time, certainly no one who counted himself an ilustrado, would have spoken in such terms of these forest-dwellers who seemed, in their untamed fastnesses, utterly remote from any urban, Hispanicized, Catholicized milieu."[48] Indeed, de los Reyes's gesture of solidarity brought him ridicule and sparked outrage among other ilustrados, who refused to see any fraternal bond with people whom they (following the Spanish) saw as less civilized races.[49]

My own family history coming from Ilocos Norte persuades me to mark the Ilocano intelligentsia as more enlightened (or progressive or antiracist) than their counterparts of the Tagalog elite. Yet de los Reyes remained subscribed to an anti-Black "two races" racial theory and sometimes retracted statements of solidarity once they threatened his position. He later claimed, for example, that his brotherhood with "jungle dwellers" was in jest. In other moments, he propelled a kind of Ilocano nationalism or even supremacy, as his "upholding of the Aeta or Negrito . . . was compromised by his ill feelings toward the Tagalog."[50] Similarly, there were plenty of peoples from Ilocos whose mode of imperial response was not solidarity and resistance but separation and collaboration. In 1902, three years into the Philippine-American War, the provincial governor of Ilocos Norte, Aguedo Agbayani, argued for a US congressional report *not* to allow voting within the province, because of "the necessity for intelligence," whereas among the peoples of Ilocos Norte "what happens is just the opposite."[51] As Dylan Rodriguez has pointed out, such intraracial prejudices from elites against other "Filipinos" are "stunningly easy to find" and were encouraged by the colonial state to buttress the thesis of Filipinos as less civilized, thus disqualifying "the majority of their (and the world's) people from recognition as inherently self-determining, rational, rightfully autonomous human beings."[52]

The collaborations and revolutions of Ilocano history cause me to revisit my own familial ruptures. I think of our gathering at the Las Vegas casino buffet, when my grandfather claimed he was not Filipino to a group of Filipino visitors, and how one could read this refusal as an act of self-hatred and American pride, or as a revolutionary gesture against the Tagalog elite whose very question "Are you Filipino?" might presume particular traits of belonging within a limited racial imaginary (based on ethnicity, language, class, non-Chineseness, and era of migration). So too these histories trace my family's own inconsistent talk-stories of our origins, and our collective narrative erasure of the "other family"—the Ilocanos in the Philippines whom my great-grandparents left behind. I wonder if, as in Bulosan's narrative of his brother Macario, Basilio's and Luciana's families had sacrificed everything for their travels to Hawai'i, had sold hectares of their land, placed all their emotional promises and investments in their future, assuming that their sons and daughters would return to them within three years' time, only to be forgotten not only by them but forever by their descendants, to be placed into the category of brown mass for whom we, the exceptional peoples in the exceptional nation, had overcome. Did they try to reunite with their families? Were my great-great-grandmother's hands like Bulosan's mother's, "big-veined, hard, and bleeding in spots," from working for her son's future? Did they sell everything, their house? Were they victims of usurers? Were they dispossessed? Did they resort to violence against the colonial regime, against the elites, against the politicians? Or did they, like us, eventually risk everything to join a new promised land?

> "Now this is hearsay, the kind of family lore that is passed
> down from generation to generation and gets more dramatic
> with every telling, so take it for what it's worth."

My great-grandfather, Basilio Fernandez Agsalud, must have seen the possibility of traveling away from the Philippines as a particularly seductive option after the hopes of the revolution had disintegrated with his family's continued poverty and displacement. When the first group of "Hawaiianos" appeared in his village, my great-grandfather must have been spellbound. Here were people like him, peasants who had fought and sacrificed yet were kept in poverty by the elite, now with money, land, stature, all the things that the revolution had initially promised. And, importantly, these travelers had come back and were adored by the peoples in the barangays. I imagine, contrary to narratives of immigration, migration, and diaspora, that my great-grandfather, longing for the adoration and security of these Hawaiianos, did not realize that by seeking out this brief and profitable adventure, he would never be coming back.[53]

Out-migration by Filipino workers in the early twentieth century rarely fits the bourgeois definitions of travel, a position that, in the Philippines, was often occupied by mestizo elites like Rizal and politicians like Teodoro Kalaw, whose travelogue *Hacia la tierra del zar* (Toward the land of the czar, 1908) followed the travels of Manuel Quezon, who was to serve as president of the Commonwealth of the Philippines from 1935 to 1944. As Coráñez Bolton writes, such travels often worked to fashion the elites "as the very rehabilitated subjects assimilated into US colonial regimes" and as "the beneficiaries turned well-traveled agents of benevolent rehabilitation."[54] In comparison to this form

FIGURE 2.2. Basilio Agsalud in *Out of This Struggle*.

of "enlightened" travel that conceptualized Filipino identity against Chinese, Japanese, and Russians, "lower" migratory travel was rarely depicted within the desire for new experiences and intellectual insights. My great-grandparents' travels are thus measured within the plantation fields of brown mass, that is, of migrants defined solely as workers rather than thinkers, fieldhands rather than creative minds, whose cognitive capacity, education, and aesthetic sensibilities were not fit enough to experience the worldliness of "travel," nor did they have the historical awareness to narrate their own stories—except, perhaps, through talking.

In an image from *Out of This Struggle*, my great-grandfather Basilio stands in his attire from World War I next to a caption that names him one "of the earliest Filipino arrivals" (figure 2.2). From archival documents, we know Basilio arrived in Honolulu on November 22, 1916, at the supposed age of twenty-four, on the transport vessel the *Shinyō Maru*, the same ship that, during World War II, would be pressed into military service by Japan and would later be known as a "hell ship" after 668 Allied prisoners of war were killed when the SS *Shinyō Maru* sank.[55] Basilio is identified as passenger number 24 on the *Shinyō Maru*, boarding in Hong Kong on a twenty-three-day journey to Honolulu, where he was listed as one of over 386 passengers, most identified as either "Asiatic Philipinos for Honolulu from Hong Kong," "Asiatic Chinese," or "Asiatic Japanese."[56] These Japanese ships carrying Filipino laborers often made stops in Hong Kong, Shanghai, Kobe, and Yokohama, giving their passengers a sense of a wider world far from either the Philippine archipelago or the Hawaiian Islands. It was common to feel that work on the Hawaiian plantations, though higher paying, was far more difficult than the same positions in the Philippines and was worsened by the lack of family and community life.[57] Yet in this photograph my great-grandfather shows little sign of resignation. According to family talk-story, Basilio was a rebel who left the Philippines under cloudy circumstances. Was his choice to enlist in the American military, only two years after his arrival, part of his rebellion?[58] If so, rebellion against what?

No record could be found for my great-grandmother Luciana Castro's passage, though one figure has arisen: a woman of the same name who lived in the same province, near Laoag City, where my family believes Luciana came from. But this woman was born over a decade earlier than Luciana said she was born, and was pronounced dead in 1924. Though my family believes Luciana came before Basilio (before 1916), no archival evidence suggests this. It seems possible—and kind of fun to imagine—that Luciana took the path of many migrants and that on her arrival in the 1920s, she made herself ten years younger and perhaps found some way to have herself pronounced deceased in the Philippines to escape family debt or violence, or simply to disappear. It could have just as well been possible that Luciana did leave before 1916 and simply never wrote back to her family, leading them to assume that she, like other migrants, had died on the ship during passage to Honolulu, her body tossed somewhere in the Pacific.[59] Neither Basilio nor Luciana mentioned their parents' names or family in the Philippines, and no one in my family seems to know their names either. Their parents' names were not included on their obituaries or on any other official documents. It is as if my great-grandparents were born on arrival.

Before the Hawaiian Islands could shift from an agriculture-based subsistence economy based on a communal society to a form of US-controlled maritime commerce, certain key events had to occur.[60] First, the traditional land tenure system had to be replaced by one of private property that could enable large-scale agribusinesses to buy up acreage, a goal that was achieved with the Great Mahele Division in 1848 that reallocated land. Then the Kuleana Act in 1850 created a fee- and commodity-based system that allowed land to be purchased by settlers. The second event was the removal of Native Hawaiian workers, who had remained the majority of plantation workers until 1876 but were replaced by more exploitable populations of Japanese and Chinese migrants—peoples who were constrained by their own migrations (of being "out of their homelands"), who were less likely to refuse work and thus more likely to accept lower wages.[61] The third event was the absence of viable markets for Hawaiian-made products, a problem that was solved with two events: the Gold Rush migration to California, which produced new markets for Hawaiian coffee and sugar, and the Spanish-American War, which effectively closed off the sugar trade coming from the West Indies.[62] Later, the Spanish-American War would result in an even more effective outcome for the sugar companies of Hawai'i: the availability of a new colonized people to perform the most difficult and lowest-paying tasks on the plantations, Filipinos.

Ilocano migration to Hawai'i was a shared opportunity for many different interests: (1) the American companies, who sought docile, exploitable labor; (2) the American colonial officials, who sought ways to expatriate the poorest classes of Filipino males, who were most likely to take part in insurgent activities; (3) the elite collaborators and senators of the Philippine colonial state, who sought ways of gaining remittances and enriching their pockets with large licensing fees; and (4) the Ilocanos themselves, who had been dispossessed of land, were encumbered by debt, and, in many cases, were subjected to disease and starvation.[63] Ilocanos, who made up the majority of sakada migrants, were the first large wave of labor out-migration encouraged by the Philippine colonial state, which would later lead to the Philippines, by the 1980s, becoming what Robyn Rodriguez has called a "labor brokerage state" that promotes "legal human trafficking."[64] As Labrador writes, for the sakadas, "travel to Hawai'i extended this tradition of out-migration and 'temporary absence' into the international sphere, and transformed them into an agri-industrial proletariat."[65]

Between 1906 and 1946, over 125,000 Filipino laborers arrived to work on Hawai'i's plantations. They were brought by the Hawaiian Sugar Planters' Association (HSPA), an agricultural federation that "held a viselike grip over island politics" and needed a new exploitable class of laborers to break up the Japanese, who made up 7 percent of plantation workers and were gaining power through labor strikes.[66] The first group of Filipino laborers arrived in Hawaii in 1906 after negotiations with American colonial officials but yielded only fifteen workers, mostly Ilocanos. These new colonial subjects seemed to fit the ideal image of a hardworking yet docile worker, "with their extended history of colonial subjection and economic privation."[67] Initially, the HSPA sought to encourage migration to Hawai'i as a family activity, hoping to entice more women to come to the plantations, bringing with them their children and perhaps extended family to "capitalize on the larger kinship structures of Ilokanos in Northern Luzon."[68] Landowning elites in Hawai'i believed that migrant workers could be more productive within these family networks and that the racial reproduction of Filipino workers could create a permanent impasse between the Japanese and Chinese labor organizers. These efforts from 1906 to 1910 mostly failed, yet were made more urgent as planters became more "concerned about the increasing organizational capacity of Japanese workers."[69] Recruitment strategies for Filipinos were then replaced with a new tactic: taking advantage of the "feet" of the sakadas by stressing the transient status of plantation work and promising fully paid fare back to the homeland after three years of work. This tactic resulted in bringing over Filipinos who, for the most part, "were neither interested in nor committed to a long-term stint in the way of life that characterized the isolated plantation towns of Hawaii."[70] Even so, the initial desire to bring over semipermanent workers was fulfilled in other ways—in placing workers into cycles of debt and, eventually, eliminating the return-fare clauses in the workers' contracts.[71] Many sakada migrants who had planned on leaving Hawai'i after a brief and profitable adventure thus found themselves held captive within cycles of debt from the initial ticket to Hawai'i, the debts they had in the Philippines but were unable to pay off after three years, and then the inflated plantation prices, remittances, gambling, and debts gained from leaving contracts to work on plantations with better treatment or higher wages. In effect, many adventurous sakadas were remade into debt fugitives with no legal way off the island.[72] By 1940 around half of the Filipino sakadas had been able to leave, and many who remained, even those with children born in the plantation towns, continued to be seen, and to see themselves, as a transient population without strong community-wide institutions.[73]

The steady stream of Filipino workers to Hawai'i from 1910 onward is often read as a symbol of American multicultural origins, where the exceptional state of the United States gave refuge to hardworking brown men seeking greater opportunity and a better life. Indeed, this is the narrative I was often told around family talk-stories. It was never presented as fact but as the only narrative available to us through US educational systems and nationalist media. The story, as it often gets told, is that Filipinos were the most abused group on the plantations and to this day remain one of the less fortunate racial classes on the islands. Thus, our family had struggles that other families did not. Yet it is important to situate how brownness entered the Hawaiian Islands in many different instances, from the Kānaka Maoli, later identified as Polynesian, who were systematically depopulated through disease and dispossessed of their lands, to the Japanese and Chinese workers who were brought to replace them, who were fleeing famine and political catastrophe and who experienced such virulent racism and suspicion that both groups were eventually excluded from entering the United States.[74] Indeed, one of the most important laws governing contract labor in the United States was directed at the Asian (mostly Chinese) coolie labor that had emerged to replace Black slave labor and create new pools of exploitable peoples for working on railroads and in service work like laundries. The 1885 Foran Act, written three years after the 1882 Chinese Exclusion Act, banned contract labor, deeming it too easy to exploit "alien" labor with contracts, but was obviously meant to keep out Asian workers.[75] Filipinos, as colonial subjects, were not immigrant aliens according to the law, and thus had the right to travel to the United States, but were also subjected to exploitive contract laws, what many call today a system of debt peonage, or a "captive-worker model of immigration" that grew out of the abolishment of slavery, when large-scale industrial employers were seeking forms of exploitable labor that offered particular benefits chattel slavery did not: no need to provide housing, clothing, food, or care; no initial purchase or capital investment in workers; and, most important, the power of the contract to limit the workers to only being present in the United States during the most productive years of their lives, to leave before they could make any political impact or "dilute the race."

My great-grandparents, as evidenced within both my family's talk-stories and the archive, slide among forms of movement. They were not immigrants but precarious migrants; they were not aliens but colonial subjects; they were not refugees fleeing the Philippine-American War to take refuge within labor camps but merely hard workers seeking a better life than the unfortunate circumstances of their births.[76] They were not political dissenters who came from a lineage of peasant revolutionaries and militarized collaborators, but worshippers breaking from Catholicism and seeking the salvation of a Protestant god. They were not starving masses emerging from the poverty and near starvation wreaked on generations by Spanish dispossession, but tough and docile workers meant to break strikes in the plantation camps. They were not exiles or travelers who were trapped and held captive, separated from their families through cycles of unending debt, but settlers seeking the gifts of American civilization. They were not subjected to some of the harshest labor conditions only made possible through their precarious position as colonized peoples, but were grateful to build a new life for their children, their children's children, and me, a tenured professor at a top-tier institution, whose academic success is all the evidence anyone would need to prove their hardworking immigrant narrative true.

> "No one remembers when or how they got married. We just
> know that she was abused by her first husband."

As is often the case, the elites of Hawai'i didn't seem to consider the long-term consequences of their attempts to pluck the Ilocanos out from the brown mass and domesticate them. In the 1920s, labor organizers began to shift the narrative of Hawaiian labor from one of travel, riches, and return, to family and investment in local communities, helping to create the conditions for workers who may not have intended to stay on the island permanently to imagine themselves living on the island for the long term. Without the trust of diasporic movement and free return, and now with families and communities to care for, "work" would shift meaning from a brief venture to a livelihood demanding more livable earnings and working conditions.

It is difficult to say whether Basilio or Luciana had initially carried the mindset of settling in Hawai'i or, like many early migrants, had always intended to leave but found themselves later unable or unwilling to do so (figure 2.3). Historians seem to agree that the early wave of migrants, which would include Basilio and Luciana, mostly did not plan on staying in Hawai'i, as family life on the island was incredibly scarce and was, among men, highly competitive.[77] In the years when my great-grandparents met, there were 1,394 Filipino men for every 100 Filipino women, a ratio of almost 14 to 1, and many of these women came in families and were already married.[78] How Basilio ended up marrying Luciana after she had already been married and had two children has remained

FIGURE 2.3. Basilio and Luciana Agsalud and their children (*left to right*) Deborah, Florita, and my grandmother Prisca, in *Out of This Struggle*.

a mystery within my family's talk-stories, one that brings the excitement and creativity of speculation. Was Luciana abused and abandoned, and later rescued by Basilio? Did Basilio secretly do away with Luciana's husband and appear as her shoulder to cry on? Perhaps Luciana was something of an older sister to Basilio, and their marriage was merely for show, a way perhaps to hide their true lovers—and besides, couldn't they be queer too? Or was the whole thing a situation of coboy coboy, a rare but well-known plantation practice where a man would steal away (kidnap?) a woman and later elope? Perhaps, yet the plantations also witnessed high divorce frequencies, as women had their pick of the crowd. In all these family speculations, one has remained of constant entertainment: the many racial possibilities of the mystery man, Luciana's first husband. Was he Filipino, or perhaps Native Hawaiian? Was he a haole (white), Japanese, or Chinese plantation overseer (or luna)?

Like for many families, our speculations have brought us to sharing DNA tests like cocktail recipes, revealing the many mixtures that make us who we are. Yet even DNA tests shift dramatically when DNA companies update their databases, or whenever we send our DNA data to a different company (a Chinese company identified us as Gaoshan peoples or Indigenous Taiwanese; an American company identified us as Malay and Polynesian). The likelihood of my grandparents having some Chinese ancestry seems substantial given that Ilocos Norte is only about 363 kilometers from Taiwan, nearly the same as the distance from Ilocos Norte to Manila (351 kilometers), and that our Chineseness has been a rumor in family talk-stories since before my birth.[79] When one compares DNA data from organizations with varied interests, DNA tests reveal their own population limitations and state/capitalist-centered stakes. The Israeliowned company MyHeritage found that I was 53.7 percent "Filipino, Indonesian, and Malay," while the American (Mormon-founded) company Ancestry.com in 2018 named me 32 percent East Asian and 15 percent Polynesian, with the rest from Europe (Great Britain, Ireland/Scotland/Wales). Only two years later, an Ancestry.com update recategorized me to having no "East Asian" or "Polynesian" ancestry at all but named me as 49 percent "Northern Philippines" from "Ilocos Region & Central Luzon." WeGene, a Chinese-owned company out of Shenzhen specializing in Southeast Asian populations, did not name me as Filipino at all but 41 percent Chinese, including 26 percent Gaoshan peoples (Indigenous "mountain people" in Taiwan), as well as 5.54 percent Southeast Asian and 4.33 percent South Asian (see figure 2.4). Dna.Land, a universitycentered organization run by MIT, NYU, and Tel Aviv University, also pinpointed my Asian heritage as from Taiwan but as only 4.7 percent Chinese, with 24 percent "Taiwanese," 12 percent "Southeast Asian," and 5.5 percent

"Cambodian/Thai." Clearly, these DNA results reveal the limitations of such lineage tracing when it comes to national belonging and racial categorizations, especially concerning how far back one's lineage is traced (none of these companies gave options for the time period proclaiming one's "origins"). They also seemed to fit the nationalist racial categories of the DNA companies: The most American company simplified me as "Filipino American," while the Chinese companies found my heritage more in Taiwan and mainland China.[80] And yet, having only revealed here my own DNA tests, I can only hint at how such DNA tests have shifted the talk-stories in my family, from some proclaiming they "knew it all along," to others holding true to our Ilocano origins, to others expressing criticism of any tale of our "origins" (or dismissing the importance of race/identity entirely). For Caroline Hau, such shifts of racial meanings are produced within a context of Asian orientalism often propagated by multiple state interests in ways that highlight "the unsettled and shifting meanings not only of 'Chinese' and 'Chineseness,' but of mestizoness, 'Filipino,' and 'Filipinoness' as well."[81] These talk-stories are thus never just the stories of migration or of national belonging but stories of our ever-shifting brown movements.

Regardless of my family's speculations, Basilio and Luciana would have met as mutual members of the ethnicized sakada community within the towns bordering the plantations, likely in Waipahu, a town created by and for the Oahu Sugar Plantation, where 75 percent of its residents worked.[82] Speaking Ilocano with firm memories of their homeland, perhaps Basilio and Luciana shared stories of the families they had left behind, or perhaps they helped each other forget these families by creating their own. Perhaps they gained a semblance of stability together through belonging within what some writers today call "the Ilokandia homeland," the diasporic construction of an Ilocano diasporic identity present throughout the Philippines, Oceania, and the United States, one that continues today among Ilocano domestic workers, construction workers, seafarers, and nurses worldwide.[83] As some of the first Ilocano migrants to leave the Philippines proper, perhaps my great-grandparents spun new memories and found in each other an answer to their feelings of rootlessness, family absence, invisibility, and alienation.

No marriage record exists between Basilio and Luciana, though we can presume through family talk-story that they likely married sometime between 1927 and 1930, between the birth of the children Luciana had with the "mystery man" (who include my grandmother, Prisca Agsalud) and the children she had with Basilio (who include Joshua Agsalud, who would help write and edit *Out of This Struggle*). Younger than Luciana, Basilio must have been a kind father to the children—hers and his own. As my mother tells it, "I don't know

All Ancestry Composition

Chinese	41.43%		Southeast Asian	5.54%		European	48.13%
Gaoshan	26.10%		Cambodian	3.08%		Hungarian	22.67%
Mongolian	4.47%		Kinh	1.88%		Spanish	13.51%
Dai	4.38%		Thai	0.56%		Finnish/Russian	6.81%
Southern Han Chinese	3.92%					English	5.13%
Lahu	2.52%					French	0.00%
Tungusic	0.00%		South Asian	4.33%		Sardinian	0.00%
Northern Han Chinese	0.00%					Balkans	0.00%
Naxi/Yi	0.00%		Sindhi	2.97%		Ashkenazi	0.00%
Uygur	0.00%		Indian	0.69%			
She	0.00%		Bengali	0.66%			
Tibetan	0.00%					African	0.00%
Hmong-Mien	0.00%		Central Asian	0.00%		Mbuti	0.00%
						Yoruba	0.00%

FIGURE 2.4. My DNA test results from the Chinese-owned company WeGene.

the real story [about the previous husband] other than when the man came over, the kids would hide."

In the 1920s the HSPA had dealt with tenuous political coalitions among Filipino and Japanese plantation workers, and in response to this, coupled with the fears of insurgency and sedition before and during World War I, "the US state's capacity to monitor and criminalize revolutionary movements and inter-racial solidarities expanded conspicuously."[84] Part of this expansion was fronted by Hawaiian elites who redoubled their efforts to keep workers divided and distracted in two ways: first, by bringing in more Filipino women to keep the workers occupied with families and invested in the plantation cities; and second, by recruiting almost entirely from the Ilocos region, as they believed the Visayans they had recruited during the 1910s had been the prime instigators of the 1920 labor uprising.[85] Alongside this move, the Hawaiian legislature passed a series of laws to cripple union action and lobbied the US Congress to give Hawai'i an exemption from the Chinese Exclusion Act so they could bring in Chinese strikebreakers.[86] Even so, throughout the 1910s–1930s, Ilocanos remained at the center of labor disputes, which often turned to violence, as in the Hanapepe Massacre in September 1924, when striking Filipino workers on Kauai disputed with police, resulting in sixteen Filipino laborers and four police officers dead, alongside over 150 arrests.[87] In response to anti-Filipino agitation across the United States, as well as anticolonial movements in the Philippines, the United States passed the Philippine Independence Act, restricting Filipino migrants to a mere fifty a year, tantamount to exclusion.[88] If my family was affected by this widespread, state-sanctioned racism, they certainly do not say so in their talk-stories, which revert continually back to my great-grandparents' belief in the power of American citizenship. In his World War II draft card, Basilio is listed as Filipino, dark brown, with a "flag and eagle" tattoo on his right arm.[89]

"Luciana always had stewed prunes and Jell-O in the
refrigerator. . . . I remember how she gargled with
Listerine every night."

The third photograph of my family in *Out of This Struggle* shows the grave of my great-uncle John Agsalud, the twin brother of the book's editor, Joshua Agsalud, and the namesake of Joshua's first son, John (figure 2.5). Though I do not remember anyone in my part of the family—that is, Prisca's—going to lengths to frame our migration as a "struggle," we have many stories that name the dead. John died soon after childbirth. Two of my great-uncles, Moses and Samuel, died young, perhaps as toddlers, perhaps as old as twelve. For these three, no records exist of their lives or their deaths, only talk-stories stating that they were all healthy boys and were perhaps poisoned by a plantation chemical or something in their diets. And we have this photograph.

Luciana appears here as she does in her other photo: hard, determined, clutching her children. Nothing like the traditional image of the Filipina as shy, retiring, and defenseless. Most likely Luciana had no formal education, and perhaps, when she arrived, she could not read or write.[90] In Hawai'i women

FIGURE 2.5. Luciana Agsalud with her three children (*left to right*) Florita, my grandmother Prisca, and Deborah, in *Out of This Struggle*.

were discouraged from working on the plantations proper, but my great-grandmother may have worked by selling goods or food (often after fishing), tending to gardens or chickens or other livestock, operating services like bath-houses, doing laundry, or providing boarding services.[91] As Hawai'i turned more toward a tourist economy after World War II, it's plausible that Luciana found work there (Filipinos still make up the majority of workers in the hotels and tourist spaces of Waikīkī).[92] With four children to raise at home, however, it's just as plausible that Luciana's home life was indeed her work.

> My mother remembers: "We visited them maybe once or twice a month.
> I was very young so there was not that much communication. Apobakit
> always greeted me with her nose to my cheek and sniffing me."

Apobakit was the name my mother had for Luciana, Apolakai for Basilio, which could be translated into "respected older woman" ("Apo Baket") or "respected older man" ("Apo Lakai"). The latter is often used today as an informal and endearing title for the Ilocano dictator Ferdinand Marcos. The story my family tells of my great-grandmother, Luciana, is of a strong and admonishing woman who made Filipino food and was proud to come to America; she pressed her children to speak good English and spoke Ilocano or Spanish only at Thanksgiving or Christmas when she read from her Bible. No one in my family seems to know when, how, or why we became Protestant (nondenominational, as my family will remind me). Given that the ilustrado writers of the late nineteenth century characterized the normative Filipino subject as one of Hispanic Catholic civilization, Protestantism likely came to my great-grandparents via the Americans, either during colonization or on arrival in Hawai'i.[93] As one of my uncles tells it, Luciana was determined to become American, and for her children to be American as well. Perhaps this was due to her own perceived escape from the Philippines and again from her abusive first husband—a desire for assimilation spurred by a sense of survival and care for her descendants.

Unlike their children Moses, Samuel, and John, Basilio and Luciana would be recorded in death, and their graves would be marked in stone. Basilio went first. He died of cancer in December 1974. Luciana died, according to my uncle, of "natural causes" in October 1983 at the age of ninety-five, after living an adventurous widowed retirement, becoming independent and traveling the world alone, always speaking English, and bringing back pictures of her travels, especially to the "holy land of Jerusalem." When she could no longer travel, she would take buses around the island of Oahu. Due to Basilio's service in World War I, he and Luciana are both buried at the National Memorial Cemetery of the Pacific in Honolulu. Their children would pass on stories of them and wonder about their commitments and their racial backgrounds. Their offspring would drift far from their Filipino communities, both in space (moving across the world) and in relations with non-Filipino families, with Kānaka Maoli, Black, Chinese, Japanese, Cambodian, Korean, Scotch-Irish, and Portuguese peoples. Their great-grandson, me, would feel so muddled by these racial mixtures that he would grow up assuming his mother's family was Native Hawaiian, and then accept that they were mixed Hawaiian "local," and then learn that he was Filipino, and only as a teenager would he hear, among talk-story laughter, that he was descended from Ilocanos (who may have been Chinese mestizos too).

"Some things nobody knows."

While moving alongside the stories, archives, and presences of my great-grandparents, I've come across several splits—branches that deviate from default migrant narratives, pressuring me to choose from many potential modes of historical interpretation. One branch leads to the quandary that wherever I encounter claims that Filipinos (and particularly Ilocanos) were the easiest migrants to domesticate for their docility and colonial mindsets, I find just as many claims, often written by the descendants of the sakadas, that they were racialized "as unskilled, hot-tempered, untrustworthy migrants" who

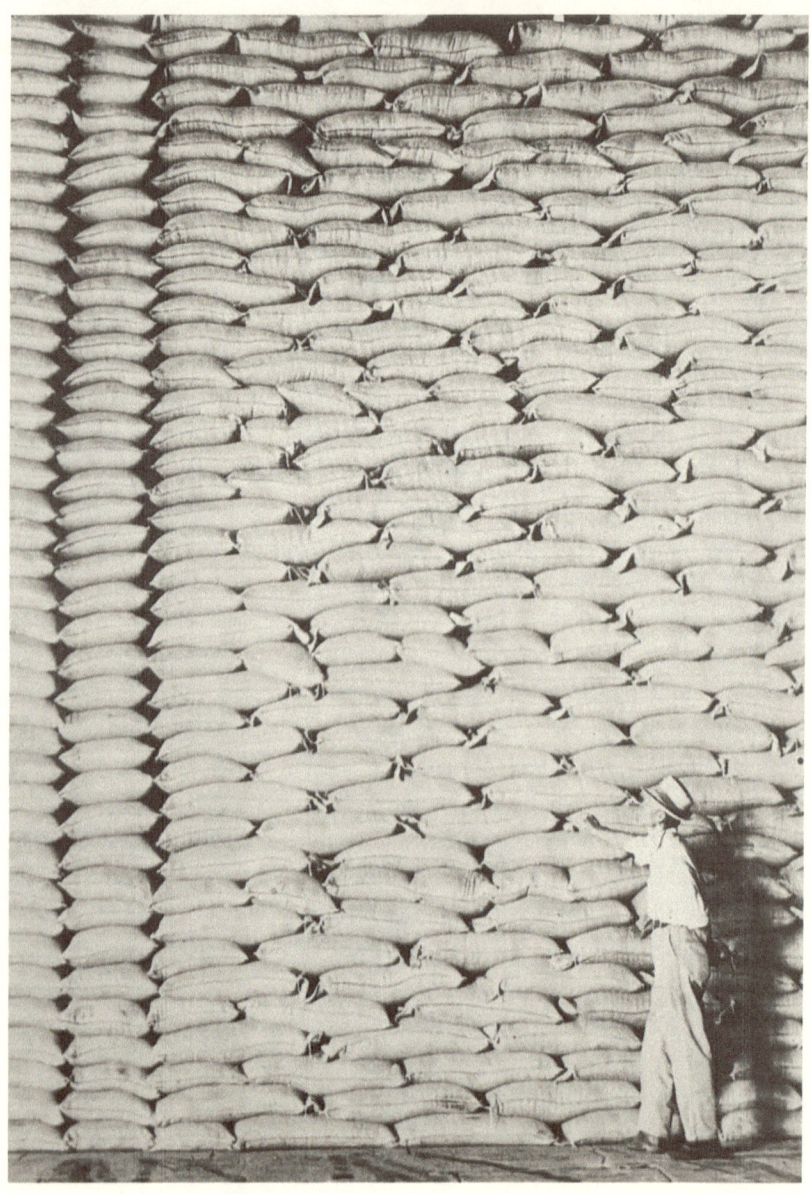

FIGURE 2.6. Basilio Agsalud and a wall of bagged sugarcane at the Oahu Sugar Company, 1957, in *Out of This Struggle*.

were "unassimilable laborers."[94] This inconsistency in racialization comes as no surprise given the fungibility and proliferation of racial forms depending on context and convenience to those in power, yet these deviations also impact those who live these experiences as well—the family narratives, the ballasts of our affective bonding. To follow this branch backward, however, is to note that the very division between "domesticated laborers" and "unassimilable laborers" still sees these migrants within the confines of this common term, *labor*. The question of "Who were the Ilocanos?" becomes an implicit gesture toward naming the migrant group as either docile or unruly workers—in effect, characterizing the migratory past through the work, rather than the creativity, the play, the ideas, the travels, of migrant peoples. The image of Basilio standing with a wall of sugar is the last image in *Out of This Struggle* and has been reused by other scholars, most notably in the book *Filipinos in Hawai'i*, by Theodore Gonzalves and Roderick Labrador, which features my great-grandfather beside the caption, "Basilio Agsalud contemplates a wall of commodities" (figure 2.6).[95] He is featured beneath the title of the book's third section, "Labor."

My concern with the repetition of the title *laborer* is that it can distance those of us who write these histories—we intellectuals, we creatives, we thinkers, we artists—from those we are seeking to represent. Situating ancestral migrant narratives through labor implicitly insists that contemporary immigrants must deal with the same conditional hospitality of the host country as our ancestors, while also refusing to see these ancestors as even capable of producing similar (unwritten, unappreciated) narratives as ourselves, or of seeing their work as communal, beautiful, and important (as we academics tend to tell ourselves), or of living intellectual and creative lives similar to our own. As Jody Blanco observes, for Filipino Americans writing Filipinx histories, "the first and most prominent category of reflection is that of labor" as "it signifies for us, more than any other consideration, our 'right' to a sense of national belonging in the US, regardless of whether or not it should."[96] As Wendy Hui Kyong Chun, Grace Kyungwon Hong, and Lisa Nakamura put it, the reinscription of ancestral migrancy as immigrant labor can reinforce the "Asian American family's place as either 'valued guests' or unwelcome invaders," figuring Asian migrants "as negligible and nonagential people whose right to exist in the US and Canada is secured by the invitation of white people."[97] In Asian American studies particularly, the primacy of Marxian analysis and materiality as the primary locus through which we conceive of "History" can have the effect of relegating creative expression to the purely subjective or parochial domain. To refer to our histories solely within the terms of labor is already a form of historical domestication, one that divides us not only from history but also from the present-day laborers whom we may now expect to follow a similar generational path or otherwise remain in their segmented historical space. The presumptions of travel for nonwhite peoples reinstate the binary of the exile and the nomad, here revised within this time period as the anti-imperialist and nationalist figures (José Rizal, King Kawika Kalākaua) and the nomadic "laborers." This recurring binary leads us, the familial descendants, to envision our ancestors primarily within the affects of sacrifice and struggle, and to place them on a developmental path leading to us—in a sense, domesticating their stories as tales of empowerment for the "we" who identify as multicultural American citizen-subjects whose work resembles not labor but vocational awe.[98]

Another deviating branch in the historical narratives of Filipino migrancy is the relations between Filipinos and Kānaka Maoli, which tend to deviate from tales of active settlement and marginalization of Natives to meaningful moments of solidarity with Indigenous peoples. In both the Philippines and Hawai'i, state narratives have proudly taken up anticolonial narratives of Indigenous uprising against past (and non-American) colonizers, from stories of Lapu Lapu killing Ferdinand Magellan at the battle of Mactan to those of the ali'i high chief Kalaimanokaho'owaha (also known as Kana'ina) killing Captain James Cook at Kealakekua Bay. These stories, however, do not seem to deter incorporation into Americanization, nor do they necessarily compel solidarities with present-day Indigenous movements such as the Native opposition to Mauna Kea Observatories or the Indigenous groups whom the Philippine state routinely labels as terrorists or communists. Like the Ilocanos, who both belittled and defended Igorot peoples, the early relations of Filipino migrants to Native Hawaiians seem to rely heavily on the relationship of Filipinos to those races who were above them on the plantation hierarchies: the Chinese, the Japanese, and the haoles. As Kim Compoc argues, it is common for plantation histories to "mask the colonial dispossession of Kānaka Maoli with the virtuous work ethic of Filipinx/immigrant labor."[99] Many scholars consider it historical fact that Filipinos were the lowest rung on the plantation labor hierarchies, a point of pride for some of their descendants, except that those very plantations required the dispossession and domination of Indigenous peoples.[100]

My own familial relation to Indigenous dispossession comes through my great-uncle, coeditor of *Out of This Struggle*, Joshua Agsalud (Uncle Joe to me growing up). At the time of editing *Out of This Struggle*, Joshua was the director of the state Department of Labor under Governor Ryoichi Ariyoshi, and he would later become vice president of the University of Hawai'i before serving as chief of staff for Governor John David Waiheʻe III and then retiring in 1994. In a 2008 article, the scholar and activist Dean Saranillio takes an excerpt from my great-uncle's 1981 autobiographical speech to a Filipino conference in Honolulu to illustrate the relations between Filipino migrants and Indigenous peoples. Saranillio compares my great-uncle's sentence, "The [Filipino] children all considered themselves natives of the land" with Haunani-Kay Trask's famous statement on Asian settlers who "claim Hawaiʻi as their own, denying indigenous history, their long collaboration in our continued dispossession, and the benefits therefrom."[101] My great-uncle's speech, made in the same year as the publication of *Out of This Struggle*, provides context for an understanding of how settler colonialism, militarized colonization, and imperial dispossession work in tandem, so that for children "growing up on the sugar plantations in the late 1940s and 1950s, there was no other known option for a national identity afforded to Filipinos besides being American."[102] Saranillio's use of my great-uncle's autobiography signals an understanding of migrant-Indigenous relations that my uncle also carried with him, as an educator and high school principal widely critical of the mechanisms through which colonization operates. As Joshua Agsalud wrote, "All the influences which shaped my views on the Americanization process were natural outcomes of the plantation experience. They were congruent to the scenario that was evolving. These influences—family, church, school and the plantation itself, along with a major world event taking place at that time, World War II—the views that were shaped, and the process, were all American. They were not conflicts among the variables, one pulling or pushing against the other—they all seemed to flow in the same direction, a direction which was inevitable under the circumstances . . . Americanization."[103] While Saranillio reads this paragraph alongside the postcolonial calls against colonial education, I wonder how we might use it to reframe all of Joshua's projects, from his editorship of and writings in *Out of This Struggle*, to his work as an educator, to his autobiographical speeches. Perhaps all his works were not about reclaiming or empowering a marginalized identity but about accounting for the "flows" of "Americanization": the ways that, even before the Philippine Revolution, Ilocanos had been chosen for certain forms of domestication. To live within the present of that history was to see "conflicts among variables"—or in this case, deviations and inconsistencies among the events and language used to describe those events. Yet all variables too tend inevitably to flow right back into Americanization, that is, back to empire. Perhaps this flow leads us to ask how this very direction of historical recovery, the focus on our marginalized backgrounds (of once being the lowest rung on a racial hierarchy) and on standing in solidarity with Indigenous peoples wherever convenient, might be yet another way of flowing in the same direction.

> "I remember vividly when grandma died and there was
> a Filipino tradition of holding the casket up with all the
> family around her."

Returning again to *Out of This Struggle* now, after years of repeated reading, has illuminated the levels of pride and shame I once felt when approaching the text. *Out of This Struggle* was once an energizing read. Then it became a particularly problematic and shameful one. Now I find in its contents a brutal honesty about Filipinos of the past. In its epilogue the book's authors see the early Filipino migrants as adopting a psyche of "resignation" after being disillusioned by the Philippine Revolution, then unknowingly being cut off forever from their families and finding terrible conditions and prevalent racism in their new homes in Hawai'i. The writers also see the descendants of these migrants as no exceptions to the bigotry of the islands, as they would "swing between 'local' culture and 'white' culture," find "hostility toward Hawaiian or Samoan groups" and resent other Filipinos with heavy accents who could travel without the same labor contracts that their parents were once subjected to.[104] A closer reading of the book invokes not pride or shame but a feeling of loss. I wonder at my own family's reactions to my aunt's Native Hawaiian husband and the many children that emerged from their marriage; or my sister's biological father, who was part Black, part Indigenous, and was never part of her life. Though I can think of no particular instances of anti-Black, anti-Indigenous racism in my family's talk-stories, I wonder how my inability to do so is brought about by my own inability to sense these racisms, or, perhaps, my selective forgetting of them when they occurred.

I see the images in *Out of This Struggle* differently too. I once marveled at the editors' attempt to show a wide variety of Filipinos and their various jobs and situations, while reminding us that most early migrants were men working on plantations. There are images of newly arrived migrants in the 1920s with their families (a rarity), as well as images of labor organizers, club organizers, Filipinos who worked on the plantation police force, tailors, celebrations of Rizal day, players in the symphony orchestra, baseball teams, schoolchildren, soldiers, beauty contestants, and tennis players. And yet, between these images of success and achievement, my great-grandfather's image lurks throughout the book as the "plantation worker," the Ilocano everyday everyman. Basilio plays the role of the only named male plantation worker in the entire photo archive of the book. Why, out of the tens of thousands of plantation workers in Hawaiʻi, my great-grandfather was the one selected for this role is a bit of a mystery, except that his son was one of the book's editors. My great-grandfather, whether posing in front of sugar or with a gun in his hand, plays the working peasant, as if he was born just to do so. His figure summons both pity and strength, the nation that was to come, surrounded by photos of high achievers. He, who is given more dedicated images than anyone else in *Out of This Struggle*, resembles an important historical phase of our racial memory: the laboring brown mass from which we have arisen.

During the four-year process of writing this chapter, five of my family members from Hawaiʻi passed away: my Ilocano step-grandmother Vee, my Indigenous step-uncle Cameron, his son (my little cousin) Kamalona, my great-uncle, Joseph Agsalud, who edited and cowrote *Out of This Struggle*, and his sister, Florita. Much of the research for this chapter, from listening to family talk-story to visiting archival spaces in Hawaiʻi, was done during processes of mourning, of funeral arranging, of check-ins, of giving and receiving care (my wife, Y-Dang Troeung, also became ill and died during this time). The quasi-folkloric form of the talk-story comes easily in times of grief. Its ambitions are not to "counter" history but to bring the memories of those who could not be present, and to break death's gripping sadness with tales of humor and joy. Talk-story grants us permission to trust each other, to renarrate our histories given our present struggles and future dreams, to simply dwell in each other's company, rather than feel isolated and in despair. For talk-stories to work in this way, they must remain open, ambiguous, speculative, so that the narratives of our past are like the narratives of ourselves, mobile (or perhaps motile), changing with our own current needs for survival. The talk-story treats the past not simply as an archive for arguing what our ancestors truly wanted or who they really were but as a shared language that proliferates the many ways they might have lived—and in doing so, multiplies our own sense of who we are and who we might become. Everyone in my family has a great-grandparent looking down on them, even if (or perhaps because) they are imagined differently.

The talk-story of my great-grandparents dazzles through formal definitions of *traveler, alien, exile, refugee, sakada, migrant, laborer, immigrant, local, settler*. These terms all remain contentious and yet cannot be pinned to totalize any single person, nor can they be used with the isolating effect of consistency. The multiplicitous and speculative form of the family talk-story rehistoricizes such peoples so that these terms appear not as historically fixed or in "hermeneutic isolation" but as "porous concepts and flexible subjectivities."[105] All these terms form different senses of movement, but in the context of family talk-story, they all also participate in the presence of brown worldmaking. Their motility manifests from movements in spaces, times, and stories that both structure and change the systems around them. We, brown peoples of the present, talk of the browned people of our past to make the brown worlds of our future. As my mother continues to remind me, it takes an entire family to hold that casket up.

You love driving, you love walking. You love planes, you love trains, you love buses, and you love ferries. You love movement, you love change.

The last time you sat still, you were at a conference on empire and the participants were anxious about the violences of the world but too comfortable to do anything about it except to theorize about their anxiety. What would "doing anything about it" even mean? You don't know, and you don't learn the answer to this question sitting down.

The only place you could ever imagine yourself staying still is floating in space, inside a shuttle, where you could watch the planets and the earth and the satellites spinning all around you. And no sun in sight, dictating your horizon.

3

Migrant Domestic Workers in the Global City

	Previously presented
2013	Seattle
2014	San Francisco
	Seoul
	Hangzhou
	Xiamen
2015	Shanghai
	Dubai
	Vancouver
	Chicago
	Kobe
	Taipei
2016	Manila
	Hong Kong
	Miami
	Shanghai
	Vancouver
	Sydney
2017	San Diego
	Hong Kong
	San Francisco
	Manila
	Vancouver
2018	Atlanta
	Madison
2019	Las Vegas
2020–23	Virtual

I contorted my body into palatable morsels for consumption, a symbol of perfection—spine curved in subordination, grateful to be tokenized, a smile affixed to a numbed and unthreatening Brownness, and eyes perpetually focused on the floor and away from an authoritative gaze. —KRISTIAN CONTRERAS, "Letter to My Daughter"

When I was young, my mother used to tell me, *Pour just enough cream in my coffee, so that the color matches the skin on your arm.* I never knew whether to take this as an insult or a compliment. Darker skinned than me, my mother grew up in Hawai'i, on the island of Oahu, where brownness can claim one's belonging as a local. As descendants primarily of Ilocano plantation workers, our shades of brown have oriented us to the place, even as some shades—those of Micronesians and Hawaiian Natives—often get subsumed into a local identity that brings solidarity and community to some and invisibility to others. My skin, as I grew up hapa haole in stark white Portland, Oregon, was of a lighter complexion—perfect, my mother would say, for a well-mixed morning coffee but not quite a flat white.

In 2000, when my family moved to Las Vegas, my own brownness began to radically shift meanings. At Basic High School, the school that proudly wore its ranking as number one in the nation in teen pregnancies, I was no longer the only brown kid in a white school. My skin read not as that of a stranger but as that of a known other: a Latino, a Filipino, a stoner, a worker, a gangster, and, after 9/11, a suspect of terror. So too I saw the way tourists would look at my mother and my older sister, not as suspects but as cleaners, caretakers, and maids. My part-Asian, part-Black, part-Indigenous sister took advantage of this and worked as a manager of Latina housekeepers, though she spoke not a word of Spanish.

I discovered an academic language for understanding these teasing vagaries of skin color when I moved to Seattle to get my PhD in literature. Critical race texts quickly reassured me that for me, as the lightest-skinned and highest-educated in my family, this language was not mere discourse but critical, erudite, knowledge-able. I was eager to show my mastery of this discourse during a home visit back to Las Vegas, when my mother brought me to her book club of almost entirely white women who had gathered to discuss *The Help*, a book about Black household servants in 1960s Mississippi. I hadn't read the book, so I decided to finish my schoolwork on the patio. An hour later my mother stormed out of the house. "What happened?" I asked her on the drive home. "They didn't like what I said," she said, shaking. "What did you say?" I prodded. "I said that it was my life we were reading about. Their lives are like mine. I am 'the help,' just on a different level." Accompanied by my recently acquired master's degree in English, I could not agree. *The Help* was a book about Black "mammies" in the Jim Crow era, I told her. And you are an operations manager for a private jet company in the era of Barack Obama. Yes, your bosses are white, but that doesn't mean you have the same life. There are no levels. Either you are the help, or you are exploiting them. It took many years for me to see the depth and complexity of what my mother was trying to communicate, and the lack of generosity and understanding in what I was, effectively and persuasively, communicating to her.

My mother, of course, would not be the only brown person who could see aspects of her own life through the stories of Black housekeepers. In 2017 Alex Tizon's posthumously published article in the *Atlantic*, "My Family's Slave," invigorated discussions about the shades of Black and brown that frame understandings of modern-day domestic enslavement. Tizon's article focused on a distant relative of his family, Eudocia Tomas Pulido, or "Lola," who was enslaved by his parents (and, in effect, by him) for nearly sixty years as an unpaid/unfree housekeeper. First provided as a "gift" to his mother from his grandfather in the Philippines, Eudocia moved with Tizon's family to America under the impression that she would be able to send money back home. Eudocia was never paid but still became a surrogate mother to the family's children, including Alex. Growing up with Eudocia as his primary caretaker, Alex soon began to see her within the framework of Black enslavement. As he wrote, the place she occupied in his family's life was something he saw "in slave characters on TV and in the movies."[1]

Responses to Tizon's article were tidal, from celebrations of Tizon's honesty in respect to his own family, to criticisms of the ways that Tizon re-created tropes of enslavement and domestic servitude by infantilizing Eudocia, "erasing her voice from his narrative, and valorizing his role as a savior."[2] Responses from the Philippines focused on the lack of understanding of Filipino culture, or the crucial economic role of unpaid domestic labor within Filipino families performed by extended-family relatives.[3] Vicente Rafael, responding to the critiques from both the Philippines and the United States, provided a brief history of familial servitude, writing, "In Tizon's narrative (and in the everyday experience of Filipinos who grew up with servants), affective ties of pity (awa), reciprocal indebtedness (utang na loob), and shame (hiya) hold together the master and servant as much as they pull them apart."[4] But perhaps the most visceral critique of Tizon was not related to either his infantilization of Eudocia or his own ignorance of Filipino cultural mores around domesticity but his desire to understand his "Lola" through the trope of the Black mammy. A follow-up article in the *Atlantic* compared Tizon to Kathryn Stockett (author of *The Help*) as two authors who were both "desperate to understand the care [they] got as unconditional love, as rising above and separate from coercion. But in this genre [of the Black mammy], that rising above always signals the growth and goodness of the narrator."[5]

Both the story of my mother encountering *The Help* and Tizon's story of his "family's slave" invoke anxieties of guilt, moral uncertainty, and attempts to solve these anxieties through forms of empathy (as becoming "like them," or as seeking to write their "story"). As Rafael writes, Filipina domestic workers emerge within a moral and religious economy that can offer servants "a kind of moral leverage," one that keeps Tizon within the confines of guilt and the desire to expiate himself as a white (lighter brown) savior.[6] Even Tizon's name for Eudocia, "Lola," invests a sense of moral elderliness (or as I will call it later, matronliness) in the figure of the migrant brown care worker, whose identification with "a grandmother as someone who cooks, cleans, etc." leads others to understand her presence as "the result of family reunification rather than exploitation."[7] As Rafael writes, Tizon's inability to see Eudocia through anything but a moral lens reinforces "the slave's ability to deflect the master's appropriative power."[8] Similarly, my mother's own difficult upbringing (becoming a single mother when she was nineteen) and various forms of service labor give her a complex relation to histories of domestic work in the United States, which today are usually (and invisibly) brown. On the global scale, however, domestic labor is understood through a variety of moral economies, and representations are rife with unstated presumptions on what brown women should be doing, on their "proper place" with their own families, secured within protective heteropatriarchal relations.[9] How can we understand or seek to revise the figure of the domestic worker as global, moralistic, and brown? Or how can we understand our own desire for understanding, for empathizing, and for establishing a single framework—a critical discourse—for a global and proliferating form of brownness? Does our understanding preclude change, or is it merely another way to domesticate?

This chapter offers a brown theoretical movement through the discourses surrounding Filipina domestic workers, who have emerged as central figures for (mis)understandings of global domestic servitude today, as representations and scholarly studies of these workers have amassed in recent decades within a global moral economy that fluctuates among the various sites where Filipina women labor worldwide. To do so, I focus on the figurations of domestic workers in literature, film, and dance, within cities that are routinely cast as sexually open, or liberated: Hong Kong, Bahrain, Honolulu, and Las Vegas. All four of these cities are unique as loci of transpacific migration, of sex tourism and illicit behavior, and as sites that are majority nonwhite, or majority brown, especially if we count the multitudinous shades of brown that enclose people within the Middle East (Bahrain), Southeast Asia and southern China (Hong Kong), Oceania (Hawai'i), and Central and South America (Las Vegas). As global transit nodes, these spaces are also racial mixtures of all of the above, where the brown domestic worker is not seen in isolation or in constant comparison to whiteness but as one of many shades of brown. I thus consider migrant domestic workers in cities that are both "sexually progressive" and "brown" to understand how these representations become vexed by underlying sexual suspicions that compel workers to perform within shades of brown, a racial optic that signifies ambiguity and mixture but also presumes brown women as lower-class migrant labor and imports colonial attitudes toward brown female sexuality.

By examining short stories, documentaries, and performance art about domestic workers, I hope to delineate a sense of brownness within highly sexualized cityscapes where workers have had to transition among shades of brown to feel at home in same-sex romances and queer cultural spaces. I see *queer* here not as a graspable identity/community formation, nor as an ungraspable "horizon" of futurity, but, as José Esteban Muñoz wrote in 1996, as "a possibility, a sense of self-knowing, a mode of sociality" that is "often transmitted covertly" and is thus meant to "evaporate at the touch" from those who are themselves not queer or aligned politically with queer life.[10] The brown theoretical movement across various global cities thus attempts to follow the various moral economies of domestic servitude around the globe, where transmissions of queerness are kept covert but are nonetheless expressed in cities that expect or encourage sexual transgression. Thus far, attempts to place a global and consistent moralism on these variations have often led researchers and audiences to transpose their own affective desires as sons/daughters and mothers/fathers onto those of domestic workers. One extreme example of this is when the scholar Geraldine Pratt, in an effort to disrupt the "culture of numbness" that dismisses the way domestic workers "leave their own children in the Philippines," included three colored photos of her own son in an article otherwise focused on a migrant worker's (Marlena's) testimony about being unable to see her own son.[11] Clearly, this transposing of the white child for the absent brown boy reiterates racist tropes that deem white children as human and brown children as disposable (Pratt admits this within the article). However, for Pratt, this tactic also serves as a desperate measure to cast attention onto the subjugation of brown women, whose circumstances, despite decades of active research and organizing, may have only worsened.[12] As with Tizon's and my mother's reactions to bearing witness to domestic servitude and unfreedom, the moral economy encircling domestic workers inevitably invokes attention to the authors/readers themselves. As Pratt writes, "I am inscribed in the text, not only in the anticipated role of research collaborator, but in a more directly compromised way: as a middleclass, white mother with the need and resources to employ Marlena."[13]

The brown theoretical methods developed in this book help reframe domestic servitude through colonial histories that have seen brown masses as wild, uncontainable threats, whose domestication often entails the need to create a consistent way to understand them within the moral (variously heteropatriarchal) standards of the colonizer themselves. Though I disagree with Pratt's methods, I share her desperation of conducting scholarly work on a globally exploited population who, despite the gargantuan amount of research about them (with well over seven thousand academic articles and books produced since 2000), seems to have progressed very little in relation to other labor organizing or state support.[14] I thus follow Laura Kang's provocation to see academic representations of abused Asian women (in her case, "comfort women"), as figures within moralistic and impassioned rubrics of violation and empowerment, as "a multivalent problematic activated and foreclosed by certain modes of expertise, contestation, and nonknowing within a particularly 'American' power/knowledge architecture."[15] This chapter makes little attempt to study the interiority of domestic workers as subjects, as these studies have been done in caring and careful ways.[16] Nor do I seek to analyze artworks by domestic workers, which I have done in other work.[17] Rather, I treat the figure of the domestic worker as a vexed locus of global understandings about servitude, unfreedom, moralism, and brownness itself, which manifests when we look at these figures "synchronically," as Neferti Tadiar suggests, "through a dynamic picture of transnational social networks of disposable and expendable populations from former and present colonies."[18]

Whereas the previous chapter sought to follow the racial imaginaries of Filipino plantation workers untethered to state and minority narratives of labor, this chapter seeks to follow the ways states, filmmakers, scholars, and authors consistently reimagine migrant domestic workers outside the bounds of labor, in discursive attempts to "rescue" them by emphasizing their motherhood, morality, and diasporic heroism—all traits that, ironically, are ideal and racially coded characteristics for migrant domestic workers. Domestic workers thus name what Josen Diaz calls a "configuration" of a brown racial and gender formation that "becomes recognizable, namable, and legible at the intersections of overlapping state and national forces" and that can be "unmade" by "directing attention to the inherent instability of each arrangement."[19] Through brown theoretical movement, I thus seek to unmake this figure of the Filipina domestic worker by tracing its cohesion as an expression of the global anxieties of colonial histories that, for authors in the Global North, can invoke the anxious instability of brown mass: being dizzyingly heterogeneous, complex, widespread, morally ambiguous, theoretically challenging, and covertly (rather than identifiably) queer. In the efforts to establish a "feminist will to global authority," as Kang calls it, the domestic worker has become a figure who must be known, cataloged, understood, and empathized with in ways that indirectly reference the brown mass as morally inferior (the brown mass of the Philippines, of Latino/a/x peoples, of the Middle East, where domestic workers are said to be the most exploited).[20]

As a global phenomenon, Filipina domestic workers capture the ways colonial discourse reiterates today on brown bodies as figures whose theoretical and personal evasions seem to demand *conceptual* domestication as the only means to rescue brown women from their *literal* domestication. Yet, in this broad and abstract conceptualizing, erasures and omissions are already embedded in any accounts of domestic workers, including those personal relations of the scholars themselves whose own upbringing was often in the care of migrant domestic workers, or who have hired migrant domestic workers themselves for various forms of child, elder, and other professional care, or who have been cared for by migrant domestic workers in hospitals, on cruise ships, or within someone else's home. To account for the way autotheory inevitably resurfaces in brown theory, this chapter chooses to integrate rather than omit the stories of brown women in my family, including my own relation to a Filipina domestic worker, Anne, during my time in Hong Kong. Starting in August 2017, just before the birth of my son, Anne worked for my wife and me until we left Hong Kong in June 2018. In the following years of writing and revising this chapter, presenting it at conferences, and publishing pieces in various journals, I chose to omit her story because mentioning her, particularly through the thematics of queerness, labor organizing, performance, and the exploitation of Hong Kong laws, would make her a target for possible state or otherwise personal attack. The alternative, then, would be to tell a story about her in a way that makes her untargetable: to discuss how much she meant to us, how she taught us to be parents, how my son missed her afterward, how she was happily treated as *one of the family*. In other words, the only way I could foresee to write about her without possibly bringing recrimination on her was to reinforce the stereotypes of brown women that this chapter is directly interrogating. Then there are complicated questions of telling someone else's story (can a previous employee ever truly give consent for their story to be told?) and of respectfully representing both the worker and my partner, who is no longer alive to share or verify stories, and whose memories I can only approach with grief and love.

Even so, in the years of revising this chapter, I've realized that this strategy of omission has only been read as evasion, obscuration, and a denial of class, national, and linguistic hierarchies that inform our many shades of brown. So too the autotheoretical engagement with our own relations to racial capitalism poses urgent questions about how and why we seek to "theorize" migrant domestic workers, how and why we seek to produce knowledge that inevitably appeals to other "theorists" living in white settler-military empires, how and why our own class-based reality informs even the ability to pose these questions. It took years for me to understand that the story of my partner and me hiring a domestic worker can, if done wisely, speak volumes about the global attention to "brown" domestic workers, and that this need to "see" and "value" domestic workers, by brown scholars for presumably North American audiences, can also work to reify international divisions of labor by obscuring class distinctions among brown subjects. I thus intersperse self-reflective sections on hiring Anne (with her consent) as a way to speak back to each global context, to the figuration of the "matronly" migrant maid, and to the issue of scholarly attention onto the domestic worker within the Global North. How might the messy, shameful, privileged, and everyday experiences of hiring a migrant worker speak to the shades of brown that make our work possible? How can we understand brown theory as emerging through our own dependencies on racialized mass and domestication—we brown authors who participate in the very exploitative racial economics our work critiques? How, similar to Tizon and Pratt, can the risk of losing the ethical authority of marginalized authorship also undo the tendency to equate or conflate instances of exploitation rooted in global economic asymmetry? By refusing to omit the omissions, this chapter seeks and hopes to encourage others to pursue a more meaningful engagement with the shame, anxieties, and contradictions of our brownness, propelled by the histories, contexts, and representations of brownness that we put under analysis, including our own.

OMISSION I

I aimed to be the best employer, so good that nobody could really call me an employer. I paid far more than my colleagues advised, and I provided rent so our worker could live outside of our home, with their new family. A host of other gestures, I made, or guilt made for me. Mostly, the burden of this guilt, and its consequences, fell on Y-Dang, my partner, whose habits of protecting her pocket-

book were being undermined by my need not to feel like an academic hypocrite.
And then there was that feeling that no matter how much we paid, or how much
freedom we tried to provide in defiance of local state laws, nothing could compen-
sate for what we received in return.

Domestic Work and the Global Sense of Brown

On the macroscale, domestic work is the persistent contrarian of human rights.
—JENNIFER FISH, *Domestic Workers of the World Unite!*

The trend toward Filipina migrant domestic work globally can be traced back to the Philippines in the early 1900s, with the formation of an ideal Filipina in the transitions from Spanish to American colonial power. American colonial race-making constructed Filipina sexuality to signify seduction, intrusion, and danger—racial stereotypes that were inherited from Spanish colonial regimes as well as the American approach to genocidal wars against Native nations during the Indian Wars, in which many American military personnel in the Philippines had participated.[21] The perceived dangers of Filipinas were in bodily threats (venereal and tropical disease); in the moral degeneration of miscegenation, infidelity, and child abandonment; and in the potential for treason—through colonial soldiers themselves becoming influenced by radical insurrectionists. Yet, as Genevieve Clutario has shown, when Americans arrived as colonial "saviors," Filipino elites shifted images of Filipina womanhood from "native" degenerates to high-class women of feminine purity, positioning the new Filipina as a "strategic tool[] with which to counter the US stereotypes of Filipino backwardness and savagery that justified the colonial project."[22] Well-traveled mestizo elites cited Filipinas who were high achievers in education and "in entrepreneurial positions as legacies of matriarchal precolonial societies," and touted Filipina women for their "moral superiority over white American women, as conveyed through their ability to preserve 'traditional' values and shun American women's wild modern ways."[23] Many of these values of family and religious adherence were rooted in Spanish colonialism and served to distinguish Filipina women from depictions of a wild and unruly mass. Inevitably, however, American women would see such admired Filipinas as inhabiting forms of mimicry, their worldliness and traveling flexibility reinterpreted as qualities best suited for forms of service and affective labor as ideal caretakers and matrons.

I use the term *matronly* to name a far-reaching characteristic commonly cast on migrant domestic workers, as it grows from the roots for "mother" and "wife" but also suggests a form of guidance for young families (as a syn-onym for *patroness* and *midwife*), as well as professional authority in do-mestic spheres, as working women in schoolhouses and women's prisons are commonly titled *matrons*.[24] *Matronly* suggests not merely sexual purity but a desire to restrict sexual desire itself, a form of self-control that perhaps has been achieved through age, motherhood, and religious moral guidance. In the Philippines this image of the mobile and matronly Filipina was converted into a reliable labor source through early nursing campaigns that began in US colonial schools in the Philippines, and in the mass exportation of Filipino workers to the United States, when the dependency on migrant labor remit-tances grew to become a mainstay of the Philippines and its diasporas. As the historian Dawn Mabalon has noted, the American colonial education re-gimes in the Philippines and the Pacific Islands trained young women toward service, putting in place "domestic science curricula required for young girls in the Philippines—cooking, knitting, sewing, crocheting, and household sanitation—[that] sought to civilize them in the model of middle-class, white Victorian womanhood or, at the very least, her perfectly trained servant."[25] From the American colonial point of view, education in domestic work was seen as a form of uplifting the Philippines by reinforcing a patriarchal cul-ture that "punished Philippine women for not committing at all times to a hetero-reproductive, domestic futurity."[26] Likewise, Neferti Tadiar has shown how this affective identity values servitude as a form of self-sacrifice built on Catholic notions of martyrdom and repayment of both spiritual and national debt, while Denise Cruz has pointed out how this figure came as a reaction to the fears of "coed" stereotypes of transnational Filipinas, who were seen as pro-miscuous, easily corrupted, and inauthentic.[27] For Cruz, the transpacific Fili-pina could not "be contained in singular types," and as a result Filipinas were identified as "focal points of tension in elite communities" who thus invested in "containing" transpacific Filipinas into "reinforced idealizations of women as representative of the nation."[28]

After independence, Filipinas came to symbolize ideal characteristics for domestic work, as many became educated in nursing and housework, and many had "a stellar competency in the English language."[29] As Robyn Rodri-guez has shown, in the 1970s the Philippines took the form of a "labor broker-age state" and attempted to police Filipina migrant identity through training regimes, advertisement campaigns, and films that shifted previous represen-tations of transnational Filipina femininity to more matronly representations that could better appeal to the needs of overseas caretaking work globally.[30] According to Anna Guevarra, brown migrant women "from Asia and Latin and Central America" have been "viewed as imbued with an ideal docility, which employers attribute to cultures with a strong work ethic and values related to family, loyalty, and authority."[31] Such migrants from the Philippines were "em-plowered" (employed and empowered) by brokerage companies to have pride in an ahistorical Filipina identity based on matronly affection and care, a vision that combines ideal femininity with the role of a responsible neoliberal subject, whose "emplowerment" "fulfills the goal of producing 'responsible' (that is, economically competitive, entrepreneurial, and self-accountable) and therefore, ideal workers and global commodities."[32] Today domestic workers are typically depicted in advertisements, political speeches, and popular media as national heroes, and their "sacrifices" account for around US$33.5 billion annually, the largest source of export revenue for the Philippines.[33]

The critical scholarship concerning migrant domestic workers has developed a counternarrative to human rights discourses, where organizations like Human Rights Watch have increasingly scrutinized domestic work as a form of modern slavery, creating new definitions, identities, and expectations for regulating fair treatment.[34] Amnesty International has documented abuses around the world, most notably in Singapore, Hong Kong, and the Gulf states. Since the targets of abuses are migrants, human rights organizations often label as "at risk" those migrants who work in countries where employers typically confiscate travel documents, invade workers' personal space, pay below the minimum wage, and put workers on call at all hours without giving them a day off.[35] But besides labeling and tracking abuses, human rights organizations have limited power to enforce changes in local laws, and their attempts to combat contemporary forms of servitude are often stymied by employment-based visa structures.[36] These limitations leave domestic workers in need of adjusting to local views of gender, religion, race, and sexuality, and the restriction of their reproductive, marriage, and sexual rights has led to cases of deportation and jail time, common for impregnated domestic workers.[37] Implied in these laws is a regime of surveillance, where migrant domestic workers, unlike casual travelers or corporate jet-setters, are presumed to give up rights to privacy as a condition of entry.

Laws that attempt to police workers' sexual relationships are represented as benevolent for the domestic worker, as they align with religious notions of sexuality and female purity that are often held sacrosanct in the workers' homelands (the Philippines, Indonesia, India, Micronesia). But such laws also reflect "an underlying fear that foreign women workers pose a sexual and social threat to families" and, in effect, accept the heteropatriarchal characterizations that these women, now free from the policing forces of their families, friends, nation-states, and religious institutions, must be kept pure by the laws and norms of the local host country.[38] In the global cities explored in this chapter—Bahrain, Hong Kong, Honolulu, Las Vegas—the matronly migrant maid contrasts with oversexualized local women, as well as migrant women working in massage parlors and brothels. The fact that much of the workers' domination comes from nonwhite clients can also mark these global cities with a veneer of multicultural fairness. Such spaces, as Vernadette Gonzalez points out, appear multicultural and tolerant, marking service workers as responsible for their own failure, or as residual remnants of history.[39] Their jobs, positions, and livelihoods are constructed as gifts within a neoliberal rescue narrative, a mode of temporary adoption that secures the space itself from being perceived within the domain of humanitarian crises. Given the limitations of human rights groups in effecting changes to local laws, attitudes, and prejudices, such groups are often co-opted into nations as rule keepers or "umpires" that maintain an ideological sense of local space as fair, multicultural, and benevolent toward outsiders.[40] Umpire logic sees human rights organizations as a (free) watchdog, representing the neoliberal state as a benevolent force that gives migrant populations the freedom to self-govern—to discipline and dominate themselves—so long as they do so within the terms of their employment and immigration laws.[41] This "governing from afar" strategy rationalizes low wages and exploitative conditions as a cost of freedom and self-accountability. Service work then becomes shaped as a mode of humanitarian assistance through affective actions that construe migrants as objects of need and pity (having a live-in maid, sharing food, leaving tips, giving gifts).

In human rights discourse, female migrants are subjected to languages of *forced, free, economic duress*, and *bounded rationality*—terms that only reinforce the supposedly universal rationality that sees some forms of affective labor (domestic work) as legitimate and others (sex work) as immoral and fraught with exploitation. Domestic workers secure forms of family and culture, resigning the migrant maid to a matronly role that supports the family unit, while the sex worker threatens this very stability. As Nicole Constable argues, domestic work and sex work overlap in their associations with migrant work and intimacy, yet human rights and neoliberal discourses have obscured their similarities as affective "contributions" that both produce "intimate surplus labor."[42] The affective characteristics of domestic workers, of course, can be reconstituted as sexual acts and can broach the excesses of commodification, breaking apart the family unit as easily as supporting it. Representations of sex work (whether as trafficked or not) abound in human rights literature as well as in Asian American literature, where it is often placed as part of a traumatic family history that reinforces the host country as a benevolent space of rescue.[43] In contrast, representations of matronly migrant domestic work remain as a symbol of the benevolence of the Global North in providing remittances and refuge.

The migrant domestic worker's perceived purity and maternal duties manifest through imperial discourses, where female brownness can signify either the religious matron who inhabits highly religious societies (the Catholic Filipina, the Islamic Indonesian) or the prostitute (often queered as bakla, khathooey, waria) who inhabits imperial zones near military bases and tourist sites. As brown women are feared to fluctuate between these two imperial racial imaginaries, their main function of sacrificing themselves to provide affective "relief" for others never ceases. Yet in being seen as brown women, domestic workers are also able to inhabit various roles of affective labor, as their "libidinal energies," as Neferti Tadiar has put it, are incorporated into the flow of global capital.[44] For Tadiar, Filipinas have been branded with an objectified affective life force characterized by their "capacities for suffering, for relieving suffering for others, [and] for using their selves as the instruments of others' relief."[45] In the context of the religious (Protestant, Catholic, and Islamic) homeland, the victimization of care work can be reframed into a transnational form of the "Madonna/Whore" binary, where self-sacrificing domestic workers are mirrored against promiscuous sex workers. As Tadiar maintains, a religious upbringing combined with traditional notions of curing and healing helps constitute the migrant maid through images of sacred women whose libidinal energies are proof of their "life-producing activity of loving performed by what can now be recognized as domestic labor."[46] Their potential as passionate healers is incorporated into value for capital, as a commodification of healing power similar to commodified traits of sex workers in the Global South, who are also marked as affective laborers capable of healing, passion, and intimacy. Thus, what remains crucial in differentiating migrant domestic intimacy from the intimacy of sex work is matronliness itself. Compared with the supposed traumas induced through sex work, domestic work appears benevolent insofar as it also appears nonsexual.

The sought-after matronliness of domestic workers is not only presumed but maintained and reinforced through laws and social gazes meant to condemn any "nonmatronly" behavior. This need to understand domestic workers as figures of moral and motherly virtue rationalizes many of the human rights abuses directed at the domestic worker: the long work hours demanding they be busy at all times, the constant surveillance from employers and the state, and the live-in rule in spaces like Hong Kong, Singapore, and the Gulf states that forces workers to live with their employers' families. As Tadiar has argued, live-in laws result in particular forms of extracting "life-times," where domestic workers function "as savers and producers of valorized and valorizable 'surplus life-time' for their host employers and their socialities," which "exemplify the conditions of unfreedom and indistinction between work and bodily life (between labor-time and life-time)."[47] Indeed, the continued iteration of domestic labor as a quantifiable form of care labor foregrounds "a concept of care that begins and ends with individual interactions," which sees family dynamics and needs as universal, and "care" as merely another type of labor.[48] This gendered and sexual moralization of migrant workers can enhance processes of "emotional extraction," which Jan Padios defines as "the transfer and extension of human emotion from one site where emotions are localized . . . to a public or private sphere where such emotions circulate for the purposes of enhancing productivity and thus profit, or surveillance and thus predictive power."[49] When depicted solely as caring mothers, migrant domestic workers can be racialized as natural caretakers swelling with emotional resource, vulnerable to the marketing and exploitation of the extractive domestic worker industry.

Following the brown theoretical triptych in the introduction, this chapter's movement through four global cities (Hong Kong, Bahrain, Honolulu, Las Vegas) deploys the terms *brown mass*, *domesticating brown*, and *shades of brown* to construct an archipelagic route where migrants confront first world peoples in intimate spaces layered with erotic suspension and suspicion. The brown triptych prioritizes the specificity of thinking through intersectional forms of power but also accounts for how state violence is played out on bodies that are inevitably grouped together within a mass. Broaching the confines of American racial politics, we see that this sense of brown shares colonial histories in Asia and Oceania, yet in domestic work is often figured through (and against) the Filipino migrant, who, as Oscar Campomanes observed in 2006, "bears the brand of the U.S. Empire on his or her forehead, its unmistakable imprints on his or her body."[50] These imprints are the signification of brownness itself, as Campomanes continues: "Empire is epidermized in Filipino brownskins, encoded in their cultural genes. Make that true for Puerto Ricans who end up in New York . . . [and] [t]hink of American Samoans, Guamenians, all those Pacific Islanders whose habitats remain shanghaied . . . [to] migrants/immigrants from Central America, the Middle East, the Korean peninsula, Vietnam, and so on—wherever the exercise of U.S. 'globalism' resulted and continues to result in massive economic displacements and tumultuous political upheavals for these peoples."[51] As a global figure of brown mass undergoing processes of domestication, the domestic worker carries a seemingly dangerous relationship to sex that can only result in contamination or self-harm. The brown mass is thus not merely an illegible muck but also a messy space of queerness and excess sexuality, one that domestic workers must seemingly be rescued from. What happens, then, for domestic workers in cities where sex work, striptease, and exotic icons are ubiquitous? How does brownness fluctuate from invoking a sense of humanitarian rescue to being associated with erotic desires for exoticized and passive brown bodies?

The remainder of this chapter moves through four global cities to grasp the way brownness itself spirals from one context to another, limning the imperial racial imaginaries that envision various senses of brown. I invoke brown theory not to study brown people but to challenge what we think we know of brown people, to emphasize the way shades of brown differentiate brown mass and domestication, to move through multisited critiques without reifying the racial imaginaries of migrant domestic workers. This chapter spirals through various genres of art by and about brown migrant workers (including my own story of hiring one) without seeking to extract emotive content from domestic workers or make legible their illegibility, but to reveal the shared discourses of sexual and moral containment that seek to discipline their movements toward higher pay, state and institutional resistance, and heterosexual unsettling. Rather than seek to reveal the subjectivity of domestic workers worldwide, this multisited voyage through the movements of racial capitalism dazzles through the unwieldy racial imaginaries of brown workers in brown cities, creating a counterassemblage of brown shards that might otherwise formulate into a brown mass whose presence in global spaces is envisioned within a long process of domestication, with no foreseeable end in sight.

OMISSION 2

When our son was born in Hong Kong, we had to learn to parent without our parents, without day care facilities. Luckily, we found a domestic worker, Anne, who could be everything we needed, who could teach us everything. But it was such a charged situation, considering the power differences.

For Y-Dang, the experience of being pregnant, giving birth, and raising an infant brought her to the brink. Everything built up, weighed on her: the overeating and desperation that came with "intrauterine growth restriction," the twenty-four hours of labor resulting in an emergency C-section, the five days our son spent in an intensive care unit, the mere ten weeks of maternity leave she received from her university, the nights of our child's screams that turned us into sleepless zombies, the postpartum depression that would last years, the anxiety of applying for tenure, the stress that came from both of us interviewing on the job market as we desperately tried to extract ourselves from the situation.

Anne was younger than us, though she asked us to call her "Tita." When we called for our own mothers, she mothered us, and our son. She taught us how to change diapers, how to feed, how to burp, how to give a bath, how to carry. She kept us alive, gave us life. She joined our family portraits and was willing, if we asked, to step out of them.

Hong Kong: Baby Ruth Villarama's *Sunday Beauty Queen*

In Hong Kong, the importation of brown women into the homes of middle- and upper-class families began when British colonizers brought Indian ayahs as maidservants, women who were seen through an orientalist gaze as exotic and undeveloped.[52] More recently, foreign domestic workers from the Philippines and Indonesia make up around 5 percent of Hong Kong's population and are subject to extremely low pay (making less than 17 percent of the local minimum wage), to a live-in law that requires domestic workers to live with their hosts (often in very tight and exposed quarters), and to work hours that can stretch to six days a week with breaks only to sleep.[53] This situation is propelled by Hong Kong's own lack of childcare accommodations: the lack of living space, the lack of paid maternity/paternity leave, and the lack of day care facilities.

Since colonial times, prostitution has been legal in Hong Kong, and migrant sex workers can easily harbor in the city on two-week travel visas, placing the brown domestic worker as a suspect for sex work, one whose forced intimacy (because of the live-in rule) inevitably conjures associations with queer and aberrant forms of sexuality. As Constable argues, domestic workers in spaces such as Hong Kong often spend their time off participating in night-life activity, "motivated largely by a desire for fun, friends, relaxation, and an escape from the narrow identity of 'domestic helper'" that intersects with work in the wider sex industry.[54] The domestic workers' relations to the Chinese/Hong Kong majority construct them as brown rather than white/Chinese, as migrants rather than locals or foreigners (foreigners can become permanent residents; domestic workers cannot), and as constant threats to the heteronormative family dynamics emphasizing marriage and reproduction. Indeed, the travel of overseas domestic workers might strike us as a curious historical moment where unprecedented numbers of women might free themselves from what Neferti Tadiar has called "their territorially bound roles as mothers, daughters, sisters, and girlfriends."[55] Yet, as Valerie Francisco-Menchavez writes, only recently has academic work on migrant domestic workers tried to account for the ways in which migrants are queered or practice alternative modes of care and intimacy.[56] For the Hong Kong scholar Amy Sim, the experiences of migrant workers who participate in diasporic same-sex communities opens new pathways for queering notions of gender and sexuality, leading to "de-naturalizing, destabilizing and rethinking amongst them of women's bodies."[57] As Francisca Yuenki Lai has argued, queer Indonesian workers in Hong Kong have remained invisible to queer studies due to most scholars' reliance on the "gay liberation model, which assumes sexuality is fixed," while these migrant women fluctuate among gendered identities and sexual preferences, and often "do not articulate a desire for same-sex relationships before migrating."[58] Scholarship on queer Filipina and Indonesian migrants in Hong Kong reveal women who live discreet, dynamic and transformative queer lives conditioned by their exploitative work, precarious migrancy and differing values between the homeland and host country.

Two documentaries from Hong Kong, *The Helper* in 2017 and *Sunday Beauty Queen* in 2016, both follow groups of domestic workers, providing them individuality and specificity while also revealing the constant tension between domestic work and sex work. The more moralistic film, *The Helper*, sees queer desire as crucial to the "rescue" of domestic workers and places aberrant sexuality as one of many forms of exploitation. Like many popular representations of domestic workers, both documentaries present the queer aspects of migrancy only as subjects under constant erasure, emphasizing the workers' shared humanity by restricting them to what Jack Halberstam, Lee Edelman, and José Esteban Muñoz have called "straight time," the conventional and normative life course leading from "childhood into adolescence, adulthood, productivity, partnership and progeny, retirement, and death."[59] Even so, these documentaries also show how attempts to capture these women through the documentary camera inevitably reveal the queer practices and desires that migrancy makes available, as the communal and nonfilial intimacies within these films also depict domestic workers within a "queer time" of nonbiological reproduction and community building, or what Muñoz defines as people who are cast as "developmentally stalled, forsaken, who do not have the complete life promised by heterosexual temporality."[60] These documentaries' missions to "give dignity" to migrant workers often mean saving them from queer time to bring them into the fold of motherhood. As Gayatri Gopinath has shown, migrant women are often presumed to be queered as corrupt, hybrid, and outside of the watchful eye of their families. Thus, the "space of the home," Gopinath argues, becomes seen as a secure space to surveil migrant women who come from mixed and uncertain

FIGURE 3.1. Jane Engelmann directs the Unsung Heroes in *The Helper*, 2017. AFP, "Filipino Migrant Mothers."

backgrounds.[61] Because domestic labor is placed within the private space of the employer's family home, the public visibility of these workers must consistently reinstate gendered norms, lest they risk deportation. In Hong Kong, public parades, performances, and pageants do the public work of maintaining gendered and sexual hierarchies by emphasizing their sacrifice as mothers.

The Helper, directed by the British Hong Kong–based filmmaker Joanna Bowers, aggrandizes maternal sacrifice through its narrative of the Unsung Heroes, a choir of domestic workers founded by Jane Engelmann, a British music teacher and head of a colonial-era performing arts school in Hong Kong (figure 3.1). Driven by her love for her own children, Engelmann seeks to help the "helpers" find their voice by writing songs for them to sing about missing their children back home ("Kiss You Goodnight") and about celebrating their "voice" ("Find Your Voice"). The film ends with each helper reaching the peak of liberal success: wearing the choir name, "Unsung Heroes: Find Your Voice, Sing Your Song," on bright blue T-shirts, singing Engelmann's hymns as Engelmann herself conducts them, their voices pleasing a crowd of local Hong Kongers and expatriates at Clockenflap, the biggest music festival in Hong Kong. As the Unsung Heroes undergo training to perform at Clockenflap, they are "rescued" from their identity as Filipina domestic workers; as Engelmann tells the workers, being domestic workers is "not who you are, [not] who you were born to be." The film continually shows images of the Philippines as a slum of discarded trash, makeshift housing, mud floors, stray animals, and naked children. Never do we see iconic Philippines vistas, beaches, buildings, or malls. For cinema scholar Elmo Gonzaga, such depictions of an entire country through its slums coincide with "the resurrection of slum terminology in the rhetoric of international aid organizations," which compels filmmakers to depict a developing country as "primeval, chaotic, and destitute" so it can be recognized by an international audience based on human rights perceptions of "the human."[62]

The visual iconography of the Philippine slum is contrasted throughout the film with one particular domestic worker's story of literal uplift as she trains to climb Mount Everest. In an interview Joanna Bower claims that her inspiration for *The Helper* came from feeling "fascinated by the visual spectacle of thousands of domestic workers sitting out on the walkways in Central." Yet the film itself is uninterested in domestic workers who occupy public space on Sundays (their one day off a week). Instead, the film highlights the story of Liza Avelino, whose Western employer tells her that to sit with other Filipinas in public spaces is "degrading, [so] go somewhere else."[63] The makeshift community space of the domestic worker areas is only briefly represented as an extension of the Philippine slums, the brown mass that has come to the cosmopolitan city of Hong Kong via the critical mass of domestic migrants. The film instead focuses on Avelino's literal uplift from the brown mass, filming her climbing Mount Everest with groups of white Westerners, literally climbing upward from the "degrading" space of migrant community.[64]

The Helper's main narrative follows the Unsung Heroes as they "find their voice" by singing songs about motherhood written by Jane Engelmann that project her (and the filmmaker's) own framing of the human as "mothers first." This trope of "giving a voice to the voiceless," Pooja Rangan writes, has remained in documentary films as "one of the most familiar and paradigmatic metaphors of humanitarian recognition and inclusion," as it simplifies the humanitarian mission by asking subjects to reiterate the desires projected onto them, visualizing their agency by seeing "speaking out" as a "liberatory act of giving expression to an interior idea, thought, opinion, or wish that inaugurates the subject's entrance into the political sphere and, indeed, into humanity."[65] In fact, the only song sung by the Unsung Heroes that is *not* about child-rearing is about voice itself, "Find Your Voice," a song that grants the domestic worker "voice" only through displays of maternal devotion. The film's director, Joanna Bowers, credits her own domestic worker, Janai, as her muse, a woman whose mother was also a domestic worker and who, after coming to Hong Kong, sought ways to "make her mum's incredible sacrifice worthwhile." Even as domestic worker unions have continually demanded changes to Hong Kong law, which include scrapping the live-in law, increasing pay, and improving work hours, Bowers's film mentions none of these demands to instead fetishize the voice of domestic workers, a voice scripted by a white woman who envisions their presumed motherhood as the primary form of shared humanity.

Despite the film's overtly maternal moralism, queer undercurrents appear in *The Helper* through the promiscuity of its subjects and the risks they take in forming new relations. In a subplot an Indonesian domestic worker, Nurul, is accused of stealing from her employer and is left homeless and pregnant without documentation, as her previous employer keeps her passport. Despite her subjection to the violence of the state and her employers, Nurul keeps the pregnancy, and in fact, the film demonizes suggestions of abortion or adoption far more than the state's neglect of Nurul herself. "The worst possible thing that could have ever happened to her," says an expatriate employer, "happened to her in Chungking Mansions." The employer here refers to a supposed South Asian immigrant (read: a brown male gangster) who suggests to the visibly pregnant Nurul that she could make US$30,000 by putting her child up for adoption. Such suggestions denying the maternal roles of these "helpers" are routinely met with rancor by the employers, particularly Engelmann herself, who describes her "cause" as "showing that these women are not workers, not Filipinos, but mothers."

The 2016 film *Sunday Beauty Queen* also documents Hong Kong migrant domestic workers but from the point of view of its Filipina director, Baby Ruth Villarama, whose mother was a domestic worker in Hong Kong. Like *The Helper*, *Sunday Beauty Queen* follows a group of workers and organizers as they prepare to put on a performance, in this case an annual beauty pageant, and focuses on speeches made by the beauty queens that overwhelmingly mention their children in the Philippines and their gratitude to their employers, and to Hong Kong for hosting them. Though both *The Helper* and *Sunday Beauty Queen* emphasize the domestic workers' maternal roles, as documentaries, these films offer distinctly different ways of depicting the migrant coded as foreign, brown, female, and (suspiciously) queer. Unlike *The Helper*, *Sunday Beauty Queen* celebrates the communities that migrant domestic workers have built while occupying the public spaces in Hong Kong's Central district. The leader and manager of the annual beauty pageant in Central is also not a "queen" herself but a transman ("tomboy") named Leo Selomenio, commonly called "daddy," who defies Hong Kong's live-in law by residing in a small apartment with his presumed lover, a woman commonly called "mama" (figure 3.2). This queer relationship is never mentioned (or "voiced") in the documentary, nor are the other visible transgender audience members who come to watch

FIGURE 3.2. Leo Selomenio and a contestant in *Sunday Beauty Queen*, 2016. O. Cruz, "'Sunday Beauty Queen' Review."

the beauty queens as they denounce any Filipinas who work in the sex industry. Yet queerness remains in the film through queer practices of pageantry, as well as in the displays of love and affection that workers show toward each other, even when doing so will risk their employment (as several employers despise beauty pageants and require early curfews).

The Helper and *Sunday Beauty Queen* both reveal the supposed matronliness of the domestic worker as a constructed configuration that must be consistently reinforced and reproduced. The domestic workers' "ultimate sacrifice" of leaving their family—as *The Helper* puts it in its advertisements and trailer—sees the victimization of domestic workers not in their vulnerability but in their separation from biological family in their "homeland" and placement instead into potentially queer communities abroad. Acts of rescue thus come in placing them into heteropatriarchal norms, envisioning them solely as loving mothers and caretakers. Yet, while *The Helper* attempts to erase any form of queerness to domesticate women into maternal narratives of sacrifice, *Sunday Beauty Queen* only does so on its surface, if one focuses solely on the voice of the domestic workers. By stressing the importance of voice through both voice-over and diegetic voices, *Sunday Beauty Queen* depicts the conscious performances of domestic workers who are persuaded to express attitudes of matronly sacrifice or else risk stigmatization, job loss, and deportation. Film scholar Pooja Rangan has argued that the documentary films' attempts to "give voice" to "dehumanized others" often result in a sedimentation of gender and racial hierarchies, where "humanity" remains within a Western, development-oriented gaze, by "invent[ing] the very disenfranchised humanity that it claims to redeem."[66] By appealing to notions of "shared humanity" that are inescapably Western, heteronormative, capitalist, and self-validating, such documentaries turn the human rights subject into a "humanitarian commodity" who contrasts with those who have a perceived *absence* of humanity—queers, prostitutes, sluts, criminals, thieves.[67] As Rangan puts it, "Documentary, especially in its most benevolent, humanitarian guises, is thoroughly implicated in the work of regulating what does and does not count as human."[68] As Genevieve Clutario has shown, since the early Manila Carnival Queen contests, Filipina beauty queens have been known for embodying "normative scripts of ideal womanhood and broadcasting successful beauty and femininity."[69] However, when reading for queer performance and unspoken forms of self-expression, *Sunday Beauty Queen* offers new ways of seeing domestic workers as migrants who creatively engage with their own depictions through clandestine methods that draw our focus away from their voice.

We can take as an example a pageant interview onstage in Central's Statue Square park, when one of the beauty queens, Mylyn Jacobo, is asked about domestic workers being confused for prostitutes. She answers:

> Being an issue that mostly Filipinos are called to be prostitutes is a big insult to us. I will cite an example of what the issue last month ago that Mrs. Regina Ip addressed to us. We, Filipino domestic helpers are working here to provide the needs and support our family in the Philippines. We are not working here not only to do bad things and I know that we have our spirit that we serve our employer well, and I will tell you, all my fellow OFWs [overseas Filipino workers] here, whatever you do in life, here in abroad you must always think not only twice, but think more before you do it, because otherwise you can affect all of Filipino society here and also our country.

This speech meets the standards of humanitarian commodification demanded by the audience and effectively separates the beauty queens from the "bad things" done by sex workers. However, Jacobo's speech also sketches the boundaries of sexual norms in the diaspora, where "bad things" could "affect all of Filipino society here," noting the surveillance of migrant women's bodies and the lack of privacy in Hong Kong, as well as the prejudice toward domestic workers exhibited by Regina Ip, a conservative politician who accused domestic workers of seeking to seduce their bosses.[70] Indeed, to presume that the film itself can only be read as supporting heterosexual recognition because of this speech would be to entrust authenticity and truth telling solely to the spoken word or the voice. Though Jacobo's voice remains within discourses of heroism that deny similarities to sex work, *Sunday Beauty Queen* presents her voice within a self-conscious presentation on a stage directed to an audience of locals, tourists, workers, and judges—people who are evaluating her performance based on the values expressed within her answers. Indeed, Jacobo's answer that domestic workers should not do "bad things" becomes so overtaken by anger that the contestant hosts agree they "should not to ask that question again."

The question that should not be asked is, "What can you say about the issue of overseas Filipino workers being tangled in prostitution or some immoral acts?" It is a question that speaks to the overlapping of pageantry and queer aesthetics commonly seen in the Philippines. As Bobby Benedicto, J. Neil Garcia, and Martin Manalansan have observed, bakla (queer) aesthetics in the Philippines have been associated with forms of pageantry and runway walking common in both lower-class transgender beauty parlors and in ostentatious displays of power, as bakla designers were widely employed by Imelda Marcos. Despite these visible displays, bakla aesthetics of cross-dressing and runway pageantry, as Garcia writes, cannot be equated with a gay-friendly tolerance, as these practices have only been allowed "in certain social classes and within certain acceptable contexts."[71] Similarly, for Benedicto, these queer/bakla aesthetics of beauty function as both a lower-class transgender culture that is anterior to Western conceptions of homosexuality and also a form of queer futurity, where its aesthetics (not its subjects) organize and design the beautification of ostentatious displays of power.[72] In effect, the pageantry of domestic workers can be seen as balancing between these two forms—it is lower-class and marginal but also permits a fantasy of power and celebration routed through queer aesthetic performance.

Rather than take the voice of the domestic worker at face value, perhaps we can read *Sunday Beauty Queen* as similar to what Martin Joseph Ponce refers to as a queer text that performs for various audiences simultaneously because its subjects are "multiply oriented" by its audiences and can thus appear progressive to some audiences and conservative to others.[73] For the human rights audience who would value the voice of the domestic worker above all else, *Sunday Beauty Queen* seems to validate their heterosexual form of humanity through speeches that overwhelmingly mention the workers' children in the Philippines, and their gratitude to the space of Hong Kong. However, these speeches always appear within the diegesis of the film and never take the authoritative form of the voice-over, what Rangan calls the "God" voice that emanates "from an unknowable off-screen space" and gives an "economical and detached delivery."[74] The speeches instead remain within a realm of interpretative play, containing what Roland Barthes calls the "graininess" of voices that inheres in the "the very precise space (genre) of *the encounter between a language and a voice,*" which carries their subjectivities and histories with them through displays of accent, affect, and performance.[75] These arguments concerning the queer erasures of the migrant worker make no claim that migrant workers are insincere about their love of family, or harbor queer desire, but rather assert that the heteronormative and humanitarian racial imaginary reinforced by documentary films about them obscures the fact that the voice audiences long to hear is often their own.

OMISSION 3

Anne told us stories of her ex-husband in the Philippines, how abusive he was, how he sucked up all her money, how impossible it was to divorce him in the Philippines, how she found new family with a Filipino tomboy truck driver in Hong Kong. Though the world would see them as lesbians, and they could only live together illegally, they seemed happy and free, mirroring the happiness and freedom that Y-Dang and I felt together.

Anne told stories about rotating through jobs in the Philippines, caretaking, nursing, and teaching, then hustling her way through training institutions to work in Hong Kong, then swaying from employer to employer (another defiance of Hong Kong laws), until she found us. Her previous employers, brought up by maids and expecting the utmost obedience, blamed her for everything, sexualized her, then hated her for being young.

We lived young and queer and free and felt a kinship with Anne, who also lived young and queer and free, in the place we rented for her in Wan Chai, Hong Kong's district of dance clubs, queer immigrants, and sex workers. We admired her ambition, her determination to be herself, to find and exploit cracks in the machinery of unjust labor laws. Together, we felt the joys of breaking these laws, of defying the migrant worker system, of celebrating travel, divorce, laughter, and dance—the kinship of queer resistance.

Bahrain: Mia Alvar's *In the Country*

The documentaries *Sunday Beauty Queen* and *The Helper* offer a sense of brown mass as a queer blur that must be made legible by "unfurling the cape" (the Tagalog idiom for "coming out") of aberrant sexuality, though *Sunday Beauty Queen* is far more ambiguous in this respect. However, if we shift mediums from film to literature, we find narratives about domestic workers that seek to complicate their relationship to sexuality within exotic and erotic spaces. If films about domestic workers have often followed the identity making of the state, literary texts—often aimed at more middlebrow reading audiences— have sought to reflect overseas maids not as mere matronly figures but as women subjected to strict sexual norms meant to manage and control them.

Mia Alvar's 2015 short story collection, *In the Country*, depicts multiple migrant workers both within and outside of the Philippines but focuses its sharpest insights on domestic workers living in Bahrain, the "playground of the Middle East," where Saudis, Emiratis, and others from the Arab states and Persian Gulf mix to gamble, drink, and hire sex workers (especially in Bahrain's own "sin city" of Manama).[76] Throughout the 2010s and prior to the COVID-19 lockdowns, Bahrain had around 99,000 migrant domestic workers (over 5 percent of the population), the majority from the Philippines (others from Ethiopia, Indonesia, India, and Sri Lanka), who were most often hidden in hotels and palaces.[77] As in many Gulf states, employers continue to rely on the kafala (sponsorship) system that restricts migrant workers' ability to change employers and enables employers to revoke sponsorship and thus trigger deportation at will. As Rhacel Parreñas eloquently summarizes, the kafala system "ultimately subjects domestic workers to the arbitrary authority of the employers," who "are the primary assessors and administrators of the law."[78] In remaining hidden, domestic workers are more subject to placement agents using legal loopholes to ensure contracts limit worker movement, and weak inspection systems make it nearly impossible for workers to take legal action.[79]

Alvar's opening short story of *In the Country*, "Shadow Families," depicts upper-class Filipina women in Bahrain who desire to help lower-class Filipina domestic workers by also subordinating them into a particular shade of brown, one marking them as matronly symbols of the home country. The story's upper-middle-class Filipina women host weekly get-togethers where they provide gifts for lower-class Filipina maids—*katulong*, also called *helpers*—whom the higher-class Filipinas try to match up with husbands by finding them pen pals in Manila, feeling, "We owed them a chance at the life we enjoyed" (95). These "lucky" upper-class women take pity on domestic servants, sending them home with leftovers and praying for them before bed, seeing them as remnants of their homeland, people who come from "farming provinces, like our fathers," and speak "Tagalog with country accents, like our mothers" (95). "Helping these helpers," as the women say, "felt like home" (95). The helpers become a symbol of Philippine national pride, as self-sacrificing maids whom the upper-class Filipinas see as "sweet, humble church [mice], who'd somehow strike us as child and granny all at once" (95).

Alvar's story focuses on the relations among Filipinas themselves to the brown mass, construed on a racial hierarchy of varying shades of brown, whose particular shade is sought after not just because of their labor but because of their moral and cultural signification as poor but virtuous brown women. Scholars focusing on Filipina domestic workers like Anna Guevarra, Robyn Rodriguez, Rhacel Parreñas, and many others have helped shape a labor-oriented discourse that resists state narratives of domestic workers as "bagong bayani," or modern heroes. In the Philippines, popular movies like *The Flor Contemplacion Story* (1995) have depicted migrant workers as martyrs and victims, while films like *The Maid* (2005) and *Ilo Ilo* (2013) in Singapore have re-worked these victimized figures into third world women who are vulnerable to first world modernity and who can cure the traumas haunting the household. This discourse of heroism appears often in presidential speeches, such as when then President Gloria Macapagal Arroyo, in 2002, called on "the work and reputation of the overseas Filipinos" to "confirm to the world that indeed, the Philippines is the home of the Great Filipino worker," or when the Philippine government declared "Migrant Heroes Week" to celebrate the signing of the Migrant Workers and Overseas Filipinos Act of 1995.[80] Guevarra criticizes this heroism narrative as "an attempt to downplay the absence of any governmental protective mechanisms for the country's overseas workers . . . by summoning a kind of nationalist spirit rooted in the belief of one's role in nation building."[81] By marking Filipina migrant workers as national heroes, the Philippine state and brokerage agencies are able to dismiss their exploitation through religious symbols of martyrdom, thus congealing the so-called danger of sexual promiscuity as not only taboo but a betrayal to the nation. In what sense, then, can we speak of a sexual migrant maid? How can we see the domestic worker as one who doesn't mind defaulting on their debts to the homeland, the host country, the family, and their prescribed roles?

Alvar's "Shadow Families" differs from previous conceptions of migrant maids because it makes no serious attempt to authentically interiorize the maids' thoughts and motivations (their voice), nor does it cast them as martyrs. Rather, Alvar's story takes aim at the bourgeois desire to rescue them and questions how these desires reinforce sexual norms and produce domestic workers as others to cosmopolitan, upper-class brown migrants. Alvar's story does this primarily by depicting these upper-class migrants from a shared gaze that only speaks in the first-person plural, a "we" narrative that lays bare all the assumptions that individual narratives would otherwise attempt to tone down or complicate by emphasizing the complexity of the individual imbricated within global capitalism. With no narrative burden to individualize the middle-class migrant's point of view, the plural narrative uncovers the crucial self-making and community building that marks the upper-class housewives as the matronly maid's opposite (as sexual, intelligent, and charitable), while also extracting the emotional labor of lower-class migrant women through a valued sense of national belonging, of feeling "like home."

The narrative of national belonging and charitable community building provided by matronly and heroic domestic workers holds up well in "Shadow Families," that is, until the upper-class Filipina women meet Baby, a Filipina office cleaner who seems to "walk on air" in translucent heels and straps and receives the housewives' hospitality as "her birthright." Baby provocatively flirts with the housewives' husbands and later accuses the husbands of attempting to touch her whenever they drive her home. While these charges may or may not be true, Baby's attitude toward the upper-class husbands, who almost all work in Bahrain's oil industry, is to feel "tickle[d]" rather than offended (101). "If you're gonna touch, touch," Baby says between laughs. "Don't pretend you want a cigarette" (101). As Baby's accusations appear after every ride home, the group of upper-class housewives become concerned for their own positions, thinking that "even the least jealous wife among us couldn't resist questioning her designated driver afterward" (103).

Baby's sexual promiscuity challenges the housewives' own sense of the matronly maid figure as a symbol of Filipina heroism and self-sacrifice. Baby's danger is not so much in departing from the Philippine nation but in bringing shame as a representative of that nation who has "the potential to circulate as unauthorized and inauthentic."[82] Baby's sexual promiscuity and accusations upset the safety of the family unit, challenging the matronly maid figure as a simplistic symbol of Filipina language, religion, and culture (Baby even claims that she forgot her Tagalog). When Baby mysteriously disappears, the upper-class women wonder about their own class security: "Just how far up did we live," they ask, "from the slop sink and the soil?" (108). As metaphor, the "slop sink and . . . soil" conjure the brown mass, the muck from which women like Baby are meant to be rescued. As Parreñas argues, the "mobility pathways" of migrant domestic workers are often seen as a form of class mobility as well as transnational mobility, a presumption that conflicts with the lived reality of remaining in "the unfreedom of poverty that initially motivated their migration, making it clear that their labor migration is ultimate a story of immobility."[83] Baby thus reveals the immobility of the domestic worker through her own attempts to improve her class position through other means (what is perceived as a form of sex work). The upper-class women, in turn, begin to see their own precarity in relation to the brown mass, and their own work in ascending the brown mass as a form of affective if not sexual exchange. No matter how rich or fluent in American-accented English, brown women can always slide back into the slop sink and soil.

Baby is later rediscovered on the street wearing a "black abaya" and living in an apartment for Muslims. Immediately, the housewives begin to frame Baby's newfound freedom as a form of descent: "Losing Baby to a world of mosques and abayas and possible polygamy set off a more desperate alarm, as if one of our children had woken with a fever and was speaking in tongues" (109). The women assume that Baby is a second or third wife of a Bahraini and immediately seek to provide rescue. While losing Baby to prostitution (her mother's profession) seems at the bottom of the ladder of success that the housewives have climbed, the thought of mixed marriage (and perhaps mixed children) to a local Bahraini represents an altogether different descent, a "world of mosques and abayas" where the upper-class women have little understanding or influence. With Baby's disappearance, the housewives cannot help but expose their own interests in policing the katulong's sexuality and cultural purity, thus replacing the role of the church, family, and nation that these migrant women have all but left behind.

The housewives' anxiety for possibly losing their privileged positions climaxes when Baby reappears at her old flatmate's wedding pregnant, claiming that the father of her child is one of the housewives' husbands. "While you were cooking in your kitchen," Baby says, "rip[ping]" with laughter, "while you were shopping in the mall, while you were in the Philippines—where did you think he was?" (112). Though Baby never reveals the father of her child, the housewives' suspicion toward their husbands remains a shared anxiety depicted through the first-person-plural narrative that refuses individualization. They all, knowingly, conform to the anxieties of monogamous, heterosexual marriage and, in turn, take revenge against Baby by reporting her pregnancy to the Bahraini police. Tellingly, their successful attempt to deport Baby back to the Philippines maintains their identities as charitable women, as they take it on themselves to rescue Baby from her sexual trespasses. As they say, "Even the so-called playground of the Gulf had no room for an unwed mother" (116). When the housewives fail to control Baby themselves, they appeal to the higher power of Bahrain's immigration laws: "The only law that could contain her," they declare, "was the one that ruled us all" (116). Bahrain's laws policing women's bodies line up uniformly with the upper-class women's interests in maintaining their social power, but also invoke their own servility to the citizens of the oil-rich state, as such laws, the women say, "renewed our awe and obligation toward our hosts" (116).

As the months passed after our son was born, Y-Dang and I began to find comfort in Anne's presence. We met her son and gave her vacation time to visit him in the Philippines as she wished. When we were away, we let her sister and her children live in our apartment.

Still, giving Anne nights and weekends off remained a struggle that worsened as the academic year moved forward. Y-Dang and I were expected to work weekends, to host scholars, to organize conferences, to always be on call for our students. Meanwhile, we continued to apply for less demanding academic jobs in cities with more reliable and affordable day care.

When our son was two months old, Y-Dang and I were longlisted for the same job at the University of British Columbia's English department and given a virtual interview. Though I could find no time to prepare, I forced myself not to use the interview as an excuse to ask Anne to come on the weekend or to stay into the evening. Nor would I put more childcare duties on Y-Dang, who was also struggling to meet deadlines and prepare for her interview. I forced my best into the interview, though I could barely make out the figures talking back to me from my laptop screen.

A year later, I asked a member of the job committee why I didn't make it past that interview. His answer was immediate: "Your affect," he told me. "You seemed tired, like you didn't really want the job."

Honolulu: Kristiana Kahakauwila's "This Is Paradise"

As we saw in Mia Alvar's story, accounting for various shades of brown allows us to perceive how the upper-class brown woman's desire to rescue domestic workers maintains her own class position through the act of policing sexual norms, keeping domestic workers within the realms of victimhood, charity, and matronliness. To further explore these brown shades, I turn briefly to Kristiana Kahakauwila's titular story from her 2013 collection, *This Is Paradise*, which attempts to provide the shared perspective of migrant Micronesian hotel maids in Honolulu, Hawai'i.[84] Whereas the turning point in the Philippines toward brokering women abroad occurred in 1974 with the overseas employment program, in the island states of Micronesia, the Marshall Islands, and Palau, the change to exporting migrant labor came in 1986, with the implementation of the Compact of Free Association, an agreement that gave the association's members the freedom to live permanently in the United States or come and go at will. Since the early 2000s, about one out of every four Micronesians has been living and working in the United States.[85]

Like Filipinas, domestic workers from Micronesia are characterized in the global market for maintaining explicit marks of colonial histories that befit service labor (use of English, Christian sexual norms, rights to travel in the United States), while their darker remnants of colonial history (cancer, environmental degradation, military recruitment) become obscured by their seemingly grateful attitudes. While women from these island states frequently go abroad to send home remittances, the men have the highest volunteer rate per capita in joining the US military and also share in the military's highest casualty rate, higher than in any US state.[86] The lack of representation of brown male migrants as at-risk figures mirrors the ways human rights organizations in areas like microfinancing often deal exclusively with women. The nonappearance of men as subjects of rescue is crucial to maintaining affective structures that see women as victims whose low-wage work also provides them refuge from brown male patriarchy. Men must either disappear or reappear only as warriors in the military, or in jobs such as seamen that do not interact with the general public. As Teresia Teaiwa notes, "In the context of war, society has an ideological stake in the reification of female bodies when male bodies are being sacrificed heroically."[87] Gender is thus deployed as a regulatory mechanism to rationalize the positioning of migrants as cheap service workers, while also lending credence to their inhabited space as providing benevolence through the "opportunities" of tourism, militarism, and the freedom to migrate.

Like in Hong Kong and Bahrain, the majority of migrant domestic workers in Hawaiian tourist areas like Waikīkī Beach are Filipino, yet in most of Hawai'i, the most exploited migrant domestic and service labor comes from Micronesians.[88] Thus, the focus on Micronesians in "This Is Paradise" plays a role similar to that of the Filipinos in *The Helper*, *Sunday Beauty Queen*, and "Shadow Families," in representing the lowest rung of migrant women's labor. Yet Micronesian migrants, like Filipinos, carry with them similar markings of American empire: weapons testing, colonial control, military bases, tourist protectorates, the buying up and continued stealing of Indigenous lands, and the need for economic migrancy and debt servitude itself. Like Alvar's "Shadow Families," Kahakauwila's titular short story from her collection, "This Is Paradise," invokes popular understandings of the migrant domestic worker as a matronly maid figure. Indeed, both Alvar's and Kahakauwila's collections have crossed a barrier in the popularity of the migrant domestic worker, as both were published by Random House subsidiaries, and both have won numerous awards and accolades.[89] Both stories also use the first-person plural *we* and third-person plural *they* to resituate migrants into mobile sisterhoods that offer a support structure while also reinforcing expectations of matronly behavior. In doing so, these stories show the ways that authors and audiences are always brought in to see domestic workers as reflections of themselves, as collectives whose domestication brings the authors and audiences into their subjectivity (as performed, affective, and domestic labor) while also refracting their privilege as clients, customers, and bosses. Their representation thus invokes the challenge (or impossibility) of theoretical categorization and calls attention to the very need for "understanding" as itself a form of conceptual domestication.

Both "Shadow Families" and "This Is Paradise" trouble the image of the matronly maid by refusing to individualize group prejudices and by focusing on the way migrant brown sisterhoods bond together through identifying (and vilifying) what Sara Ahmed calls "willful subjects": "willful women, unwilling to get along, unwilling to preserve an idea of happiness."[90] Willful women appear in the stories as those who separate from the group by refusing the duty to reproduce social and gender norms. Indeed, while the "we" narrative exposes shared assumptions of domestic workers as victims in need of rescue, it also depicts how such women are partially produced through a binary other: the willful woman, whose freedom speaks to the anxieties of sexual promiscuity and miscegenation that comes with overseas travel. Shadowing this matronliness ascribed to migrant workers, the willful woman refuses to reproduce or smile correctly and, rather than show gratitude, chooses to expect equality.

Kahakauwila's "This Is Paradise" focuses on three separate groups of brown women who all speak in a first-person plural voice. The first are young local surfer women (Cora Jones, Kaila Ka'awa, Lani Pogan, Mel Chun); the second are middle-aged and upper-middle-class women (Esther Lu, Laura Tavares, Kiana Naone, Paula Gilbert). While these first two groups of women are ambiguous mixtures of Asian, Indigenous, and white locals, the third group are hotel maids, "the women of Housekeeping" (11), who have all migrated from Micronesia, and only one, Stassi Nifon, is individually named, though we understand all their origins come from islands like "Pohnpei or Yap or Kosrae" (14). The story follows these three groups as each observes the promiscuous and careless freedom of a willful woman, Susan, a white tourist wearing a polka-dot bikini who conjures sexual anxieties in every group and who, in the end, is assaulted and killed by a local brown man sporting prison tattoos. For the most part, "This Is Paradise" represents migrant workers as matronly women who accommodate tourists by cleaning up their condoms and pornography. Unlike in Alvar's story, Kahakauwila's narrative sees the maids' matronly affections as boundless, and they are the least judgmental of all the women.

Whereas the two other groups of brown women see Susan as a dangerous and foolish young tourist, the migrant domestic workers see her as one of their own children, their "eldest daughter"; as they say, "This girl, like our girls, is the type a mother can depend on to do things: drive Grandmother to a doctor's appointment, cook breakfast for Papa, dress and feed the babies before school" (12). By speaking in a communal voice, this passage makes visible the gendering labor that transforms the sexual, effervescent energy of a young woman into recognizable labor power for caretaking and domestic work. While the other women see Susan as an object of danger or shame, the domestic workers recognize the way willfulness is so often subsumed into domesticity, where the same woman who dresses scantily and seeks adventure can later become the woman to "cook breakfast for Papa" and "dress and feed the babies" (12).

While Kahakauwila's story illuminates the contemporary struggles of Hawaiian locals and natives in dealing with tourism, poverty, and the buying up of private land, the representation of Micronesian maids as subjects of US atomic testing and military recruitment remains hidden by the workers' obligation to give approval to tourists and local Hawaiians. Even so, the bikini that Susan wears, which grabs the attention of each passing group, tells of this very past. As Oceania scholar Teresia Teaiwa has pointed out, the bikini was originally named after Bikini Atoll, a site in the Marshall Islands where the United States tested twenty-five nuclear bombs from 1946 to 1958, displacing Indigenous tribes and destroying the ecology of the archipelago. The story's focus on the maid's reactions to Susan's bikini externalizes the implicit narrative of the two-piece swimsuit, as Teaiwa puts it, to "manifest[] both a celebration and a forgetting of the nuclear power that strategically and materially marginalizes and erases the living history of Pacific Islanders."[91] The bikini is also a prominent feature of the exotic brown beach woman, a figure commonly seen in tourist advertisements in island states within both the Philippines and Hawai'i, where, as Teaiwa writes, "the female body is appropriated by a colonial discourse to successfully disguise the horror of the bomb."[92] As Vernadette Gonzalez has also pointed out, the sexualized bikini-clad brown body entices American soldiers in their routes to conquer and marks the tourist space as one in need of American security and protection.[93] The bikini-clad body thus serves to distract from the matronly maid who is meant to remain barely visible, unexciting, and unenticing. The domestic worker's desexualized but comforting nature, as well as her ability to nurture, provides both legitimacy and security to the tourist. The domestic worker shows happiness where one might expect anger and provides a symbol of moral virtue that affirms and approves of a tourist's pleasures.

While Susan's bikini serves as a constant symbol of US imperial violence in the Pacific, the Micronesian women must cover over explicit marks of colonialism (cancer, environmental degradation, military recruitment) as well as the colonial histories (the English language, Protestant notions of sexuality, employment as hospitality workers) that frame them as natural domestic workers. Indeed, the first-person plural narrative throughout the story solidifies the migrants' shared strategies in appearing as matronly, collective, invisible service labor to tourists. In contrast, the successful women are individualized by differing life choices and careers: Paula is a detective who never chose to live off the island, Kiana is a journalist, and the others are identified as a lawyer and a business consultant. Similarly, the young surfer women are differentiated by the parts of the islands they come from: Cora is from Kailua (which makes her "naïve"), and Lanie is "a Nanakuli girl and likes to pretend she's tougher" (24). While the young women visit clubs searching for appropriate men to dance with, the successful women lounge at quiet bars wondering if passing men are single, wishing they could "have the husband and the babies and the home" (30). Meanwhile, the Micronesian workers practice a group cohesion that erases any trace of sexual desire for the willingness to protect and to provide for others: those with the privilege and freedom to become sexual beings.

Kahakauwila's story of three groups of brown women in Honolulu demonstrates the ways brownness remains on various levels of domestication: domestications into neoliberal feminism (the successful women), domestications toward marriage and domesticity (the surfer women), and domestications into the migrant work of domestic labor itself (the Micronesian workers). Yet "This Is Paradise" also reveals shades of brown within these collectives by exploring forms of desire and awareness that speak to Indigenous traditions of collectivity in caretaking, spirituality, and mourning. As Leanne Day suggests, when the migrant workers discover Susan's corpse, they express a form of collective caretaking through the performance of "an Oceanic practice of care or Kanaka 'Ōiwi-aligned concepts of aloha."[94] While the other two groups of women continue to envision heterosexual marriage as the only route to happiness (even more than financial success), the Micronesian migrant maids are depicted not so much as victims to be rescued but as a collectivity who provide forms of care and spiritual relief, which the tourist industry has commodified into low-wage labor. Their ability to read as a matronly collectivity to tourist institutions thus provides flexible forms of care that see beyond divisions of migrant, local, mainlander, and tourists, and allows the other groups in the story to mourn the death of Susan, the promiscuous and willful white tourist. When the maids discover Susan's body on the beach, they conduct an act of mourning:

We form a circle around her, protecting her even though she is beyond our protection. . . . She is older than even our eldest girls, and, on any other day, we could have called her haole, foreigner, a white woman independent and capable of caring for herself. But in these few minutes before the police come running down the beach with a first-aid kit and walkie-talkie, this girl is a child. She is helpless. She is in need of a mother, and that's a job at which we are experts. . . . We are here, we tell the unmoving girl. All us mothers are here. (38–39)

Only on seeing these maids mourn for the deceased Susan can the other two groups reconnect to the "natural" purposes of heterosexual success. The career women are struck with a sense of guilt for not helping Susan: "We should have done something," they collectively say (42), while the surfers perform their own mourning ritual with flowers purchased from a nearby Safeway (45).

While Baby's sexuality in "Shadow Families" is cursed as inauthentic and unlawful, the matronly maids of "This Is Paradise" see Susan as "a white woman independent and capable of caring for herself," who in death becomes a "helpless" "child" whose spirit is in need of public mourning and protection. In both stories, the willful woman produces individual difference within a "we" collective form, symbolizing "the possibility of not being reduced to thing, of not being compelled by an external force, including the will of others, enshrined in or as law."[95] But in "This Is Paradise," the loss of the willful woman does not return the space to a status quo but results in acts of mourning that directly oppose the tourist economy's encouragement of bikini-clad beach vacations with expected sex and inebriation. For Day, the workers' refusal to return to work so they can continue their vigil for Susan's spirit notes a "shift in the precariousness of their positions as workers," for whom "motherhood" might symbolize "non-human entities" of Pacific cosmology that "call to the Micronesian women's various ancestral homes."[96] Day's reading here should not be seen as merely contextual: What some might see as a domestic worker's "matronly majesty" may in fact be a categorical way of domesticating a person's vastness and spiritual complexity: Their actions may be neither matronly nor willful but a foundational disruption of how we see matronliness itself.

OMISSION 5

After the birth of our son, Y-Dang and I did our best to equalize the parenting work. This was harder for her because she was still recovering from the birth and felt like a failure if I did too much. With Anne, my wife's feelings of failure grew, entangled with the power dynamics of migrant employment. When our child cried out, we did not know how to interpret his screams, or how to soothe him. When we failed to stop his tears, Anne took him in her arms, and he would immediately go quiet. She was teaching us how to be good parents. But her abilities with him made us feel like bad parents.

In her first week back from maternity leave, Y-Dang was humiliated at an English department meeting by her chair, who chewed her out for not doing enough work or answering emails fast enough while she was on leave.

That weekend, just before Y-Dang had another meeting that would include discussing her tenure and promotion, we realized we needed more help. We did not want to pressure Anne to work on her day off, so we found someone else. The woman came, babysat for a couple of hours, and left.

The next day, after another humiliating meeting, Y-Dang had an argument with Anne, who was enraged that we had asked someone else to babysit, someone who fed our infant son water. It was actually my idea. But Y-Dang got the blame.

We talked about this day for the rest of Y-Dang's life. She could not take the guilt of bad motherhood along with the pressure of her book being rejected, of going up for tenure and then getting rejected for that as well. After her argument with Anne, Y-Dang went for a walk, stood on a bridge, and planned how she might throw herself off. The future was bleak: losing her job, never publishing her book, staying trapped in Hong Kong's roller-coaster lifestyle, and, at the end of the day, allowing all this stress to endanger our son by keeping him away from the one person who could care for him best: not his mother, but his caregiver, Anne. After a lifetime seeking a peace that would never come, Y-Dang longed to make it for herself.

Las Vegas: Miss Di' Lovely

For most tourists, Las Vegas, a place I grew up in from 1999 to 2007, often does not register as a space of brownness, despite its enormous hospitality industry, its population where white residents make up a minority (or very slim majority), and its university (University of Nevada, Las Vegas [UNLV]), which boasts of being the most diverse campus in the United States.[97] Populated mostly by a mixture of white, Latino, and Black peoples, Las Vegas is positioned in the Southwest, a land that has remained the traditional and ancestral territory of the Southern Paiute-Shoshone Indigenous peoples since at least 1100 CE. Their land was first colonized by Spain, then by independent Mexico. After the Mexican-American War, Las Vegas was settled by Mormons, then began to develop and thrive by marketing itself as an oasis of gambling and lust. Las Vegas is a borderland that, as Gloria Anzaldúa wrote, invites migrant brown women as refugees venturing into an "unknown and possibl[y] dangerous terrain."[98]

For Anzaldúa, survival in the Borderlands came not from embracing the figure of the matronly domestic worker but from seeking refuge from it, from finding "the strength to leave the source, the mother."[99] Raised in a Catholic home, Anzaldúa was taught to see female sexuality as "carnal, animal, closer to the undivine," and thus a woman had to be "protected from herself."[100]

It would be difficult to deny in a city defined by tourism that brownness in Las Vegas also signifies the illegible and queer mass, whose main routes of escape are through service work and hospitality. As my mother sharply intuited after reading *The Help*, housekeeping can be synonymous with darker-skinned bodies. One study from the University of Nevada found that housekeeping was the most ethnically overrepresented form of hotel labor, with 62 percent ethnic minorities, most African American and Hispanic, while hotel management staff were only 25 percent ethnic minorities, and most—like my sister—managed housekeeping, or what the authors of this study call "the ghetto of hotel management."[101] As similar studies show, these working women are vulnerable to the injuries and low pay of the industry, as the majority of room cleaners who experience work-related pain and injury do not report their injuries to either management or workers' compensation, and only about half of workers who do file complaints report their claims as being accepted, while many others report being subjected to drug testing and other forms of bodily discipline. Just as African Americans were the faces of domestic work both during and after slavery, in the borderlands domestic work and housekeeping have become typified as the work of the brown mass seeking domestication.

If Las Vegas offers a counterpoint to the narratives of Hong Kong, Bahrain, and Honolulu, perhaps it is not in the arena of film or literature but in the erotic performance art found ubiquitously within "sin city": the art of cabaret, burlesque, striptease, and sex work. These forms of labor, as in our previous contexts, offer points of constant tension and anxiety as they promulgate forms of brown mass that domestic workers are often thought to be rescued from. As we have seen in narratives of domestic workers from Hong Kong to Bahrain to Honolulu, the desire to domesticate the brown migrant woman implies protecting her from her own desire by rerouting libidinal energies toward maintenance of the household, toward childcare, and toward commodification of even the wayward potentialities of matronliness. So it is too in Las Vegas, where the vulnerability of strippers and cabaret dancers to sexual violence, theft, and police harassment is sensationalized in news media that depict sexual transgression as an always risky venture fraught with danger and exploitation. Though we might find forms of expression and negotiation in various forms of erotic performance art, I focus here on burlesque for its capacity to offer critical understandings of brown eroticism in a space where brown women often fluctuate among sex work, hospitality, and service work.

Unlike strip and cabaret dancing, burlesque has, since the 1920s at least, synthesized the erotic with the comic and asserted the importance of nonnormative dancing bodies. The "Berla" of the word *burlesque*, meaning "joke" in Italian, insists on parody, aggrandizement, and caricature of everyday relations into political ironies. As Becki Ross writes in *Burlesque West*, burlesque operates as a space to discuss "politics, domestic relations, and all facets of sex," as well as to satirize heterosexuality.[102] For the cultural theorist Roland Barthes, striptease in the 1950s Moulin Rouge worked to unsettle dominant depictions of women's bodies, where to strip the body of clothing was also to strip the exotic stereotype from the minds of the audience, revealing it as mere "disguise."[103] However, for Barthes, striptease could also reinforce the audience's bourgeois and liberal class position, as well as the sexually liberated pride within French nationalism. Indeed, early burlesque in the United States was not so different: Clubs were most often racially segregated, and white dancers were known to dress in brown- and blackface, appropriating dances and costumes from women of color. White burlesque dancers like Lili St. Cyr, who was "as much a fixture in Las Vegas as the roulette wheels," routinely appropriated black and brown dance, costume, and iconography to flirt with the dangers of otherness.[104] Meanwhile, dancers of color were left in the precarious position of having no claim to their own erotic heritage, remaining "unbookable" due to the racism of management and segregated audiences. In 1952, while Lili St. Cyr was appropriating Black and brown iconography, the Black queer burlesque and cabaret dancer Josephine Baker famously went on a desegregation tour, refusing to play in segregated theaters, and was effectively the first to integrate audiences in clubs in Manhattan; Miami; Vancouver, Canada; and Las Vegas.

In response to tactics of appropriation and the denial of sexual agency, women of color in burlesque have also taken back discourses of brownness, seeing the term *brown* as itself an assertion of the centrality of the body in forming imperial imaginaries that place brown bodies within the queer mass of the exotic, the dangerous, the servile, and the extractable (in terms of affect, aesthetic, style). Whereas the brown mass is cast on workers and migrants whose individuality and specific backgrounds are deemed irrelevant to their job performance, brownness in burlesque operates as an erotic code for the artifice—the precarious mass as well as the domesticated worker—that must be stripped away. At the Burlesque Hall of Fame Museum in the Las Vegas Arts District, the 2013 exhibition *Not-So-Hidden Histories: Performers of Color in Burlesque* showcased lost histories of burlesque dancers who advertised

FIGURE 3.3. Postcard for *Brown Skin Scandals*, 1953. Ricci Cortez Collection, the Burlesque Hall of Fame.

themselves in postcards and magazines as brown bodies: Black, Asian, Latina, South Pacific Islander, and Native American (figure 3.3). As with burlesque performances today, such dancers coded with the word *brown* affirmed a sense of erotic brownness that white dancers could only partially appropriate, only to strip it bare, revealing its tenacious grip on the imagination through the erotic and the comic.

The historical staging of brownness in order to strip it away also rereads the figure of the brown woman not as a victim of her own sexuality but as a woman who negotiates her place within the open disguise that brownness affords. Early racialized performers on erotic stages inherited traditions of minstrelsy and performed for mainly white audiences, yet were able to use the "fluid structure and mutability of the variety stage" to also perform for themselves and for each other, to look "with glee at their ingenious forms of bodily malapropism and disguise."[105] The ability to inhabit various racialized performances onstage reflected the fragmentation of Black and brown women engaged both in labor (on plantations, as cleaners, as caretakers) and in their mobility, where they could express "protean abilities to slip between worlds with ease to work on the stage."[106] As the description of the *Not-So-Hidden Histories* exhibition reads, "Among the first to shamelessly bump and grind, performers of color left an indelible mark on burlesque history. . . . These performers not only existed but, in many cases, they thrived."[107] Sydney Lewis, a queer-of-color burlesque scholar and the exhibition's cocurator, points out that dances like the shimmy and the hoochie-coochie, which are both cited as dance moves fundamental to burlesque striptease, were taken from dancers in Black clubs and from brown dancers like Little Egypt, "one of many 'Oriental Dancers' who shocked and entertained in venues such as World's Fairs."[108]

By the 1970s the term *brown sugar* came to be popularized through 1970s Black women pornography, invoking the process of turning raw brown sugarcane into white sweetener as a metaphor for the domestication of Black sexuality "in need of refinement and prone to manipulation."[109] At the same time, *brown sugar* in racialized erotic performances articulated the shifting discourse of sexual Black women from merely lecherous and prurient to express, in Black communities themselves, "adoration, loveliness, and intimacy even as it articulate[d] lust, sensuality, and sex."[110] Situating brownness within the history of burlesque, many neo-burlesque groups today have invoked the term *brown* to assert the importance of sexual agency for women who might identify within a wide variety of nonwhite shades. The Los Angeles–based group Brown Betties offers courses on consent, collaboration, and forging empowerment for one's own body and desires, while the New York–based group Brown Girls Burlesque operates through its mission to "entertain, titillate, educate, and liberate."[111] The latter group's creative producer, Chicava Honey-Child, writes that as a "brown girl," she feels "empowered with each layer of clothing she pulls off," seeing her performance as much as a political statement as it is art.[112] As she says, "It's liberating because it gives us visibility.... We're owning our brown skin and our sexuality and we're putting it out there, making ourselves vulnerable for the sake of our beauty."[113] Such art forms inherited from racist forms of blackface minstrelsy, in the hands of racialized performers, reject forms of racial purity in favor of "promiscuous" forms of ambiguous self-expression that "refuse to be contained."[114]

The uses of *brown* by performers within an erotic context lend new ways to encounter the term not as a form of analysis or theoretical method but as a constant conjuring of the erotic anxieties of brown migrant women around the globe. We can see how this occurs specifically in the burlesque performer Miss Di' Lovely, a self-styled brown performer born and raised in San Diego, winner of "Best Burlesque" at the Arizona Burlesque Festival, and a contestant numerous times at the international Burlesque Hall of Fame in Las Vegas. Miss Di' Lovely offers a vision of brown that is a play on the brown mass as well as the forms of anxieties, joys, collaborations, and movements within shades of brown. Her website offers no outright identification of her racial background but amplifies her brown body within different shades: as rich mestiza, as Polynesian Tiki-girl, and as a "traveling showgirl."[115] This ambiguity places her identity within her routes rather than her roots. By using *brown* as a reference to skin and beauty as much as colonial histories, Miss Di' Lovely's persona is of movement itself, a detour through the various erotic imaginaries of colonial violence. Touring under the moniker of the "Weapon of Mass Seduction," Miss Di' Lovely's performances refuse to forget the violent histories embedded in brown figures seen as products of corruption, poverty, and war, while also evading the eyes of critical or empathetic authors who might want to place her as victim, threat, matron.

In the 2017 performance pictured in figure 3.4, Miss Di' Lovely begins her striptease wearing a famous symbol of Philippine femininity: the Maria Clara gown, named after the heroine in Dr. Jose Rizal's novel *Noli Me Tángere*, a novel famous for forming Filipino nationalism and fomenting resistance against the Spanish. During the Spanish colonial period, the gown was known as the *mestiza dress*, or the *traje de mestiza*, whose style evolved to embody the ideal Filipina beauty of Maria Clara, "a Spanish mestiza with light skin and hair and a slim, long nose; virginal, devout, and demure."[116] As a dress that has come out of the mixed histories of colonial, Indigenous, and nationalist formations, the Maria Clara gown also signifies the complex shades of brown that might threaten white colonial archetypes through its embodiment of the multitude and its use during the colonial period to intimidate American colonials with Filipina worldliness and sophistication. But from the colonial point of view, the dress symbolizes the threat of the brown mass—overly complex, mixed, and strange—which must be domesticated into a single symbol, in this case a sign of the domestic itself.

In her performance Miss Di' Lovely wears a black Maria Clara dress to queer the Paseo de Iloilo traditional dance, where men compete for the affections of a chaste and saintly woman—or, in this case, the erotic and exotic ideal of the brown woman, innocent and ready to serve (figure 3.4). Miss Di' Lovely strips the Maria Clara construct first with the slight tease of an undergarment. Then, after much enticing, her first strip of the gown comes as a ribald flashing: The initial strip is the direct exposure of her large buttocks to the crowd. As Sydney Lewis writes, in burlesque large (read: nonwhite) buttocks invoke the racisms against Black female bodies and signal the aberrant nonbeauty of stretch marks, flab, and dark skin. Lewis, who performs as Doctor Ginger Snapz, writes, "I came to Femme as defiance through a big booty that declined to be tucked under, bountiful breasts that refused to hide, insolent hair that can kink, and curl, and bead up, and lay straight all in one day, through my golden skin, against her caramel skin, against her chocolate skin, against her creamy skin . . . through

FIGURE 3.4. Miss Di' Lovely performs a burlesque of the Paseo de Iloilo traditional dance in a black Maria Clara gown (San Francisco, 2013). Lovely, "Paseo Di' Lovely."

shedding shame instead of shedding pounds, and learning that growing comfortable in my skin means finding comfort in her brownness."[117]

In the desire to shed "shame" and feel "comfortable" in her skin, Doctor Ginger Snapz also takes a more creative and erotic relationship to race as skin, naming "golden skin," "caramel skin," "chocolate skin," "creamy skin," as a means for a brown woman to find "comfort in her brownness." Indeed, while shaking her ass(ets), Miss Di' Lovely maintains her innocent smile and twirl, noting that while the clothes become undone, the skin exposed (the shame "shed," as Snapz writes), the joy of the dance itself has not changed.

Miss Di' Lovely's striptease provokes a notion of brown shades that can account for migrant domestic workers through the ambiguous erotic figure, whose sexual provocations play on the histories and presences of colonial domestication. As Denise Cruz has shown, Maria Clara's image has become so sanctified in the Philippines that even today there remains "a long-standing tradition that casts her as the epitome of virtuous Filipina femininity."[118] Yet Di' Lovely's invocation of Maria Clara is not as the saintly mestiza of virginal beauty but the tragic bastard with a "compromised heritage" whose mixture, unlike that of mixed brown men, "does not avow hybrid thinking or complex subjectivity but rather corruption."[119] Her performance in the mestiza gown of the Paseo de Iloilo, a courtship and flirtation dance, recalls the Spanish colonial aesthetic of courtship ritual where one woman was meant to dance for multiple (usually three) men, rotating about equally between them. Miss Di' Lovely's tease reinvents brown femininity not as mere erotic empowerment but as the tragic figure of brownness: the women who are meant to withhold and thus carry the burden of colonial histories of rape and enslavement, and who are in turn hidden by allegiance to the colonial power through a denial of their own sexual power (such as the tradition of the Maria Clara dress itself). By covering up one's own sexual desires, one also covers up the colonial erotic forms of power that produced them.

The sexual agency exhibited in burlesque exposes how brown women are already pathologized as sexual, as needing to be depathologized through servile matronly performances. I thus end this brown movement across global sexualized cities with a speculation: What if we read the art of the tease, the art of show dancing, alongside the art of housekeeping, as two industries that heavily employ brown women, one hypervisible and the other invisible, one meant to entice, the other to form indifference?[120] What if we, like my mother on reading *The Help*, dared to see both professions as a habituated dance—cleaning, cooking, childcaring—as well as a performance catering to imaginaries of brown sexuality: the erotic, the exotic, as well as the matronly? What if we, as Andrea Canaan wrote in her essay on brownness, saw the brown mass not as the queer threat to liberal forms of success but as a political force based on the people who have the greatest investment in creating societal change?

OMISSION 6

In November 2022, on the ninth floor of Vancouver General Hospital, I sparked memories whenever I brought Y-Dang food. We remembered how, when she gave birth five years before, I would bring her food at that Hong Kong hospital on a hill—noodles, curries, and sweets that our domestic worker, Anne, had spent the day shopping for, preparing, and cooking for us.

In the days before her death, Y-Dang's thoughts often drifted to Anne. She wanted to send Anne a letter before she died. And perhaps she might add this letter to her last book, Landbridge, *which she continued to edit from her hospital bed.*

In a soft voice, barely audible above the air vent still at max levels during COVID, *Y-Dang dictated the letter. She spoke of how Anne was her only good friend in Hong Kong, how any amount of money to compensate her work seemed undervalued, and how hard it was to face that every day. Add postpartum depression, suicidal ideation, and guilt, and friendship seemed impossible. Add academia to the mix, and the situation became completely hopeless. We were both, always, so hateful, and so grateful.*

Y-Dang and I had seen, in novels and academic books, countless tropes of a mother's jealousy of their maid, their fear of intimacy toward their husbands, their racist suspicions, their anxieties about who the child would see as the real mother, the better mother. We were prepared to be the exceptions, believing that our knowl-

edge could free us from the power structures determined to make us perpetrators. We wanted to be good people, but every time we gave Anne a break, the labor just went onto our shoulders—and mostly hers. Where does all the labor go? Not our labor, not her labor, but the labor that's needed.

Y-Dang's letter moved from memory to memory, sad and joyful, guilty and prideful. When I read it back to her, something about the letter felt disjointed, hard to place. We wondered about the watchful eyes of her book's audience of scholars and middlebrow readers. Would they understand the expectations of domestic work, especially in Asian contexts? What kind of context would a reader need to even approach this topic? Would any amount of history, any amount of artworks, any amount of cities where brown people work, ever bring a reader to understand us all enough to not convict us all? Would someone pick Y-Dang's words apart in the same way we, as academics, had been trained to pick apart the words of anyone who sought to represent domestic workers?

Y-Dang chose not to include the letter in her book. But she was determined not to omit Anne either. Her name appears in Landbridge, *within a note to our son: "She fed you and bathed you and loved you. Since our own parents could not be here, she taught us to be the best parents we could be, and we owe her so much."*

Coda: Homecoming

This chapter began with an epigraph by the poet Kristian Contreras, "Letter to My Daughter," an attempt by the author to voice brown motherhood. Yet unlike all the forms of matronly extraction we've seen in this chapter, the recipient of Contreras's motherliness is not a client, a filmmaker, an author, or an expert but Contreras's own brown daughter, who will one day occupy spaces of brown mass, will one day feel the need to route herself through domesticated forms of being, will one day need to understand the various shades of brown difference. In this sense, we can reread the poem's lines "I contorted my body into palatable morsels for consumption . . . eyes perpetually focused on the floor and away from an authoritative gaze," not as an appeal to clients or to human rights organizations but as survival tactics for a brown daughter who will grow up with the same demands cast on her. For brown theory, which seeks to flow alongside the straying movement of brownness, which seeks not capture but change, the question still remains: In what ways are the authoritative gazes that brown girls must prepare for not those of employers, bosses, or clients but those of authors seeking to film, to study, to sing, to write?

In the years of writing this chapter, I have included my own realist, fictionalized, and anonymized stories about migrant brown women, which I later chose to omit. There was our domestic worker's story, a transgender domestic worker's story, my mother's story, my sister's. I had planned, in various iterations, to weave in stories of my family in Hawai'i and Las Vegas who have worked or continue to work in service work, domestic work, sex work, hospitality, and military work. I had thought of including stories of family who have lost land, who have become diseased by toxic water and food, who became addicted to opiates, who committed suicide. These stories proliferated throughout the writing of this already beefy chapter (by far the longest I've ever written). This chapter and its many stories took me on investigative journeys as I journeyed across the globe to present new iterations of it, from Dubai to Hong Kong to Las Vegas. In every iteration the stories proliferated, each weighing on the chapter's brown movement. In efforts to give "voice," I found that, like Alvar's and Kahakauwila's stories, I could not maintain the collective "we" narrative of migrant brown women while also highlighting their individual personhood.

This chapter has attempted to spiral through the racial imaginaries of migrant domestic work not only through a brown movement across global sexualized cities but also through exposing the omissions of my own relationship to domestic work, and the way it impacted my wife until her death, and still impacts me. Neither my wife nor I had professional childcare growing up, and before my son was born, my scholarship on domestic workers was, like many nongovernmental organizations castigating brown employers, angry and unforgiving. Meeting students in Hong Kong raised by domestic workers helped change this, and taking them to domestic-worker areas of the city, guided by migrant-led NGOs, illuminated the troubling power relations at play.[121] But even so, hiring a domestic worker myself was fraught with unexpected challenges and anxieties. One of the most intense anxieties was the idea that I could ever use my domestic worker's story in my own work, that she would become just another notch in my belt counting every peer-reviewed publication. There are plenty of cautionary tales not to do so: the writer Alex Tizon's posthumous essay, which, despite impacting conversations around slavery and domestic work, made his reputation (and his still-living family) infamous; the scholar Geraldine Pratt, whose choice to replace a migrant mother's picture of her son with her own white son certainly did not enhance her reputation; my own mother, who, in tears, expressed her own feelings of being trapped in service work after reading *The Help*, only to receive academic mansplaining from her half-white son. I took all of these lessons as I imagine that anyone writing about domestic workers does: more reasons to keep the omissions omitted, more reasons not to risk my family's reputation, more reasons to stay safe, obscure, distant.

After my wife's death, I sent her letter to Anne, who received it with love and grief. Though it did not fit her final book, Y-Dang wished for her experiences to one day be made public, to be told true, because they spoke to truths we could find in none of the stories or scholarship we had encountered before. Her letter, along with my own recollections and writings of the past five years, form the omissions of this chapter. I have sought to shape them with the utmost care not to evade or expose but to speak to the shades of brown that inform brown relations with brown domestic workers. Some of these omissions express guilt; others, complicity, gratitude, and anxiety. In each, I find the ongoing desire to extract myself from the discomfort of the situation, while taking full advantage of its comforts. I find in them, too, the struggle that many brown academics charged to write about our own communities face: the struggle between criticism and humanity, between critical distance and complex personhood, between trying to see outside of the imperial racial imaginaries of our times while also accounting for our own pretensions of ever being outside those imaginaries.

Brown theory is neither theory nor autotheory—it moves through these genre expectations, as both can be life-giving and life-taking, both emotionally true and intellectually extractive, a practice of both knowing the self and omitting the self. Brown theory travels; it has a hard time keeping still long enough to produce a complete or even reliable account of a place, one that experts could turn into disciplinary knowledge. Perhaps, by telling the stories of my own relationship to domestic work, I will still be accused of omitting, of shaping certain stories to enhance rather than plummet my reputation, or perhaps, by choosing to be brief, I have missed an opportunity to comprehensively give voice to migrant brown women. And yet I have chosen to keep these omissions, flawed as they might be, as a beginning, a gesture to note the unseeable, unknowable shades of brown, of queer and subjected being, whose evasion from clients, experts, and authors was never a mere characteristic, habit, or flaw but a mode of survival. Survival: not just the longevity of one's life but one's ability, in the face of normalized violence, to feel great joys, immense pleasures, and the brown worlds that cannot be contained within somebody else's home.

A foreigner throws down a beer bottle. Another wrestles him to the ground of broken booze-coated glass.

Two expats fight in a bar, then tumble down the stairs and into the street. One mashes the other's face into the cold metal comb of an escalator step. In the subway station, a crowd interprets their slurry English. Something about swapping women, trading wives, sharing the market, horses in a race. They call each other white, colonial, racist. The crowd tweets, instas, shoots, shares.

One of the men apologizes, and they walk away in a half-hug, balancing each other toward the escalator. Claps ring out like the clinking of two butcher knives. A subway train stops, and bystanders guide the arriving passengers around bits of blood.

4

Organic and Inorganic Chinas

HONG KONG AND THE QUESTION OF CHINESE BROWNNESS

Christopher B. Patterson with Y-Dang Troeung

2007	My (Chris's) first visit to China (Tianjin and Beijing, via Seoul)
2011	visits to Taiwan and Hong Kong
2012	visits to Shanghai, Suzhou, Hangzhou, Nanjing, Xi'an, Chengdu, Taiwan, Hong Kong
	Y-Dang moves to Hong Kong
2013	I visit Guangdong, Guanxi, and Yunnan
2014	I move to Nanjing, China
	visits to Xi'an, Xiamen, Shanghai, Taiwan
	I meet Y-Dang in Hong Kong, visit the Umbrella Revolution and occupations
2015	I move to Hong Kong
2016	Fishball Revolution
2018	We leave Hong Kong
2019	Hong Kong protests on college campuses
2020	COVID-19 pushes protesters to virtual spaces
2022	resurgence of protests

Interlude

In February 2014, two months after receiving my PhD in English literature, I moved from Seattle to the People's Republic of China (PRC) to take a post as an assistant professor in Nanjing at the New York Institute of Technology. Before working in the PRC, I had traveled to mainland China three times, and I had taken Mandarin courses for two years, so I had some idea of what I was getting into. Even still, as I'd learned in my many excursions around South, Southeast, and East Asia, the economic and political rise of the PRC had embroiled its neighbors in confrontations with the PRC government, its exported laborers, its tour groups, its infrastructure projects, and its debt imperialism. My biggest fear while moving to the PRC was that my background in organization, activism, and subversive online writing would make the trip short-lived.[1] I was nervous, not because of the PRC's famed censorship and pollution, but because, as a mixed-race Filipino-Chinese American, I was unsure how my brownness would fly as an American studies and creative writing professor.

Within days of teaching, I found that my position as a successful brown American already fit into a particular Chinese nationalist narrative. I was not seen as a fake American but as an American minority hero, whose uphill struggle into academia provided evidence for the failure of American multiculturalism, while my arrival in China spoke to the success of China's social harmony and economic development. For many of my students, my lessons exposing histories of slavery, Indigenous genocide, yellow peril, and anti-Chinese riots emphasized the injustices of a country they saw as their global competitor. For them, I had voted with my feet—abandoned the racist, religious, and uber-capitalist America to live in a world of social harmony, a place where Chinese descendants would eventually return. Or, as the propaganda leaflets in my local coffee shop read in Chinese: "Taiwanese and huaren [people of Chinese ethnicity in the diasporas], mother has cooked a great meal for you, please come home."

Determined not to be compliant in this emerging empire, I changed my course content to focus on forms of oppression in China and encouraged students to write about their own experiences involving state institutions and propaganda. This was a risky venture—how risky, I would soon find out. Hearing of my new assignments, my dean warned me that students could report me for saying anything critical of China or Chinese policies. Particularly, I was to avoid the "three Ts": Tiananmen Square, Tibet, and Taiwan. I continued to test how far I could go before my dean's warnings turned into consequences. My students wrote critiques of their national news media, of the PRC's censorship regime, of the state's oppression of Muslim communities in Xinjiang. I lectured on the riots of 1989—not the Tiananmen Square riots but the anti-Black/anti-African riots that had occurred in Nanjing the same year.

Within one week I was reported. It happened during the Sunflower Student Movement in Taiwan, when one of my students brought to class "a new friend": a young woman in a cottony pink dress who spent the entire lecture smiling and listening with perked ears.[2] Afterward, she introduced herself with an Anglo name (let's call her Mary). Mary was a military informant for the Communist Party. She told me directly, as if it were a common thing. And then she invited me to tea.

Being invited to tea (hē chá, 喝茶) is a euphemism for being questioned by the authorities.[3] The phrase emerged after 1989 to put a face to the Communist Party while still issuing warnings. But being invited to tea was no laughing matter. My colleagues had told me stories of two American professors who were asked to tea after breaking the "three *Ts*" policy. Both were promptly deported. One, the authorities learned, was actually trying to get deported to get a free ticket back to America. So the authorities sent him to Pakistan without his belongings.

As Mary walked next to me on the school's gravel path, rocking about in high heels that were clearly a nuisance for her, my mind raced through a torrent of fears—harassment, financial insecurity, jail time, deportation. Mary took me to an empty Thai restaurant where we ordered lunch (no actual tea) and the interrogation began. First, she asked me about Taiwan, claiming she had heard that I told students Taiwan was a country, not a province, and that I was publishing research and organizing meetings on Taiwanese independence. I parried by interrogating her about how she got her information. Perhaps I was playing dumb—it was obvious how she had heard of it (informants, surveillance). But she also couldn't say so and risk breaking our trust. I was, after all, that Filipino-Chinese American who had voted with my feet and abandoned the racist enterprise of America to live in the social harmony of China. We had a long verbal bout, until she seemed satisfied that she had at least confused me. By the time we ordered dessert, Mary was confiding that she did not really like the Communist Party but had to join because of her parents, while all she really wanted was to attend a Justin Bieber concert. She showed me pictures of herself with her last boyfriend—American, white. "He helped me learn English," she told me.

The next day, as I reeled from the confusion of that encounter, I began to understand that Mary's interview with me was, perhaps, a means of checking off a box to inspect this new foreign teacher for insurgent (Western imperial) forms of contamination. I had many students who were in the Communist Party, and about half, I would say, frequently expressed criticisms in their es-says and creative works, either political grievances (about the pollution, Tibet) or cultural ones (the antiqueer crusades). Later, after conversations with col-leagues, I found that Mary's light treatment of my seditious behavior was ex-ceptional. Usually, the party would have already deported me, or forced some change in my curriculum, or discouraged students from taking my class. But quite the opposite happened. My courses were full. Students in the party con-tinued to seek my mentorship, even when I encouraged them to write critically about China. And I was free to fly frequently to Taiwan, Hong Kong, and other places of potential radicalization. In time, I began to wonder how my own brownness figured to this other empire—if they saw my own colonial histories as an asset, or as simply fangless, and therefore tolerable.

Introduction: On Brown Chinas

I begin this chapter with an interlude about my time in Nanjing to frame how we might be able to conceive of a shade of brownness that isn't necessarily his-torical, identitarian, or based in racial science, but one that shadows how em-pires tend to shape colonized and diasporic populations (in this case, huaren) within brown racializations (seeing them as uncontainable and contagious mass, as domesticatable subjects), and in the way these populations see them-selves, and can perform, within many shades. This form of brownness grows out of my experiences teaching and researching at the New York Institute of Technology in Nanjing (2014–15), at the Chinese University of Hong Kong (2015–16), and at Hong Kong Baptist University (2016–18). Before moving to China, I had taught English in South Korea (2007), I had traveled considerably in Asia, I was a program director for the Seattle Asian American Film Festival, I was the founder and host of the *New Books in Asian American Studies* podcast, I had organized half a dozen Asian American speaker events at the University of Washington, and I had written over a dozen short stories exploring "Asian American themes." These experiences littered my CV and were crucial to my acceptance as an assistant professor in mainland China and Hong Kong, as they came up in my many academic job interviews in Asia. My record colored me into an identity type that I found enabling but also felt unsettled within. Being half Filipino/Chinese and half white, I was unable to pass as a local, and most students and colleagues presumed I was some splendid variation of "Eur-asian." The routes I, as an inheritor of brown and colonized communities, had taken to resist forms of imperial domestication within one empire (the United

States) had placed me in a unique position in the domestication of another (the PRC). My position within these global educational networks shaped how students saw my own racialized body as living proof of American multicultural exceptionalism or as its very opposite: the exilic Chinese who had come to my true home. And yet there was also a third meaning made from my presence that would take me years to fully grasp: a relation to political insurgencies in the diaspora (namely, Taiwan and Hong Kong) that marked me with a form of Chinese and foreign mixture—an altogether different shade of brown.

This chapter navigates through brown theory to reframe American Cold War discourses that conceive of Chinese cultures as two Chinas: the communist People's Republic of China (PRC) and the "other China" (Taiwan), "Greater China" (Hong Kong, Singapore, Taiwan), or what has more recently come to be called the Sinophone: "a network of places of cultural production outside China and on the margins of China and Chineseness."[4] These definitions carry spatial connotations, as the first China is bound to the imperial center of Beijing, while the countries and cultures that make up Greater China can be cast as peripheral or within the hinterlands. But in an age where China has been recognized as a global imperial force, scholars have debated the productive value of the two-Chinas paradigm. On one hand, the paradigm can help develop counterimaginaries to stereotypes of communist mainland Chinese, but on the other, it risks dismissing the shared cultures and politics among the two Chinas: the transnational sharing of digital cultures, queer cultures, the unanimous attempts to modernize via capitalist economic structures. This Cold War imagining has greatly affected scholarship on China even in Asia, where the two-Chinas discourse aligns neatly with various claims from the PRC, such as the presumption that Marxism, capitalist critique, and class solidarity are discourses owned by the PRC. For Petrus Liu, two-Chinas logic presumes that the Greater Chinas of Taiwan, Hong Kong, and Singapore function as pure products of neoliberalism, rather than as historical negotiations among capitalist and grassroots forces concerned with environmental protection, community and cultural preservation, and unionization.[5] Similarly, Wang Xiaoming has argued that seeing Chineseness through binaries such as "traditional/modern, closed/open, conservative/reformer, market/planned, socialism/capitalism, [and] communist/anti-communist" conforms to the contemporary historical narrative encouraged by the PRC, which fosters a "dual identity" in order to distance itself from the Cultural Revolution and to stifle "any social awareness of crises."[6]

While the two-Chinas discourse has perhaps lost its relevance to geopolitical nation forms, it remains prescient in capturing political and cultural forms of Chineseness, and in noting the ways in which China's contemporary imperial rise both relies on and transforms existing racial forms of yellow and brown. Whereas one China resembles a mysterious competitive enemy characterized by authoritarianism, one-party rule, censorship, and seemingly blind patriotism, the other offers forms of collaboration and, for the West, "subimperial" intervention, characterized by democracy, a free press, and participatory protest. We can thus understand Chineseness through Lily Wong's description of the term "as a morphing affective structure" that circulates in mass media and thus remains "deterritorialized from fixed, and often exclusionary, authenticity discourses."[7] Perceived politically, these two forms of Chineseness expose a unique kind of orientalism, where neither is characterized as timeless or lost to history as in classic orientalist discourse. Yet as a "morphing affective structure," both remain reified in two mutually constitutive forms: an *inorganic* authoritarian society bent on homogenization and control, and an *organic* merger of Chinese tradition with capitalism and globalization—read as English speaking, Western allied, collaborative, and domesticatable.[8]

I reread these two forms of Chineseness through brown methods of mass, domestication, and shades, to consider how they speak to colonial relations that pattern characterizations of brown. I thus explore how "organic Chineseness" slides into forms of brown Chineseness, whose intense complexity (its "mass") has remained open to domestication by Western empires through histories of global capitalist labor and hybrid cultural expressions. Organic China is often rendered brown by colonial powers for its hybrid relation to those powers, whether in colonial histories (the British in Hong Kong and Singapore, the Portuguese in Macau, the Portuguese and later the Japanese in Taiwan) or in more recent appeals made to Western powers (Tibet, Xinjiang). The nationalisms of organic China thus have a similar relation to mainland China as mestizo nationalisms in the Philippines do to the Americas, where "the mestizo racialized body consolidated its meaning around its fundamental difference from the Asian body."[9] This organic brownness of colonial mixture stands in binary relation to the inorganic yellowness of the Communist Chinese as Western competitors and enemies, who are, as Vivian Huang writes, often cast as "inscrutable others" whose thoughts and feelings are "inaccessible from an outside perspective."[10] Through these figurations, I from here on resist tethering brown theory to mere color itself, though many routes could be taken to understand some racial imaginaries of Chineseness as colored brown: the darker skins featured in Hong Kong and Taiwanese cinema versus Beijing cinema; the racial mixtures of Chinese diasporas in Taiwan and Southeast Asia; the colonial relations of the communist state toward darker-skinned

Tibetans, Muslims, and Indigenous peoples in Taiwan and the Southwest; the histories of colorism in China that include modern skin and beauty regimes that emphasize light skin as well as the class signals of dark skin between rural communities and large cities or Beijing royalty, whose skin, far before European intervention, was praised for its fairness.[11] All these notations of brown as skin pigmentation pervade studies of brownness that emphasize the central importance of darker skin, where brown as a color seems to invoke instinctual symbolisms whose quintessence resides in its association with dirt and dung.[12] Yet, for what I have been naming brown theory, brown is not merely about color or tone but about the lifeworlds that we brown people inhabit, and it emerges in colonial contexts in ways that skin color can both inform and obscure. In this chapter Chinese brownness will thus not appear through skin-lightening regimes or class presumptions related to "tanned" or "untanned" skin, but will regard the peoples whom some empires (of the East) will see as wild, unruly, and corrupted, but whom other empires (of the West) will see as fungible, as usable, as a "little brother," as domesticable. To reframe our understanding of brownness as untethered to mere color, I will call the shades of brownness that best capture this colonial relation "inorganic" (yellow) and "organic" (brown) types of Chineseness, and will refer to the "inorganic/organic binary."

The movements through yellowness and brownness in this chapter continue from similar points in chapter 1, only to turn in new directions based on a very different imperial context. Whereas chapter 1 reread the Mongol Empire from an amalgam of brownness and yellowness to show how the Mongols' history distinguishes comparable forms of yellow and brown, this chapter rereads common understandings of contemporary Chinese empire from distinct forms of yellowness, as inorganic and organic Chineseness, to conceive of the many proliferating forms where brownness and yellowness overlap, where they blur to such an extent that distinctions fail and are revealed for their imperial allegiances. If empires of the past have remade brownness in ways that seem natural today, empires of the present use and reshape these brown racializations in ways that appear so incoherent and obscured that to name them brown as such can seem speculative, provocative, or even socially problematic. Rather than claim brownness, this chapter questions its absence given the similar racializations and colonial violences in Hong Kong, and asks what possibilities might arise were we to consider the making of Chinese brownness within imperial racial imaginaries of the present.

Whereas chapter 1 primarily sought to center yellowness to interrogate understandings of brownness (from the Mongols to West Asian, South Asian, and Southeast Asian states), this chapter focuses on brownness to interrogate yellowness, to consider how, of all racial forms, yellow seems to be the *least* prone to mixture, the least organic. As explored throughout this book, many racialized groups have self-identified as brown in North America: Black, Latinx, South and Southeast Asian, Indigenous, and Arab—yet East Asian claims to brownhood seem almost nonexistent. Though some, like Japanese migrants, were often seen as brown, Japanese migrants have overwhelmingly positioned themselves within discourses of East Asian and yellow belonging. While brownness can be conceived globally within spaces that range from dark skin color (in South Asia or Melanesia, for example) to more white-passing mixtures (Southwest Asia and North Africa region and South America, for example), this range and flexibility of brownness seems to snap apart once yellowness is invoked, which appears only to contrast or compare with brownness, rarely to blend, except perhaps with food or other cultural hybridities. Why do brown forms of whiteness, Latinxness, Indigenousness, Blackness, and Arab/Middle Easternness seem more intuitive than a brown form of yellowness? What would it mean to make visible, to understand, or to try and imagine forms of colonial brownness that mix with yellowness? What would a Chinese form of brownness look like?

Asiatic Blurs of Yellow and Brown: Chinos, Hakkas, Coolies

The racial imaginary of two Chinas today supersedes more overtly racist East/West binaries that have sought to contain Chineseness within forms of yellowness—that is, as a foreign and unassimilable presence within an otherwise diverse (often brown) populace. As Sony Coráñez Bolton writes, Spanish colonists in the colonial Philippines sought to subjugate Filipinos by differentiating their modern and hybrid characteristics from the yellowness of "a depraved Orient—an existential container of impairment, perversity, and bodily abjection."[13] As the colonial powers of Spain and later the United States sought to frame the Filipino colonial subject within the intersections of Asian and Indigenous ("indio"), the figure of Chinese outsiders played a crucial binary role as a figure of distance and foreignness, differentiating "Filipino Asianness as itself a form of Indigenous rehabilitation and philosophical distance from depraved Chineseness."[14]

While distinctions between (yellow) Chinese and (brown) Filipino Asians in the Philippines hardened during Spanish colonization, the galleon routes from Manila to Spain's colonies in the Americas had a blurring effect, where the vast majority of the free and unfree laborers who stepped off Spanish ships became known collectively as *chinos*, regardless of their racial or geographic origin. As Diego Javier Luis writes, the invented term *chino* in colonial Mexico "slotted Asian peoples into New Spain's casta (caste) system, alongside more familiar casta designations that variously defined Afro-Mexican and Indigenous peoples as 'indios,' 'mulatos,' and 'negros.'"[15] As Filipinos moved alongside their Chinese counterparts, so did their brownness. Once the mixed Indigenous domesticated subject, they were now part of the foreign and unassimilable *chino* designation that restricted their ability to work in certain trades and made them "legally vulnerable to enslavement and the Inquisition," and their presence "conjured up the expectation of servitude, criminality, and un-Catholic behavior."[16] Meanwhile, in the British colony of Jamaica, the term *Hakka* came to massify Chinese laborers coming from British treaty ports in southern China and Hong Kong. In China, *Hakka* (客家 Kèjiā), translated from Mandarin as "guest family or people," named nomadic Chinese peoples mostly inhabiting southern China and Taiwan, while in Jamaica, the term came to name Asian migrants who would occupy roles of indentured servitude.[17] This brown racialization of *Hakka* remains in use today to differentiate mixed Asian diasporas "in relation to individuals of Black, white, and Asian descent in Jamaica, the United States, and Canada."[18]

Both *chino* and *Hakka* were inheritances of sixteenth-century European colonial expansion into Asia, which produced the term *coolie*, perhaps the most well-known term globally for laborers who were both yellow and brown—South Asian (often Tamil) and Chinese. As Moon-Ho Jung writes, the abolition of slavery in the nineteenth century "remade 'coolies' into indentured laborers in high demand across the world" by ascribing to them "a conglomeration of racial imaginings."[19] This cross-racial (Indian/Chinese) form of brownness was tied ultimately to indenture and meant to contrast with Black, Indigenous, and white forms of unfree and free labor. In colonial Hong Kong, forms of "coolie labor" coming from South Asia were racialized differently than the coolie labor being exported from Hong Kong (as local Hong Kongers or Cantonese Chinese). Brownness in Hong Kong was thus produced through various migratory and colonial iterations, becoming activated and dulled as each iteration waned, and, like brownness everywhere, was shaped as more a colonial condition than a recognized communal identity.[20]

While all the above examples of *chino*, *Hakka*, and *coolie* are deeply contextual and are not interchangeable, they speak to a time when, "within the colonial order of things, brownness conjured the fantasy of free, unbonded labor."[21] Today global Chinese populations are reimagined within the legacies of indentured labor combined with Cold War rhetoric to imagine Chineseness within differentiating types of yellowness—often referred to as the *two Chinas*. For many Westerners, the two-Chinas binary hides racist presumptions against Chinese generally with the plurality of two contrasting types, while giving value to the type more likely to benefit Western interests. For those within these Chinas, such discourses obviate intraracial hierarchies through a national affect of racial harmony. In our contemporary imperial context, invoking brown forms of Chineseness names the continued presence of colonial conditions rather than recognized communal identities. Brownness here can thus help chart alternative political genealogies that read against the tendency to reduce Chineseness to any stable binary but rather can move alongside the desires and anxieties that necessitated the binary in the first place.[22]

To reimagine Chinese senses of brown, this chapter focuses on the anxieties of inorganic/organic Chineseness that have emerged through representations of China and Hong Kong during and after the 1997 handover. As Pheng Cheah has written, Hong Kong's precarious position has envisioned "the global" as "a prescriptive norm to strive for—a dream or an aspiration."[23] This dream has been foundational to transforming the two-Chinas discourse from Cold War–era anxieties about communism to anxieties about Chinese-majority countries entering the global community, reconstituting Chineseness as either "inorganic" (signifying one-party rule and social/cultural engineering) or "organic" (signifying cultural hybridity and laissez-faire capitalism).[24] Such dichotomies, I argue, reproduce attitudes of yellow peril and orientalism by directing anti-Chinese sentiments toward inorganic forms of Chineseness while being inclusive and empowering toward organic forms.

This chapter imagines Chinese forms of brownness by seeking to understand how the inorganic/organic binary has appeared in texts that articulate Chineseness as global, and thus as a main competitor to forms of Western cultural, economic, and military imperialism. It moves through texts that depict binary forms of Chineseness as inorganic and organic: the popular 2012 video game *Sleeping Dogs*, which encapsulates the dream of Hong Kong's organic Chineseness, and two texts produced during and immediately after the 1997 handover: Wayne Wang's 1997 film *Chinese Box* and Yu Suzuki's 2001 video game *Shenmue II*. Though they speak to vastly different audiences, these filmic and gamic texts each refract and unsettle the inorganic/organic binary through their representations of Hong Kong as an organic space of cultural and gendered flexibility that has served to elicit fears of takeover by mainland China, which is imagined as an inorganic force of purified national heritage. As each of these texts was produced by transnational agents and was intended for global audiences, they construct Hong Kong's fluctuation within the inorganic/organic binary through the shared motif of global fatigue, which articulates not a desire for the global but a disillusionment with its liberating myths. These multimedia representations cast attention onto the structural violence of Hong Kong, envisioned as an organic and dynamic "global city" but one whose globality obscures and even legitimates its precarious position as a shared colony of multiple capitalist and imperial forces—a colonized space whose unique form of imperial subjugation includes its own colonial position being constantly disavowed as such. As a "global" dependency, Hong Kong has rather been imagined as a geopolitical and discursive battleground, a metaphorical bargaining chip in the New Cold War rhetoric between China and the United States.[25]

One last authorial note: most of this chapter was written in collaboration with my late wife, Y-Dang Troeung, whom I met in Hong Kong in 2014 at her home university, City University of Hong Kong. We lived in Hong Kong together from 2015 to 2018. Having lived in Hong Kong before me (since 2012), Y-Dang introduced me to the many ways of adapting to brown personhood in Hong Kong, and the ways our Chinese brownness could flow within a brown lifeworld of art and protest. We confronted brown forms of Chineseness together, as we could both speak decent Chinese (me Mandarin, her Cantonese), and we traveled frequently to Taiwan, Shanghai, Nanjing, Guangzhou, Xiamen, and the many Southeast Asian countries within China's orbit (Cambodia, the Philippines, Vietnam). Our dual presence in many Chinas revealed the granular shades of brown and yellow that, context by context, dissolved binaries of two Chinas to instead reveal many forms of Chineseness. By being centered not in US discourses of multiculturalism but in alternative (often Chinese imperial) forms of recognizing diversity, the plurality of Chineseness operated around race less as skin color per se and more as an amalgam of language, dialect, class positioning, and the many political and pseudoscientific discourses that remake race differently and always in relation to racial capitalist empire. As we traveled, Y-Dang and I carried with us a racial ambivalence that spoke to our colonial histories as part-brown, part-yellow subjects (my Filipino-Chinese heritage, Y-Dang's Khmer-Chinese heritage). We were often seen as more yellow/East Asian in Southeast Asia and more brown/Southeast Asian in East Asia. Our shades of brown offered unexpected provocations to whomever we encountered. We were often positioned to explain, time and again, how our brown Chineseness recalled histories of xenophobia, scapegoating, massacre, and genocide. Centered within my and Y-Dang's experiences as brown Chinese living within many Chinas, this chapter will thus weave in and out of the first-person singular and first-person plural narrative to note our divergent narratives and shared experiences.

In October 2019 Y-Dang and I had been living in Vancouver, Canada, for only a year when we saw what would have awaited us had we remained in Hong Kong. On global news media, we saw our university students being rounded up in the aftermath of intensely criminalized protests against the Beijing-installed Hong Kong government. Our students were accused of creating blockades by gluing cement blocks to the streets and byways that our offices once comfortably sat above. It was an open secret that many of these student groups were crowdfunded by communities in the West: South Korea, the United Kingdom, Australia, and America, while many of the university administrators and faculty were being replaced by Beijing loyalists. Y-Dang and I feared for our students as well as our colleagues in Hong Kong, many of whom would leave over the next two years or find themselves laid off. At the same time, we were realizing how the narrative of protest had been radically transformed in North American media, as well as among scholars who were reigning in typical (and Beijing-condoned) narratives about protesters misunderstanding neoliberal capitalism or misunderstanding Karl Marx. We saw our students, many of whom lived in "coffin homes" (tiny apartments of less than five hundred square feet) with their families and were the children of service and sex workers, risking their lives and futures only to be labeled by Western intellectuals as "privileged students" nostalgic for British and American imperialism. As Ben Ehrenreich wrote in the *Nation*, "The more doctrinaire quarters of the left have sniffed imperialist interventionism behind the Hong Kong and Iranian protests while affirming the legitimacy of pretty much every other popular movement on the planet."[26] The only alternative to this "critical Marxist discourse," it seemed, was to romanticize the movement, to see the student uprising as a rebellion against global capital and neoliberalism even if it wasn't voiced (to the Global North) in an academic language. What we saw appearing before our eyes was a familiar yet reframed discourse of two Chinas, one that fused both the American and the Chinese popular views, where one China was cast as a competing and undemocratic communist power rising from poverty, and the other as a liberal yet uber-capitalist lackey to the West.

A month after these protests seemed to hit their peak, on November 27, 2019, the United States nearly unanimously passed the Hong Kong Human Rights and Democracy Act (HKHRDA), requiring the US government to impose sanctions against Chinese and Hong Kong officials found responsible for human rights abuses in Hong Kong. Initially proposed during the 2014 Umbrella Movement, the HKHRDA was reintroduced in 2019 following the protests and occupations in Hong Kong responding to the 2019 Hong Kong Extradition Bill. Though most protesters in Hong Kong seemed to celebrate the HKHRDA, some writers and scholars argued that the act reiterated a Cold War myth of "China-versus-the-West," while also undermining the possibilities of solidarity among protesters and dissenters within mainland China, who shared many of the same grievances of "inequality, a lack of stable jobs, unaffordable housing, corruption, and unaccountable elites."[27] This "China-versus-the-West" discourse was not merely nationalist but also acted as a means of protecting "globality" within a Western form of global capitalism secured by an American Pacific garrison.

The imagined splits between China and Hong Kong during and after the Occupy movements represent what we will refer to as an imagined inorganic/organic binary, where China's inorganic style of globality is represented as reflecting the artificial nature of its party rule, while other Chinas contrast with this inorganic form, appearing organic in their seemingly natural democratic growth and early tethering to laissez-faire capitalism. *Inorganic* is here not imagined as artificial or robotic but more as biomechanical, as in engineered and reproduced unnaturally, through a one-party state intent on social engineering through a massive propaganda apparatus that holds a tight grip on media and information, the false reporting of the gross domestic product (GDP) and artificial currency manipulation, the fake brands of counterfeit culture, and the phenomenon of copied cities.[28] In contrast, Hong Kong's organic form of globality is routinely depicted in global media and writings as the product of a long postcolonial process that has matured into a dialogue of protest, uncensored film and art, and global education, resulting in more creativity and critical thinking. As in the case of the HKHRDA, this binary limits abilities to account for organic processes of protest, resistance, and creativity within inorganic forms and spaces, as well as the inorganic elements in Greater China, such as the one-party rule of Singapore's People's Action Party or the forms of exclusion and racial hierarchies experienced by ethnic minorities and domestic workers in Singapore, Taiwan, and Hong Kong.

By tracing the conventions of the organic/inorganic binary, we can better recognize its iterations within texts that participate within a racial imaginary constructed through the emerging desires for globality (as modern, economically successful, multicultural), as well as through the contested definitions of what globality entails. While the inorganic notes order and purity (even if it is seen by some as mere simulation), the organic, like the brown mass, is burdened by excess. It is the hybrid, the mixed-up, the contaminated, still far from the original not because it is a copy but because it lacks purity or a stable identity. Appearing through nonthreatening forms of masculinity like passive spiritual males (the Dalai Lama) or through erotic and diasporic heroes like Bruce Lee, organic Chineseness does not elicit fears of being incorporated or invaded but has itself already been domesticated into Western societies. As a shared dependency that has recently been the site of multiple protests and occupations, Hong Kong has recently represented a rupture in the separation of organic and inorganic, feminine and masculine. Lo Kwai-Cheung has pointed out that Hong Kong has occupied a "symbolic 'female' position for the construction of masculine Chinese identity."[29] As a subempire of America, Hong Kong has also been subjected to a long feminizing discourse of Asian effeminacy marked with "the racialized fetishes of an older white male for the diminutive and effeminized Asian."[30] Hong Kong's feminized role has been a source of tension between the mainland and the West; in 1997 Hong Kong appeared to be handed over to a patriarchal lover, yet her sanctity and purity would go on under the watchful eye of the West. In this regard, for Lo, organic Hong Kong receives "the other's *jouissance*," as both China and the West can also congratulate themselves for successfully preserving Hong Kong's way of life.[31]

As the visual iconography of Chinatowns in San Francisco, Seattle, New York, and Toronto often appears more similar to that of streets in urban Hong Kong and Taiwan than in Beijing, the futurity of organic Chineseness remains as an accepted and domesticable form predicated outside and against inorganic China, which has come to represent a ghastly other, monstrous in its ecological waste and in its chase for unfettered capitalism. We thus call this the *inorganic/ organic binary* to provide an example of what Eric Hayot calls "an ecliptic," a "perspectival relation" that occurs when we assume a universal, even if that universal is evidently false.[32] The binary reveals China's repeated casting as the horizon of globality, as a measurement to understand globality as chiefly Western, at least *for now*. Taking note of the inorganic/organic binary allows us to perceive its many guises, even when globality is not the point but the target. James Scott's *The Art of Not Being Governed*, for example, thematizes "the ubiquity of the encounter between self-governing and state-governed peoples—variously styled as the raw and the cooked, the wild and the tamed."[33] These binaries, claimed as natural the world over (at least since the time of the Mongols, as noted in chapter 1), are rendered visible in Chinese contexts and give greater value to organic forms of self-governance within what Scott calls "shatter zones," the "regions of bewildering ethnic and linguistic complexity." Here, the brown anarchic zones of self-governing populations can be domesticated by the West to carry over the "good" values of globality—the pluralism, the diversity, the flexibility—without the "bad" conditions of state control, capitalist exploitation, and environmental degradation. To typify these self-governing zones as "exceptionally diverse" in agriculture, culture, and language thus relies on presuming that "state-governed" China has remained exceptionally homogeneous/inorganic even in its "precocious early expansion."[34]

In the following analyses, we explore the inorganic/organic binary through texts that attempt to portray Hong Kong as a global presence that fluctuates within the binary due to its position as a former British colony and current colony of mainland China (as a special administrative region [SAR]). As Wing Sang Law has observed, Hong Kong colonialism has rarely been acknowledged as colonialism, and scholars instead have tended to "either treat Hong Kong Colonial Rule as an exception or turn colonialism into an entirely positive factor, if they do not totally neglect its presence."[35] To understand colonialism in Hong Kong, Law points to the threat of collaboration, pointing out how businesspeople and educators have been enticed by the promise of access and privilege, uprooting the culture and autonomy of Hong Kong from the inside. While those in the mainland could remain "chauvinist" and "prideful," those in Hong Kong were not expected to rehearse the same uniform nationalism, so that "whatever happens to Hong Kong becomes simply a sideshow compared with China's national-revival struggles."[36] We thus ask how Hong Kong's depiction as a space of hybridity, organic cultural and gendered flexibility, has served to elicit fears of takeover by mainland China as an imagined inorganic space of purity and national heritage.

As Stuart Hall wrote, the Cold War was a force that polarized "every topic by its remorseless binary logic," where new identities (like Chineseness) operated in film and television as the front line of a "war of positions."[37] Following Hall, we look at popular visual and interactive media to trace new positions and battlegrounds, focusing on film and video games, two forms of media that dominate global cultural networks and produce spatial imaginaries of global cities. As texts produced during and immediately after the 1997 handover, both *Chinese Box* and *Shenmue II* offer meditations on the inorganic/organic binary by questioning the desires for globality itself (as modern, economically successful, multicultural) and by tracing the forms of shared oppressions and repressions done in the name of globality. Where globality since the end of the Cold War has, according to Pheng Cheah, come to be "characterized by flexibility and pluralism," the inorganicism of the PRC represents an altogether opposing type of globality seen as a threat to the global order.[38] Indeed, given the high stakes of these discourses in the context of economics (the Trans-Pacific Partnership turned trade war), the contestation over the South China Sea, and the difficulty in theoretically conceptualizing the "rise of China," we ask how the discourse of two Chinas evolved from a Cold War imaginary into a global racial imaginary that continues to persist and shape the region, and how global media texts like *Sleeping Dogs*, *Chinese Box*, and *Shenmue II* have refracted, unsettled, and produced alternative understandings of Chinese globality.[39]

Of course, Hong Kong's own organic representation flies in the face of its real history, particularly the social engineering of its Chineseness by British colonials who sought to position themselves as an ideal other for colonized Chinese subjects to aspire to, but whose identity they could never claim. Later, Chineseness in Hong Kong became 'engineered' with the demands of global capital, and a standard form of Chineseness became whatever was more easily incorporated into the global market. As Lo Kwai-Cheung writes, Hong Kong has maintained a flexibility in deciding what can pass as a cultural tradition, making its vision of Chineseness appear organic and practical.[40] As a result, Hong Kong localist culture today is nearly synonymous with consumer products, from films to pop music to fishballs, the last being the main symbol for the 2016 Fishball Revolution during Chinese New Year. Yet we would contend that what appear to be free are actually necessary adjustments for the continuous growth of global capital, the city's main reason for being since it was created as a colonial outpost for British and Chinese trade. Its claims to pluralism seem difficult to articulate given that the colony remains 94 percent Han Chinese.

With the limiting boundaries of this two-Chinas discourse, the front lines of the new Cold War have remained firmly in place, at least ideologically, while American empire remains an absent presence and, along with it, the Chinese diasporas who play no marginal role in activating this discourse. Asian American cultural production, from the literature of Maxine Hong Kingston to movies like *Crazy Rich Asians* to the televised adaptation of Eddie Huang's *Fresh off the Boat*, has reinforced the notion that organic Chinas like Singapore (the locale of *Crazy Rich Asians*), Taiwan (Eddie Huang's diasporic connection), and Hong Kong (Bruce Lee's) remain subempires of Western imperial power and capital, while inorganic China remains a main competitor to American power in the Pacific. In the eyes of many Asian Americans, peripheral spaces like Singapore, Hong Kong, and Taiwan are constructed as nostalgic homelands, a "stand-in for the Chinese identity lost to the motherland," and in the light of Tiananmen Square and other human rights atrocities such as the Cultural Revolution, Hong Kong itself becomes "a symbol of Western strength that is supposed to prevail along with a system of Western values, institutions, civil liberties, and democracy."[41] Meanwhile, mainland China remains visible mostly through an imperial gaze as a space of trauma and patriarchy, as we see in the fiction of Kingston and

Amy Tan and in the transnational films of the early Zhang Yimou. Such discourses have thus marked more recent immigrants to America from mainland China as imperial agents unless proven otherwise. Thus, artworks and novels from new Chinese immigrants in the United States (much like my own presence in Nanjing) must either be persistently critical of their home countries or otherwise leave any racial or political meaning out of their work entirely. In turn, we find that globally circulating and transnationally produced texts, like some films and video games, rather than novels or artworks, perform a more direct confrontation with the racial imaginary of organic/inorganic Chinas in ways that reveal the histories and ramifications of both.

Wayne Wang's *Chinese Box*

The gray sky was falling in big soft wisps of tumbled stuffing, like a cushion torn open—but not one of those stinky straw-filled Chinese cushions.—PAUL THEROUX, *Kowloon Tong*

The above sentence is from the opening page of Paul Theroux's novel *Kowloon Tong*, a fictionalized account of the 1997 handover published in the same year.[42] The novel expresses the anxieties of expatriates having to confront mainland China, when for so long they had grown accustomed to a type of Chineseness developed under British tutelage. Theroux's single em dash extends the metaphor of "a cushion torn open" to specify the type of cushion for a transnational audience, while, in this need for specificity, casting a racist gaze onto the "stinky" Chinese type. Indeed, this sentence expresses the novel's themes of chauvinist racism, as it reflects the interior monologue of a British colonizer who "believed [he] knew the Chinese," despite rarely eating Chinese food and never bothering to learn a Chinese language (30). The Chineseness the British have come to know is characterized only by the locals' relationship with global capitalism and empire, where they have had to survive on the lower rung. Chinese cultural traditions, taken as racial essences, thus reflect practices of frugality, as Theroux's main character, the middle-aged Englishman Bunt, believes: "The Chinese were frugal first of all, but not mean; they were self-denying and Spartan. . . . They liked simplicity more than ingenuity, because ingenuity costs more" (10). As the handover becomes a reality, Bunt's self-assurance ruptures when he is confronted with "a China he did not know" (43), an inorganic China of "enforcing the law," "subversion and disloyalty," a "Chinese system of threats and bribes and crookery" (86). In the arrogance of believing he knows the real China, Bunt remains totally unprepared for the upset of Chineseness coming from the mainland. This new Chineseness manifests in Mr. Hung, an ex-military investor who buys out Bunt's textile company and forces him to leave Hong Kong forever.

Like much of his work, Paul Theroux's novel of the handover mocks British arrogance by depicting their imperial gaze as racist, but also as producing race. "The whole point about the Chinese," Bunt states, "was that every one of them was equally broke and pathetic" (91). The production of Chineseness in Hong Kong cannot be separated from the colonial violence that necessitated Chinese identity; as Patrick Wolfe writes, "Racial identities are constructed in and through the very process of their enactment," so that race itself can be seen as "colonialism speaking."[43] Though Hong Kong's Chineseness has been reproduced and reshaped since the early colonial era, the contemporary conflicts over Chineseness and localism have reemerged in political responses to the PRC's "slow induction" of antidemocratic policies that officially began in 1997.[44] In *Kowloon Tong*, the racial division between Hong Kong Chineseness and mainland Chineseness relies on histories of divergent social reproductions (organic and inorganic) that reinstate the stability of given cultural identities.

Wayne Wang's 1997 film *Chinese Box* is based loosely on Theroux's novel and explores the same anxieties as *Kowloon Tong*, but with a more sentimental and realistic portrayal of the city.[45] The film reimagines Hong Kong urban space as an imperial borderland that must contend with multiple forms of Chinese globality within the rush to maintain its stature as a global city, "rent-free borrowed space on borrowed time."[46] The film intersperses shots of the Hong Kong cityscape with a visual collage of fish and chickens being skinned, gutted, and prepped, with reiterating shots of their beating hearts, brutally exposed for the camera's eye. This ambivalent imagery is suggestive of the film's attempt to express the uncertain future of Hong Kong's cultural identity after the handover. Wang's protagonist John Spencer (Jeremy Irons) contends with a masculinized Chinese man, Chang (Michael Hui), who deals in corruption with mainland investors. Chang secures the heart of Vivian (Gong Li), John's longtime love interest and a bar owner from Beijing. Vivian's gendered service work reflects John's own comparison of Hong Kong to a "whore" who will have to cope "with her new pimp." John has become disillusioned with the meaningless world of British finance in the colony and takes up documentary filmmaking in order to seek deeper truths about Hong Kong before the cultural shifts that will inevitably come with the handover. Whereas Theroux's Bunt is filled with the arrogance of believing he knows everything about China, Irons's John Spencer is filled with the dread that he knows nothing.

At the film's beginning, Spencer is diagnosed with leukemia and given three to six months to live. His impending death drives him to capture a perpetually elusive Hong Kong essence, seeking to make meaning out of the colonial violence of which he has thus far been a beneficiary. The film is self-consciously critical of both the PRC's colonization of Hong Kong and the imperial legacy of racism and rapacious capitalism that the British are leaving behind. John's disillusionment with the financial world, coupled with his terminal illness, leaves him no sentiments or nostalgia for British privilege but, rather, a regret for the price of that privilege, that he could never really know the local people. His desire to capture the essence of Hong Kong drives his desire for Vivian; as John says, "So much of Hong Kong exists below the surface.... If they could see what I see hidden in [Vivian's eyes]." Vying for the same woman, John and Chang both create disturbances over Vivian: John attacks Chang (comparing Chang to a pimp) in a show of masculine bravado, and Chang gets into a bar brawl with Cantonese-speaking men who insult Vivian for being a mainland immigrant. The film allegorizes Hong Kong's position as a feminized commodity caught between two colonizers at the same time that it dramatizes entrenched forms of prejudices targeted at mainland Chinese.[47] Indeed, John's masculinity attempts to retain the privilege he once had, and Chang's own claim to Vivian causes John to suspect that her love for him was merely a product of his privilege. Despite John's critical attitude toward British colonialism, his British superiority toward the colonized keeps him from revealing his sickness to Vivian. Only after she disappears into a nightclub and masks herself as a prostitute named Jenny is John able to reveal his disease, as he attempts to break through barriers of their imperial identities through the democratizing (and empathetic) specter of death. Throughout the film death serves as a consistent metaphor through Wang's dreamy shots of wet markets, where red-filtered still shots feature chopped-up animals, their hearts still beating, their eyes still gazing out.

If Vivian represents an outcast or victim of a yellow and inorganic China, with its restrictions on sex work and its bodily surveillance, then the other leading female character, Jean (Maggie Cheung), represents the victimized brown and organic Hong Kong local, made precarious not by Chinese patriarchy but by a combination of British colonization, its imposed class hierarchies, and rampant global capitalism. First spotted on the street selling DVDs, Jean seems to withhold an authentic glimpse into a city that John is eager to understand. Her personality as a "strange, funny girl" is similar to the elusive "manic pixie dream girl," a Hong Kong cinematic staple associated with both Cheung and the singer/actress Faye Wong.[48] Whereas the manic pixie in Hollywood helps

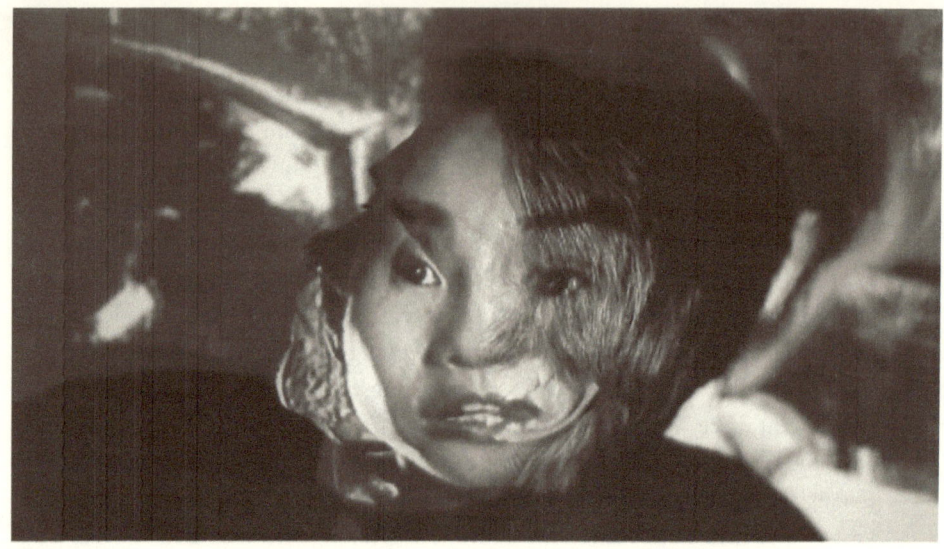

FIGURE 4.1. *Chinese Box*: Jean (Maggie Cheung) superimposed onto John (Jeremy Irons). Screenshot by authors.

young men mature into adulthood, in Hong Kong cinema the manic pixie often shares a symbiotic relationship with the (already adult) male lead, who believes the woman's shallowness is merely a veil to protect her from the male (and often colonial) gaze.[49] Thus, rather than allow herself to be interviewed about the handover, Jean takes control of John's camera to tell her own story about her upbringing but refuses to reveal the origins of her facial scar, unwilling to divulge its history. The story she tells, real or not, is, in a way, the "truth" that John is seeking: graphic details of familial abuse, sexual trauma, rape, and violence. As John watches her own filming of her story, Jean's face is superimposed onto John's through manipulation of the projector, and the audience watches her perform her supposedly true story with John's desire pinned beneath her (see figure 4.1). Though Wang never reveals if her story is true or false, her image, visually mapped onto John's, exposes how her performance continues to be managed by the colonizer's expectations even when she seems to be in control.

Whereas John seems to lament Vivian's involvement in sex work, he also seems to accept that Vivian will always be out of his reach, that the yellow "inscrutable other" can, by her very impenetrable withholding, always evade the incorporation of an assimilationist narrative.[50] Yet John continues to investigate Jean, believing he can penetrate her suspicious story of surviving childhood sexual abuse and violence. For him, Jean's story seems to belong in the annals of Asian female victims in need of a white savior, akin to *The World of Suzie Wong* (1960). Even John sees that Jean's story is typical of Hong Kong Chineseness, where sexual victimhood is wrought within its very comparison to a more conservative sexuality on the mainland.[51] Distrusting Jean's story, John discovers her "true story" in an archival microfilm, but this too seems a typical story of colonial encounter: Jean, as a "jilted teenager," attempted suicide over her English boyfriend, William Campbell, after they had made a suicide pact together, though William hadn't done the same. When John chases her to question her about this story, his sickness reemerges, and he collapses on Queen's Road. As with Vivian, it is only after seeing John's weakness that Jean volunteers her story, which unfolds from one Orientalist myth (that she is in need of a white savior) into one more akin to Giacomo Puccini's *Madame Butterfly*: that she was abandoned and driven to suicide by the betrayal of her white male lover. But even as the film plants itself in the discursive tradition of *Madame Butterfly* and *Suzie Wong*, it takes a critical distance when John arranges for Jean to reunite with her former lover, William (Jared Harris), who pretends not to remember her, reopening and redoubling old wounds of abandonment. Like in Britain's colonial betrayal of Hong Kong, William feels no obligation toward Jean, now squeaking out a meager existence on the streets. William seems little more than a tool of British colonization, a blond-haired, gray-jacketed financier whose obedience has yielded a routine forgetting of the inconveniences of the past. Jean is no Madame Butterfly or Suzie Wong. Her vociferous disobedience of her family, her society, and William himself (she slaps him midsentence) remains an active force. After receiving the slap, William's anger gives rise to a typically passive-aggressive response: "I'm sorry, I really don't appreciate this."

In this scene, John's gaze, prominent in the center of the camera, catches our attention (see figure 4.2). We watch him watching the interaction, his own desire to understand Hong Kong Chineseness finally coming to pass in Jean's suffering. Similar to the desire for the "voice" of domestic workers in chapter 3, John's need to discover realness and authenticity in the brown colonized woman's story can only be satisfied in a way that alleviates his own imperial guilt, ending his own life narrative not through imperial violence but through his own exceptional heroism, establishing that he is not like the other colonizers. Jean's rewriting of her own narrative was never enough to satisfy him in the way that her real tears, placed on his broad shoulders, can. As his gaze moves from Jean

FIGURE 4.2. *Chinese Box*: John and Jean confront William (Jared Harris). Screenshot by authors.

to the camera, breaking the fourth wall, we become aware that John and Jean, despite their similar names, are not nearly as alike as John and Jean's betrayer, William Campbell. Faced with John's mirror image in William, we have little to separate the two, since we know almost nothing about John's own circumstances besides his fatal disease. Indeed, the film's first line of dialogue is from John's wife back in Britain, who reminds him via his answering machine to "call the kids," a message he immediately ignores, leaving the audience to only speculate how his family might react to his impending death. We see only through a gaze that demands the other's story, that demands to know the truth behind both Chinas, one of purity, cultural authenticity, and racial intercourse (Vivian), the other of mixture, cultural hybridity, and interracial intercourse (Jean). To please John's gaze, both must be seen as exploited; both must reveal their suffering; both must be somehow in need of his—the white colonizer's—presence in their lives.

Global Fatigue in *Chinese Box*

Through *Chinese Box*'s depiction of a fatal disease, John himself stands in for the British position during the Hong Kong handover, out of breath, exhausted, and emasculated in the face of an approaching end. John's imminent death reflects the anxieties of living in a colony where the uncertainty of local culture enacts what Ackbar Abbas has called a cultural politics of disappearance, wherein "the anticipated end of Hong Kong as people knew it was the beginning of a profound concern with its historical and cultural specificity."[52] If a new subject position can be "coaxed into being by the disappearance of old cultural bearings and institutions," then we can understand John's anxieties as the need for the Western colonizer to remain relevant to various forms of Chinese globality.[53] His masculine competition with Chang can be read less as a fight over a woman's love and more as a means of resisting the termination of his right to belong in Hong Kong, given the inevitable shift in power from one global racial imaginary, where globality is represented by British colonialism, to another, one centered on Asian megacities. Indeed, one could read John's confrontation with inorganic and organic Chineseness as a symptom of an anxiety not so much focused on the loss of rulership as on the fear of death, of fading away from the global city and into irrelevancy. Yet this story is not just John's story, it is also Hong Kong's. Wang's filmic techniques disrupt the desire for globality through a local realism that borders on docudrama, as the handheld on-location shots are juxtaposed with documentary sequences of crowds and tanks.[54] The film entangles fact and fiction as its narrative romance is constantly interrupted by political activity: A student activist commits suicide just before John and Vivian can reunite, and later the bus carrying John and Jean is gridlocked in traffic by a bomb at the city council. Like the death of the fish in the wet market, Wang's frequent images of a caged dog on a treadmill become an extended metaphor of Hong Kong's exhaustion, where the push to rush on a never-ending treadmill recurs despite who is in the position of colonial owner, manager, or pimp. The film's spatial story climaxes when John collapses on Queen's Road while chasing Jean, begging her for her real story (see figure 4.3). His impending death entices Jean to help him and articulates a power shift told through the dynamic city-space of Hong Kong. Queen's

FIGURE 4.3. *Chinese Box*: John collapses at the intersection of Queen's Road Central, Bonham Street, Wellington Street, and Jervois Street. Screenshot by authors.

Road, constructed by the British in 1843, was the colonial hub of the city for much of its lifetime, home to governors and military men, as well as squatters and coolies. The junction where John collapses connects the streets webbed throughout the colonial island and was the location where, in 1851, the British military decided to destroy a number of Chinese homes in order to buffer a fire in Chinese-dominated Sheung Wan before it ravaged the Central Business District. The intersection connects the business district of Central with the roads associated with prostitution and opium dens, but also with Chinese housing, medicine stores, and hawker stalls. Metaphorically, the intersection signals the inheritance of the organic postcolony once imagined as the horizon of colonial division, a place where the civility of the colonizer ended and the hazardous chaos of the colonized began.

John's collapse in Sheung Wan, the district where the British Army officially landed in 1841, enacts the exhaustion within Hong Kong's shift from hybrid colony to organic global presence. His collapse is precipitated by the sound of honking cars, jackhammers, and the sights of the heavy construction work that would, only a year later, result in giant office towers and a renewed public square. In being more economically and technologically advanced than its colonizer Britain, Hong Kong, with its rise to the status of a global city, is reframed in Wang's work into a story of exhaustion, a global fatigue that opposes the desires for a globality that assures no equal growth or democratic structure but rather grants privilege to people like John and creates boundaries between him and the city's inhabitants. Hong Kong has long claimed to be "Asia's World City" but has competed with Singapore, Seoul, Tokyo, Taipei, Beijing, and Shanghai over the title. Wang's film explores the costs of such globality, emphasizing the spaces of bars and clubs that have disappeared from Hong Kong's urban space.

And yet the film's global fatigue is partially produced through its reiterating of Hong Kong as a particularly organic shade of brown, where the once-domesticated space (like the dog on the treadmill, or the caged chicken, or the other shots of domesticated animals spliced throughout the film) is in constant danger of outgrowing its colonial overseer, of spilling into excessive population and extreme capitalist development, of no longer being of use. Indeed, routed through brown theory, we could reframe the central anxiety of the film: It is not merely that the colonizer needs to remain globally relevant (to live, in John's case) but that to do so, Hong Kong must remain a brown colony not of Britain but of the world itself. The brown and organic Chineseness that the film helps produce is one where the global city of Hong Kong is no longer directly Britain's but belongs to all the colonial masters of the world: China, America, Europe. Indeed, the form of brownness revealed in the film is that of a global city that lacks its own empire, a tale that we can see reiterated in other brown Chinese spaces like Taipei and Singapore. *Chinese Box* reveals this not only in the film's characters and plot but also in the audience's awareness of the film's transnational collaborations, with its global group of screenwriters and producers made up of Wayne Wang, Paul Theroux, French novelist Jean-Claude Carrière, and the American screenwriter Larry Gross.[55] The film's international cast stars a range of cross-cultural actors, from the polyglot Maggie Cheung, the first Asian actress to win a prize at the Cannes Film Festival for performing in the French film *Clean* (2004), to Jeremy Irons, a Shakespearean actor turned Hollywood star, whose role in David Cronenberg's *M. Butterfly* (1993) (an adaptation of David Henry Hwang's play of the same name) cast him as a colonial man with a fetish for an exotic Asia. Similarly, Gong Li, who became famous for her performances in banned Chinese films critical of the PRC, repeats her well-trodden role of a Chinese prostitute hardened by the sexual oppression of the mainland.

While *Chinese Box* may have seemed an opportunity for Chinese megastars like Cheung and Li to reach Hollywood, this opportunity for the global only resulted in reconstructing the limits of their national stardom by containing their roles into distinct racialized extremes of a two-Chinas discourse. As Song Hwee Lim has written, transnational films about China and the Chinese diaspora "serve to reinforce notions of national identities and to safeguard ethnic boundaries."[56] Or, as Georgette Wang and Emilie Yueh-yu Yeh observed in their analysis of *Mulan* (1998) and *Crouching Tiger, Hidden Dragon* (2000), such films gain transcultural standing alongside the risk of performing stereotypical or inaccurate traditional practices (indeed, local critics panned *Chinese Box* for its spatial inaccuracies).[57] As reflected in its modest box office returns, *Chinese Box* expresses not the rush toward global success nor the conservation of a localist identity but an exhaustive attempt to make legible— through organic/inorganic Chineseness—the otherwise illegible ways of being attached to Hong Kong as a shared colonized dependency: the temporary and flexible movements of its many shades of brown.

Playing the Organic in *Sleeping Dogs*

Wayne Wang's *Chinese Box* reimagines Hong Kong space from an aesthetic and romantic style typical of martial arts films and the films of Wong Kar-wai into one of social realism and political turmoil that expresses the fatigue of global competition in a multiply colonized global city. This fatigue is driven in part by the Western colonizer's (John's) desire to capture the organic essence of Hong Kong (through Jean) before the inorganic encroachment of the PRC. This fear of inorganic Chineseness carries a binary, mutually reinforcing relationship with the desire for organic Chineseness, where the inorganic depictions of Chinese as homogeneous, synthetic, obedient, and overly simple are set against organic depictions of Chinese as flexible, hybrid, heterogeneous, and overly complex. The binary operates as an affective aura that produces atmospheric qualities, symbolizing forms of gender (rigid versus flexible masculinities and femininities), political economy (socialist/controlled versus laissez-faire), and futurity (a dystopian cyberpunk world of hackers and mercenaries versus a dystopian future of robotic copies and state control). Inorganic and organic thus cannot be mapped easily to a country, region, or single culture but manifest through two aesthetic racial imaginaries that produce Chineseness as an object of either fear or desire. Where inorganic Chineseness seems an outdated and racist stereotype and reiteration of yellow peril, the organic becomes its saving grace, the means through which Chineseness can enter the global but only as a domesticated form of brownness that can broach intimacies with global colonial power without threatening the definitions of "humanity" within it (seen as Westernized, English speaking, capitalist). Like yellow peril discourses of the past, the fears of inorganic China are of replacement and invasion—fears of becoming overpowered, enveloped, and swallowed by an inscrutable force. Representations of inorganic China induce not only the anxieties of competitive economic and political power but also, as Lo Kwai-Cheung has argued, a fear of its "excess masculinity" manifesting in war, military adventures, and autocratic patriarchs who make grand sacrifices in the name of a futuristic utopia (Mao Zedong, Deng Xiaoping, Lee Kuan Yew).[58] Its common tropes are militaristic rhetoric, an obedient and uniform populace, and women as resilient victims and heroes (as depicted in the early films of Zhang Yimou). Though these depictions are not always directed at a particular state or nation, they are often coupled with fears of a rising communist China, where males outnumber females by thirty-three million, and sex-identification technologies have been used to eliminate female fetuses. While the inorganic is cast as a mere simulation of something real, the organic (as we see in both Jean and the Hong Kong cityscape) is cast as hybrid, mixed up, contaminated, still far from the original not because it is a copy but because it lacks a stable identity.

While *Chinese Box* captures the fears of the inorganic and the desires for the organic, mainstream video games about Hong Kong use virtual spatial representations to capture the organic as a space burdened by complexity and capitalist artificiality. The social and political representation of space has often been a central focus in video games, particularly in open-world games that allow players to interact with a space by walking or driving through it and by speaking to (and sometimes abusing) its inhabitants. Such games reimagine space within a global racial imaginary that is made accessible to players from all over the world but retains enough of its foreignness to appeal as a mode of virtual tourism. Espen Aarseth's frequently quoted essay "Allegories of Space" sees computer games as building spatial imaginaries as symbolic and aesthetic spaces, yet it is important also to note the social-political function of these virtual spaces and the way they redesign cities according to a global audience.[59] Open-world games can unsettle or placate global imaginings by simulating them for the player to wander undirected, allowing players to concoct permutations and porousness within given racialized spaces.

In video games, Hong Kong space has been most famously constituted in the 2001 game *Shenmue II* and the 2012 game *Sleeping Dogs*, both of which construct Hong Kong as an organic postcolonial form of Chineseness that attempts to either erase inorganic forms (as in *Sleeping Dogs*) or see the mixtures of inorganic/organic as forming their own hybrid subcultures (as in *Shenmue II*). The more recent game, *Sleeping Dogs*, developed by both a Canadian studio (United Front Games) and a UK studio (Square Enix London) in conjunction with Japanese designers and distributors (Square Enix), has garnered a sequel and movie (both in the works), attracting attention from Chinese diasporic audiences through its articulation of Chinese globality through hybridity,

FIGURE 4.4. Driving on Hong Kong Island in *Sleeping Dogs*. Screenshot by authors.

diasporic mobility, and global capital.[60] *Sleeping Dogs* takes the point of view of a Hong Kong–born man, Wei Shen, who has recently returned from living in America for fifteen years and has infiltrated the Sun On Yee (新安義) triad as a member of the undercover police. Like many open-world games, the game centers on mechanics of fighting, driving, shooting, and running through stylized cityscapes like a parkour artist. Inspired by Hong Kong cinema traditions of kung fu and police films, *Sleeping Dogs* uses Hong Kong space to provide players an adrenaline rush of percussive action, where players weave through hanging meats, vault over construction, collide with fish tanks, and crash through chicken coops. The game encourages rapid movement through a city free of traffic jams but full of pedestrians whose regional charm comes through their Cantonese cursing when players inevitably run them over (see figure 4.4). Even missions to gain face, which usually begin with small favors like running errands or helping someone decide on a dress to wear, end in violence.

The popularity of *Sleeping Dogs* across the Chinese diaspora is due in part to its imagining of Hong Kong as purely organic, constructing the city as if the 1997 handover never took place. As Tara Fickle and I have pointed out in previous work, Asian Americans have a high rate of video game play compared to other diasporic groups, and are ubiquitous as players and developers, though they are almost invisible in terms of representation.[61] This situation makes the appearance of *Sleeping Dogs'* protagonist Wei Shen much more impactful for Asian American players, as the diasporic Chinese martial artist provides an empowered representation of Asian American masculinity set to

FIGURE 4.5. *Sleeping Dogs*: The same stores and restaurants repeat. Screenshot by authors.

the nostalgic tone of organic Chineseness, here rendered as the sole form of Chinese globality. Through representations like Wei Shen, Asian Americans have been both symbols of organic Chineseness and its main political force, as representations of the organic Chinas of Hong Kong, Taiwan, and the pre-communist mainland have often been centerpieces of diasporic tales nostalgic for a lost homeland (*Joy Luck Club, Woman Warrior, Fresh off the Boat*). In depicting Wei Shen as an English-speaking hero on par with Bruce Lee, *Sleeping Dogs* envisions organic Chinese masculinity not as a force of competition or invasion but as an American minority already incorporated into the West. Here the imagining of organic Chineseness as a tolerable future becomes all encompassing, as the mixture of Cantonese and English throughout the game erases Mandarin from the city and stylizes Hong Kong less like a multiracial and dynamic global city and more like an exaggerated theme park of an American Chinatown, with Cantonese effortlessly code-mixing with English.[62] Even the city's map reimagines Hong Kong Island as a solitary island without a bridge, tunnel, or airport connecting it to the mainland, while Hong Kong flags can be seen implanted throughout the city.[63]

If globality is envisioned and put into practice by what Cheah calls "the internalization of a virtual image," *Sleeping Dogs*, in its rendering of a playable Hong Kong, goes a step further in inviting players into an entirely virtual city defined by its globality.[64] Unlike open-world games like the *Grand Theft Auto* series, the developers of *Sleeping Dogs* attempted to re-create Hong Kong not to parody it but to be "as realistic and as authentic as possible" and to "capture that essence of Hong Kong" by including major landmarks but altering the city's layout to focus on "the driving and the free-running missions."[65] The city is meant to be experienced only in blurred form, with landscape not meant to be savored but bulleted through. In this world of exteriors, there are very few buildings that the player can go inside, and if they dare to walk through the city rather than speed through it, they will find that the names of the restaurants and cafés steadily repeat, with the same shops looping again and again (see figure 4.5). Even the people inside of these shops turn out to be wallpaper images, and the pedestrians on the street mere copies of each other. A second glance only uncovers the cardboard walls of the glitzy cityscape. What emerges in a slow "close play" of *Sleeping Dogs* is the plasticity of the organic—its very inorganic opposite planted already within it.[66] As Cheah writes, plasticity is a feature built into the competitive atmosphere of a global city "because it is always in the process of making and remaking itself, or being made and remade, in response to global flows."[67] The organicism, flexibility, and complexity that have defined Hong Kong are rendered an artificial commodity exported for a global audience, a homogenization of racial forms (Chineseness) in a city fully imagined as a space of global domestication.

Shenmue II and the Many Chinas

The speed and cinematic gameplay of *Sleeping Dogs* come to a standstill in the 2001 open-world game *Shenmue II*, where the player paces slowly through a minutely detailed Hong Kong. Like *Sleeping Dogs*, *Shenmue II* is also meant to feel like an authentic, realistic experience of the harbor city, but as an open-world game produced just before the genre became popular (*Grand Theft Auto III* was released in the same year), *Shenmue II* stages a social realist representation of Hong Kong that encourages players to ambulate through the monotony of everyday movement (see figure 4.6).[68] *Shenmue II* is microdetailed in the sense that picking up items, gazing on them, and working part-time jobs can feel more difficult and tedious in the game than in real life. In turn, acts of wandering become purposeful in themselves, as the player can always discover more details that the developers spent labor, time, and money on. For instance, the player can take a part-time job lifting boxes for pocket money, spend hours carrying books out of a library, or simply saunter around the city. The game takes the form of a "virtual walking simulator," allowing the player to move without direction and without a clearly defined goal, so that the game appears "open ended (much like real life)."[69] Indeed, *Shenmue II* can be understood

FIGURE 4.6. *Shenmue II*: Ryo in Wan Chai. Screenshot by authors.

as an antithesis to fast, violent games like *Sleeping Dogs* and is, rather, a process-driven game with a slow, purposeful accumulation of experiences. While Alexander Galloway reads *Shenmue*'s form as "ambient," the game also delivers a sense of frustration with its slow loading times, its lack of maps, and the need to run through the city, adding to its conception of Hong Kong space as slow and rhythmic.[70] Like *Chinese Box*, *Shenmue II*'s organic depiction of Hong Kong enacts a sense of global fatigue in its preoccupation with Hong Kong as a space of collapse, a space resigned from the desire for the fast, abstract sense of globality of *Sleeping Dogs*. Yet unlike *Chinese Box*, the global fatigue of *Shenmue II* reveals the many shades of brown within both inorganic and organic Chinas, while still remaining aware of the encroachment of Chinese and American capitalist empire. The game's slow and experiential pace, its shifts in spatial genres (from hyperrealist to kung fu dystopia to village), and its cast of over seven hundred unique characters rupture the racial imaginings of two Chinas and reveal the varying shades of brown once rendered illegible under the universalizing (and imperial) rhetoric of globality.

In 2001 *Shenmue II* was the most expensive video game ever produced and, along with its predecessor, took over six years of development. Made for a global audience after the worldwide success of the first *Shenmue* (1999), *Shenmue II* attempts to depict Chineseness outside of its ideological and political connotations to offer a spatial poetics reliant on the rhythm and patterns of daily life, inviting players to become intimate with and knowledgeable about the game's virtual space, its hundreds of characters and shops. Its predecessor, *Shenmue*, sees the player-character Ryo in Japan fighting Chinese martial artists to avenge the death of his father, and its depiction of 1980s small-town Japan includes Chinese gangs as well as Chinese immigrants who own restaurants and barbershops.[71] Like *Shenmue*, *Shenmue II* offers an intimate, hyperrealist portrayal of so many unique characters, symbols, and spaces that the game evades offering a binary view of Chineseness but rather strives to create more intimate bonds between the player and the city's minutely detailed spaces.

Shenmue II gives the Western player a hyperrealist Hong Kong without being viewed as a white foreigner but instead as a young Japanese visitor, Ryo.[72] Western players are thus able to see Hong Kong through the estranged embodiment of a foreign Japanese man, permitting a view of Chineseness and Asianness in general as more than fetishized otherness that is always represented in reference to whiteness. By shifting the basis of comparison from whiteness or Americanness to forms of Chineseness and Japaneseness, here the available references are not British or American, as in *Chinese Box* and *Sleeping Dogs*, but inter-Asian, exposing altered forms of the inorganic/organic (yellow/brown) binary. The forms of Chineseness in *Shenmue II*'s Hong Kong thus do not appear as a competitive form of globality but as a network of possible solidarities and intimacies. In this non-Western global racial imaginary, no language barrier exists, and even when characters comment on Ryo's accent, they do so through English or Japanese voice actors. Though the game was released in the Japanese language, the vast majority of characters in *Shenmue II* would not know any Japanese, and the game's main love interest, Shenhua, speaks Japanese but has never even heard of Japan.

The organicism of Hong Kong Island shifts dramatically in *Shenmue II* when Ryo ventures into the epic kung fu setting of Kowloon Walled City in the 1980s, when it was known as an ungoverned enclave run by triads, before it was demolished by the Hong Kong government (see figures 4.7 and 4.8). The hyperrealism of the game's beginning on Hong Kong Island complements the epic nature of Kowloon by carrying over the feeling of authenticity and realism even into this strange setting. Hong Kong's cityscape here does not offer a space to be dominated by Western forms of culture and capital but rather a space to be submitted to, where the inorganic auras of excess mascu-

FIGURE 4.7. Kowloon Walled City before demolition. Photo by Ian Lambot. From Girard and Lambot, *City of Darkness*.

FIGURE 4.8. *Shenmue II*: Kowloon, by Sega. Screenshot from Fandom.com.

FIGURE 4.9. *Shenmue II*: Ryo and Shenhua strolling to Bailu village. Screenshot by authors.

linity, despotic control, and dystopian futurities are mixed intimately with the organic, violent, and anarchic spaces of street fights and crumbling high-rises. The space carries an aesthetic of the global slum, a space of transience and ruin. Spaces like "Ghost Hall Building" are mythical in their decay, with large holes, crumbled gaps, and caved-in rooftops. Whereas Western depictions of Hong Kong in *Chinese Box* and *Sleeping Dogs* see its organicism as a truly hybrid form of globality in need of preservation, *Shenmue II*'s Kowloon reminds us of the shared structures that have conditioned the rise of both mainland China and Greater China. Ghost cities, urban decay, and poverty are characteristic of both inorganic and organic forms, just as globality has only been possible through labor exploitation and resource extraction. As Sit Tsui and Wong Tak Hing have pointed out, modern China has been depicted mainly from its largest urban centers, whose affluence was built through the extraction of surplus labor from rural regions and decaying cities.[73] This extraction has created an "internal colonialism" that treats the countryside as a reservoir of resources and labor, similar to the relationships between the power centers of Greater China and their neighbors (between Hong Kong and the Pearl River Delta, between Taiwan and southwestern China, between Singapore and Malaysia or Indonesia).[74] *Shenmue II* thus complicates views of Chinese globality by staging the rise to globality itself as exploitative and uneven, pointing us to a political and economic conception of China that moves from an organic and inorganic binary to a model of overlapping power centers, where global cities, whether organic or inorganic, whether colonial centers or domesticated outposts, harbor deep structural inequalities and rely on the low wages and environmental exploitation of nearby dependencies.

In the ending of *Shenmue II*, Ryo ventures from Kowloon to Bailu, a small village in Guilin of less than fifty people in rural southern China that resembles neither an organic nor an inorganic space but a form of Chineseness outside of the binary, a revolutionary space that has maneuvered past the bounds of capital and the state. Compared to Hong Kong Island and Kowloon, Guilin appears mythical, with place-names like "bai lu" (white deer) and "Bai Sha" (white sand). It is an antiglobal refuge devoid of both the eyes of the PRC and imperial global capitalism. Here the player finds no Chinese flags or Communist Party slogans but a revolutionary tradition that, implicitly, provides an alternative to both organic and inorganic Chinas through a history of exile that has lasted for centuries. As the village girl Shenhua tells Ryo, Guilin's origins trace back to the Tang dynasty, when nobles were expelled from "the city" by the emperor and built "the village" of Bailu after reaching a place totally enclosed by mountains (see figure 4.9). This exile group has retreated into the rural not to reeducate themselves in communism/state allegiance or to return to a lost purity but to evade both the capitalist industry and the Communist Party, both inorganic and organic Chinas. They are insurgents bound by exilic experience and thus find alliance with the Japanese protagonist, Ryo. In Bailu we thus have an antiglobal imaginary, an antithesis to the rush for globality of the capitalist state, one that does not invoke the local as its counterforce but rather the political and social exile. The rural village, stripped of its allegiance to state ideology and free from the grip of capitalist exploitation, here posits an alternative form of Chineseness, one that rejects the aspiration to global racial forms where one will always remain in what Dipesh Chakrabarty calls the "waiting room of history."[75]

If Wayne Wang's *Chinese Box* expresses fatigue resulting from Hong Kong's competition as a global city, *Shenmue II* expresses this fatigue by rejecting the desire for globality from the point of view of a Japanese character, whose homeland too was once put forward as *the* form of Asian global modernity (or even postmodernity) and was once also a racialized competitor to the West. Japan, once perceived as global threat and yellow peril, has also been routed through colonial forms of domestication, has also constructed senses of yellow against its own brown colonial outposts (such as the Indigenous peoples of Okinawa). From this view, Chineseness does not elicit anxiety as it enters the global stage but an intimacy bound through a shared colonial racial frame. *Shenmue II* offers a slow, rhythmic interaction with a space most often presented as global in order to reveal its complexity, breaking with the fast-paced rise of organic and inorganic Chineseness. Like *Chinese Box*, *Shenmue II* visualizes this urban space as overpowering, mythic, and difficult to register, one whose narrative still continues to unfold. In contrasting Hong Kong's middle-class hybrid spaces with the decrepit slums of Kowloon Walled City and the exiles of Bailu Village, the game evades discourses of two Chinas to account instead for the relationship between centers of power (Beijing, Shanghai, Hong Kong, Taipei, Singapore), their peripheries, and their exilic communities. *Shenmue II* thus invokes the view that despite Western fears, most frequently it is not organic or inorganic forms of Chineseness that are most vulnerable but those unseen and unvoiced peoples living on the periphery who are the victims of these power centers, whose health wavers in ecological catastrophe, whose lives are rendered fearful and limited to party slogans, who find themselves at the mercy of repetitious, exploitative factory work.

Conclusion: Racial Imaginaries, Global Nightmares

This chapter has sought to challenge global discourses of two Chinas, first by revealing their imperial and racial presumptions through the binary of inorganic and organic Chineseness and, second, by showing how this binary misunderstands the nuances of power, race, statecraft, and the many shades of brown that reveal forms of complicity and resistance, which remain outside the purview of global racial imaginaries. I have invoked the inorganic/organic binary as a starting point to deconstruct the binaries that are meant to contain Chineseness into two extreme but contradicting racial forms, one that follows more from fears of yellowness (as homogeneous, imperial yellow peril) and one that follows more from brownness (as plural, subjugated domesticable mass). I have seen organic and inorganic Chineseness, as conceived through brown theory, as a means of moving alongside the shifting forms of racial imagination, to take the reader along for the brief ride of organic/inorganic binary thinking to reveal its presence in global narratives of Chineseness, as well as the ways in which American and Chinese imperial projects invest heavily in binary depictions of Chineseness that sometimes overlap, sometimes deviate.

As with previous chapters, I have sought to read brownness beyond the castings of colorism or shadism to consider shifts in perspective where highly politicized migrant or minority populations might be racialized to fit one racial form (yellow) for one imperial power but might read differently (brown) to others. I have read brownness within those who are often cast as yellow but who occupy traits of brownness via their relationship to colonial powers. Rather than seek to establish simple characteristics for these racial forms (brown/organic as domesticatable, yellow/inorganic as inassimilable), the movements of brownness challenge such naming and refuse the tendency to name brown Chineseness as an auxiliary form of brownness, as a "lighter shade of brown," or as a form that is less authentic than, perhaps, the Filipina domestic workers focused on in the previous chapter. While we may gravitate toward widely accepted instantiations of brownness, such gravities still orbit the imperial power of our time, which shapes the way we see, understand, and identify brown peoples. The colonial racial desire to domesticate brownness also hierarchizes brownness, seeing some as more authentically brown and others as more hybrid and inauthentic. While this chapter focused on Hong Kong, brown Chineseness could be conceived in various other contexts: during the war in Vietnam, where Vietnamese were often called *brown* by both US military and antiwar activists; in colonial Mexico, where Asian migrants from Manila were massified by Spanish colonial laws as *chinos*; or in contemporary Taiwan, Tibet, and Xinjiang. Indeed, we could also ask what brown Chineseness might look like were we to center Maoist philosophy and the Cultural Revolution within discourses of Indigeneity, rural poverty, and colonial subjugation against the Chinese urban elite as well as imperial Japan. Could even the "yellowest" people of our racial imagination, in a different time and comparative context, also be called *brown*?

Movements of brownness complicate attempts to ascribe authenticity to any particular form of brownness, as doing so misses out on the stories of movement and colonial desires that brownness can otherwise reveal. This chapter's movement through inorganic/organic Chineseness points brown theory in other, wayward directions, by excavating the racial, gendered/sexual, and imperial overtones of two-Chinas discourses in ways that help perceive alternative conceptual patterns. Cultural texts that attempt to articulate Chineseness within global media often reiterate an inorganic/organic binary strikingly similar to discourses of yellow peril, anticommunism, and racial castration. As a space bounded within the orbits of British colonial history, neoliberal globalization, and colonial administration by the PRC, Hong Kong is often depicted as an exceptional and organic melting pot, a narrative that not only reproduces the space as an American and British subempire characterized by diversity but also presumes that the Hanicization of the mainland has been totalizing among those who, on the surface, identify as such. Such narratives that maintain an image of Hong Kong as organic, pluralist, and free hide the less visible social engineering of global capitalism, while the PRC mainland represents, by contrast, an impossibly direct control over Chinese culture, identity, and behavior. As a space of colonial encounter, Hong Kong's Chineseness continues to define the city despite generations of immigrants, refugees, migrant workers, and expatriates who do not share in the familial belonging of the city, what John Erni has called Hong Kong's "hegemonic model of *family solidarity*."[76]

Narratives supporting stark dichotomies between two Chinas speak to neocolonial tensions but, in doing so, risk reproducing Cold War optics that forget those who have lost lives and livelihoods to the mutual desire for globality—the poor, migratory, and marginalized populations for whom "the dream of globality is lived as a nightmare."[77] Indeed, contrasting these two Chinas preoccupies the readings of Asian cultural products with questions of marginalized types of Chineseness, thus reproducing Chineseness as the main logic in organizing various texts, and limiting the diverse cultural expressions that abound throughout "China" and "Greater China." As Erni argues, the preoccupation over Chineseness in Hong Kong has resulted in a "dearth of attention paid to the role racial and ethnic difference played in the identity politics of the local."[78] Similarly, these narratives also construct the mainland and Han Chinese themselves as impermeable, joining ethno-state narratives that suppress groups of linguistic, racial, religious, and political difference.

Through a frame of brownness, we might also see Hong Kong differently, not as experiencing a slow (and inevitable) incursion of a growing global power, one who shares similar racial, cultural, and linguistic traits and to whom they are destined to one day return, but as a colonized nation that is under violent and oppressive colonial occupation. To refuse the racial mapping of Chineseness as singular, in other words, insists that the "slow incursions" of the PRC into Hong Kong map onto forms of colonial violence that must be taken seriously and with the same vigor as colonial spaces of the past and present. To see the mechanics of the inorganic/organic binary thus revises the fifty-year "slow integration" of Hong Kong into the PRC as less a conquering of the organic by the inorganic and more a different form of globality being forced on those who—as we have seen in the disruptive tactics of the 2014 Umbrella Movement and the 2019 protests—refuse the imperative of globality altogether. The stakes of reproducing the organic/inorganic binary are as high as ever in Hong Kong's struggle for democracy, where aspirations and losses are being drowned out by the renewal of Cold War rhetoric, rather than envisioning Hong Kong protesters within multiple genealogies of protest as well as concurrent uprisings against neoliberalism and empire in non-Chinese contexts.[79] Rather than rely on constructed binaries, Wang Xiaoming has stressed the importance of studying how regimes based on globalization, efficiency, and short-term success have begun to erode "longer-term interests of individuals, organizations, and regions" and have led to environmental, educational, and governmental deterioration.[80] Binaries can cast a false sense of security as they confine a "bad China" to one type of people (Han Chinese), one type of government (totalitarian, communist), and one social practice (inorganic). They can also continue to dictate Chineseness and its margins as the main conceptual paradigm through which Hong Kong and mainland China are made visible. As "the most difficult and unprecedented case of social change in twentieth-century history," in the words of Wang Xiaoming, China breaks through such conceptual limits.[81]

On a beach of artists, someone mentions that the straight white guy you met last night was a Pisces, which explains why the group actually liked him. On the topic of star signs, someone insists on playing games about the mind. The cube you imagine represents yourself, the ladder your support system, the horse your passions and sex, the flowers your artistic projects. In another game, the color purple is your self, the horse your ideal partner, and the ocean your passions and sex, but there is no artistic project.

You sink your hand in sand that was once dinosaur and dog, ancestor-ash. Each grain passing through your fingers was once a quarry, a stone for sitting or for beating a heretic. You recall that the first short story you ever wrote, "Mud Man," was about a hero created from toxins, a brown monster with dripping skin, oily with chemical waste. The mud that made him oozed off and became part of the earth. He could fight crime, but only in the sun, where his soft skin hardened into a swingable fist.

Lyrics to a song come, slip away, but you don't want to pull out your phone here. For a moment, while you're lying on your back and they are looking down at you, you believe this might be the moment you touch. Instead, you tell them that artists cannot build hope from nothing. You can only project the images throbbing inside you: the plainness of organs whose sole purpose is to move things around. You wish to find more projects like that. It would, you imagine, feel a lot like sunshine.

Brown Crafts

A CREATIVE PRAXIS FOR OUR PRESENT

Christopher B. Patterson (as Kawika Guillermo)

2018	*Stamped: an anti-travel novel*
	Transitive Cultures: Anglophone
	Literature of the Transpacific
2020	*All Flowers Bloom*
	Open World Empire: Race, Erotics,
	and the Global Rise of Video Games
2023	*Nimrods: a fake-punk self-hurt anti-memoir*
	"Brown Theory: A Storied Manifest of Our World"

Once, at a writing conference, a white man asked me if destruction was necessary for art. . . . "No, sir, destruction is not necessary for art." I said that, not because I was certain, but because I thought my saying it would help me believe it. But why can't the language for creativity be the language of regeneration? —OCEAN VUONG, *On Earth We're Briefly Gorgeous*

Writing is a product of loss: Great suffering begets great art. This is a common cliché that has bled into countless Hollywood films, when a story about a person's traumatizing experiences ends with the victimized figure publishing a book about their traumas (*The Help*; *Green Book*; *Hidden Figures*; *Precious*; *Slumdog Millionaire*; *The Namesake*; *The Reluctant Fundamentalist*; *The Perks of Being a Wallflower*; *Wild*; *Eat, Pray, Love*). In these narratives systemic oppression is resolved with the act of creative expression, cemented by a final scene where the victim-turned-author signs books for an awaiting crowd.[1] Rather than resolve an injustice with a change in law, social order, or the everyday habits of colonial violence, such films—like the books they are often based on—see the power of creative expression as the pinnacle of justice itself. Publishing is seen as resolution, conclusion, foreclosure. Rarely do such narratives follow the social impact of these books. In a context where publishing one's story with a large press is already a far-fetched dream, these narratives tell us that the change promised from a bestselling book is no longer the goal. Simply placing our personal tragedies into the discourse of "literature" is all that justice requires.

As Ocean Vuong writes in the epigraph above, conflict, oppression, and trauma are often the only gateways through which marginalized peoples are permitted to make creative acts. This is not merely an outside condition: We creative artists too presume this not only when we write but also when we read literary texts—how we are drawn to texts that were (as it may say on the book's jacket) written during times of duress, when the writer was experiencing trauma, illness, or worse. As both a literary scholar and a creative writer myself—and as someone suspicious of magical commodities—I wonder, as Vuong does, about the competitive and warlike way we attend to creative acts: as products gunning for awards, written by marginalized authors whose main desire for justice is merely to be read, to be understood, for the audience to know them. If, as Olúfẹ́mi Táíwò has argued, "oppression is not a prep school," then can we also say that "trauma is not a creative writing program"?[2] What do we writers of color lose, and what do we gain, in shifting our creative acts from forms of productive trauma to something more wayward, made more directly for us?

In 2019, just before the release of my second novel, *All Flowers Bloom*, a far more renowned writer on a panel explained to me how unique my upbringing was, how politically interesting my family was (uniquely mixed, with Black, Indigenous, East and Southeast Asian, and white members), and how writing about this could have some useful impact beyond my fiction writing.[3] Only in retrospect, on the publication of my "anti-memoir," *Nimrods: a fake-punk self-hurt anti-memoir*, did this same writer also guide me to understand just how unusual my writing career has been, how my casting of creative and academic work (under separate pseudonyms) has offered a unique circumstance to illuminate creative pathways for those who seek to do both.[4] Rare, that a theory of creativity might emerge from (and about) the creator themselves, based on their own work; rarer still, that this theory comes within a critical discourse that brings together both their creative and their academic work, seeing them not as bifurcating paths or different personas but as coming from shared affects, political ideas, histories, or, as I will name it in this chapter, brown crafts.

While my prose-poetry anti-memoir *Nimrods* sought to capture some unique circumstance of my and my family's embodiments, this chapter seeks to trace some of the unique stages of my own creative and academic work as a means of making what I will call *brown crafts*. This chapter thus slides away from the more distancing (and constantly moving) view of brown theory to instead consider the ways brownness can serve as a basis for creative worldmaking, and to see our acts as scholars, students, and workers as already within the realm of brown craft making. This focus on creativity in brownness helps spotlight the pitfalls of scholarly and popular works that tend to fetishize or romanticize hybrid identities, including mestizo/a consciousness, hybridity, or colonialism itself. Like the forms of suffering presumed inherent for marginalized people to write novels or memoirs, such forms of colonial violence that produced the brown author could be understood as resolvable by creative acts that disperse new genre forms and stylistic innovations. Such romanticizations we can understand when writing our brown crafts not as traits inherent to brownness but as stories and experiences that obtain structural meaning through their colonial context, meanings that can be revelatory for middlebrow literary audiences, as well as for students within an educational state institution. As Sony Coráñez Bolton argues in his rereading of Gloria Anzaldúa's *Borderlands*, such romanticizations of brown creativity (as mestizo/mestiza) not only are limited to the particular contexts in which they take place (often ignorant of transnational marginalizations) but are commonly ablest, anti-Black, anti-Indigenous, and anti-Asian (or in our case, antiyellow), especially when they see the hybrid mestiza/o as containing an almost supernatural capacity to intellectualize and to create art in ways that "reify[] the lens of 'mestizos' to read social reality better than the rest of us."[5] Exploring forms of "brown creativity" thus also means wrestling with narratives of other color-coded racializations as being anticreative or limited in imaginary scope (as the term *Mongoloid* often did in chapter 1, "labor" did in chapters 2 and 3, and the "inorganic" forms of Chineseness did in chapter 4). In other words, we could see the romanticization of hybridity as a form of imperial domestication itself—a complex means of differentiating peoples from a brown mass through an artful practice of what I will later call *brown power*. Thinking through brown craft takes a different view of the fetishization of brownness, by looking more specifically at the practice of creating artwork through the meanings that brownness provides.

This chapter seeks to retool brown theory into a usable form of brown creative praxis, first by reanimating this oft-used term for writing, *craft*, in a way that makes it theoretically generative, critical of the inequalities within reading and publishing, and salvageable for our own writing. I will insist that when we think of the term *craft*, we think not of the white working-class craftsman honing a skill but of a sea vessel, a ship that sails the water and the wind. In so doing, we can understand brown craft making as a creative act that does not come from a natural or organic endpoint to oppression or trauma. To think in terms of brown craft refuses the narratives of marginalized peoples that see our creative acts as a resolution to oppression, that see publishing a novel or an academic book, hard as this may be, as an act of justice in itself. Since at least the seventeenth century, the term *craft* has been used for ships, to mean "a vehicle designed for navigation in or on water or air or through outer space."[6] Commonly, it is used to mean a small vessel that can be made by a factory but is often made by hand in a do-it-yourself, piecemeal fashion, and usually with a team of other builders. In this sense, crafts are seen less as praiseworthy original works and more as translations of our experiences, our communities, our ways of seeing. "Translation," as Teju Cole has written, can be traced etymologically to the Latin *ferre*, "to carry," and shares relation to the English word *ferry*. Translation of our lives to the page thus places the writer as a "ferry operator, carrying meaning from words on that shore to words on this shore."[7] Unlike the way we are taught to see well-crafted novels and books of poetry, a craft is not meant to stick around—it is built for the express purpose of getting from one place to another.

As we often talk of language as seas of words, or narratives as oceans of stories, our writing can be the crafts we build to venture through words and stories, to carry us from one moment in our life to the next, and to invest in a particular moment, a craft for these seas, to cross these waters, to deal with this climate, to flee from that oncoming storm. We don't craft stories or essays just so they can sit in our virtual clouds, but to help us get past the shoals, the rough surf on the coast, so we can navigate the open possibilities of the open ocean. In practice, this means understanding creativity as a craft not within the weight and (e)valuation of artistic gatekeepers, critics, and historians but as diary entries, as reflections of who we believe we are, because the person who started the project will always be different from the person who ends the project, and that separation can only grow with time. For this reason, this chapter will tether arguments concerning creativity and craft making with reflections on all the crafts I have made that were themselves not given the advantage of time: my first poems and short stories from 1997 to 2017; my first two books, which were both released in 2018, *Stamped: an anti-travel novel* and *Transitive Cultures: Anglophone Literature of the Transpacific*; and my second pair of books, which were both released in 2020, *All Flowers Bloom* and *Open World Empire: Race, Erotics, and the Global Rise of Video Games*. I end focusing on my debut prose-poetic anti-memoir, *Nimrods* (2023), and its relation to this very book, *Domesticating Brown*. These reflections will attempt to invoke a form of brown craft that embraces the changes in our selves and the changes in our time. This chapter thus bookends the introduction with a refractive mirror of the introduction's hybrid creative/critical essay form. Similarly, this chapter's first half is devoted to a more critical, genealogical view to establish the context and possibilities for brown craft making today. The second half embarks from this traditionally critical approach to offer reflections on my own experience as both a scholar of literature and a creative writer in the hopes of generating a second "brown triptych," one that prismatically refracts the introduction's triptych of "brown mass \ domesticating brown / shades of brown" by turning the reparative potentialities of brown movement toward acts of creative expression.

This chapter also deviates from most academic theories of creativity not only by examining the discourses and effects of creativity with a critical lens but also by seeking to reframe craft to open pathways for those who may not see themselves or their writings as creative. I hope to relay and amplify the creative urge as it responds to our contexts and as it builds our crafts anew. Thinking in brown crafts resists creativity as a category that brown authors must earn first through experiencing personal tragedy, then by investing incalculable amounts of time in struggle, reflection, and hyperproduction. Yet to categorize our acts as creative is not something granted to us by either a higher power or ourselves. Rather, our brown crafts can serve as everyday forms of conceptual survival, of time-capsuling our own understandings of our eras and ways of being from our own marginalized, brown perspectives, but not necessarily as marginalized and brown perspectives. Though these crafts are survival rafts, they are also not necessarily made to float us toward the white, progressive, capitalist utopias, but to drift to other, wayward isles. Thus, our crafts are not just toward the future but are also a form of bereavement, of building memory through words, where, as Sandra Ruiz writes, "difference always evolves [and] mourning also becomes something other in movement."[8] To put it in the words of brown theory, brown craft making depicts brown masses not to separate "us" from "them" but to evade imperial domestication. The brown crafts sail us away from those seeking to incorporate us; they reveal and revel in our shades of brown. They may indeed resist, challenge, or otherwise respond to oppressions and traumas, but this is only one of their features, one tethered to the cultural/capital value cast on them. Because brown crafts are not mere responses to white oppression, they are often invisible to the larger reading world and are rarely even classified as creative (and even more rarely as successful). There are a multitude of ways these crafts transport us, usher us along the tides of our desires and our contexts, to a planned but ultimately unknowable destination.

On Craft

Though craft is often claimed to be apolitical or "noncommitted writing," craft today follows literary analysis as a process of revelation: It is about deep truths; it is about exposing hidden desires and psychological depths through form, style, or subtext.[9] Like an expert craftsperson, the writer creates a chair not just to have a place to sit but to build something strong and sturdy, something that will stand the test of time. Though these notions of craft emerged when literature in the West was routinely seen through binaries of artistic/political, universal/particular, committed/noncommitted, today the art of writing has congealed to see literature simultaneously as time-tested art and as exposés for the truths of our social world, and the truths of our minds. I too have sought to reveal such depths in my writing, though this has been but one stray—and what Eve Kosofsky Sedgwick might call paranoid—component of my work.[10] Following Sedgwick, perhaps we can ask how the desire for literature as exposure, whether social or psychological, often erases the power dynamics of the literary industry and those between author and reader. When we consider a text written by a marginalized artist read by audiences who do not share the artist's communities, what exactly does the audience want to see exposed, and under what conditions was such an exposure produced? What

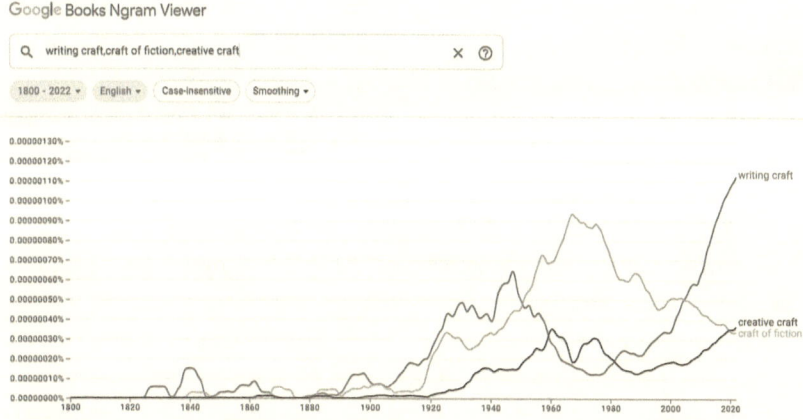

FIGURE 5.1. The search results for "writing craft," "craft of fiction," and "creative craft." Google Books Ngram Viewer, 2023.

must be revealed about the writer and their communities that will satisfy the readers, editors, agents, and award committees?

The term *craft* is commonly associated with the turn away from forms of committed, political, or responsive writing affiliated with leftist writers (and muckrakers) in the late 1800s and early 1900s. Sinclair Lewis, one of the most famous authors of this period and the first American to win the Nobel Prize in Literature in 1930, shares a tipping point away from both the age of leftist political writing and the Harlem Renaissance. As we see in simple charts from Google Books Ngram Viewer, the turn against politicized writing also took place around the time that *craft* emerged not just to think of the craft of building but to discuss the art of creative writing (figure 5.1).

Perhaps the most well-known early use of *craft* in terms of writing was in Percy Lubbock's 1921 book, *The Craft of Fiction*. Lubbock's book was not a writing guide for fiction authors but a collection of literary criticism focusing on Leo Tolstoy, Charles Dickens, and Henry James, essentially arguing, as Mark McGurl writes, that "narrative perspective has profound aesthetic consequences."[11] The aesthetic framework of craft helped lead to what McGurl influentially called "the Program Era," when, after the Harlem Renaissance and the Red Scare, and during the ideological battles of the Cold War, creative writers began to concentrate more on form, style, and craft, as a way to distinguish their work as innovative and creative, while authors of color, leftists, and communists in countries like Russia (which Lubbock's book initially praised in 1921) were deemed too realist, political, or merely ideological. We see examples of this today, as when the speculative fiction author N. K. Jemisin was awarded her third consecutive Hugo Award for her *Broken Earth* series and argued in her acceptance speech against the divide of craft and politics, calling out her naysayers who believed that "when they win it's meritocracy, but when we win it's 'identity politics.'"[12]

While creativity can sometimes seem like the abstract work of thinkers and intellectuals, creative writing programs, as Viet Thanh Nguyen wrote in the *New York Times*, have attempted to invoke "the nobility of craftsmanship, physical (not intellectual) labor—and masculinity."[13] Mark McGurl's *The Program Era* (2009) was one of the first major studies to show through historical evidence that "the rise of the creative writing program stands as the most important event in postwar American literary history."[14] *The Program Era* spawned the discipline of program studies: scholarship that compares the institutionalized master of fine arts (MFA) to other literary cultures and follows the imperial outreach of MFA programs to understand how their forms of craft aesthetics have served to deradicalize insurgent literary forms.[15] Eric Bennett's 2015 book *Workshops of Empire* examines how MFA programs emerged during the Cold War to institutionalize creativity in ways that degraded political writing, aggrandized the new Pax Americana, and gained funding from bankers and oil tycoons like the Rockefellers. As Bennett argues, "The institutions of the Cold War—meaning the brokers of power and signatories of checks outside the university—played a larger role in the institutionalization of creative writing than any one poet, novelist, or professor did."[16] During the Cold War, MFA workshops worked to demobilize the growing threat of anti-imperial collective action on US college campuses by domesticating creative thinking with seemingly timeless proverbs: to "write what you know," to "make it new," to "show, not tell," to "find your voice," and to write as sparingly and as masculinely as Ernest Hemingway and Raymond Carver. As Monica Popescu has also argued, in Africa, Europe, and parts of the Middle East, literary projects funded by the Central Intelligence Agency (CIA), like the Congress for Cultural Freedom and its associated African and Oriental studies programs, promoted abstract expressionism as an artistic model across the globe as the accepted way to express creative freedom, while high modernism and later postmodernism became the literary form of freedom writing.[17]

Globally, scholars in the Philippines, Taiwan, and Hong Kong, and writers of color in the United States, have shown that the universalization of craft-based aesthetics has, over time, included people of color only to deny their interiorization (Cathy Park Hong), to devalue politically engaged and com-

mitted fiction in colonized spaces (Conchitina Cruz), to promote the appropriation of nonwhite stories while reducing minority writers to single ethnic
narratives (Junot Díaz, Viet Thanh Nguyen), to replicate the racializations of
China and Chinese as political and cultural others (Yi-hung Liu), and to become a way for white middle/lower-class writers to self-marginalize without
remaining committed to a political cause (Elif Batuman, Fredric Jameson).[18]
In Asia, workshop aesthetics were weaponized through the CIA's Congress for
Cultural Freedom, the Asia Foundation, and many of the literary festivals and
award systems still in place across the world today.[19] As Conchitina Cruz has
shown, the students trained in these workshops often went on to create writing
programs in other places, like the University of the Philippines (UP) National
Writers Workshop, whose leaders spotlighted "the primacy of craft . . . as a
catchall explanation for the lack of emphasis on social consciousness."[20] These
English-language and CIA-sponsored creative writing programs can be traced
back to educational experiments in the Philippines, which, as Paul Nadal has
argued, attempted to keep Filipino intellectuals within the cultural and imperial orbit of the United States by creating "a hedge against its former colony's
nascent isolationism."[21] As these researchers and writers have shown, "craft"
was rarely just a way of producing "good writing" but rather sought to define
good writing as featuring what Fredric Jameson has called a political form of
"restraint."[22] So too it shaped the (white) Western author as creative, and the
rest as merely propagandic, autobiographical, or plagiarizing.

To view writing as a craft on the seas rather than the act of crafting helps
us understand the vast and continuous inequalities of massive institutions
like the literary industry—to see works as crafts that are in collaboration
with multiple editors, agents, publishers, and the presumed middlebrow and
often majority-white audience. In this way, books by marginalized authors
are not pure statements of authorial or cultural authenticity but are the crafts
of lifeboats, floatation devices made to transport on the rough tides of racial
inequality. As Richard So has shown through mass data collection, from 1950
to 2000, during the height of multiculturalism and the so-called ethnic literature turn, the racial demographics of the mainstream US literary industry as a
whole hardly changed at all. Its authors remained 97 percent white, recipients
of book prizes remained 91 percent white, and writers of bestseller novels remained 98 percent white.[23] So writes that part of this unbreakable racial hegemony was due to big publishers tokenizing their popular writers of color,
like Toni Morrison, and then literary educators running with this narrative to
mark all of literature as diverse. Random House's authors, despite Morrison,
remained 97 percent white for fifty years, though we can discern a slight blip

TABLE 5.1. US Novelists, 1950–2000.

Race of author	Publishing (%)	Book reviews (%)	Bestsellers (%)	Book prizes (%)
White	97	90	98	91
Black	2	6	0.5	5
POC	1	4	1.3	4

Source: So, *Redlining Culture*, 4.
Note: Percentage of novelists by racial identity (white, Black, and person of color [POC]—Asian American, Latinx, and Native American) in four contexts: mainstream publishing as represented by Random House, US book reviews, US bestsellers, and US prizewinners between 1950 and 2000.

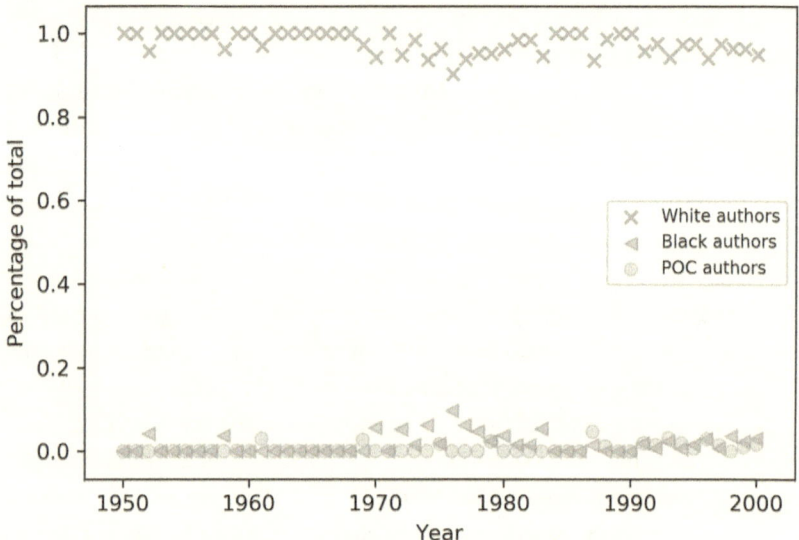

FIGURE 5.2. Race and publishing over time. From So, *Redlining Culture*, 3.

when Morrison joined the editorial staff from 1967 to 1983 (see table 5.1 and figure 5.2).

Besides the literary industry, the other cause of what was known over social media in 2020 as #publishingsowhite has been literary educators presuming that there had been "cultural wars" or "canon wars" that successfully diversified literature. However, as So proves, this never happened except within some academic institutions. Rather, mainstream literature has not strayed much from the white hegemony it was associated with in the 1950s. In fact, So argues that the easy celebration of the supposed multicultural turn in literature can actually impede the work of activist organizations like Kundiman or Voices of Our Nation and the many other small presses in North America that attempt to create a more equitable literary culture. To rectify this, So asks educators to stop seeing multiculturalism in mainstream literature as a given sea change but to instead regard it as a marked failure whose promises did not result in much more than tokenization and the heightening of the literary industry as well as of North American multiculturalism during the Cold War and later the war on terror—wars fought against supposedly monocultural others.[24] Though So focuses on the top five (now top four) literary houses, studies of the US literary industry have shown that even if we move away from mainstream publishing and account for trade publishers, review journals, literary agencies, and university presses, publishing in the United States as a whole has since 2000 remained anywhere from 75 to 80 percent white identified, with editors remaining 85 percent white, and book reviewers and agents 80 percent white.[25] Even more telling is that the main diversity in the industry comes not from writers but from interns, many of whom are unpaid, and about half of whom are people of color. As for the books themselves, even as recently as 2018 only 11 percent of mainstream books were written by nonwhite writers.[26] While literary educators could certainly do better in how they historicize multiculturalism as a failure rather than a success story, creative writing programs too replicate this narrative by either ignoring the inequalities of the industry or, worse, pretending as if literature is a comfortable or even ideal industry for writers of color.

As Andrea Canaan wrote in *This Bridge Called My Back*, "Part of our victimization is self-oppression. Our adaptations were creative, the end goal, survival."[27] Canaan writes of the creative works of mixed-race Black cultures in the US South, where the humor and parody that targeted white people also compelled Black audiences to revere brown or light-skinned Black men. Yet even within these creative acts of adaptation and survival, there remained "an insidious[,] terrifying, self-negating desire—even need—to be white."[28] For Canaan, to truly be creative one had to break from the "isolated categories" of self-oppression that reduced marginalized people to demographic data and stereotypes, "brownness and whiteness, maleness and femaleness."[29] Speaking as a brown author myself who deliberately takes on "Asian Americanness" as an identity signifier (though I am mixed Chinese/Filipino/white, though I haven't lived in "America" since 2013), I feel Canaan's words causing me to wonder how the promise of the literary—of becoming a creative author—is, in the end, my own way of creatively disavowing my desire for whiteness. Are these two forms of creativity—one of adaptation and survival, the other of boundary breaking and liberation—even distinguishable? To what extent does the desire to write in a way that is creative, boundless, and liberating also speak to forms of self-oppression and self-hate?

The traditional narrative of craft is one of domestication, one that, for marginalized authors, casts proximity to whiteness as its end goal, a goal that can be achieved by offering one's intimate stories, so they may be "plucked out" of the brown mass. At the same time, for white authors, craft has a redeeming, liberating effect, as it offers a means of reinstating authority over universal themes like climate/environment, emerging technology, or postmodern and innovative writing styles. As Fredric Jameson points out in his response to *The Program Era*, the "dirty little secret" of the impact of writing programs has altogether been part of an anti-intellectual trend in US literary cultures compared to those in other nations.[30] The aesthetics of workshops, which McGurl saw as individualistic and self-oriented ("autopoetics"), Jameson sees as an aesthetics of shame—shame in being an artist within an intellectual institution, shame in being white and telling stories of marginalization and of being othered. For the author Elif Batuman, craft has functioned to resolve the shame of white writers who feel they have nothing to write about, so they may pursue authorship as a form of universal (read: colonial) authority.[31] Craft solves this sense of shame by allowing budding white authors to identify their writing with lower-class forms of craftmanship like welding or woodwork, or even the crafts making of so-called women's arts. As Batuman writes, "Shame explains the cult of persecutedness, a strategy designed to legitimize literary production as social advocacy, and make White People feel better (Stuff White People Like #21: Writers' Workshops)."[32] Craft thus resolves the multicultural crisis in creative writing by allowing the white writer who can afford the sometimes exorbitant fees of an MFA program to disavow the costs, privilege, elitism, and whiteness of MFA programs in general.

To be clear, I am not saying that so-called white writers should feel a sense of shame, or that any author has nothing to say, but that these are the social anxieties and affects that structure the supposedly multicultural system of creative writing, where craft has presented a way to resolve such anxieties. As a generalization, craft says that writing centers are not places for stuffy, leftist, or woke intellectual theorizations but are spaces of labor within a material workforce of woodsmen, welders, and of course craft beer. Craft has thus remained a means of denying the racial inequalities of mainstream literature by saying that "we too are minority-like and racially adjacent," or, as Joyce Carol Oates puts it when describing walking through a Black neighborhood, "Like me they are outcasts in this country. Not like me: they are true outcasts."[33]

On Brown Craft

Life's momentum often mirrors art and art's momentum parallels life. These are the very stages of the everyday as the everyday is always staged. —SANDRA RUIZ AND HYPATIA VOURLOUMIS, *Formless Formation*

Today many writers of color have become critical of MFA programs and of craft in general. Critiques have ranged from Junot Díaz's 2014 "MFA vs. POC" article in the *New Yorker* to similar works by Viet Thanh Nguyen, Nam Le, Cathy Park Hong, and many others, like the Palestinian American poet Noor Hindi and her poem "Fuck Your Lecture on Craft, My People Are Dying." One phenomenon that we can attribute to the tokenization and surface multiculturalism of craft is that readers casually see white authors as writing about the universal, and marginalized authors as writing about themselves (their own marginalization), which is meant to bring not shame but pride. This can be tracked in how the bestselling books by writers of color since the 2020 resurgence of the Black Lives Matter movement have aligned with the already-peaked popularity of memoir and autobiography to create what Melissa Phruksachart has called "The Literature of White Liberalism," that is, the memoirs of a "self-reflective, emotionally regulated white (or white-adjacent) antiracist person who can be incorporated into US political modernity."[34] Whereas white liberalism once functioned through novels like *The Help* and other white or white-adjacent depictions of people of color, the new white liberalism "eschews the novel and coheres around the genres of nonfiction, autobiography, and self-help."[35]

Of course, the lineage of ethnic autobiography tells a vastly different story, where classics like Maxine Hong Kingston's *The Woman Warrior*, *The Autobiography of Malcolm X*, the works of *This Bridge Called My Back*, and nineteenth-century slave narratives have long proven to be politically resistant, deeply reparative, and undeniably creative. The problem in the literature of white liberalism is in both how these texts are written (through the expectations and standards of craft) and how they are read, marketed, and edited to elicit what I briefly referred to earlier as (paranoid) exposure or cultural authenticity. This is what the scholar Betsy Huang has called the "autobiographic imperative" that casts "all Asian American fiction as forms of life writing," and has kept in place an atmosphere where budding writers of color are expected to produce art catering to editors, agents, and white audiences, all of whom may not understand the artists' experiences of racial embodiment or who otherwise pressure the artist to speak from an anthropological point of view about themselves and their cultural background and, worse, their own psyche.[36] As Y-Dang Troeung has argued, "The normalising of the ethnic autobiography in American ethnic literature comes from a history of exclusion, wartime violence, and colonisation," and many mainstream forms of (even fictionalized) life writing provide "a fantasy of authenticity and allow[] us to forget that even the deepest forays into one's backstory are often written through the American arts of compromise and self-invention."[37] For Troeung, Southeast Asian refugee authors like herself whose stories both enabled and conditioned their arrival in host countries reveal the similarities of desire and pain in forms of refugee performance, testimonial, interrogation, forced confession, and mainstream literary authorship.

To be clear, I don't mean to dismiss the importance of movements like #ownvoices and #publishingsowhite but to show how the writings of white liberalism have been drawn from the separation of craft and politics, and to trace the ways that craft has calcified textual expectations so that the so-called diversity of literature is not even located within fiction anymore but within how-to guides and memoirs that are presumed—again, regardless of how they're written—as direct gateways into the authentic lives of others. As Cathy Park Hong has argued, these presumptions about books by racialized authors represent a "stay in your lane politics" that "reduces racial identity to intellectual property."[38] Of course, many writers of the self defy this tradition, such as Claudia Rankine, Saidiya Hartman, Christina Sharpe, Sandra Ruiz, Cathy Park Hong, Ocean Vuong, Y-Dang Troeung, and others, yet these writers explicitly seek to resist mainstream memoir as a form. Vuong, for example, published his so-called memoir as a novel, *On Earth We're Briefly Gorgeous*, even after two of its chapters were originally published as autobiographies in the *New Yorker*.[39] We see this continued "reality hunger," as David Shields has called it, in the acknowledgments pages of memoirs written by women of color where an agent or editor is named as the person who first insisted that the author write the memoir (see, for example, Jesmyn Ward's memoir, *Men We Reaped*).[40] Following authors whose memoirs seek to critique memoir itself, I hope this reanimation of craft as a ferrying floatation allows us to move away from these traditional ways of seeing the craft of writing, to otherwise see our own empowerment empire and the gutter guards of creativity that understand race and capitalist critique through personal narratives that may be artistic, creative, and imaginative but are too rarely read or marketed as such. For many writers, this desire to stay in our lanes can also keep us from realizing that we're all still driving toward the same national utopia: to socioeconomic success, to the erasing of the inequalities of our industries, to the end of the film when the oppressed figure finds justice not in realizing political or social change but in publishing their story with a mainstream press.

If craft is about movement, it is about, in a sense, getting out. As Toni Morrison once said, her love for writing is propelled by movement, "because otherwise I'm stuck with life."[41] As Adrienne Maree Brown writes of imagination, "I often feel I am trapped inside someone else's imagination, and I must engage my own imagination in order to break free. . . . The more people that collaborate on that ideation, the more that people will be served by the resulting world(s)."[42] So too I see craft making as a form of getting out not as an individual but as an artist in community and in collaboration with others, a form of "worldmaking," which Dorinne Kondo describes as the collaborative and productive processes of race and identity making that "evoke[] sociopolitical transformation and the impossibility of escaping power, history, and culture."[43] Worlds, like genres, are imagined within communities as sets of norms and conventions yet can be remade so long as they "always work with this givenness."[44] If genres are world makers, then these worlds are responding to and refracting the "real-world" genres of race, class, sexuality, gender, nation, and so on. For Sylvia Wynter and Alexander Weheliye, white supremacy has been inescapable due to the overarching standard of whiteness within "different genres of the human," where white subjects are seen as more human than others.[45] Worldmaking is thus a collaborative and interactive process that can offer reparative responses to the "genre of man" by inviting audiences to take part in remaking their already genre-based worlds.[46] As Kondo stresses, in a world structured by race, worldmaking allows us to trace "the production of race—racialized structures of inequality, racialized labor, the racialized aesthetics of genre, racialized subjectivities, racial affect." Creative worldmaking, in other words, is not only about making an alternative space for a particular group but also about "making and unmaking race."[47]

This chapter's second half reframes my own brown crafts, made as both a scholar and an artist, to generate a "creative brown triptych," one that creatively refracts the triptych from this book's introduction by following alongside brownness within forms of creative work, such as inspiration, travel, love, feeling, and community. This creative brown triptych is:

feeling stamped / brown power \ self-referencing

"Feeling stamped": feelings of needing to perform elements of the brown mass as they are conceived from one context to another; "brown power": the forms of empowerment and worldmaking that are often within a subimperial frame of domestication that reproduces imperial violence onto other marginalized and brown peoples; "self-referencing": understanding our own ways of seeing and being not through a single author or even through our selves but through multiple shades of creative expression, the various ways we see "selves" scattered throughout the world and the ways we seek to express them in our work.

Unlike the first triptych, these terms are not ways of analyzing or flowing alongside brownness so much as tools for making brown crafts, for pushing us toward creative action within our own contexts. These terms can thus be understood as "repertoires," which Diana Taylor conceived of as "embodied memory: performances, gestures, orality, movement, dance, singing—in short, all those acts usually thought of as ephemeral, non-reproducible knowledge."[48] While some scholars like Theodore Gonzalves have reconceived of repertoires in contexts of teaching and activism, for writers such embodied memory is also expressed in the ways we understand genres and forms (as academic, social realist, poetic, etc.), in the way we shape characters or peoples, in the way we write from our own interior monologues, in our sense of plot and style, and through the unconscious habits that recognize what does and doesn't flow.[49] In other words, our repertoires are the gamut of embodied experiences as readers, scholars, and peoples that we have "practiced and tested over time," which are imbricated with our contexts—the people we meet, our daily career habits, the events on the morning news that day. These repertoires also reveal how so many of our habits come from whiteness, empire, and ableist notions of body and excellence. Repertoires can thus lead us to—as Mel Chen, Alison Kafer, Eunjung Kim, and Julie Avril Minich argue—"an installation of new habits, ones that refuse the laws of coherence in order to make more pathways for present and future work."[50] While I previously called the pieces of brown theory in the introduction shards (following José Esteban Muñoz), here I use the term *repertoire* to follow how these terms express embodied knowledges that are difficult to trace within physical and published archives (and in this case can only be written about in retrospect by the author).

If we imagine our craft as a floating vessel, we should also understand that we are already using our imaginations to do so. We are, already, practicing the purpose of poetry for Audre Lorde, whose first reason for writing was "my need to say things I couldn't say otherwise when I couldn't find other poems to serve."[51] The vessels we build are articulations of our expressions that do not follow the rules of language that publishing industries, critics, scholars, imperial apparatuses, the CIA, or mainstream audiences can expect or even comprehend. Mel Chen calls such creative thinkers "animate theorists," a "term for creative language users" who work within the constraints of language and grammar to "enliven and animate" given terms.[52] In the next section, I present my own work within the triptych of brown crafts, as moments in my life where writing served to explore an open ocean, to respond to a particular climate or context, to migrate, to transition, to ferry from one context, and one self, to another.

"Feeling Stamped": *Stamped* and *Transitive Cultures* (2018)

In my first year as an undergraduate at the Community College of Southern Nevada, I embarked on the creative path, joining writing workshops and seeking mentors. But I quickly began to feel out of place. I couldn't place why, until during a workshop at the University of Nevada, Las Vegas, our class read George Orwell's classic "Shooting an Elephant" as an example of ideal craft-based writing. The story, written in 1936 and set in Burma when it was a British colony, takes on the voice of a British policeman who was "all for the Burmese and all against their oppressors, the British."[53] I have never forgotten this story's end, its prevailing insight that "every white man's life in the East was one long struggle not to be laughed at."[54] But my fellow students and instructor only sought to understand the story as an example of craft: how the elephant turned from an "it" to a "he"; how he operated as an analogue to the people of Burma. To me, these formal attributes weren't half as interesting as the forms of race and empire that the story distilled so visibly for Orwell's audience. Was it possible, I wondered, to contain such a private life of doubt, even as a soldier within a violent and racist empire? Isn't this story about all of us in this room? When I tried to discuss these points, I was criticized for not reading like an artist, and told that I was too taken in by the political realm that just so happened to make up the background of the story. I was making the mistake of viewing the story through my heritage as a mixed-race Filipino and descendant of colonial subjects (I was also one of only two people of color in that workshop). I thus found myself in the same situation described by Junot Díaz when he was enrolled in the Cornell MFA: "We never talked about race except on the rare occasion someone wanted to argue that 'race discussions' were exactly the discussion a serious writer should not be having."[55]

Offput by MFA writing courses and agog to see the world, I scuttled my plans for an MFA, graduated with a BA in English, and took the path of travel, holding dear to the notion that it was more important to have something to say than to discipline myself into saying it well. For five months in the summer of 2006, I wandered North America, hitchhiking, ride-sharing, couch surfing, hosteling, and seeking out strange encounters. Then, in 2007, I spent nearly a year teaching English in South Korea and then spent my graduate school summers from 2007 to 2013 maxing out my credit cards by flitting briefly from country to country—Japan, China, the Philippines, Indonesia, Malaysia, India, and others—before settling to live for two years in Nanjing, China, and for two and a half more in Hong Kong.

While away from North America, I wrote a wealth of fevered prose about wanderlusting around Asia while teaching and researching at the University of Washington, where I specialized in Asian American studies and literatures concerning empire, race, and travel. What came forth was my debut novel, *Stamped: an anti-travel novel*, which was written mostly in 2007 and 2008 but went through a decade of submission and revision until it was published in 2018. *Stamped* is the blurred product of my frequent travel excursions and time spent living in Asia, as well as my academic research, which manifested in my first academic book, *Transitive Cultures: Anglophone Literature of the Transpacific*. Written over the same ten-year period, both books were formed through a set of wayward travel experiences within the cultural mosaics of Asian cities and asked similar questions about how movement in Asia could disrupt North American views of race and identity. Both these academic and prose works explored how undirected and sporadic forms of travel emerged within global multicultural settings that encouraged travelers to parrot colonial attitudes (or colonized subjectivities) while getting high on exotic local trappings.

I began writing both *Stamped* and *Transitive Cultures* in 2008, when I first visited Bangkok and ended up taking the typical Banana Pancake tour from Thailand through Laos, Vietnam, and Cambodia. The trip was a political coming-of-age. I was twenty-two, fresh from my first year in graduate school, where I was beginning to specialize in Asian American studies and literatures concerning empire, racism, and travel. Being in Southeast Asia for months at a time gave palpable presence to histories of bombing, war, and colonization. At the same time, a recession and unprecedented presidential election in the United States flashed on the television screens of every sleazy expat bar I visited. All of this I wanted to bring back with me, to let spring whatever work could emerge, and to create disruptions in places complicit in, but largely unaffected by, the violences across the sea. The opening lines of *Stamped* follow this vision:

> The plan is to travel until the pain runs you over. But Bangkok was the worst place to start. It's just too easy here, in the land of smiles. Instead of a long, pathetic decay, you find food so cheap you couldn't possibly starve. People so beautiful you couldn't possibly be lonely. A police-force strictly for foreigners. A hotel room for seven dollars. Cheap massages that taunt your hopes of perishing in a blaze of hardcore travel glory.

And because you are as brown as the fried cricket snacks that tantalize every street stall, you get to stroll into historic temples through the locals-only line. You can slide into an American coffee shop and shoot the breeze with ladyboys about their foreigner clients. You laugh at them, the white men, calling them big, hairy gorillas. Here, the rules of the game have changed. Your race card has turned wild.[56]

In the above paragraph, written in haste at a crowded air-conditioned bar in the Khao San backpacker district, forms of brownness emerge both explicitly ("you are as brown as the fried cricket snacks") and implicitly in the ways I give a somewhat naive trust to the reader with linguistic risks that speak to the shades of brown I had grown up with and found throughout my time in Asia: the somewhat unconscious choice to situate suicidal ideation ("until the pain runs you over") alongside sex work ("people so beautiful"), spaces of worship ("temples"), potentially offensive language ("ladyboys," "big, hairy gorillas"), and an awareness of brown performativity ("Your race card has turned wild"). Looking back on this paragraph seventeen years after I wrote it, all of this signals attention to brown audiences. This could also partly explain why the book, after nearly a decade of failed submissions, found a receptive editor only in a brown woman who happened to acquire books for a micropress (Westphalia, a small imprint of an academic publisher).[57] Today, with a few years of experience in the North American publishing industry, I immediately see this paragraph for its many red flags that, for white and established editors at the time, must have rendered the entire novel unpublishable.

With *Stamped*, I sought to unearth the lived experiences of minority, queer, and poor youth who find their homespun identities unspooling when they attempt to settle elsewhere. The novel is about people looking through playful mirrors—seeing themselves, then being unable to account for the violence that emerges from the twisted funhouse of constant movement. Resolving never to go back to America, the characters weave through the afterlives of colonial histories: the Cambodian genocide, the Philippine-American War, and the many military bases throughout the Pacific. One of the central focuses of the book is confrontation, and the anger that follows. Anger, as Audre Lorde wrote, should not be feared but should be something we learn to deal with, to orchestrate from cacophony into symphony, "so that [those furies] do not tear us apart."[58] While writing *Stamped*, I wanted to explore how the anger that manifests from travel can be reshaped by galvanizing forces but can also be domesticated through ready-made narratives: local nationalist propaganda, the tourist industry, internalized imperial attitudes. These forces turn anger from discordance into anthem, shifting the blame by trumpeting a gruesome chorus of self-hate, racism, and dispossession. Anyone is susceptible to this, even *Stamped*'s cadre of frequently sloshed queer, Black, and POC travelers who act on Asia with whatever privilege they afford, chasing their own ends until they are undone by the road. How does one get out of this chronic mess? What risks does one need to take? What comes with the loss of an identity that has, time and again, made and remade the self?

In *Transitive Cultures* I would call the global forces of state and institutional identity making "pluralist governmentality," an art of government that expects individuals to visibly and transparently express their difference via given group identities and, in doing so, to represent imperial state power as neutral, universal, and benevolent. While *Stamped* was the result of my decade-long desire to depict colonial confrontation by forgoing the elements of craft and minimalism as a universal aesthetics (one reviewer called the book "maximalist"), its core sources of anger and frustration were heavily informed by critical race studies and my desire to theorize my own racial embodiment alongside other marginalized travelers I had met. Only in retrospect did I see the book's title and main thematic, "stamped," as forming a nexus of the travel/racial experience, one that would be captured in those opening lines, "your race card has turned wild." In my academic work, I would reframe this feeling into theory by reanimating the term *transitive cultures* to refer to processes of unceasing ethnic and cultural transitions that shift with every new context—processes that "can be controlled, reimagined, and, with enough savvy, made pleasurable."[59]

Both *Transitive Cultures* and *Stamped* saw brown movement in brown migratory and diasporic authors within brown spaces (Southeast Asian diasporic peoples writing in Southeast Asia and Oceania). These browned travelers moved not for the pleasures of the grand tour but within intellectual and social exile, as Edward Said defines it, as a "state of never being fully adjusted . . . [of] tending to avoid and even dislike the trappings of accommodation and national well-being. Exile for the intellectual in this metaphysical sense is restlessness, movement, constantly being unsettled, and unsettling others."[60] For me as a young brown writer living in North America, claiming racial identities often felt like living in a dust-layered filter that only let through the most sanitized ways of being. The limitless plurality of possible selves, our shades of brown, felt always reduced to a few. But when I traveled, racial being proliferated, turned to strangeness, to the unknown. The constraints of racial otherness remained, yet no longer was I pinned to the same set of familiar types. *Transitive Cultures* and *Stamped* both sought to spotlight practices of brown transition that occur in travel: the way changing, shifting, and renaming occurs through migrancy and strategic planning, so that what appears inauthentic does not also appear apolitical. In *Transitive Cultures* I called texts that do this *transpacific anglophone texts*, using the term *anglophone* to account for marginalized literary traditions within the United States as well as in Asia that do not fit easily into the multiculturalist spectrum but are seen as foreign, corrupted, or inauthentic.

The shared impulse behind both *Stamped* and *Transitive Cultures* was an anger aiming at forms of pluralist governmentality, or what I call in this brown triptych "feeling stamped": the ways of feeling the racial and colonial structures of global racial capitalism while within brown movement. As these feelings so often emerge in our art practices, I casually repurpose the title of *Stamped* here to consider authorship within creative and academic industries that promote marginalized writers as stamps who (1) authenticate the industry and institution as liberal and multicultural; (2) flatten authors and their works; and (3) provide readers access across racial borders that seem natural but have in fact been imposed by such industries and institutions themselves. To feel stamped is to feel flattened, stomped on by a modern colossus crushing anything in its path. The desire for knowledge and travel that compelled me to live in Asia was stamped too with my desire to leave behind an Asian American identity that I felt had become one-dimensional. And yet to be stamped was also to have access. The same stamp that was created through flattening one's identity also enabled mobility, and some amount of privilege and access. The very things one tries to escape—the apparatus validating the stamp—also provides inclusion into new spaces.

For me as a writer, my anger against MFA programs was partly a reaction to feeling stamped when I wrote under either my patriarchal name, Christopher B. Patterson, or my matriarchal name, Kawika Guillermo. These names led editors to pin my writing into categories of white or ethnic, universal or particular, which I spent many stories and articles trying to resist (my fiction as Kawika Guillermo was often about white travelers, racists, and Nazis, while my articles as Christopher B. Patterson were about racial capitalist resistance in literatures by writers of color). My separate names too presented a form of brown movement that revealed structures of racism as well as my own feelings of being stamped within them. Writing fiction for me thus never resembled a freedom associated with sparse, ambivalent prose but was a way to account for my own responsibility as an English-speaking lighter-skinned brown Filipino American with the privilege to travel and a close proximity to intellectual power. The brown craft of *Stamped* and *Transitive Cultures* responded to the structural affect of feeling stamped by attempting to s(t)imulate the act of seeing, of bearing witness to the atrocities of the past, and of recognizing the reach of empire. As Arundhati Roy writes, "The trouble is that once you see it, you can't unsee it. And once you've seen it, keeping quiet, saying nothing, becomes as political an act as speaking out. There's no innocence. Either way, you're accountable."[61] These curiosities concerning power, art, and accountability, even from authors who feel marginalized, alienated, and ashamed, would grow in my next two writing projects, which would consider the ways that seemingly marginalized peoples enact imperial power onto those whom they have never met, and those whom they love.

Brown Power: All Flowers Bloom and
Open World Empire (2020)

Whereas my first two books, *Stamped* and *Transitive Cultures*, both sought to follow alongside brown migration, excursion, and travel, my second pair of books, *All Flowers Bloom* and *Open World Empire*, published within one month of each other, considered brown movement over narratives of history, emerging technology, and transitions bound by love and erotics.

Both *All Flowers Bloom* and *Open World Empire* were primarily written from 2014 to 2018 in Nanjing and Hong Kong, when I taught creative writing and literary/games courses situated at the intersections of intellectual rigor and creative freedom. After the near decade of failures trying to publish *Stamped*, my own feelings on workshop methods and American literary cultures were, to be blunt, antagonistic. I found that my writing, which had always playfully and often unconsciously crossed genre (as well as gendered and racial) lines, could foster much more outside of the traditionally gatekept fields of either Asia studies (as in *Transitive Cultures*) or mainstream social realist literature (as in *Stamped*). I found more flexible writing styles in reading communities that were fairly new and experimental (game studies) or that took on "genre defiance" as one of their main attributes (speculative fiction). Concerning the latter, I was inspired by authors like Ken Liu, who, like many speculative fiction writers, has criticized the writing norms of the MFA workshop as presumptive of the shared experiences of white and European/North American experiences. "To write from resistance," Liu wrote in a tweet, "telling is sometimes far superior [to showing]. 'Showing' is great when you're relying on a shared, implicit understanding."[62] Guided by Liu and the speculative fiction of Ursula Le Guin, Octavia Butler, and Filipino speculative fiction authors gathered in anthologies by Charles Tan, Mia Tijam, Dean Francis Alfar, and Joseph Frederic Nacino, my role as both an Asian American author and a critical scholar living in Asia allowed me to fashion my antagonism into an iconoclasm, giving myself free rein to criticize an industry that was and remains overwhelmingly North American and white.[63] Living in Asia and believing, at the time, that I was to live there permanently, I presumed my readers would always be those nearest to me: my colleagues, my students, my audiences in conferences and writing groups, almost none of whom were white or North American. The publishing industries felt far away, and questions of how normative audiences—white, middle class, middlebrow—might react to my work were of little concern. As a teacher, I taught books that weren't manufactured through big publishing and urged students not to see their own value as writers through the lens of an industry whose aesthetic norms might only seek to gentrify or exploit their stories. As physical books from North America or Europe were hard to get a hold of (and students could hardly afford them anyway), I promoted digitized and other free forms of literary artwork that marginalized people were creating every day, from electronic literature, to punk DIY literary movements, to art anthologies by migrant domestic workers, which all circulated online in the forms of e-zines and independent literary magazines.[64]

For my students in Hong Kong, their most influential role models were not the Saint Hemingway and Saint Carver of craft minimalism, nor were they the magical realist aesthetics that Ramón Saldívar has quite convincingly argued were dialectically opposed to the workshop methods.[65] The creative works that my students most appreciated were those built on the politically charged context in Hong Kong after the 2014 Umbrella Movement, during the 2016 Fishball Revolution, and before the 2019 occupation of college campuses (see chapter 4 for more on these protests). In this highly politicized atmosphere, the craft methods of the workshop were no longer received as universal styles but as American imperial imports associated with white and English-language authors. Close reading and close attention to form were also seen as a handover from colonial education, and their universalism was persistently questioned as either colonial or bourgeois. More illuminating for me was many of my students' belief that literary fiction was far less interesting than the more overt political allegories of science fiction, fantasy, and young adult novels. Even the fidelity to the language of English, which, as Conchitina Cruz argues, has been one of the most clear-cut colonial remnants of the MFA workshop, was under suspicion.[66] With only moderate encouragement from me, students dared to set the English language adrift, playing with language through pidgins, accents, and hybrid forms.[67]

Though it was entirely coincidental that my first two books were published in the same year, I was more intentional in the dual publications of *All Flowers*

Bloom and *Open World Empire*, as I found that both writing forms (academic, creative) could be drawn out of the same impulses, the same feelings, the same questions, the same craft. I found inspiration in Virginia Woolf's *A Room of One's Own* (1929), a book based on lectures she gave in October 1928, published the very same month that Woolf also published her queer speculative novel, *Orlando*. Both *Room* and *Orlando* feel eerily similar in their distrust of traditional writing and publication industries, as well as in their desires to imagine writing differently. In *Room*, Woolf famously defined fiction as "imaginative work" that is "not dropped like a pebble upon the ground . . . but [is] the work of suffering human beings, and [is] attached to grossly material things, like health and money and the houses we live in."[68] This treatise on writing was written alongside her tall tale of the queer yet still imperial poet Orlando, who throughout *Orlando* defies gender roles while also reiterating orientalist writing tropes. All the while, *Orlando* itself ruptures genre expectations (it is subtitled "a biography" though Orlando lives over three hundred years without aging). Delving deeper into the multigenre works of other writers like W. E. B. Du Bois, Sui Sin Far, Zora Neale Hurston, Audre Lorde, Gloria Anzaldúa, and more contemporary authors like Viet Thanh Nguyen, Saidiya Hartman, Shirley Geok-lin Lim, Claudia Rankine, Fred Moten, and Larissa Lai, I began to see such groupings of books, articles, and artworks alongside my own not as distinct and isolated texts but as crafts that help understand how multiple writings can belong within the same journey.[69] *Room* is a book of essays with the language of an autobiography; *Orlando* is a novel with the language of a biography. Yet they work as pairs—one cannot see the journey of the craft as an exploration of writing and life writing fully without understanding them both.

Open World Empire is about the ways that race works in video games, as imperial products manufactured and often innovated on in Asia, and the forms of erotic play emerging from games that can resist their dominant ways of being seen. *All Flowers Bloom* is a queer speculative novel about two souls who reincarnate throughout human history, one ("S") who repeatedly invests in radical political projects, the other ("871") who usually collaborates with imperial violence in order to love and capture the other. Though there is no explicit link between these two books, reviewers have often pointed out how *All Flowers Bloom* feels like a video game, with every life and death reminiscent of a single life in a game, while *Open World Empire* can often feel like queer fiction, with the repeated emphasis on the player's intimate relations with games and the forms of erotic play within them. As these books were both "second projects" written in the more flexible genres of game studies and speculative fiction, I felt freer to cross genres and experiment with language and form. *All Flowers*

Bloom, for example, features handwritten notations within the text; *Open World Empire* features asides about my own erotic relationship to video games. For academic audiences, I attempted to navigate these experiments by taking on the role of a writer pretending to be an academic, and for literary audiences, that of an academic pretending to be a writer. Both roles kept me in the attitude of an amateur, harnessing my curiosity by focusing on the elsewheres that invite categorical crossover and play, because in other contexts such mixing of discrete disciplines can risk career suicide. As Saidiya Hartman has said of her own work, creative writing in the academy brings about new homes by bridging theory and narrative and does not tell stories so much as commit to "a storied articulation of ideas."[70]

The brown craft of imaginative work was also made through concurrent events that questioned my own relationship to imperial power as a marginalized author-other. The Occupy movements, Black Lives Matter in 2014, and the movements in Hong Kong, Taiwan, and South Korea (which, as described in chapter 4, often cast me as a brown Chinese radical or coconspirator) all influenced the forms of imperial complicity that are at the heart of *All Flowers Bloom* and *Open World Empire*. While writing both, I continued to think of a line I had heard from a history podcast: "Given the right circumstances, all of us could be a saint or a gas chamber assistant."[71] This line bothered me on both spiritual and political levels but also focused my craft onto embarking from the feelings of anger within personal conflict to feelings of responsibility, especially in seas where love and pleasure were the primary currents. Both books were carried on the waves of love, desire, and pleasure, and both are about the risks and responsibilities involved when we choose erotic love, whether as a gamer or a reincarnating soul. We often say that love can move mountains, but you also can't move a mountain without crushing something. In my own life, I was falling in love and becoming a parent, two events that brought unexpected value and commitment.

The shared craft of *All Flowers Bloom* and *Open World Empire* was carried by the desire to understand how love and erotic desire both fulfilled and failed us within contexts of imperial complicity, incorporation, and domestication. *All Flowers Bloom* seeks to do so from a grand historical perspective, to show how the imperial domestications of the past and future can be normalized for those living through them, yet obvious to those of us living in the present. *Open World Empire* uses a different tactic: It asks how an overlooked medium (video games) tells the story of our own domestication and, if played erotically, can reveal how normalized and habituated we already are to our own complicities with imperial violence. Both books, in a sense, are meditations on "brown power," which I reanimate here not to suggest an identity-based rallying cry but a subimperial power that might come in the form of expressing marginalization, love, and solidarity, but that in practice can often be routed into complicity, incorporation, domestication, and normalization to imperial violence. Brown power thus contains an ambiguity, a complexity, that can mean refusing one form of imperial power (in a domestic, institutional, or personal sense) while capitulating to another. Both *All Flowers Bloom* and *Open World Empire* attempt to understand brown power through shifts in representation and perspective within those who, by attempting to empower themselves from their own domestication, might domesticate others. *All Flowers Bloom*'s story explores how love and violence in various historical and futuristic moments (from 600 BCE to 731 "Post-Terra"), various bodies (genders, races, ages), and various relations (colonial, friendly, familial, erotic) can breed both chaos and redemption. In an early chapter of *All Flowers Bloom*, the main character, Soul 871, is reborn as a Viking woman who helps encourage men to conquer foreign lands by emasculating them if they don't go viking. She too is complicit with what's happening elsewhere even though she's not bashing in any skulls, even though she has to deny her yearning for her lover (who dies overseas) and herself dies regretful and alone.

With Vikings, popular media mostly depict their violence rather than their commodities, whereas in IT technology, most media only know the commodities rather than the violences of obtaining them. Thus, in *Open World Empire*, the forms of brown power come in the erotic forms of imperial participation, whether from playing a militarized tourist in a video game, purchasing an iPhone, ordering a gift from Amazon, or narrating the advancements and pleasures of new technology without questioning its production process. *Open World Empire* attempts to explain how the erotic pleasures that manifest through technological commodities create new and obscured relations with others across the globe, recalling Edward Said's appeal to read English literature during the British Empire as "contrapuntal": that we can understand all games, and many of their play styles and mechanics, as always tethered to spaces, experiences, and power dynamics far outside of their explicit meaning.[72] For both books, love and erotics offer different forms of self-realization that can allow us to understand the broader effects of our actions, even when such acts are voiced through narratives of oppression and trauma. When allowing time and reflection (or the building of a craft), love and pleasure can operate as truth-telling affects to help understand the underlying motivations and willingness to participate in systems that deliver exploitation and slow death to others.

As a reanimation of brown power movements, *brown power* is not meant to be a parody or appropriation of a term once used for solidarity among Chicano, Filipino, South Asian, and other brown communities who have rallied around this call. It is instead meant to insist on the movement of brown movements, to sense the complexity and ambiguity within such calls, to tread with certainty and purpose, and to leave room for the ways our own forms of power can become oppressive to others outside of our intention, whether it is the heteropatriarchal, ableist, or transnational capitalist forms of power that our movements inevitably participate in. Brown power thus does not offer an outside, an ideal form of organizing or pure and universal framework that will dispel any possibility of abuse or complicity. Indeed, the movement of brown theory is also the movement of movements themselves, the persistent need to readjust, rethink, and restructure. The craft of brown power thus embarks from questions of the value of marginalized identities within the power of institutional empowerment: the forms of competition, of patronage, of claiming power in the act of reading or publishing books rather than evident structural change (a kind of "trickle-down power"). Brown power is power from the marginalized in a context where anyone can be granted a marginalized identity, and its craft was made at a time when Donald Trump, America's rich, white male president, could occupy the space of victimhood by claiming to be the target of various witch hunts. In *All Flowers Bloom*, several of the chapters (or "lives") feature moments where the two reincarnating characters begin to realize their own abuse of power, but always too late: Their current life ends, and the next life starts without any memory of what happened in their past lives. Writing during the ongoing war on terror and the Hong Kong protests often felt like experiencing a similar erasure. One day, in 2016, US bombs killed ninety-seven civilians in a market in Yemen, including twenty-five children, and the next day every news source was still talking about which political candidate was going to best represent the United States.[73] Brown power was my repertoire when I needed to ponder power in the face of powerlessness: the ways that atrocities remain constant, tolerable, embattled. Writing in that time often felt like being reborn, starting over and over again in a video game or within a new body, plodding forward without any memory at all.

Self-Referencing: *Nimrods* and "Brown Theory" (2023)

Before my first novel, I was a prolific short-story writer. I would write a story in one sitting, usually under a thousand words and usually about wandering somewhere, sometimes to a different place, sometimes to a historical moment, sometimes to another world. Many of these stories came while researching for my PhD, and I reimagined the racial histories I absorbed from a multitude of texts. Often these stories came from an urge to respond imaginatively to a novel I admired. In 2013 I wrote a queer thousand-word story inspired by a queer novel. I finished the story after briefly traveling to the country where the novel takes place, and I found a small, online-only publication willing to post it. In my excitement I wrote a blog piece about how the story was influenced by the novel I admired. Perhaps naively, I sent my story and accompanying blog piece to the novel's author, believing that my work would show how their novel impacted me, and my wish to honor that influence. Immediately, the author wrote me back accusing me of plagiarism. They detailed the legal ramifications of what could happen to me unless the story was immediately taken down, and they claimed to be in discussions with their lawyer about me. They also threatened to ruin my reputation as a writer, which at the time did not exist. I was shocked and broken but mostly confused that my story could be seen as plagiarism, since the story itself was less than a thousand words, had no linguistic similarities to the novel as far as I could tell, came with no monetary reward (it was a free publication), and was published with a very obscure online-only journal that perhaps a dozen people would read. Yet still, by writing about similar characters in a similar situation, I had peeved this author who had a large amount of cultural power, enough to end my writing career before it began. I asked the editor of the journal to take down the story, and I deleted my blog post about it.

As the years passed, I tried to learn from this experience, but the lesson was unclear. Was I, like many marginalized authors, supposed to find inspiration only in the great white writers of the past? Or was the inspiration I took from other marginalized, living authors supposed to remain something unspoken and unvoiced, so that my audiences would never know the soils from which my creative works grew? Over time, I only grew more incensed at this author for making me feel as if I had directly copied someone's work (or would ever need to). I wondered if they had written similar emails to other budding writers, if they had made the place and time period of their novel (about marginalized migrants living in a Southeast Asian country) difficult for any upcoming authors to ever write about, or if they had threatened other young marginalized and queer authors with lawsuits and community expulsion. The people who were our subjects as authors surely did not deserve for their narratives to be gatekept by a single author, one who did not even live in the country they wrote about. In defiance, I chose to republish this story as a chapter of *All Flowers Bloom* and suffer whatever consequences might come. But the accusations of plagiarism never came again, at least not to my face.

In book touring for *All Flowers Bloom*, I began publicly discussing the marginalized authors who influenced my work, many of whom were still alive and who might have seen similarities in my work and theirs. With my next book, *Nimrods: a fake-punk self-hurt anti-memoir*, I wanted my influences to be part of the story itself, similar to the way every chapter of this book begins with a timeline of potential influences. Like brown theory, brown craft tracks our works, documents where they come from, legal ramifications be damned. I have come to call this method of explicit influence tracking *self-referencing*, a reanimation of a term often used to overshare, gossip, or participate in forms of self-indulgence (in academia, "me studies"). Self-referencing, for this brown craft, expands and does not deny all these characteristics, to include forms of embodied cross-referencing, or the act of discovering different selves, different shades of our own brownness in the works of others, and then referencing those other selves through the way we express our own selves.

Though I grew up writing poetry, and in my young adulthood pursued open mic nights to hone and share my poems, once I began graduate school in 2007, I stopped writing poetry entirely. In an English department, being expected to know and care about poetic terms, forms, and discourses kept me from seeing the magic and imaginative release of poetry. But in 2017 poetic lines reawakened in a time of hardship, with the complicated birth of my son, and in my own anxieties and fears of becoming like my (white) father. These lines eventually became part of the prose-poetry book *Nimrods*, a project that also broke a promise to myself as an author that I had held for my first four books: never to write in the mode of an ethnic autobiography (for what is memoir but the unabashed plagiarizing of words, styles, plots, characters, from reality?). I thus pursued *Nimrods* by seeing the self not as myself but as a collaborative project in conversation with the many "self-writing" crafts of the past. The poems in *Nimrods* cross-reference other poems, novels, academic texts, and popular culture, which contain expressions similar to my own embodied practices, experiences, and ways of seeing—similar shades of brown. Seeking to follow the poet Douglas Kearney's advice that "writing poems just to express oneself is like using the Internet just for email," I thought of *Nimrods* not as a stamp of our true authentic selves but as a craft like all crafts, as a way of floating, a temporary and localized means of self-reflection in order to escape, to explore, to venture out, to last, and to get to the next thing.[74]

A nimrod is three things: a biblical figure of the first ruling patriarch, a word that my father claimed to have invented as an insult, and the title of a 1997 album by the pop punk band Green Day. Like its title, *Nimrods* seeks to tell my own experience within a form of writing that consistently exposes the multiple influences, inspirations, and violences that placed the words on the page. Written from 2017 to 2023, *Nimrods* takes a hybrid prose-poetic style to give an honest account of my experience being raised by two preacher's kids in a chaotic mixed-race family, witnessing my father's breakdown into alcoholism and suicidal ideation, growing to understand my own queerness and Filipino background, and becoming a father, academic, and creative writer. To do so, the book takes on forms of direct collaborative cross-referencing: queer punk poetry and musical ekphrasis that lifts, remixes, and splices apart lyrics and forms; the use of odes, sonnets, rhyme royals, haibuns, and triptychs, to recall forms of othered and imperial techniques; the constant notations and disruptions that reveal sources of inspiration, context, or forms of violence (figure 5.3). Self-referencing also appears in *Nimrods* in various notational forms: as haikus in a haibun, as literal footnotes, as poems in italics, as words in gray, as redactions, and as asides in the poetic narrative itself. Twice, the prose-poetry narrative about my father is interrupted by references to Jesmyn Ward's *Salvage the Bones*, whose words inspired the very words on the page. All of this self-referencing becomes explicit in the last section, "Envoi," which combines a notes section with an acknowledgments section, thanking authors, colleagues, and friends, alongside citations marking quotations and influence (see figure 5.4).

The subtitle of *Nimrods* labeling it an "anti-memoir" is reframed in the book's poems as hiding a (dis)empowering phrase within it, "anti-me," as well as a phrase that turns intense anger into authorship, "me/more/ire." *Nimrods* explores these twin feelings of self-hate and ire as starting points for a type of self-rehearsal less about reflecting on one's life and more about feeling anger, hate, and repugnance for the person in the mirror—the domesticated brown author. And yet smashing this mirror through anger and self-hate creates shards that act as gateways into deeper emotions and events: grief, death, shame, and loss. *Nimrods* begins with anger and self-hate only to point to communities and collectives who reveal the political and social stakes of these emotions. *Nimrods*, then, can be read as a form of "family memoir," a phrase Y-Dang Troeung used to describe her book *Landbridge*, which captures the multiple voices coming from Cambodian diasporic peoples, or "collective memoir," which Jordy Rosenberg uses in his book *Confessions of the Fox* to mean speculative memoirs written from multiple perspectives that use the past of a single person or event to form a "we," a union of editors and creators who create and re-create the text together.[75] The "Envoi" section of *Nimrods* explicitly names the family of editors and storytellers who collectivity made the book's craft, who are also mentioned within the text through blatant callouts that sometimes fracture narrative flow.

my white grandfather wrote twelve educational books on christianity   I still keep his last book on my shelf *Search for True Discipleship in Church History*

Supreme, sovereign, infinite deity planned it from the beginning: a teaching/discipling church—a Growing Christian Teaching/Discipling Church.

octopedal   church
moist consentacled
church   growing erecting
disciplining   church

I awry his funeral strive
to bring peace plan an
epode

In a world gone awry since the Garden of Eden God has striven to bring to all mankind his saving plan.

The most highly skilled, intensive care available must be provided if the suffering patient is to survive.

before he went into intensive
care that highly demented
man did not recognize me but
when he looked at me he talked
about how he saw a lot of asian
whores during the war but did
not see their suffering or what
else those folks did to survive

the ode the Lord's pants
falling saying to his wife   oh
just let them fall   no cure with
each step pants searching
down stain boxers didn't care

We owe it to ourselves, as well as to our Lord, to search and find the best possible care and cure

and to see that it is administered before it is too late.

nothing ministered against women gays us he gives
me none of this he hated the pulpit believed in
small communities working things out before it is
too late perhaps his glares were just meant to see

FIGURE 5.3. A page from *Nimrods* that shows excerpts from my grandfather's book *Search for True Discipleship in Church History*, alongside my creative reworking of those same lines, which also lifts language from Naomi Clark's card game "consentacle."

Envoi

page

2 Judith Butler, *Gender Trouble.*

8 W. E. B. Du Bois, "How does it feel to be a problem?"

8 Ellen D. Wu, "the success of a success story."

9 Gray text is taken from a bench owned by UBC (outside Buchanan Tower).

11 Audre Lorde, *Zami*, "to whom do I owe . . . I have become?" (3).

12 Christina Sharpe, in italics.

13 Mahalo to my family in Hawai'i and all the Guillermos abroad.

14 Saidiya Hartman, "violence of abstraction," in conversation with Patricia J. Saunders.

19 Thank you, Chanel Guillermo, who gave me the third text in gray. The rest are common sayings from friends after meeting my father.

20 Thank you to my teachers in Las Vegas—Marc Smereck, Anne Stevens, Vincent Perez, and Felicia Campbell—for changing my life by changing my worldview.

23 Thank you to my mentors and colleagues in Asia/America, too numerous to mention.

31 Thank you to Micheal James Drake for helping guide me through these hardships of youth.

36 James Joyce, "dark-plumaged dove."

36 Tony Kushner, "mangled guts pretending."

36 Against Me!, "rough surf on the coast," from the song "Transgender Dysphoria Blues."

36 David Henry Hwang, "big western arms."

36 Susan Sontag, "the coarsest, commonest pleasures."

39 Gracias to Allen Baros and other friends in Seattle who saw me through this period.

FIGURE 5.4. The first page of the "Envoi" section of *Nimrods*. Sources, citations, acknowledgments, and inspirations all come in reference to the poetic pages that they inspired.

Nimrods participates in self-referencing not as referrals to the self but as a form of embodied cross-referencing similar to the way historians and journalists seek to confirm the veracity of an event by researching multiple points of reference. Self-referencing is thus less about affirming an identity and more about validating (and thus realizing) shared ways of being, seeing, and interacting with the world, which do not easily get leveraged toward political ends, nor do they remain stagnant within a sole representative text, character, or author. Rather than see brown crafts as boats built by a single (often tokenized) authorial voice, one determined by the outside value of publishers and experts, self-referencing pinpoints the shared ways of being and seeing expressed in our creative artwork, and, rather than entrusting the authority to portray ourselves solely in our own writing, explicitly cross-references ourselves with the many selves we've found while journeying through various novels, poems, and artworks. Movements of self-critique and self-inquiry arise when we trace our selves through others. Just as there is no exemplar, no perfect representation of brownness that can grant empowerment, so is there no one expression of our ever-changing selves, even when it comes from our own pens. Rather, for those of us who have been rendered nonhuman, parahuman, or merely not counting in the way those around us count, our sense of self comes not from a universal consensus of the human but from forms of cross-referential verification that validate our selves to ourselves. Our self-referencing acknowledges all the sources we've found that say yes, our way of seeing, our way of being, our shade of brown, is true, and we can prove it, because our selves are traceable through multiple accounts. Our sense of self transpires in our shared contexts and in our collaborations with others, even if those others do not offer refuge but guilt, danger, and pain. Often such self-imagining happens without direct intention. It is usually called *inspiration* or *influence* when one sees or reads a way of being similar to (but also distinct from) one's own and feels the urge to write about oneself—such as my own feelings as both colonial subject and colonial actor in reading Orwell's "Shooting an Elephant," feelings that grew while writing *Stamped*. Acts of self-referencing in our brown crafts make this visible by archiving our multiple selves through other shades of brown.

In 2023, the same year that *Nimrods* was published, another piece of this craft also was released: my article "Brown Theory: A Storied Articulation of Ideas," which became the introduction to this very book, *Domesticating Brown*. Both that article and this book are part of the same craft of self-referencing that made *Nimrods*. But with *Domesticating Brown*, such cross-referencing does not occur through deliberately overshared notations but in forms of writing that explore the shades of brown within our families (introduction), our racial histories (chapter 1), our ancestors (chapter 2), our relations to other brown(ed) peoples (chapter 3), our political and cultural contexts (chapter 4), and our works (chapter 5). By referring to the self in reference to our other selves expressed by others—some nearly exact and some only briefly so—self-referencing challenges any imaginative consensus of brown people. For writers and artists, it allows us to move alongside our various selves, to flow through the ways we see parts of ourselves in others, and them within us.

Coda: a kind of navel-gazing

I end this movement through brown crafts by tracing two sources of inspiration for this chapter that came from writers in very different contexts.

The first source came on February 20, 2020, just weeks before the COVID-19 lockdowns on my campus, when Ta-Nehisi Coates came to speak to a full on-campus auditorium (I was part of the committee who had invited him). An audience member asked Coates why he thought his work had become so popular, especially among white people. Coates gave an answer that mostly evaded the question: He tried not to think about it because he believed that "that kind of navel-gazing" didn't help him write ethically in the world. I remember feeling very disappointed in this answer, because I, who had maybe one-thousandth of the success of someone like Coates, thought about this question all the time. Why did I write? And who was it for? And was my conscious decision to care about my audience also the reason my writing was only one-thousandth as successful as that of someone like Coates? Had my turn away from MFA programs, academic writing, and craft resulted only in the lack of the large audience that all these conventions promised?

The second writing source came in 2014 at a lecture by the Malaysian Chinese American academic and creative author Shirley Geok-lin Lim at a small event held for Hong Kong writing students. A student prompted Lim with the question, "How do I write in a way that will get me recognized by large audiences?" Rather than answer this question with modes of craft or self-discipline, Lim turned the question around: "What if you just wanted to write for small audiences?" I took Lim to suggest many inquiries: What if you never became a known artist? What if you just wrote for the people near you, the ones who might need it the most?

Brown crafts ask us to wonder about all the works that are made not for the world but for our families, our friends, our selves; that bring us from place to place; and that use the repertoires of all the crafts we sailed to arrive here.

Indeed, reflections on who we are for our audiences are pivotal in this process, as thinking of craft as an imagined ship demands that we locate ourselves, that we take an account of where we are and what journeys we are already on, which necessitated building this craft. When asked about my audience, I think of my communities, friends, and colleagues, whose works (and whose reactions to my work) inspire me to continue drifting along, or to create new blueprints for the next craft. Without them to help navigate, there is the ever-present danger of floating into the windless doldrums of my inner self, the stagnating waters of racist, sexist, patriarchal imperialism, without any land in sight—just a marooned ship eating itself to death. As all of my crafts were made pretenure, one of the greatest doldrums I've had to evade is professionalization itself, and I've repeatedly had to resist the academic institution's desire to domesticate our pens. Still, academia continues to move me through all the brown crafts: the feelings of being stamped, the temptations of brown power, the communal creativity found in self-referencing. At panels and talks, I am often asked by scholars facing the anxieties of professionalization how their desire for creative writing can be routed to meaningfully count for tenure or promotion. My answer has often followed Lim's: What if your writing didn't count as anything? What if your decision to write only harmed your career or your paycheck? Would it still be an act of service, even if it didn't count as "service"?

Crafts are rarely made for single sailors. They are made with others and shared among travelers, migrants, pirates, soldiers, and statespeople too. Crafts can move from place to place, from genre to genre, from person to person, and they are always collaborations of a sort. Even the timber needed for flotation comes from the earth. The person writing things down, the assistant, the notetaker, plays one of many roles within a motley crew. So too, for those of us writing brown crafts, it is not so much ourselves as our families, our support system, our children, our editors, our nights out listening to music or walking for hours, our enriching conversations and our traumatizing ones, that are all part of the craft we build—they are our fellow crew who move us along the open seas. To think of crafts in terms of movement, of ships, stresses the importance of the communities, big and small, who are moved by our work, and understands how our works are collaborations with them. Our crafts come in novels, in academic articles, in poems, in letters we write to lift those around us, which allow us all to stay afloat.

Perhaps you have to find yourself at the top of the mountain before you can smell the gargantuan pile of shit you just spent decades climbing up.

Though you began your ascent with your nostrils paper-plugged, you got used to the odor, and you joined the collegial parades who declared it an acquirable taste. They had their ways, when you pointed out the stench, of making you believe that the home from which you came, before you attempted the climb, reeked of worse waste.

Then again, maybe you've scaled your way up, and found no smell at all. Just the mountain's vast view: beautiful, broad, and distant. None of this seems fair without her here.

In memory of those unwell, those who fell from the summit, those who couldn't stand the scent, and those who walked away, you remind your collegial climbers: Yes, you are funk and refuse and manure. You are the fertility of fertilizer. Despite it all, you still have your color.

Afterword

Chapters cut from *Domesticating Brown*

on the Eaton sisters and movements from
Canada to America to Jamaica

on wild brown girl travel, featuring
Anna May Wong and Josephine Baker

on representations of the jungle in
the Philippine tropical gothic

on the race radical tradition
in American literature

on pedagogy in Nanjing and
the 1989 anti-African riots

on the emotional automation of
refugees in virtual reality

on brownness in video games
and making brown isles

on brown futurity and
the imperial leviathan

I first saw José Esteban Muñoz speak in January 2013, at the Modern Language Association conference in Boston. On a roundtable of scholars discussing "Queer Theory in a Postcolonial World," Muñoz presented upcoming work on theories of brownness, an expansion of his ideas on brown feelings that he had been revising since the late 1990s. After his talk I retreated into a bathroom stall and wrote down a flood of notes inspired by his presence: his focus on postcolonial queerness and on the worlds hardly represented in queer theory at the time; his defiant mannerisms and tics that resonated with my own neurodivergence; his desire to insist on his own embodiments of guilt and shame as well as pride and love; most of all, how all these brought forth a theoretical "sense of brown." Back in Seattle, I jumbled the notes into a short essay, which I hoped to include in my dissertation. But due to time and page constraints, that chapter was cut from the submitted manuscript. At my PhD defense that December, my committee encouraged me to keep working on brownness, calling it a missing piece of my thinking thus far. Three days after my defense, Muñoz died. Five years later, my dissertation came out as a revised book, *Transitive Cultures*, which included my chapter on brownness. Like many scholars, writers, and artists, I was deeply indebted to Muñoz in the brief time I saw him. He was able to plant a seed that could sway in whichever direction fostered its growth.

~

The growth of brownness resulted in a book that was planned to be far larger than *Domesticating Brown* has become. Originally, I had intended for this book to be a magnum opus, as ambitious as recent theoretical works like Lisa Lowe's *The Intimacies of Four Continents* and Neferti Tadiar's *Remaindered Life*. In that previous schema, many of the chapters in the book's second half were to dwell on brown futurity: the image of a future where "we are all brown," where mixture has become so common that race has lost its structural and social meaning. I wanted to show how brown theory could generate radical imaginings that resist postracial narratives of this future "beyond race" by reframing race not as a problem or trauma to overcome, but as an integral part of our lives, our histories, and our futures that we would never want to lose. Brown theory, I had hoped to say, changes the questions around race because it moves alongside race's ever-shifting nature. Thus, rather than pinpoint race, racism, or even racial capitalism as the leviathan whose waves propel racial hierarchies and inequalities, brown theory sees racialized peoples as already submerged within this ocean, as those who have, for generations, already been encountering various forms of domestication that come from entangled and vastly distributed representatives of power, some of whom can offer less precarious situations, and some, only crumbs of survival that prolong illness and death. We are not merely faced with these choices; we are already the products of them. Race in brown theory appears not as a hierarchical mechanism that must be erased but as a useful weight to help anchor ourselves in these ever-shifting seas. Where *race* is often conjured as a disruptive term that incites fear, agony, or memories of trauma and genocide, brown theory imagines the ways race can invite hope, laughter, sly and shy grins, and transformative movement.

I hoped to expand on all this over a sprawling set of chapters that would follow chapter 5. But speculations on brown futurity, whether optimistic or dystopic, seemed to always arrive as a way of dealing with race in the inevitable, always protracted future. The brown future became impossible for me to write about, because, as Muñoz wrote over a decade ago, brownness is already the world for the vast majority of us. We have been living in the brown world for so long that we have forgotten that many peoples—Japanese, Italians, Chinese, light-skinned peoples of the Middle East and North Africa, African American mulattos, Indigenous Native Americans and Polynesians—were once called *brown.* To even reflect on brown futurity presumes that most of the world, for the past century perhaps, is not already living in the brown futurity presaged in societies far before we were born—we, with our mixtures, our melting and melding, our migrations. We are living in a brown future, just not *our* brown future. For generations far before us, we have already arrived at the end point of race as a useful category.

And yet.

While struggling to write these missing chapters, I realized that to even pretend there could be a brown future merely leaves open the possibility of redemption from our own racist ways of being, our own imperial violences, our own collaborative and complicit allegiances. I began to have the same nauseating feelings for brown futurity as I did for most science fiction narratives about time travel: that to give any possibility of such an easy redemption seemed to diminish the lives of those who lived through these times—or, just as wrong, to see them solely as victims in need of our redemption. And who are we to long so desperately for the redeemable?

~

In the death of brown futurity as a concept, I began to take risks in a different direction that one editor told me was one of "self-indulgence." They meant this negatively, probably. But even so, I latched on to this word, as it marked a practice of brownness that seemed characteristic of many shades. Brown self-indulgence suits the "excess" associated with brown styles, aesthetics, tastes, sexualities.[1] We are always too much. In writing, this "too much" is the maximalist styles, the inclusion of the irrelevant, the slide into irreverence, the highlighting of particular concepts not because they are logically intertwined but because they give a pleasurable rhyme.

In academia, the indulgence for our selves marks an inability to do proper scholarship, particularly when the cultural backgrounds we research remain within a brown political ambiguity: when they are often used to serve either nationalist propaganda elsewhere (the American colonial era in the Philippines) or American warmongering (Taiwan, Hong Kong, Tibet) and capitalist legitimacy (the Cambodian genocide, the Chinese Cultural Revolution). This fear of brown indulgence is also the fear that the author could be enacting the very forms of imperial influence that they are writing about—that when we research our selves and our histories (the "we" who is not stamped as the "most affected" or "most marginalized" in the room), there is some tendency to valorize the lives of the complicit, the domesticated.[2] By seeking to redeem the violence of the past, we create redeemable others who, in turn, become our redemption from the violences of the present. By indulging in my many messy and excessive selves, I have explored throughout this book my own longing for redemption through redeemable others: Mongols, settler ancestors, migrant workers, "good" Chinese, racialized authors.

Of course, the excess associated with self-indulgent writing is racialized and can be deconstructed: A white scholar indulging in their own European background by researching William Shakespeare will never seem self-indulgent, yet my writings about histories of Southeast Asia and Oceania will always be typed as some form of "me studies." Making this choice to indulge thus usually means overcoming the hierarchies of academic excellence, choosing one's self over the committees, the directors, the reviewers. Indulgence could also be considered a form of amateur research, what Edward Said defined as "the desire to be moved not by profit or reward but by love for and unquenchable interest in the larger picture, in making connections across lines and barriers, in refusing to be tied down to a specialty, in caring for ideas and values despite the restrictions of a profession."[3] By writing about our selves and our histories, we are already admitting a lack of scholarly expertise, of critical distancing, and we know with some certainty that others will always see our work in this way. We write with the "amore" of the amateur: out of care, out of coping, out of our desire to find love for ourselves in an academy that has taught us our stories are irrelevant, excessive, forgotten. This brazenness to indulge in us, in our own worlds, in our isles and our oceans, is what I've tentatively called *brown theory*, for which, no doubt, others will use different words to reflect their own lifeworlds, for that is what it means to move. What is brown theory then but the brazen choice to indulge?

~

For brown theory, the personal is not only political; it is also theoretical. It frames our ways of seeing, our styles, our tool sets. This is not the same as autotheory, though it is informed by it (more so, "theory of the flesh"). Brown theory expands modes of self-authorship to consider the author as one of many shades of brown: a shade whose racial present is shaped irrefutably by historical narratives of those who came centuries before us (as in chapter 1); a shade whose migration history generates, reproduces, and responds to the structures and networks around them (as in chapter 2); a shade whose sense of self only comes through similar shades of creative, embodied, and explicit *self-referencing* (as in chapter 5). Like the acts of erasure and obscurity in chapter 3, brown theory does not see our writing about others as merely telling our side of the story but works in collaboration and sometimes settles on fictionalization, redaction, or heart-in-throat honesty. Sometimes brown theory is an act responding to political distress, as in chapter 4, of shifting the very terms of racial thinking to reveal the violences of our colonial present. We embark on brown theory for those who could not join us, for those who grant us the love and burden to include them. Our indulgence is not merely meant to form our *selves* but, as in chapter 5, to understand how we are stamped, how we enact power, and how we can trace our selves by referencing others so we can understand our many senses of brownness within the communities with whom our stories are enmeshed.

~

The little space left of this afterword will lean fully into the excesses of self-indulgence by following one particular straying movement that has thus far remained sunken beneath this book's argumentative horizon. If, to refer to the terms of chapter 5, my first craft of books (*Transitive Cultures, Stamped*) was propelled by anger, and the second (*Open World Empire, All Flowers Bloom*) was moved by love, then this craft (*Nimrods, Domesticating Brown*) has been driven primarily by fear. *Nimrods* was compelled by the fear of reproducing patriarchy in my child, the fear of my father and others in my family passing away, as well as the fear of not counting, of not being seen, of being without community, without home, a fear that pervades many brown academics as they find themselves achieving academic success, being plucked from the muck. *Domesticating Brown* too has been propelled by the fears that come with the domestication of the dead: the fear that those who have passed will either be forgotten or remembered as mere figures of victimhood or collateral damage, the fear that the conceptual tools and the disciplinary frames we have to remember them do little to reveal the complexity of their lives, the fear that we will have nothing to know what they meant to us but the abstract language of the academy. These fears too are how we grieve.

As discussed in various moments of this book, *Domesticating Brown* was written in a time of illnesses and death within my personal orbit. The most impactful of these was the illness and death of my wife, soulmate, and partner, Y-Dang Troeung. Though her name shares credit on only a few of my published works, all my work since we met in 2014 has undertaken some form of collaboration with Y-Dang. Our conjoined thinking fostered the first sprouts for this book, and she shared its craft-making as coauthor, editor, companion, researcher, and heartfelt supporter. After her death in November 2022, I returned to expand this manuscript, believing I might add another few chapters leading to brown futurity. But in the end, I was only able to edit the current five. After her death this book became ethereal and intimate, an archive of our discussions and our fears. I see her presence in this book just as much as I see myself. I hear her voice alongside my own.

Y-Dang's impact has been substantial in all my works, but in *Domesticating Brown* more than any other. From the day we met, we formed brown lifeworlds together and nurtured those who were part of them.[4] Through our love we wed the brown worlds we had, and found new homes in spaces where our brownness could meld, both with the strangers there and with our own families, those given and those found. Y-Dang encouraged me to pursue this work on brownness even in times when I grew paranoid that this project was cursed, because every time I came to work on it, something tragic would happen (sickness, trips to the emergency room, a family member's suicide, Y-Dang's own terminal illness). Chapter 2, focusing on my own lineage and family talk-story, was written entirely in the last year of Y-Dang's life, as we were shuttling among doctors, hospitals, chemo visits, and brief sunny getaways so we would remember her last year in a warmer light. These moments are tethered to this chapter in a way that created something sacred, not merely a set of ideas or a reworking of histories, but the words and deeds of the dead, who have no say in this chapter's alterations.

~

Color has no still existence. The colors we see are only light waves of varied wavelengths, vibrational cues triggering affectional hues in our retinal cones. In emotional advertising, brown is a risky color for one's brand. Certain brown shades may invite ideas of freshness and fecundity: soil, farms, chocolate, bread. Others will conjure the opposite: decay, rot, feces, death.[5] On the Willcox color wheel, which my son's school used to enhance his "emotional intelligence," brownness signifies "scared": the confusion, fear, anxiety, and helplessness of facing an overwhelming loss.[6]

Brown theory too moves through the waves of fear, mourning, bereavement, coping. Perhaps more than anger, more than desire, fear motivates our self-indulgence, our excess. We do our work not because we love ourselves but because we fear the dread of hating ourselves, of losing our selves and our loved ones to the stark white void. And when those of us within our brown world begin to die, and we see the value and complexity in them that others cannot, it adds urgency to this research. In many ways, all our works could be considered ways of discovering parts of ourselves in others. But in bereavement, something shifts in our capacity to distance ourselves from the lives of the dead. Saying their names, crying out their history, intimating our shared love, even to that uncaring void, claims importance for those we mourn. Perhaps it is a choice no longer: It is the only way we can continue to move.

~

The fear that comes from mourning is a fear for the future, for how our loved one's absence might redefine our selves. Y-Dang and I first met only months after I had been titled with a PhD. My entire being as a scholar came through her. Often my scholarship grew as a way to impress her. Often it was through discussions with her that my ideas were able to shape themselves into words. To be with her, I took a position in Hong Kong in a cultural studies department. Through her, I became a spousal hire in Vancouver and earned a job I never would have even been short-listed for (I had applied to over two hundred positions by that point and nearly all failed to even get long-listed). All my scholarship, my thinking, my career, my livelihood, came through Y-Dang, from our discussions, our intimacies, our shared brown worlds. I, Christopher B. Patterson, the scholar, was created through her. Without her, there is no such person. Only the writing dead.

This book has sought to capture many forms of brown domestications: domestications of history (chapter 1), domestications of our lineages (chapter 2), domestications of peoples (chapter 3), domestications of our political and social perceptions (chapter 4), domestications of our creative imaginations (chapter 5). Perhaps this book's very focus on domestication was due to the fear of my own emerging context while writing it: the fear of my own work being domesticated. This epilogue, then, ends not only this book but also my story as an academic writer. It ends the domestication of intellect, of scholarship. It does so through a practice of cease.

~

Part of the intention behind so much of this writing of the self, this self-indulgence, is to conclude something new about the self that, on reflection, has conditioned the very terms of one's writing. I thus offer conclusion here by untitling my academic self with a performative phrase: This book, *Domesticating Brown*, will be the last sole-authored academic monograph I will ever write. With bereavement comes a refusal, not an awakening—an action based on the understanding one has always had. In this case, my understanding is of the administrative violence of universities: their investment in state-sanctioned narratives of the human; their desire to exploit the languages of protest by putting on a grotesque theater of social justice performed solely for their own marketing schemes so that good-willed students will flock to them in droves; the obscene standards of excellence that pervade budgets, grants, job postings; the carrots and sticks of tenure and promotion that destroy our mental and physical health; the vast extraction of knowledge from communities that attracts far more grant money for researchers than funding and support for those living in those communities; the exploitation of students and educators, who are encouraged to work with a sense of "vocational awe," grateful for any employment within a prestigious space no matter how precarious; the many colleagues who, since my tenure, have revealed to me all the ways we do not prioritize the next generation but instead our own self-reproduction, gaining more and more for ourselves because we, the secure class, have earned our place, because we deserve it, because the university *wants* so badly to shower us with rewards until we, the brown academics, see our individual accomplishments as collective victories for the brown communities supporting us: the muck from whom we have risen and whom we have left behind.[7] All of these violences are enhanced by a stultifying language used even by so-called critical academics, whose very radicalism offers notable prestige to the university.[8] Much of this prestige comes from our ability to continue writing, to always have our next project, a pitch that the university can then use to obtain endowments, grants, students, and renown. The fear propelling the craft of *Domesticating Brown* is also the fear of becoming part of all this: the fear of overstaying, of turning into the gatekeeping, unchanging, prideful, narcissistic academic, of whom we all know so many, whom we are all destined to become the day we lose ourselves to the institutional (de)void. Then let the curse of brownness that once brought only fear come true. Let the end of the brown project bring death—the death of a comfortable, grant-seeking, excellence-pursuing, domesticated form of scholarship.

Our scholarship becomes domesticated not when we cease to speak truth to power but when we do so only through an academic language that is so difficult to parse that power becomes obscured for the vast majority of readers, or when our notion of power becomes so abstract ("global capitalism") or so diffuse ("power is all of us") that no direct action can impact it. The implication of this language is often a specific form of knowledge dissemination: that our writing will go to influence students and activists, who will interpret it in their own contexts and take direct action, while we return to our single-family homes in quiet neighborhoods. We become domesticated, as Mimi Thi Nguyen writes, when we "so-called critical academics" accuse such direct actors of being "insufficiently radical because their platforms did not include mention of X (the scene of [our] academic capital)," and when our "radical critique" acts to constrain, destabilize, demobilize, or dispose of the very "forms of life we should defend."[9] Our readers become the cannon fodder, the collateral damage, the front-line soldiers; we, the generals safely ensconced within garrisons of higher knowledge. As Cornel West has pointedly argued, power becomes fetishized when it is depicted as "almighty, magical and unremovable" and contains little "connection to collective action."[10] I too feel like too much of my scholarship has fit this description; West too has ceased to write academic monographs.

~

The brown earth resembles a time before the evolution of flowers, before the greenery of trees, to over 400 million years in the past, when the Earth was a world of towering fungi. These *Prototaxites*, or protomushrooms, were the tallest organisms on land, reaching heights of up to twenty-four feet, with wide trunks that grew on the deceased, finding life and difference in decay. Brownness has since remained on our Earth as mycelium. Brownness grows on the legacies of colonialism in anastomosing, hyaline threads of spored bodies, creating new fungal colonies. What grows from the rotten soil of violence and death can also become violent and deadly, suffocating other life inhabiting the soil.

~

Attempts to trace the mycelial threads of brownness in this book have meant placing trust in the spiral, remaining open to wherever their substrates lead. Fungal threads overlap; they bring us to the decay from which they feed. Where can such movement end? How far does the spiral sink? What happens when we reach a dense, gravitational center and find only the death of our own domestication?

In the practice of cease, I hear her voice, reminding me that our love was never without scholarship: how we first met at an academic conference called "Fashion in Fiction" in a Hong Kong arts center surrounded by supermodels;

how one of our most romantic moments was at a Shanghai shisah bar fangirling over Edward Said's *Representations of the Intellectual*; how our love bloomed the first time we traveled to Cambodia together and embraced on a beach while from her laptop Slavoj Žižek pontificated in front of gigantic mounds of trash; how our experience writing academic articles together brought us to an electrifying level of synchronicity. The spiral does not spin neatly within itself, nor does it settle on a particular darkness—to long for an end, in a way, is still to long for redemption, for an easy way out.

The spiral may reveal the death and dearth of domestication, and yet we brown peoples are always prepared to turn, to see the end point of the spiral as no end at all. As Y-Dang wrote in *Landbridge*: "When we enter into that space [of trauma, loss, and survival], we delve into a spiral of infinite darkness, but we also swirl into a field of life: a lifeworld, a meditative, repetitious space of beauty, creativity, and regeneration."[11] The spiral's center is not an end but a turn from spiral into swirl, a movement that proliferates into more unpredictable turns, where life goes on, becoming "habitable, viable, and sometimes even beautiful."[12] *Domesticating Brown* was written while she was still alive, as was all my significant work as an academic. Our love too was a swirl spun by the force of our ideas, our politics, our critique, our insight, and our knowledge. This choice to cease is not a refusal of academic language, of the words that brought us both so much understanding, joy, and community. It is simply another turn: an acceptance that, after the completion of this last book written in her presence, these words have dried up their flow.

Sometimes the craft we build is not a vessel for the seas but a bridge over a river, a rail over a mountain, a balloon through the air. To build a new craft, perhaps, means dismantling the one that brought us here and using its wreckage to pursue the next thing. Without her, this craft of scholarship, run aground and washed ashore, is no longer worthy of the sea. Alone, I have only the ability to move around, to expand, or to reduce the words our dwelling together produced. With my name written across her granite grave, our ashes will one day share the same dirt. Perhaps, with death, I'm just at a loss for words. I may still dabble, tinker, edit, collab, wrangle together. Like all brown presences, ours too will turn, until this spiral becomes a swirl. But she will never write another academic book again, and neither will I. May the brown, straying movements that began when our bodies first danced, together, finally rest.

Your first encounter with brown theory was in Bible classes, where brown was
    the color of both life and death, the beginning and the end. Brown was
    there when God made
        Adam out of mud
        and it remains there
        in the dark
        trail to Hell

In many religions, brown represents stability, earth, comfort, cycles of life.
    Brown is the soil that covers our bodies, the earthworms who eat us, the
    fungi that grow from us, the
        trees that mark where our
        ashes lie so our
        descendants
        can return

FOREWORD

1. While some have argued that academia has homogenized brownness around the experiences of "high-caste Indian scholars who can access its spaces" (Borisa and Brown, "Intimate Borders," 96), it is also common in Canadian scholarship for *brown* to be interchangeable with *South Asian* or *South Asian diasporas* (Shah, "Brown Identities").

2. Smilges, *Crip Negativity*, 2–3.

3. Ruiz and Vourloumis, in Harney et al., "Resonances."

4. Glissant, *Poetics of Relation*, xxii.

5. Glissant, *Poetics of Relation*, 55.

6. Ricoeur, *Lectures on Imagination*, 285.

7. Glissant, *Poetics of Relation*, 100.

8. Ricoeur, *Lectures on Imagination*, 218.

9. In *The Difference Aesthetics Makes*, Chuh writes of the "need to activate ways of going beyond the sometimes strenuous demands of disciplinarity and professionalization, ways that are not so much interdisciplinary but are instead deliberately promiscuous" (4).

10. T. Chen, "Transpacific Turns," 2.

11. Ruiz, *Left Turns*, 8.

12. Rafael, *White Love*, 15–16.

13. Glissant, *Poetics of Relation*, 199.

14. Glissant, *Poetics of Relation*, 199.

15. Troeung, *Landbridge*, 68–69.

INTRODUCTION

Parts of this introduction were published previously as Christopher Patterson, "Brown Theory: A Storied Manifest of Our World," *positions: asia critique* 31, no. 1 (2023): 91–116.

1. Clifford, *Studies in Brown Humanity*, vii.

2. Clifford, *Studies in Brown Humanity*, 40; for a deeper reading of Clifford's work, see Holden, "Dissonant Voices."

3. Clifford, *Studies in Brown Humanity*, 18.

4. Clifford, *Studies in Brown Humanity*, 18.

5. Blumenbach, *Anthropological Treatises*, 269.

6. Sharma, "Brown."

7. E.-B. Lim, *Brown Boys*, 9.

8. E.-B. Lim, *Brown Boys*, 20.

9. London, *Revolution, and Other Essays*, 326.

10. Far, "Leaves," 225; Yao, "Black-Asian Counterintimacies," 199.

11. Manuud, *Brown Heritage*.

12. Melamed, "Racial Capitalism," 77.

13. Patterson, *Transitive Cultures*, 15.

14. Isaac, *American Tropics*.

15. Caronan, *Legitimizing Empire*, 5.

16. M. Chen et al., "Introduction," 18 (original in bold); Teaiwa, "bikinis," 96.

17. I use *brownness* in ways that can also signify a more fluid form of Blackness; as Margo Natalie Crawford writes, "The space that Muñoz gives 'brown,' the way he allows it to be amorphous and a collective feeling, is similar to the lowercase 'blackness' that moves in and out of the settled identity of 'Black.'" Crawford, "What Time Is It," 154.

18. Canaan, "Brownness," 235.

19. Muñoz, *Sense of Brown*, 122.

20. M. Chen et al., "Introduction," 12.

21. Rather than "claim latinidad," Sony Coráñez Bolton offers "Filipinx Hispanidad" as an alternative to understand "the regulatory and disciplinary rubrics through which we come to know of ourselves in racial, ethnonational terms." Coráñez Bolton, *Crip Colony*, 5.

22. Patterson, *Transitive Cultures*, 16.

23. Curaming, "Rizal and the Rethinking," 327.

24. L. Sullivan, *Racial Types*, 55–56.

25. Curaming, "Rizal and the Rethinking," 326.

26. Coráñez Bolton, *Crip Colony*, 24.

27. Aboitiz, *Asian Place, Filipino Nation*, 37.

28. Aboitiz, *Asian Place, Filipino Nation*, 37.

29. Coates, *Rizal*; see also Curaming, "Filipinos as Malay."

30. Quoted in Capino et al., *Rizal's Life, Works*, 227.

31. Arvin, *Possessing Polynesians*, 4.

32. Arvin, *Possessing Polynesians*, 40.

33. Desmond, "Picturing Hawai'i," 486.

34. Armstrong, *Around the World*, 144.

35. Silva, *Aloha Betrayed*.

36. Zeiler, "Basepaths to Empire," 192; Coráñez Bolton, *Crip Colony*, 60.

37. Saranillio, *Unsustainable Empire*, 42.

38. Saranillio, *Unsustainable Empire*, 43.

39. Princess Orig, "Kayumanggi Versus Maputi." For more on how Americans established cross-racial hierarchies, see chapter 2.

40. Kramer, "Race-Making and Colonial Violence"; Rafael, *White Love*.

41. Rafael, *White Love*, 35.

42. Du Bois, *Health and Physique*, 32–33. See also Haidarali, *Brown Beauty*, 27.

43. Haidarali, *Brown Beauty*, 144.

44. Hurston, "How It Feels," 155.

45. Haidarali, *Brown Beauty*, 8.

46. Justice George Sutherland's decision depriving Bhagat Singh Thind of citizenship on the basis of race relies on these racial distinctions while also providing forms of allyship among Asiatic groups, writing that "the framers did not have in mind the brown or yellow races of Asia." Daksha Pillai, "United States v. Bhagat Singh Thind," 14. For an analysis of the *Thind* decision through a "critical brown studies" analytic, see Boge, "US v. Thind."

47. Man, *Soldiering Through Empire*, 108.

48. Y. Espiritu, "Critical Transnational Perspective," 109.

49. Y. Espiritu, "Critical Transnational Perspective," 109; see also Bradley, *Imagining Vietnam and America*, 55–56.

50. See, "Language Run Amok," 371.

51. Dunne, *Delano*, xiv.

52. Harrison, "Muhammad Ali Draft Case," 81.

53. Tu, *Experiments in Skin*, 28.

54. Martin Manalansan conceives of "messy" as characterizing his ethnographic research (of queer Filipinx diasporic peoples) where "everyday life is not a mere conglomeration of routines and clear tactics," reflected in his field notes, which are "filled with contradictory and often disconnected ideas, quotes and scenes." Manalansan, "Queer Worldings," 566.

55. Hong and Junio, "Dazzle," 137. In *Transitive Cultures*, I define *transitive cultures* as "a set of shifting cultural practices tactically mobilized in contexts where identity is defined as fixed and authentic." Patterson, *Transitive Cultures*, 4.

56. Deleuze, *Francis Bacon*, 61 (italics in original).

57. Musser, *Sensual Excess*, 15.

58. Muñoz, *Sense of Brown*, 118.

59. Puar, *Right to Maim*, 60.

60. Spillers, "Mama's Baby, Papa's Maybe," 67; Cheng, "Ornamentalism," 416.

61. Mel Chen uses the term *reanimate* to understand how queer authors "animate" terms for new forms and collectives that express "beautiful collectivity/assemblage /reengagement of self with animate force." M. Chen, *Animacies*, 53.

62. Coráñez Bolton, *Crip Colony*, 133.

63. "Image Complex" was coined by Meg McLagan and Yates McKee to describe the infrastructure that produces and circulates visual experience. See McLagan and McKee, *Sensible Politics*.

64. Abbasi, "Trypophobia."

65. Ahmed, *Cultural Politics of Emotion*, 98.

66. Ahmed, *Cultural Politics of Emotion*, 97.

67. Vancouver Art Gallery, "Scott Eaton."

68. Kaplan, *Aerial Aftermaths*, 2.

69. Yapp, *Minor China*, 73–74.

70. Zimanyi, "*Human Flow*," 377 (italics in original).

71. These analyses of *Human Flow* were made in conversation with Y-Dang Troeung while we cotaught her last class together, a graduate seminar on critical refugee studies and debilitation.

72. Here I use imagination to conjure Hannah Arendt's "exertion of the imagination," which she believed was required for moral political thought (see more in chapter 5). Arendt, "Truth and Politics," 237.

73. Singh, *America's Long War*.

74. See Wolfe, *Traces of History*; Arvin, *Possessing Polynesians*.

75. I make these animalia comparisons to recognize, as Antoinette M. Burton and Renisa Mawani write, that within imperial discourses "the human/animal distinction [has] served as a recurrent reference point for who was expendable and who would flourish." Burton and Mawani, *Animalia*, 1.

76. W. Anderson, "Racial Hybridity," s105.

77. Heidi Nast writes that the domestication of the dog brought standardization and control as traits of British Empire and that "selective breeding commenced to create dogs physically tailored for war, hunting, herding, and even the sleeve or lap." Nast, "D Is for Dog," 46.

78. Musser, *Sensual Excess*, 3.

79. Pérez, *Taste for Brown Bodies*, 34.

80. Musser, *Sensual Excess*, 5.

81. Weinbaum, *Wayward Reproductions*.

82. Tadiar, "Himala (Miracle)," 724.

83. Coráñez Bolton, *Crip Colony*, 95.

84. Coráñez Bolton, *Crip Colony*, 31.

85. Ahmed, *Cultural Politics of Emotion*, 97.

86. Chun et al., "'Understanding' Asians," 432.

87. Chun et al., "'Understanding' Asians," 432.

88. Bow, *Racist Love*, 2.

89. Chun et al., "'Understanding' Asians," 433.

90. A. Chen, *Ilo Ilo*.

91. Johnson, *Knives Out*.

92. Lien et al., "Introduction," 4.

93. Tsing, "Nine Provocations," 232.

94. Manalansan, "Messy Mismeasures," abstract.

95. Muñoz defined a "brown commons" as people and things rendered "brown because they share an organicism that is not solely the organic of the natural as much as it is a certain brownness, which is embedded in a vast and pulsating social world." Muñoz, *Sense of Brown*, 2.

96. Cacho, *Social Death*, 150.

97. Melamed, "Racial Capitalism," 82.

98. Trask, "Settlers of Color," 2.

99. Saranillio, *Unsustainable Empire*, 17.

100. Táíwò, "Being-in-the-Room Privilege."

101. Muñoz, *Sense of Brown*, 87.

102. Muñoz, "Race, Sex," 112.

103. Coráñez Bolton and Ku, "Transregional Postcolonialisms."

104. I am thankful to the readers who evaluated this manuscript for Duke University Press, who provided many of the insights and language for this paragraph.

105. Hartman, "On Working with Archives."

CHAPTER 1. CROSSING THE CAUCASUS

Thank you to Christine Kim (University of British Columbia) and Helen Hok-Sze Leung (Simon Fraser University), who gave feedback on a 2018 version of this chapter that was later rejected by *Inter-Asia Cultural Studies*.

1. Saunders, *Mongol Conquests*, 12.

2. Chambers, *Genghis Khan*, 23.

3. Benjamin, *Empires of Ancient Eurasia*, 85.

4. Fijn, "Domestic and the Wild," 284.

5. Halberstam and Nyong'o, "Introduction," 454.

6. As Marianne Elisabeth Lien, Heather Anne Swanson, and Gro B. Ween write, "most scholars today agree that domestication is, at least, a two-way relationship." Lien, Swanson, and Ween, "Introduction," 15.

7. Morgan, *Mongols*, 5.

8. Deleuze and Guattari, *Nomadology*, 97.

9. Tsing, "Nine Provocations," 242.

10. *New York Times*, "E-Book Nonfiction."

11. Fusco, *Marco Polo*; Bodrov, *Mongol*.

12. Myadar, "Rebirth of Chinggis Khaan," 841.

13. Morefield, *Empires Without Imperialism*. See also Biran, "Mongol Empire."

14. Myadar, "Rebirth of Chinggis Khaan," 841.

15. Deep thanks to anonymous reader 2 for providing many of the insights of this paragraph, some of which have been revised from the reader's comments.

16. For more on One Belt, One Road and other Chinese imperial projects, see Miller, *China's Asian Dream*; Michel, "When China Met Africa," 39; Moyo, "Perspectives on South-South Relations"; and E. Wong et al., "One Belt, One Road."

17. Said, *Representations of the Intellectual*, xvi.

18. Said, *Representations of the Intellectual*, 76.

19. K.-H. Chen, *Asia as Method*, 18. Chen employs the term *subempire* "to refer to a lower-level empire that is dependent on an empire at a higher level in the imperialist hierarchy."

20. Morgan, *Mongols*, 33.

21. Down syndrome was once itself called Mongolism, and to have Mongolian traits often meant birth defects or ill health.

22. Bow, *Racist Love*, 2.

23. Hendricks, "Coloring the Past."

24. Hendricks, "Coloring the Past."

25. Heng, *Invention of Race*, 19.

26. Britton and Coles, "Spenser and Race," 3.

27. Coles, in Britton et al., "Spenser and Race," at 17:35–38.

28. Keevak, *Becoming Yellow*, 31.

29. Keevak, *Becoming Yellow*, 2.

30. Keevak, *Becoming Yellow*, 2.

31. Keevak, *Becoming Yellow*, 2.

32. M. Chen, "'Stuff of Slow Constitution.'"

33. Coles, in Britton et al., "Spenser and Race," at 22:30–34.

34. Again, deep thanks to anonymous reader 2 for providing many of the insights of this paragraph, some of which were revised from the reader's comments.

35. Gilley, "Case for Colonialism," 1.

36. Dawes and cosignatories, "Open Letter"; A. Rodriguez, "Case Against Colonialism."

37. Heward-Mills, "Addressing 'The Case for Colonialism.'"

38. Heward-Mills, "Addressing 'The Case for Colonialism,'" 2.

39. Carlin, "Wrath of the Khans."

40. Edward G. Browne, "1902," in Browne, *Literary History of Persia*, 4:426–27.

41. Morgan, *Mongols*, 64–65.

42. Korhonen, "Common Culture," 411.

43. The Republic of China in Taiwan only once ever used their veto at the United Nations, to keep Mongolia from being recognized. Morozova, *Socialist Revolutions in Asia*, 81. See also Bat-Ėrdėniĭn Baabar's "The Great Purge," which details the lamas, dissidents, and others imprisoned and shot during the Stalinist purges starting in 1937.

44. B. Lewis, *Islam in History*, 190.

45. Morgan, *Mongols*, 64–65.

46. Garten, *From Silk to Silicon*.

47. Nicolle, *Mongol Warlords*, 7.

48. Weatherford, *Quest for God*, 13.

49. Quoted in Watkins, "Genghis Khan"; see also Weatherford, "Jack Weatherford Says."

50. McNeill, *Plagues and Peoples*; Morgan, *Mongols*, 118.

51. Winchester, "Empire of Tolerance."

52. *Secret History of the Mongols*, 180.

53. Akim, *Just One Genghis Khan*, 142–43.

54. Harl, *Empires of the Steppes*, 288.

55. Haqqi, *Chingiz Khan*, xiii.

56. Haqqi, *Chingiz Khan*, 269.

57. Weatherford, *Quest for God*, 9.

58. Weatherford, *Quest for God*, 12.

59. Weatherford, *Quest for God*, 20.

60. Giffney, "Que(e)rying Mongols," 16.

61. Kublai Khan's policy of racial segregation: "The Chinese were forbidden to learn the Mongol language, marry Mongol, or carry arms." Saunders, *Mongol Conquests*, 124.

62. Reddy, *Freedom with Violence*.

63. Morgan, *Mongols*, 118; McNeill, *Plagues and Peoples*, 134.

64. Anievas and Nişancıoğlu, *How the West*, 72.

65. Harl, *Empires of the Steppes*, 410.

66. Morgan, *Mongols*, 66–67.

67. Morgan, *Mongols*, 38.

68. Morgan, *Mongols*, 81.

69. Saunders, *Mongol Conquests*, 95.

70. Harl, *Empires of the Steppes*, 307.

71. Harl, *Empires of the Steppes*, 330.

72. Harl, *Empires of the Steppes*, 331.

73. Morgan, *Mongols*, 56.

74. Gabriel, *Subotai the Valiant*, 78.

75. As amateur historian and podcaster Dan Carlin puts it in his "Wrath of the Khans" series, "Anyone with a skill that seemed useful to the Mongols—they'd just grab 'em." Carlin, "Wrath of the Khans," June 13, 2012.

76. Kenneth Harl writes that Genghis Khan's appreciation of Islam only arrived when he "toured the caravan cities of Transoxiana and eastern Iran, which his warriors had so ruthlessly sacked just years before." Harl, *Empires of the Steppes*, 290.

77. Moyo, "Perspectives on South-South Relations," 64.

78. Rossabi, *Mongols*, 112.

79. Reid, *Sojourners and Settlers*, 17.

80. Reid, *Sojourners and Settlers*, 17.

81. Morgan, *Mongols*, 120.

82. Peers, *Genghis Khan*, 70.

83. Andre Wink writes that "the Indian subcontinent has always been ecologically unsuitable for extensive pastoral nomadism, and . . . this is the main reason why it never invited the mass immigrations of nomadic peoples." Wink, "Post-Nomadic Empires," 124; see also Saunders, *Mongol Conquests*, 61.

84. Polo, *Travels of Marco Polo*, 97.

85. Wong, *Ali Wong: Baby Cobra*.

86. Saunders, *Mongol Conquests*, 112.

87. Saunders, *Mongol Conquests*, 112.

88. Saunders, *Mongol Conquests*, 117.

89. Weatherford, *Making of the Modern World*, 206.

90. Weatherford, *Genghis Khan*, 205.

91. McLynn, "Brutal Brilliance."

92. Anievas and Nişancıoğlu, *How the West*, 68–69.

93. McLynn, "Brutal Brilliance."

94. Muñoz, "Wildness," 658.

95. Saunders, *Mongol Conquests*, 89.

96. Winchester, "Empire of Tolerance."

CHAPTER 2. ILOCANOS ON THE RUN

Thanks to the readers of this chapter who gave valuable insights: Renisa Mawani, Allen Baylosis, and my family members Cameron Patterson, Chanel Guillermo, Dion Guillermo Glenn, and Mark Guillermo. Thanks to all the members of the Guillermo family who have continued to provide talk-story.

1. Teodoro, preface to *Out of This Struggle*, x.

2. Teodoro, preface to *Out of This Struggle*, xiv.

3. 1 Samuel 15:3 (NIV), accessed May 3, 2023, https://biblehub.com/niv/1_samuel/15.htm.

4. Byrd, "Beast of America," 600.

5. Cheung, *Articulate Silences*, 120.

6. Kim, "Korean American Literature," 170.

7. Saraf, "'We'd Rather Eat Rocks,'" 158.

8. Goodyear-Ka'ōpua, "Protectors of the Future," 190.

9. Vang, *History on the Run*, 8.

10. Vang, *History on the Run*, 6.

11. Vang, *History on the Run*, 6.

12. Said, *Reflections on Exile*, 149.

13. Zalloua, *Continental Philosophy*, 97.

14. E. Espiritu, "Vexed Solidarities," 24.

15. Tadiar, "Challenges for Cultural Studies," 23.

16. Tadiar, "Challenges for Cultural Studies," 23.

17. D. Rodriguez, "Not Classifiable," 155.

18. Coráñez Bolton, *Crip Colony*, 12.

19. Labrador, *Building Filipino Hawai'i*, 133.

20. Labrador, *Building Filipino Hawai'i*, 133.

21. Rafael, *White Love*, 33.

22. De Leon, "Sugarcane *Sakadas*," 56.

23. Chu and Hau, "Region and Microhistory," 300.

24. Coráñez Bolton, *Crip Colony*, 10.

25. Chu, "Including the Excluded."

26. De Leon, "Sugarcane *Sakadas*," 54.

27. Bulosan, *America*, 5.

28. Blanco, "Labor of History," 150.

29. Blanco, "Labor of History," 150.

30. Blanco, "Labor of History," 150.

31. De Leon, "Sugarcane *Sakadas*," 51.

32. Bautista, "ILIW," 36; Xenos, "Ilocos Coast Since 1800," 47.

33. Xenos, "Ilocos Coast Since 1800," 53.

34. Coráñez Bolton, *Crip Colony*, 6.

35. De Leon, "Sugarcane *Sakadas*," 52.

36. The Scouts were deemed a "military necessity" after the official end of the Philippine-American War, when US soldiers returned to the United States and left only US Regulars and Scouts. Kramer, *Blood of Government*, 114.

37. Kramer, *Blood of Government*, 114.

38. Marple, "Philippine Scouts," 118.

39. Thomas, "Isabelo de Los Reyes"; Kramer, *Blood of Government*, 65.

40. Kramer, *Blood of Government*, 65.

41. B. Anderson, "Rooster's Egg."

42. B. Anderson, *Age of Globalization*, 13.

43. B. Anderson, *Age of Globalization*, 228.

44. Kramer, *Blood of Government*, 68.

45. B. Anderson, *Age of Globalization*, 93n63.

46. Kramer, *Blood of Government*, 68; B. Anderson, *Age of Globalization*, 14.

47. De los Reyes, *Folk-lore filipino*, 20, quoted in Aguilar, "Tracing Origins," 615; also quoted in Kramer, *Blood of Government*, 68.

48. B. Anderson, *Age of Globalization*, 17.

49. Aguilar, "Tracing Origins," 616.

50. Aguilar, "Tracing Origins," 623n23.

51. Quoted in D. Rodriguez, "Not Classifiable," 153.

52. D. Rodriguez, "Not Classifiable," 153.

53. "The adventuresome Filipinos who came to Hawaii to work on the plantations typically went through their early working years with the singular goal of saving money in order to return to their barrio (rural neighborhood) with enough wealth to establish their social and economic security. That ambition was never achieved by the Filipinos who remained in Hawaii." R. Anderson et al., *Filipinos in Rural Hawaii*, ix.

54. Coráñez Bolton, *Crip Colony*, 100.

55. Mazza, "American Prisoners of War."

56. Ancestry.com, *Honolulu, Hawaii, US, Arriving and Departing Passenger and Crew Lists*.

57. R. Anderson et al., *Filipinos in Rural Hawaiʻi*, 10.

58. Basilio Agsalud enlisted in World War I in July 1918 to fight in the American army as a private and was discharged a year later, in September 1919. He received a draft registration card for both world wars, but it is unclear if this was the primary reason for his enlistment.

59. R. Anderson et al., *Filipinos in Rural Hawaiʻi*, 7.

60. Labrador, *Building Filipino Hawaiʻi*, 40.

61. Teodoro, *Out of This Struggle*, 7.

62. Teodoro, *Out of This Struggle*, 8.

63. Baldoz, *Third Asiatic Invasion*, 50.

64. Of the Filipino plantation workers, 37,114 (or 55.9 percent) came from Ilocos Norte from 1916 to 1928. Teodoro, *Out of This Struggle*, 13. See also R. Rodriguez, "Critical Filipino Studies Approach," 34.

65. Labrador, *Building Filipino Hawaiʻi*, 42.

66. Baldoz, *Third Asiatic Invasion*, 49.

67. Baldoz, *Third Asiatic Invasion*, 50.

68. De Leon, "Sugarcane *Sakadas*," 59.

69. Baldoz, *Third Asiatic Invasion*, 50.

70. R. Anderson et al., *Filipinos in Rural Hawaiʻi*, 3.

71. R. Anderson et al., *Filipinos in Rural Hawaiʻi*, 6.

72. De Leon, "Sugarcane *Sakadas*," 60.

73. Teodoro, *Out of This Struggle*, 21.

74. Labrador, *Building Filipino Hawaiʻi*, 41.

75. Hutchinson, *Legislative History*, 91.

76. Likely, were these migrations to occur today, they would be denied asylum as refugees, being labeled instead as *economic migrants*, a term "used in many instances to deny refugee claims, according to national protectionists who seek to disqualify applicants on the grounds that migrants who move for better economic opportunities cannot be considered refugees, who are deemed to be politically persecuted." Vinh Nguyen and Phu, "Critical Refugee Studies," 7.

77. Bautista, "ILIW," 37.

78. Teodoro, *Out of This Struggle*, 14.

79. These figures were made through the Google Maps tool "measure distance."

80. See my own experiences with being "brown Chinese diasporic" in chapter 4.

81. Hau, *Chinese Question*, 5.

82. Coulter, "Oahu Sugar Cane Plantation."

83. Perez, "Translation Politics," 212.

84. Jung, *Menace to Empire*, 150.

85. Baldoz, *Third Asiatic Invasion*, 56.

86. The Criminal Syndicalism Law of 1919, the Anarchistic Publications Law of 1921, and the Anti-Picketing Law of 1923. See Alcántara, "1924 Strike."

87. Alegado, "Blood in the Fields"; Bautista, "ILIW," 43.

88. Teodoro, *Out of This Struggle*, 21.

89. Ancestry.com, *U.S., World War II Draft Registration Cards, 1942*.

90. Teodoro, *Out of This Struggle*, 35.

91. R. Anderson et al., *Filipinos in Rural Hawai'i*, 27.

92. Cachola, "Beneath the Touristic Sheen," 285.

93. Kramer, *Blood of Government*, 68.

94. Perez, "Ilocano Immigrants' Renegotiation," 80.

95. Teodoro, *Out of This Struggle*, 45.

96. Blanco, "Labor of History," 148.

97. Chun et al., "'Understanding' Asians," 432.

98. Ettarh, "Vocational Awe and Librarianship."

99. Compoc, "Considerations," 271.

100. Teodoro, *Out of This Struggle*, 13.

101. Saranillio, "Colonial Amnesia," 262–63; Trask, "Settlers of Color," 2.

102. Saranillio, "Colonial Amnesia," 263.

103. Agsalud, "My Perceptions of the Plantation Experience," 12.

104. Teodoro, *Out of This Struggle*, 65.

105. Vinh Nguyen and Phu, "Critical Refugee Studies," 7.

CHAPTER 3. MIGRANT DOMESTIC WORKERS IN THE GLOBAL CITY

Thank you to Cathy, Guy, and Hsiu-chuan, who gave feedback on and helped publish a version of the paper I presented in Taipei in 2015: Christopher B. Patterson, "Matronly Maids and Willful Women," in *The Subject(s) of Human Rights: Crises, Violations, and Asian/American Critique*, ed. Cathy J. Schlund-Vials, Guy Beauregard, and Hsiu-chuan Lee (Temple University Press, 2019), 109–26.

Thank you to John Erni, who read and helped publish a version of this chapter based on the 2017 Hong Kong presentation: Christopher B. Patterson, "Queer, Brown, Migrant: Documenting the Hong Kong 'Helper,'" *Cultural Studies* 33, no. 6 (2019): 1008–28.

1. Tizon, "My Family's Slave."

2. Maich, "Domesticated Democracy?"

3. Reyes, "Filipinos Are Defending."

4. Rafael, "Lola's Resistant Dignity."

5. McElya, "Faithful Slave."

6. Rafael, "Lola's Resistant Dignity."

7. Nadurata, "Who Cares?," 347.

8. Rafael, "Lola's Resistant Dignity."

9. For deeper theorizations concerning Filipina domestic workers' relation to slavery, see the concepts of "unfreedom" in Parreñas, *Unfree*, and "disenfranchisement" in Tadiar, *Remaindered Life*.

10. Muñoz, "Ephemera as Evidence," 6.

11. Pratt, "Circulating Sadness," 6.

12. Pratt, "Circulating Sadness," 6.

13. Pratt, "Circulating Sadness," 13.

14. I gathered these statistics by using Google Scholar, with the keywords "Philippines 'migrant domestic workers.'" Searching for "Filipina domestic workers" resulted in over 4,500 texts, and "'OFW' domestic workers" over 9,800 texts.

15. Kang, *Traffic in Asian Women*, 35.

16. See the works of Rhacel Parreñas, Anna Romina Guevarra, and Robyn Rodriguez.

17. See Patterson, "Queer, Brown, Migrant"; and Patterson, "Matronly Maids."

18. Tadiar, *Remaindered Life*, 180–81.

19. Diaz, *Postcolonial Configurations*, 8–9, 25–26.

20. Kang, *Traffic in Asian Women*, 35.

21. Winkelmann, *Dangerous Intercourse*, 8.

22. Clutario, *Beauty Regimes*, 12.

23. Clutario, *Beauty Regimes*, 12.

24. *Online Etymology Dictionary*, "matron," accessed December 2, 2018, https://www.etymonline.com/word/matron.

25. Mabalon, *Little Manila*, 35.

26. Mendoza, *Metroimperial Intimacies*, 101.

27. Tadiar, "Himala (Miracle)"; D. Cruz, *Transpacific Femininities*.

28. D. Cruz, *Transpacific Femininities*, 6–7.

29. Mabalon, *Little Manila*, 10.

30. R. Rodriguez, *Migrants for Export*.

31. Guevarra, *Marketing Dreams*, 10.

32. Guevarra, *Marketing Dreams*, 8.

33. Yeung and Bacani, "When Love Is Not Enough."

34. See Human Rights Watch, *Maid to Order*; and Human Rights Watch, *Swept Under the Rug*.

35. Human Rights Watch, *Maid to Order*.

36. Human Rights Watch, for example, is limited to only seeing violations of domestic workers' human rights that rise to "the level of forced labor and debt bondage." Human Rights Watch, *Maid to Order*, 57.

37. Human Rights Watch, *Swept Under the Rug*, 80.

38. Human Rights Watch, *Swept Under the Rug*, 81.

39. Gonzalez, "Military Bases," 45.

40. I have previously expanded on the umpire as a neocolonial form of governance that seems to "exist outside of history" and acts in the name of "overcom[ing] the imperial violence and capitalist exploitation that defined all of history before it." Patterson, *Open World Empire*, 15.

41. Guevarra, *Marketing Dreams*, 8.

42. Constable, "Reproductive Labor," 46–47.

43. See, for example, *The Joy Luck Club* (by Amy Tan) and *The Woman Warrior* (by Maxine Hong Kingston).

44. Tadiar, "Himala (Miracle)," 724.

45. Tadiar, "Himala (Miracle)," 724.

46. Tadiar, "Himala (Miracle)," 724.

47. Tadiar, *Remaindered Life*, 98, 156.

48. Minh Nguyen et al., "Beyond the Global Care Chain," 200.

49. Padios, "Mining the Mind," 210.

50. Campomanes, "On Filipinos," 29.

51. Campomanes, "On Filipinos," 29.

52. Constable, *Maid to Order*, 53.

53. Hutton, "Domestic Workers' Rights Advocates."

54. Constable, *Maid to Order*, 52.

55. Tadiar, "Himala (Miracle)."

56. As Francisco-Menchavez writes, most academic work on migrant domestic workers has only seen domestic workers within a "vertical kinship structure" wherein "heteropatriarchal lineage takes primacy." Francisco-Menchavez, *Labor of Care*, 109.

57. Sim, "Sexual Economy of Desire," 14–15.

58. Lai, *Maid to Queer*, 14.

59. Rice et al., "Imagining Disability Futurities," 216. See Halberstam, *In a Queer Time and Place*; Edelman, *No Future*; Muñoz, *Cruising Utopia*.

60. Muñoz, *Cruising Utopia*, 98.

61. Gopinath, *Impossible Desires*, 56.

62. Gonzaga, "Cinematographic Unconscious," 103–4.

63. This point of view contrasts with Yun-Chung Chen and Mirana May Szeto's claim that Filipina workers have had an educational effect on Hong Kong society and that Sunday pageantry has "redefined Central for Hong Kong from the weekday space of capital to the weekend place of multiculturalism and quotidian diversity." Y.-C. Chen and Szeto, "In-Your-Face Multiculturalism," 56.

64. Avelino makes this connection more explicit in her TEDx Talk, where she says that climbing Mount Kilimanjaro "made me realize how far I have come from my roots

in the Philippines," and then shows an image of a slum in Davao City with broken concrete, focused on a nude child walking unattended. Avelino, "Breaking Notions."

65. Rangan, *Immediations*, 105.

66. Rangan, *Immediations*, 1.

67. Rangan, *Immediations*, 3.

68. Rangan, *Immediations*, 8.

69. Clutario, *Beauty Regimes*, 65.

70. Regina Ip Lau Suk-yee is the founder and current chairperson of the New People's Party (新民黨), a pro-Beijing conservative group in Hong Kong. Her comments sparked domestic worker protests in April 2015. Lam, "Regina Ip Accused."

71. Garcia, "Male Homosexuality," 13. See also Manalansan, *Global Divas*.

72. Benedicto, "Queer Afterlife," 582.

73. Ponce, *Beyond the Nation*, 20–22.

74. Rangan, *Immediations*, 110.

75. Barthes, "Grain of the Voice," 181 (author's italics), quoted in Rangan, "In Defense of Voicelessness," 102.

76. Alvar, *In the Country*. All subsequent cites of *In the Country* are given parenthetically in the text.

77. European Centre for Democracy and Human Rights, "Bahrain—Migrant Workers' Rights."

78. Parreñas, *Unfree*, 4.

79. Buhejji, "Bahrain's 'Third Millennium Slavery.'"

80. Arroyo, quoted in Guevarra, *Marketing Dreams*, 3. On Migrant Heroes Week, see R. Rodriguez, *Migrants for Export*, 75.

81. Guevarra, *Marketing Dreams*, 33.

82. D. Cruz, *Transpacific Femininities*, 193.

83. Parreñas, *Unfree*, 24.

84. Kahakauwila, *This Is Paradise*. All subsequent citations of *This Is Paradise: Stories* are given parenthetically in the text.

85. Hezel and Samuel, *Micronesians Abroad*.

86. Letman, "Micronesians in Hawaii."

87. Teaiwa, "Bikinis," 91.

88. See Day, "'This Is Paradise.'"

89. Alvar's book won the 2016 PEN/Robert W. Bingham Prize for Debut Fiction; Kahakauwila's was short-listed for the William Saroyan International Prize for Writing and was named a 2013 Barnes and Noble Discover Great New Writers Selection.

90. Ahmed, *Willful Subjects*, 2.

91. Teaiwa, "Bikinis," 87.

92. Teaiwa, "Bikinis," 92.

93. Gonzalez, *Securing Paradise*, 13.

94. Day, "'This Is Paradise,'" 40.

95. Ahmed, *Willful Subjects*, 143.

96. Day, "'This Is Paradise.'"

97. US Census Bureau, "Las Vegas City, Nevada"; UNLV Media Relations, "UNLV Most Diverse Campus."

98. Anzaldúa, *Borderlands/La Frontera*, 12.

99. Anzaldúa, *Borderlands/La Frontera*, 16.

100. Anzaldúa, *Borderlands/La Frontera*, 19.

101. Costen et al., "Racial and Ethnic Minorities," 65.

102. Ross, *Burlesque West*, 10.

103. Barthes, *Mythologies*, 84.

104. Quoted in Ross, *Burlesque West*, 95; and S. Sullivan, *Va Va Voom!*, 280.

105. J. Brown, *Babylon Girls*, 5–6.

106. J. Brown, *Babylon Girls*, 12.

107. Honeychild et al., "Not-So-Hidden Histories."

108. S. Lewis, "Looking Forward to the Past," 180.

109. Miller-Young, *Taste for Brown Sugar*, 19.

110. Miller-Young, *Taste for Brown Sugar*, 19.

111. Brown Girls Burlesque, accessed January 23, 2019, browngirlsburlesque.com.

112. Stretten, "Beautiful Brown Women."

113. Stretten, "Beautiful Brown Women."

114. J. Brown, *Babylon Girls*, 7.

115. Miss Di' Lovely website, accessed May 1, 2023, https://missdilovely.com/.

116. Clutario, *Beauty Regimes*, 48.

117. S. Lewis, "Looking Forward to the Past," 25.

118. D. Cruz, *Transpacific Femininities*, 2.

119. Coráñez Bolton, *Crip Colony*, 68, 73.

120. See, for example, the Clean Labor Art Project by Brendan Fernandes, which creates dance from domestic work. Fernandes, "*Clean Labour.*"

121. Thank you to Doris Lee at Open Door Hong Kong for facilitating these excursions. Thank you to the workers and volunteers at Las Filipinas, Enrich, and Bethune House Migrant Worker Refuge, for inviting my students and me into your collectives.

CHAPTER 4. ORGANIC AND INORGANIC CHINAS

Thank you to *Amerasia*, who helped edit and publish a smaller version of this chapter: Christopher B. Patterson and Y-Dang Troeung, "Organic and Inorganic Chinas: Desire and Fatigue in Global Hong Kong," *Amerasia Journal* 45, no. 3 (2019): 280–98.

1. During the 2011 Occupy movements in the United States, I had helped organize and participate in panels, sit-ins, walkouts, and marches for groups advocating greater democratic participation, immigrant rights, and economic equality. In the two years I had spent with the Seattle Asian American Film Festival, we had worked closely with organizations advocating Taiwanese nationalism and with the former Black Panthers.

2. The Sunflower Student Movement in Taiwan was a collective student-led protest that emerged in March 2014 as a response to the government's attempt to approve the Cross-Strait Service Trade Agreement, a free-trade pact with China. Student protesters occupied the Parliament for twenty-four days and organized a mass demonstration of about 700,000 people.

3. Wu, "Tea?"

4. Shi, *Visuality and Identity*, 4.

5. P. Liu, *Queer Marxism*, 17. As Liu writes, "The coexistence of two Chinas . . . limits the usefulness of nation-centered history. From the BEGINNING, the creation of two Chinas signals a sedimentation of multinational interests and conflicts" (16).

6. Wang X., "Manifesto for Cultural Studies," 287, 290.

7. L. Wong, *Transpacific Attachments*, 6.

8. L. Wong, *Transpacific Attachments*, 6.

9. Coráñez Bolton, *Crip Colony*, 27.

10. V. Huang, *Surface Relations*.

11. See, for example, Johansson, "White Skin, Large Breasts."

12. See Glenn, *Shades of Difference*; and Al-Solaylee, *Brown*.

13. Coráñez Bolton, *Crip Colony*, 106.

14. Coráñez Bolton, *Crip Colony*, 10.

15. Luis, *First Asians*, 6.

16. Luis, *First Asians*, 6–7.

17. Cox, "What Is a Hakka?," 117.

18. Cox, "What Is a Hakka?," 111.

19. Jung, "Coolie."

20. Brownness, as Najnin Islam, Kaneesha Cherelle Parsard, and Neelofer Qadir point out, was not always cathected toward indenture, but, rather, the need for indentured labor across the British, Spanish, and later American empires after the abolition of slavery produced particular iterations of brownness. Islam et al., "Indenture, Iteration," 19.

21. Islam et al., "Indenture, Iteration," 3.

22. Thank you to the anonymous readers of this manuscript, who lent clarity on the ideas of this paragraph and elsewhere in this chapter.

23. Cheah, "Global Dreams and Nightmares," 194.

24. For a similar theorization of Chinese inorganic racial form, see D. Wong, "Inorganic Asian North American Lives."

25. Chien and Tse, "'Hong Kong Card.'"

26. Ehrenreich, "Global Rebellion Against Neoliberalism."

27. T. Chow and Werner, "Congress's Hong Kong Bill."

28. For a discussion of the PRC's phenomenon of copied cities, see Bianca Bosker's *Original Copies*.

29. Lo, *Chinese Face/Off*, 80.

30. E.-B. Lim, *Brown Boys*, 389.

31. Lo, *Chinese Face/Off*, 111.

32. Hayot, *Hypothetical Mandarin*, 11.

33. Scott, *Art of Not Being Governed*, 3.

34. Scott, *Art of Not Being Governed*, 24.

35. Law, *Collaborative Colonial Power*, 10.

36. Law, *Collaborative Colonial Power*, 13.

37. Hall, "First New Left," 180.

38. Cheah, "Global Dreams and Nightmares," 196.

39. I previously defined a *global imaginary* as "the utopic imaginings of pluralist governmentality as a globally equalizing force" that "restructures the world upon a hierarchy of tolerance, where tolerance signifies global civility, and intolerance the provincial, violent, and uncivilized." Patterson, *Transitive Cultures*, 4.

40. Lo, *Chinese Face/Off*, 4.

41. Lo, *Chinese Face/Off*, 11, 15.

42. All subsequent citations of Theroux's book are given parenthetically in the text.

43. Wolfe, *Traces of History*, 5.

44. Examples include the proposal of Article 23 in 2003 that would enforce laws criminalizing treason, sedition, and secession; the moral and national curriculum changes in 2012; the decision for the Beijing government to preselect high-ranking electoral candidates in 2014; the barring and disqualifying of democratically elected candidates in 2016; and the proposed (and failed) extradition bill in 2019, which led to the forced imposition of national security laws imprisoning activists in 2020. All of these "encroachments" led to mass protests.

45. W. Wang et al., *Chinese Box*.

46. Luk, "Hong Kong as City/Imaginary," 79.

47. Rey Chow argues that Hong Kong in the 1990s was marked by a "double impossibility" of submitting to either Chinese nationalist repossession or British colonialism. R. Chow, *Ethics After Idealism*, 151.

48. Dowd, "California Dreamin.'"

49. See Schwyzer, "Real-World Consequences."

50. V. Huang, *Surface Relations*, 5.

51. Wing Sang Law writes, "In comparison with the 'pure' Chinese national body, Hong Kongers [have been] lamented for their sexual and amoral unpredictability." Law, *Collaborative Colonial Power*, 114.

52. Abbas, *Hong Kong*, 7.

53. Abbas, *Hong Kong*, 7.

54. Luk, "Hong Kong as City/Imaginary," 81.

55. Wang is a noted transnational filmmaker who has made films in English, Mandarin, Cantonese, and Japanese, describing himself as neither Chinese nor Chinese American but as "a bird without landing gear." Blair, "Filmart."

56. S. Lim, "Is the Trans-," 45.

57. G. Wang and Yeh, "Globalization and Hybridization," 190.

58. Lo, *Chinese Face/Off*, 74.

59. Aarseth, "Allegories of Space," 163.

60. Square Enix, *Sleeping Dogs*; K. Wong, "What *Sleeping Dogs*."

61. See Patterson and Fickle, *Made in Asia/America*.

62. Zhang, "Stroller in the City."

63. Since the 1997 handover, Hong Kong flags are only displayed alongside a PRC flag beside (and usually above) it.

64. Cheah, "Global Dreams and Nightmares," 195.

65. Sochan, "Interview."

66. See Edmond Chang's definition of "close play" in "Gaming as Writing."

67. Cheah, "Global Dreams and Nightmares," 197.

68. Suzuki et al., *Shenmue II.*

69. Cross, "'Walking Simulators.'"

70. Galloway, *Gaming,* 10.

71. Suzuki et al., *Shenmue.*

72. Nakamura, "Race in/for Cyberspace."

73. Sit and Wong, "Rural China," 50.

74. Sit and Wong, "Rural China," 50.

75. Chakrabarty, *Provincializing Europe,* 8.

76. Erni, "Who Needs Strangers?," 82.

77. Cheah, "Global Dreams and Nightmares," 197.

78. Erni, "Who Needs Strangers?," 79.

79. Ehrenreich, "Global Rebellion Against Neoliberalism."

80. Wang, "Manifesto for Cultural Studies," 287.

81. Wang, "Manifesto for Cultural Studies," 287.

CHAPTER 5. BROWN CRAFTS

Parts of this chapter were previously published as Christopher B. Patterson, "The Programmatic, the Problematic, and the Radical Racial Tradition (or, On Being Stamped)," in *Creative Writing Scholars on the Publishing Trade,* ed. Marshall Moore (Routledge, 2021), 127–39.

1. Often these books, like *The Help* and *Green Book,* are about the process of writing the very book the characters will publish; others, such as *Hidden Figures* and *Precious,* are about reflections on a lost past, while others like *Eat, Pray, Love* and *Wild* are about transformative journeys that culminate in a book publication. In all these cases, the books are published in a familiar trope some have called the "Instant Book Deal." TV Tropes, "Instant Book Deal."

2. Táíwò, "'Oppression.'"

3. Many thanks to David Chariandy, whose thoughts on writing have impacted my own. Thank you to my writing, thinking, and loving community: Elif Sari, Kim Bain, Danielle Wong, Crystal Webster, Christine Kim, Madeleine Thien, Rawi Hage, Ayasha Guerin, Justin Alger, Alifa Bandali, Ayesha Chaudhry, Rumee Ahmed, Vincent Ternida, Rebecca Monnerat, SF Ho, Doretta Lau, Mila Zuo, William Brown, Nathalie De Los Santos, JP Catungal, Jasbir Puar, Jordy Rosenberg, Jemima Pierre, Jan Padios, Tara Fickle, Lily Wong, and Anida Yoeu Ali.

4. I consider both my patrilineal name, "Christopher B. Patterson," and my matrilineal name, "Kawika Guillermo," pseudonyms, as both names were given to me by my parents and both misrepresent me in about equal measure. I see my real name located within the many pet names I have with friends, family, and lovers.

5. Coráñez Bolton, *Crip Colony,* 45.

6. *WordNet 3.0, Farlex Clipart Collection,* "craft," retrieved from *The Free Dictionary,* accessed May 6, 2024, https://www.thefreedictionary.com/craft.

7. Cole, "Carrying a Single Life."

8. Ruiz, *Left Turns,* 130.

9. See Jean-Paul Sartre on committed versus noncommitted literatures. Sartre, *"What Is Literature?"*

10. Sedgwick saw "paranoid readings" as those that overvalued transparency and exposure while seeing pleasure and self-nourishment as merely systemic, while "reparative readings" were those that conferred "plentitude on an object" when "the culture surrounding it is inadequate or inimical to its nurture." Sedgwick, *Touching Feeling*, 149.

11. McGurl, *Program Era*, 49.

12. Quoted in Flood, "NK Jemisin."

13. Viet Nguyen, "Dislocation Is My Location."

14. McGurl, *Program Era*, ix.

15. Besides those cited below, see also Kamola, *Making the World Global*; and Nadiminti, "Global Program Era."

16. Bennett, *Workshops of Empire*, 58.

17. Popescu, *At Penpoint*.

18. See Hong, *Minor Feelings*; Cruz, "(Mis)Education of the Filipino Writer"; Díaz, "MFA vs. POC"; Viet Nguyen, "Dislocation Is My Location"; Y. Liu, "World Comes to Iowa"; Batuman, "Invisible Vocation"; Jameson, "Dirty Little Secret."

19. Iber, "Spy Who Funded Me"; Best, "Stolen History"; Bennett, *Workshops of Empire*.

20. C. Cruz, "(Mis)Education," 6.

21. Nadal, "Cold War Remittance Economy," 559, 560.

22. Jameson, "Dirty Little Secret."

23. So, *Redlining Culture*.

24. See Melamed, "Spirit of Neoliberalism," 1.

25. Lee and Low Books, "Where Is the Diversity."

26. Lee and Low Books, "Where Is the Diversity."

27. Canaan, "Brownness," 232.

28. Canaan, "Brownness," 233.

29. Canaan, "Brownness," 233.

30. Jameson, "Dirty Little Secret," 207.

31. Batuman, "Invisible Vocation."

32. Batuman, "Invisible Vocation," 255.

33. Oates, *I Lock My Door*, 40, quoted in Batuman, "Invisible Vocation," 255.

34. Phruksachart, "Literature of White Liberalism."

35. Phruksachart, "Literature of White Liberalism"; Stockett, *The Help*.

36. B. Huang, *Contesting Genres*, 7.

37. Troeung, "Between Forced Confession," 225.

38. Hong, *Minor Feelings*, 80.

39. Vuong, "Letter to My Mother."

40. Shields, *Reality Hunger*; Ward, *Men We Reaped*.

41. Morrison and Lebowitz, "Conversation."

42. A. Brown, *Emergent Strategy*, 15.

43. Kondo, *Worldmaking*, 29.

44. Kondo, *Worldmaking*, 29.

45. Weheliye, *Habeas Viscus*, 2–3.

46. Wynter and Thomas, "ProudFlesh Inter/Views."

47. Kondo, *Worldmaking*, 25.

48. Taylor, *Archive and the Repertoire*, 20.

49. Gonzalves, "Repertoires on Other Stages."

50. M. Chen et al., "Introduction," 12.

51. Lorde, *Sister Outsider*, 82.

52. M. Chen, *Animacies*, 72.

53. Orwell, "Shooting an Elephant," 31.

54. Orwell, "Shooting an Elephant," 35.

55. Díaz, "MFA VS. POC."

56. Guillermo, *Stamped*, 3, italics removed.

57. Thank you, Rahima Schwenkbeck, my publisher at Westphalia, for believing in my work and for taking a chance on it.

58. Lorde, *Sister Outsider*, 129.

59. Patterson, *Transitive Cultures*, 4.

60. Said, *Representations of the Intellectual*, 53.

61. Roy, *Power Politics*, 7.

62. Ken Liu, "On showing vs. Telling: 'To write from resistance, telling is sometimes far superior. "Showing" is great when you're relying on a shared, implicit understanding,'" Twitter (now X), April 28, 2017, https://twitter.com/kyliu99/status/857760139146911744; quoted in Bodard, "Showing vs Telling."

63. Tan and Tijam, *Philippine Speculative Fiction Sampler*; Alfar and Nacino, *Farthest Shore*.

64. Thank you, Freya, for guiding me through Hong Kong's combative and enriching hidden art world. Chou et al., "Afterwork."

65. Saldívar, "Second Elevation."

66. C. Cruz, "(Mis)Education."

67. For more on my experience teaching bilingualism, see Patterson, "How to Drown."

68. Woolf, *Room of One's Own*, 35.

69. For more on these authors and what I call their "radical racial tradition," see Patterson, "Programmatic."

70. Hartman, "On Working with Archives."

71. I recall that this line came while listening to a podcast by Dan Carlin, though I am unable to locate it. Carlin, *Hardcore History* (podcast).

72. Said, *Culture and Imperialism*, 66; Patterson, *Open World Empire*, 32.

73. Human Rights Watch, "Yemen."

74. Kearney, "Sharpened Visions."

75. Troeung, *Landbridge*; Rosenberg, *Confessions of the Fox*.

AFTERWORD

1. Hernandez, *Aesthetics of Excess*.

2. Táíwò, "Being-in-the-Room Privilege."

3. Said, *Representations of the Intellectual*, 76.

4. Thank you to everyone from Y-Dang's lifeworld who has come into my own and supported my life and work: Heung and Yok Troeung, Sophia Troeung, Pheng Troeung, Mary Tsoi, Vinh Nguyen, Thy Phu, and many others. Thank you to the late Donald Goellnicht for bringing us together and guiding us along.

5. Aslam, "Are You Selling," 22.

6. Willcox, "Feeling Wheel."

7. Ettarh, "Vocational Awe and Librarianship."

8. As Fred Moten and Stefano Harney write of "the critical academic," "to be a critical academic in the university is to be against the university, and to be against the university is always to recognize it and be recognized by it, and to institute the negligence of that internal outside, that unassimilated underground, a negligence of it that is precisely, we must insist, the basis of the professions." Moten and Harney, "University and the Undercommons," 105.

9. Mimi Nguyen, "Getting Over Ourselves," 346.

10. West, "Ta-Nehisi Coates."

11. Troeung, *Landbridge*, 258.

12. Troeung, *Landbridge*, 258.

Aarseth, Espen. "Allegories of Space: The Question of Spatiality in Computer Games." In *Cybertext Yearbook 2000*, edited by Markku Eskelinen and Raine Koskimaa, 152–71. University of Jyväskylä, 2008.

Abbas, Ackbar. *Hong Kong: Culture and the Politics of Disappearance*. University of Minnesota Press, 1997.

Abbasi, Jennifer. "Is Trypophobia a Real Phobia?" *Popular Science*, July 25, 2011. http://www.popsci.com/trypophobia/.

Aboitiz, Nicole CuUnjieng. *Asian Place, Filipino Nation: A Global Intellectual History of the Philippine Revolution, 1887–1912*. Columbia University Press, 2020.

AFP. "Filipino Migrant Mothers in Hong Kong Sing for Their Distant Children." *Coconuts*, October 1, 2017. https://coconuts.co/manila/features/filipino-migrant-mothers-hong-kong-sing-distantchildren/.

Agsalud, Joshua. "My Perceptions of the Plantation Experience: Influences That Shaped My Views on the Americanization Process." Paper presented at the Philippine Studies Conference at the Center for Asian and Pacific Studies at the University of Hawai'i, "in commemoration of the 75th anniversary of the coming of Filipinos to Hawai'i," June 28, 1981.

Aguilar, Filomeno V., Jr. "Tracing Origins: 'Ilustrado' Nationalism and the Racial Science of Migration Waves." *Journal of Asian Studies* 64, no. 3 (2005): 605–37. https://www.jstor.org/stable/25075827.

Ahmed, Sara. *The Cultural Politics of Emotion*. Routledge, 2013.

Ahmed, Sara. *Willful Subjects*. Duke University Press, 2014.

Akim, Hatagin Gotov. *Just One Genghis Khan on Earth: The Sitting Pretty of Blue Mongols*. Jack Weatherford Foundation, 2014.

Alcántara, Rubén R. "The 1924 Strike." In *Filipino History in Hawaii Before 1946*, chap. 5. University of Hawai'i Press, 1988.

Alegado, Dean. "Blood in the Fields: The Hanapepe Massacre and the 1924 Filipino Strike." *Positively Filipino*, November 26, 2012. https://www.positivelyfilipino.com/magazine/2012/11/26/blood-in-the-fields-the-hanapepe-massacre-and-the-1942-filipino-strike.

Alfar, Dean Francis, and Joseph Frederic F. Nacino. *The Farthest Shore: An Anthology of Fantasy Fiction from the Philippines*. University of Hawai'i Press, 2014.

Al-Solaylee, Kamal. *Brown: What Being Brown in the World Today Means (to Everyone)*. HarperCollins, 2016.

Alvar, Mia. *In the Country: Stories*. Alfred A. Knopf, 2015.

Ancestry.com. *Honolulu, Hawaii, U.S., Arriving and Departing Passenger and Crew Lists, 1900–1959*. Lehi, UT: Ancestry.com Operations, 2009. https://www.ancestry.com/search/collections/1502/.

Ancestry.com. *U.S., World War II Draft Registration Cards, 1942*. Lehi, UT: Ancestry.com Operations, 2010. https://www.ancestry.com/search/collections/1002/?redirectFor=db.aspx. Original data: United States, Selective Service System. Selective Service Registration Cards, World War II: Fourth Registration. Records of the Selective Service System, Record Group Number 147. National Archives and Records Administration.

Anderson, Benedict. *The Age of Globalization*. Verso Books, 2013.

Anderson, Benedict. "The Rooster's Egg: Isabelo de los Reyes and *El folk-lore filipino*." Blog, Verso Books, June 15, 2016. https://www.versobooks.com/blogs/2705-the-rooster-s-egg-isabelo-de-los-reyes-and-el-folk-lore-filipino.

Anderson, Robert N., Richard Coller, and Rebecca F. Pestano. *Filipinos in Rural Hawaii*. University of Hawai'i Press, 1984.

Anderson, Warwick. "Racial Hybridity, Physical Anthropology, and Human Biology in the Colonial Laboratories of the United States." *Current Anthropology* 53, no. S5 (2012): S95–S107.

Anievas, Alexander, and Kerem Nişancıoğlu. *How the West Came to Rule: The Geopolitical Origins of Capitalism*. Pluto, 2015.

Anzaldúa, Gloria. *Borderlands/La Frontera: The New Mestiza*. Aunt Lute Books, 1987.

Arendt, Hannah. "Truth and Politics." In *Between Past and Future: Six Exercises in Political Thought*, 227–64. Penguin, 2006.

Armstrong, William N. *Around the World with a King*. F. A. Stokes, 1904.

Arvin, Maile Renee. *Possessing Polynesians: The Science of Settler Colonial Whiteness in Hawaii and Oceania*. Duke University Press, 2019.

Aslam, Mubeen M. "Are You Selling the Right Colour? A Cross-Cultural Review of Colour as a Marketing Cue." *Journal of Marketing Communications* 12, no. 1 (2006): 15–30.

Avelino, Liza. "Breaking Notions and Finding Freedom in the Mountains." TEDxTinHauWomen, November 3, 2017. YouTube, posted November 28, 2017. https://www.youtube.com/watch?v=3jk9BmR6G98.

Baabar, Bat-Èrdèniïn. "The Great Purge." In *The History of Mongolia*, edited by David Sneath and Christopher Kaplonski, 3:1001–12. Leiden: Brill, 2010.

Baldoz, Rick. *The Third Asiatic Invasion: Empire and Migration in Filipino America, 1898–1946*. New York University Press, 2015.

Baldwin, James. *Notes of a Native Son*. Beacon, 1955.

Barthes, Roland. "The Grain of the Voice." In *Image, Music, Text*, translated by Stephen Heath, 179–89. Hill and Wang, 1977.

Barthes, Roland. *Mythologies*. Translated by Annette Lavers. Hill and Wang, 1984.

Batuman, Elif. "The Invisible Vocation." In *MFA vs NYC: The Two Cultures of American Fiction*, edited by Chad Harbach, 241–61. Farrar, Straus and Giroux, 2014.

Bautista, Elma P. "ILIW: Longing and Belonging in Ilokano Narratives of Displacements." *International Journal of Humanities, Philosophy, Language* 1, no. 4 (2018): 34–46. https://www.ijhpl.com/PDF/IJHPL-2018-04-12-03.pdf.

Benedicto, Bobby. "The Queer Afterlife of the Postcolonial City: (Trans)gender Performance and the War of Beautification." *Antipode* 47, no. 3 (2015): 580–97.

Benjamin, Craig. *Empires of Ancient Eurasia: The First Silk Roads Era, 100 B.C.E.–250 C.E.* Cambridge University Press, 2018.

Bennett, Eric. *Workshops of Empire*. University of Iowa Press, 2015.

Best, Emma. "The Stolen History of the CIA and the Asian Foundation." MuckRock, November 2, 2017. https://www.muckrock.com/news/archives/2017/nov/02/taf-1/.

Biran, Michal. "The Mongol Empire in World History: The State of the Field." *History Compass* 11, no. 11 (2013): 1021–33. http://doi.org/10.1111/hic3.12095.

Blair, Gavin J. "Filmart: How Wayne Wang Rebuilt 'While the Women Are Sleeping' as a Japanese Story (Q&A)." *Hollywood Reporter*, March 13, 2016. https://www.hollywoodreporter.com/news/how-wayne-wang-rebuilt-women-874983.

Blanco, Jody. "The Labor of History in Filipinx Historiography." In *Filipinx American Studies: Reckoning, Reclamation, Transformation*, edited by Rick Bonus and Antonio T. Tiongson Jr., 148–60. Fordham University Press, 2022.

Blumenbach, Johann Friedrich. *Anthropological Treatises of Johann Friedrich Blumenbach*. The Anthropological Society, 1898.

Bodard, Aliette de. "Showing vs Telling." Aliette de Bodard's website, April 28, 2017. https://www.aliettedebodard.com/2017/04/28/showing-vs-telling/.

Bodrov, Sergei, dir. *Mongol*. Kinokompaniya CTB, 2007.

Boge, Andrew Parayil. "*US v. Thind* and the Rhetorical Labors of 'Where Are You From?'" *Ethnic Studies Review* 46, nos. 1–2 (2023): 69–92.

Borisa, Dhiren, and Gavin Brown. "Intimate Borders of South Asian Queer Diasporas in the UK." In *The Routledge Companion to Gender and Borderlands*, edited by Zalfa Feghali and Deborah Toner, 94–104. Taylor and Francis, 2024.

Bosker, Bianca. *Original Copies: Architectural Mimicry in Contemporary China*. Hong Kong University Press / University of Hawai'i Press, 2013.

Bow, Leslie. *Racist Love: Asian Abstraction and the Pleasures of Fantasy*. Duke University Press, 2022.

Bowers, Joanna, dir. *The Helper*. Cheeky Monkey Productions, 2017.

Bradley, Mark Philip. *Imagining Vietnam and America: The Making of Postcolonial Vietnam, 1919–1950*. University of North Carolina Press, 2003.

Britton, Dennis Austin, and Kimberly Anne Coles. "Spenser and Race: An Introduction." *Spenser Studies* 35, no. 1 (2021): 1–19.

Britton, Dennis Austin, Kimberly Anne Coles, and John Yargo. "Spenser and Race: A Discussion with Dennis Austin Britton and Kimberly Anne Coles." *Literary Studies* (podcast), New Books Network, July 12, 2022. https://newbooksnetwork.com/spenser-and-race-a-discussion-with-dennis-austin-britton-and-kimberly-anne-coles.

Brown, Adrienne M. *Emergent Strategy: Shaping Change, Changing Worlds*. AK Press, 2017.

Brown, Jayna. *Babylon Girls: Black Women Performers and the Shaping of the Modern*. Duke University Press, 2008.

Browne, Edward G. *A Literary History of Persia*. Vol. 4, *Modern Times (1500–1924)*. Cambridge University Press, 1959.

Buhejji, Hana. "Bahrain's 'Third Millennium Slavery.'" European Commission, 2011. Accessed April 5, 2015. https://ec.europa.eu/europeaid/sites/devco/files/article -hanabuhejji_en.pdf.

Bulosan, Carlos. *America Is in the Heart*. Harcourt, Brace, 1946.

Burton, Antoinette M., and Renisa Mawani. *Animalia: An Anti-Imperial Bestiary for Our Times*. Duke University Press, 2020.

Byrd, Jodi A. "Beast of America: Sovereignty and the Wildness of Objects." *South Atlantic Quarterly* 117, no. 3 (2018): 599–615.

Cacho, Lisa Marie. *Social Death: Racialized Rightlessness and the Criminalization of the Unprotected*. New York University Press, 2012.

Cachola, Ellen-Rae. "Beneath the Touristic Sheen of Waikīkī." In *Detours: A Decolonial Guide to Hawai'i*, edited by Hokulani K. Aikau and Vernadette Vicuña Gonzalez, 283–92. Duke University Press, 2019.

Campomanes, Oscar V. "On Filipinos, Filipino Americans, and US Imperialism: Interview with Oscar V. Campomanes." Interview by Antonio T. Tiongson. In *Positively No Filipinos Allowed: Building Communities and Discourse*, edited by Antonio Tiongson, Edgardo Gutierrez, Ricardo Gutierrez, and Ricardo Valencia Gutierrez, 26–42. Temple University Press, 2006.

Canaan, Andrea. "Brownness." In *This Bridge Called My Back: Writings by Radical Women of Color*, edited by Cherrie Moraga and Gloria E. Anzaldúa, 232–37. Kitchen Table, Women of Color Press, 1983.

Capino, Diosdado, Maria Minerva A. Gonzales, and Filipinas E. Pineda. *Rizal's Life, Works, and Writings: Their Impact on Our National Identity*. Goodwill Trading, 1997.

Carlin, Dan. *Hardcore History* (podcast). 2006–23. https://www.dancarlin.com /hardcorehistory-series/.

Carlin, Dan. "The Wrath of the Khans." *Hardcore History* (podcast), 2014–15. https:// www.dancarlin.com/product/hardcore-history-wrath-of-the-khans-series/.

Caronan, Faye. *Legitimizing Empire: Filipino American and US Puerto Rican Cultural Critique*. University of Illinois Press, 2015.

Chakrabarty, Dipesh. *Provincializing Europe: Postcolonial Thought and Historical Difference*. Princeton University Press, 2000.

Chambers, James. *Genghis Khan*. History Press, 2012.

Chang, Edmond. "Gaming as Writing, or, World of Warcraft as World of Wordcraft." *Computers and Composition Online*, Fall 2008. http://cconlinejournal.org/gaming _issue_2008/Chang_Gaming_as_writing/index.html.

Cheah, Pheng. "Global Dreams and Nightmares: The Underside of Hong Kong as a Global City in Fruit Chan's Hollywood, Hong Kong." In *Hong Kong Culture*, edited by Louie Kam, 193–211. Hong Kong University Press, 2010.

Chen, Anthony, dir. *Ilo Ilo*. Golden Village Pictures, 2016.

Chen, Kuan-Hsing. *Asia as Method: Toward Deimperialization*. Duke University Press, 2010.

Chen, Mel Y. *Animacies: Biopolitics, Racial Mattering, and Queer Affect*. Duke University Press, 2012.

Chen, Mel Y. "'The Stuff of Slow Constitution': Reading Down Syndrome for Race, Disability, and the Timing That Makes Them So." *Somatechnics* 6, no. 2 (2016): 235–48.

Chen, Mel Y., Alison Kafer, Eunjung Kim, and Julie Avril Minich. "Introduction: Crip Genealogies." In *Crip Genealogies*, edited by Mel Chen, Alison Kafer, Eunjung Kim, and Julie Avril Minich, 1–57. Duke University Press, 2023.

Chen, Tina. "(The) Transpacific Turns." In *The Oxford Encyclopedia of Asian American Literature and Culture*, edited by Josephine Lee. Oxford University Press, 2020.

Chen, Yun-Chung, and Mirana May Szeto. "In-Your-Face Multiculturalism: Reclaiming Public Space and Citizenship by Filipina Immigrant Workers in Hong Kong." In *Worlding Multiculturalisms: The Politics of Inter-Asian Dwelling*, edited by Daniel P. S. Goh, 55–74. Routledge, 2014.

Cheng, Anne Anlin. "Ornamentalism: A Feminist Theory for the Yellow Woman." *Critical Inquiry* 44, no. 3 (2018): 415–46.

Cheung, King-Kok. *Articulate Silences: Hisaye Yamamoto, Maxine Hong Kingston, and Joy Kogewa*. Cornell University Press, 1993.

Cheung, King-Kok, ed. *An Interethnic Companion to Asian American Literature*. Cambridge University Press, 1997.

Chien, Chris, and Ellie Tse. "'The Hong Kong Card': Against the New Cold War." *The Abusable Past, Radical History Review*, October 23, 2019. https://abusablepast.org/the -hong-kong-card-against-the-new-cold-war/.

Chou, Freya, Cosmin Costinas, Inti Guerrero, and Qinyi Lim, eds. "Afterwork." Para Site, May 18, 2016. https://www.para-site.art/exhibitions/afterwork/.

Chow, Rey. *Ethics After Idealism: Theory—Culture—Ethnicity—Reading*. Indiana University Press, 1998.

Chow, Tobita, and Jack Werner. "Congress's Hong Kong Bill Is Giving Cover to Nationalism." *Nation*, November 27, 2019. https://www.thenation.com/article/archive /hkhrda-hong-kong-congress/.

Chu, Richard T. "Including the Excluded: The 'Chinese' in the Philippines and the Study of 'Migration' in Filipinx American Studies." In *Filipinx American Studies: Reckoning, Reclamation, Transformation*, edited by Rick Bonus and Antonio T. Tiongson Jr., 128–37. Fordham University Press, 2022.

Chu, Richard T., and Caroline Hau. "Region and Microhistory: Writing the Chinese Diaspora in the Philippines." *Kritika Kultura*, no. 21/22 (2013): 299–306.

Chuh, Kandice. *The Difference Aesthetics Makes: On the Humanities After Man*. Duke University Press, 2019.

Chun, Wendy Hui Kyong, Grace Kyungwon Hong, and Lisa Nakamura. "'Understanding' Asians: Anti-Asian Racism, Sentimentality, Sentiment Analysis, and Digital Surveillance." *Critical Inquiry* 50, no. 3 (2024): 425–51.

Clifford, Hugh Charles. *Studies in Brown Humanity: Being Scrawls and Smudges in Sepia, White and Yellow*. G. Richards, 1898.

Clutario, Genevieve Alva. *Beauty Regimes: A History of Power and Modern Empire in the Philippines, 1898–1941*. Duke University Press, 2023.

Coates, Austen. *Rizal: Philippine Nationalist and Martyr*. Oxford University Press, 1968.

Cole, Teju. "Carrying a Single Life: On Literature and Translation." *New York Review of Books*, July 5, 2019. https://www.nybooks.com/online/2019/07/05/carrying-a-single -life-on-literaturetranslation/.

Compoc, Kim. "Considerations from the US-Occupied Pacific." In *Filipinx American Studies: Reckoning, Reclamation, Transformation*, edited by Rick Bonus and Antonio T. Tiongson Jr., 267–74. Fordham University Press, 2022.

Constable, Nicole. *Maid to Order in Hong Kong: Stories of Filipina Workers*. Cornell University Press, 1997.

Constable, Nicole. "Reproductive Labor at the Intersection of Three Intimate Industries: Domestic Work, Sex Tourism, and Adoption." *positions: asia critique* 24, no. 1 (2016): 45–69.

Contreras, Kristian. "Letter to My Daughter." *Intersections: Critical Issues in Education* 4, no. 1 (2020). https://digitalrepository.unm.edu/intersections/vol4/iss1/6.

Coráñez Bolton, Sony. *Crip Colony: Mestizaje, US Imperialism, and the Queer Politics of Disability in the Philippines*. Duke University Press, 2023.

Coráñez Bolton, Sony, and Ryanson Alessandro Ku. "cfp: Transregional Postcolonialisms: Queer Remainders of Disappearing Imperialism (acla 2019)." *H-Net*, 2018. https://networks.h-net.org/node/5293/discussions/2273334/cfp-transregional -postcolonialisms-queer-remainders-disappearing.

Costen, Wanda M., Alison G. Cliath, and Robert H. Woods. "Where Are the Racial and Ethnic Minorities in Hotel Management? Exploring the Relationship Between Race and Position in Hotels." *Journal of Human Resources in Hospitality and Tourism* 1, no. 2 (2002): 57–69.

Coulter, John Wesley. "The Oahu Sugar Cane Plantation, Waipahu." *Economic Geography* 9, no. 1 (1933): 60–71.

Cox, Jordan Lynton. "What Is a Hakka? Tracing the Development of Hakka Ethnic Identity in Jamaica." *Verge: Studies in Global Asias* 10, no. 1 (2024): 108–35.

Crawford, Margo Natalie. "What Time Is It When You're Black?" *South Atlantic Quarterly* 121, no. 1 (2022): 153–72.

Cross, Katherine. "How 'Walking Simulators' Allow Us to Touch Other Worlds." Game Developer, August 13, 2015. https://www.gamedeveloper.com/design/how-walking -simulators-allow-us-to-touch-other-worlds.

Cruz, Conchitina. "The (Mis)Education of the Filipino Writer." *Kritika Kultura*, no. 28 (2017): 3–34.

Cruz, Denise. *Transpacific Femininities: The Making of the Modern Filipina*. Duke University Press, 2012.

Cruz, Oggs. "'Sunday Beauty Queen' Review: Enthralling Reality." *Rappler*, December 27, 2016. https://www.rappler.com/entertainment/movies/156745-mmff-2016 -sunday-beauty-queen-review/.

Cuarón, Alfonso, dir. *Roma*. Netflix, 2018.

Curaming, Rommel A. "Filipinos as Malay: Historicising an Identity." In *Melayu: Politics, Poetics and Paradoxes of Race*, edited by Maznah Mohamad and Syed Muhd Khairudin Aljunied, 241–74. National University of Singapore Press, 2011.

Curaming, Rommel A. "Rizal and the Rethinking of the Analytics of the Malayness." *Inter-Asia Cultural Studies* 18, no. 3 (2017): 325–37.

Dawes, Simon, and cosignatories. "Open Letter to Third World Quarterly on the Publication of 'The Case for Colonialism.'" *openDemocracy*, September 20, 2017. https://www.opendemocracy.net/en/open-letter-to-third-world-quarterly-on-publication-of-case-for-coloniali/.

Day, Leanne P. "'This Is Paradise': Transpacific Labor, Indigeneity, and 'Undocumented' in Hawai'i's Hospitality Industry." In *Transpacific, Undisciplined*, edited by Lily Wong, Christopher B. Patterson, and Chien-ting Lin, 29–49. University of Washington Press, 2024.

De Leon, Adrian. "Sugarcane *Sakadas*: The Corporate Production of the Filipino on a Hawai'i Plantation." *Amerasia Journal* 45, no. 1 (2019): 50–67.

Deleuze, Gilles. *Francis Bacon: The Logic of Sensation*. University of Minnesota Press, 2003.

Deleuze, Gilles, and Félix Guattari. *Nomadology: The War Machine*. Translated by Brian Massumi. Semiotext(e), 1986.

De los Reyes, Isabelo. *El folk-lore filipino* [Philippine folklore]. Translated by Salud C. Dizon and Maria Elinora P. Imson. University of the Philippines Press, 1994.

Desmond, Jane. "Picturing Hawai'i: The Ideal Native and the Origins of Tourism, 1880–1915." *positions: asia critique* 7, no. 2 (1999): 459–501.

Diaz, Josen Masangkay. *Postcolonial Configurations: Dictatorship, the Racial Cold War, and Filipino America*. Duke University Press, 2022.

Díaz, Junot. "MFA vs. POC." *New Yorker*, April 30, 2014. https://www.newyorker.com/books/page-turner/mfa-vs-poc.

Dowd, A. A. "California Dreamin' on a Hong Kong Night." *A.V. Club*, August 22, 2014. https://www.avclub.com/california-dreamin-on-a-hong-kong-night-1798271515.

Du Bois, W. E. B. *The Health and Physique of the Negro American: Report of a Social Study Made Under the Direction of Atlanta University, Together with the Proceedings of the Eleventh Conference for the Study of Negro Problems, Held at Atlanta University, on May the 29th, 1906*. Atlanta University Press, 1906.

Dunne, John Gregory. *Delano: The Story of the California Grape Strike*. University of California Press, 2008.

Edelman, Lee. *No Future: Queer Theory and the Death Drive*. Duke University Press, 2004.

Ehrenreich, Ben. "Welcome to the Global Rebellion Against Neoliberalism." *Nation*, November 19, 2019. https://www.thenation.com/article/archive/global-rebellions-inequality/.

Erni, John Nguyet. "Who Needs Strangers? Un-Imagining Hong Kong Chineseness." *Chinese Journal of Communication* 5, no. 1 (2012): 78–87.

Espiritu, Evyn Lê. "Vexed Solidarities: Vietnamese Israelis and the Question of Palestine." *Lit: Literature Interpretation Theory* 29, no. 1 (2018): 8–28.

Espiritu, Yến Lê. "A Critical Transnational Perspective to Asian America." In *Oxford Handbook of Philosophy and Race*, edited by Naomi Zack, 102–13. Oxford University Press, 2016.

Ettarh, Fobazi. "Vocational Awe and Librarianship: The Lies We Tell Ourselves." *In the Library with the Lead Pipe*, January 10, 2018. http://www.inthelibrarywiththeleadpipe .org/2018/vocational-awe/.

European Centre for Democracy and Human Rights. "Bahrain—Migrant Workers' Rights, June 2019." Accessed September 7, 2025. https://www.ecdhr.org/wp-content /uploads/2019/06/2019.06_Bahrain_Migrant-workers%E2%80%99-rights.pdf.

Far, Sui Sin. "Leaves from the Mental Portfolio of a Eurasian." *Independent* 66, no. 3138 (1909): 225–32.

Fernandes, Brendan. "*Clean Labour.*" Brendan Fernandes's website, 2017. http://www .brendanfernandes.ca/clean-labour.

Fijn, Natasha. "The Domestic and the Wild in the Mongolian Horse and the Takhi." In *Taxonomic Tapestries: The Threads of Evolutionary, Behavioural and Conservation Research*, edited by Alison M. Behie and Marc F. Oxenham, 279–98. Australian National University, 2015.

Fish, Jennifer N. *Domestic Workers of the World Unite! A Global Movement for Dignity and Human Rights*. New York University Press, 2017.

Flood, Alison. "NK Jemisin: 'It's Easier to Get a Book Set in Black Africa Published If You're White.'" *Guardian*, May 2, 2020. https://www.theguardian.com/books/2020 /may/02/nk-jemisin-its-easier-to-get-a-book-set-in-black-africa-published-if-youre -white.

Francisco-Menchavez, Valerie. *The Labor of Care: Filipina Migrants and Transnational Families in the Digital Age*. University of Illinois Press, 2018.

Fusco, John, creator. *Marco Polo* (series). Netflix, 2014–16.

Gabriel, Richard A. *Subotai the Valiant: Genghis Khan's Greatest General*. Greenwood, 2004.

Galloway, Alexander. *Gaming: Essays on Algorithmic Culture*. University of Minnesota Press, 2006.

Garcia, J. Neil C. "Male Homosexuality in the Philippines: A Short History." *IIAS Newsletter* 35 (2004): 13.

Garten, Jeffrey E. *From Silk to Silicon: The Story of Globalization Through Ten Extraordinary Lives*. Amberley, 2016.

Giffney, Noreen. "Que(e)rying Mongols." *Medieval Feminist Forum: A Journal of Gender and Sexuality* 36, no. 1 (2003): 15–21.

Gilley, Bruce. "The Case for Colonialism." *Third World Quarterly* (September 2017): 1–17.

Girard, Greg, and Ian Lambot. *City of Darkness: Life in Kowloon Walled City*. Watermark, 1993.

Glenn, Evelyn Nakano, ed. *Shades of Difference: Why Skin Color Matters*. Stanford University Press, 2009.

Glissant, Édouard. *Poetics of Relation*. Translated by Betsy Wing. University of Michigan Press, 1997.

Gonzaga, Elmo. "The Cinematographic Unconscious of Slum Voyeurism." *Cinema Journal* 56, no. 4 (2017): 102–25.

Gonzalez, Vernadette Vicuña. "Military Bases, 'Royalty Trips,' and Imperial Modernities: Gendered and Racialized Labor in the Postcolonial Philippines." *Frontiers: A Journal of Women Studies* 28, no. 3 (2007): 28–59.

Gonzalez, Vernadette Vicuña. *Securing Paradise: Tourism and Militarism in Hawai'i and the Philippines*. Duke University Press, 2013.

Gonzalves, Theodore S. "Repertoires on Other Stages." In *Filipinx American Studies: Reckoning, Reclamation, Transformation*, edited by Rick Bonus and Antonio T. Tiongson Jr., 308–19. Fordham University Press, 2022.

Gonzalves, Theodore S., and Roderick N. Labrador. *Filipinos in Hawai'i*. Arcadia, 2011.

Goodyear-Ka'ōpua, Noelani. "Protectors of the Future, Not Protestors of the Past: Indigenous Pacific Activism and Mauna a Wākea." *South Atlantic Quarterly* 116, no. 1 (2017): 184–94.

Gopinath, Gayatri. *Impossible Desires: Queer Diasporas and South Asian Public Cultures*. Duke University Press, 2005.

Guevarra, Anna Romina. *Marketing Dreams, Manufacturing Heroes: The Transnational Labor Brokering of Filipino Workers*. Rutgers University Press, 2009.

Guillermo, Kawika [Christopher B. Patterson]. *All Flowers Bloom*. Westphalia, 2020.

Guillermo, Kawika [Christopher B. Patterson]. *Nimrods: a fake-punk self-hurt anti-memoir*. Duke University Press, 2023.

Guillermo, Kawika [Christopher B. Patterson]. *Stamped: an anti-travel novel*. Westphalia, 2018.

Guzmán, Joshua Javier. "Brown." In *Keywords for Latina/o Studies*, edited by Deborah R. Vargas, Nancy Raquel Mirabal, and Lawrence La Fountain-Stokes, 25–28. New York University Press, 2017.

Haidarali, Laila. *Brown Beauty: Color, Sex, and Race from the Harlem Renaissance to World War II*. New York University Press, 2018.

Halberstam, Jack. *In a Queer Time and Place: Transgender Bodies, Subcultural Lives*. New York University Press, 2005.

Halberstam, Jack, and Tavia Nyong'o. "Introduction: Theory in the Wild." *South Atlantic Quarterly* 117, no. 3 (2018): 453–64.

Hall, Stuart. "Life and Times of the First New Left." *New Left Review*, no. 61 (2010): 177–96.

Haqqi, Anwarul Haque. *Chingiz Khan: The Life and Legacy of an Empire Builder*. Primus Books, 2010.

Harl, Kenneth W. *Empires of the Steppes: The Nomadic Tribes Who Shaped Civilization*. HarperCollins, 2024.

Harney, Stefano, Fred Moten, Sandra Ruiz, and Hypatia Vourloumis. "Resonances: A Conversation on Formless Formation." *e-flux journal*, no. 121 (2021). https://www.e-flux.com/journal/121/423318/resonances-a-conversation-on-formless-formation/.

Harrison, Benjamin T. "The Muhammad Ali Draft Case and Public Debate on the Vietnam War." *Peace Research* 33, no. 2 (2001): 69–86.

Hartman, Saidiya. "On Working with Archives: An Interview with Writer Saidiya Hartman." From a conversation with Thora Siemsen. *Creative Independent*, April 18, 2018. https://thecreativeindependent.com/people/saidiya-hartman-on-working-with-archives/.

Hau, Caroline S. *The Chinese Question: Ethnicity, Nation, and Region in and Beyond the Philippines*. National University of Singapore Press, 2014.

Hayot, Eric. *The Hypothetical Mandarin: Sympathy, Modernity, and Chinese Pain*. Oxford University Press, 2009.

Hendricks, Margo. "Coloring the Past, Rewriting Our Future: RaceB4Race." In *Gender and Sexuality in Ancient Greece*, edited by Jody Valentine. The Claremont Colleges Library, 2019. https://pressbooks.claremont.edu/clas114valentine/chapter/coloring-the-past-rewriting-ourfuture-raceb4race/.

Heng, Geraldine. *The Invention of Race in the European Middle Ages*. Cambridge University Press, 2018.

Hernandez, Jillian. *Aesthetics of Excess: The Art and Politics of Black and Latina Embodiment*. Duke University Press, 2020.

Heward-Mills, Leon. "Addressing 'The Case for Colonialism' Viewpoint Essay, 26th September 2017." Taylor and Francis website, September 26, 2017. https://www.tandfonline.com/pb-assets/TWQ-response-Sept-2017.pdf.

Hezel, Francis X., and S. E. Samuel. *Micronesians Abroad*. Micronesian Seminar, 2006.

Hindi, Noor. "Fuck Your Lecture on Craft, My People Are Dying," *Poetry*, December 2020. https://www.poetryfoundation.org/poetrymagazine/poems/154658/fuck-your-lecture-on-craft-my-people-are-dying.

Holden, Philip. "Dissonant Voices: Straits Chinese Appropriation of Colonial Travel Writing." *Studies in Travel Writing* 2, no. 1 (1998): 181–89.

Honeychild, Chicava, Dustin M. Wax, Janelle Smith, Sydney F. Lewis (Doctor Ginger Snapz), and The Shanghai Pearl. "Not-So-Hidden Histories: Performers of Color in Burlesque." Burlesque Hall of Fame, 2013. https://www.burlesquehall.com/exhibition/not-so-hidden-histories-performers-of-color-in-burlesque/.

Hong, Cathy Park. *Minor Feelings: An Asian American Reckoning*. One World, 2020.

Hong, Greyson, and Kiam Junio. "Dazzle: A Conversation on Transgender Subjectivity with Greyson Hong and Kiam Junio." Interview by Jan Christian Bernabe and Laura Kina. In *Queering Contemporary Asian American Art*, edited by Laura Kina and Jan Christian Bernabe, 129–37. University of Washington Press, 2017.

Huang, Betsy. *Contesting Genres in Contemporary Asian American Fiction*. Palgrave Macmillan, 2010.

Huang, Vivian L. *Surface Relations: Queer Forms of Asian American Inscrutability*. Duke University Press, 2022.

Human Rights Watch. "Maid to Order: Ending Abuses Against Migrant Domestic Workers in Singapore." December 6, 2005. https://www.hrw.org/report/2005/12/06/maid-order/ending-abuses-against-migrant-domestic-workers-singapore.

Human Rights Watch. "Swept Under the Rug: Abuses Against Domestic Workers Around the World." July 27, 2006. https://www.hrw.org/report/2006/07/27/swept-under-rug/abuses-against-domestic-workers-around-world.

Human Rights Watch. "Yemen: US Bombs Used in Deadliest Market Strike; Coalition Allies Should Stop Selling Weapons to Saudi Arabia." April 7, 2016. https://www.hrw.org/news/2016/04/08/yemen-us-bombs-used-deadliest-market-strike.

Hurston, Zora Neale. "How It Feels to Be Colored Me." In *I Love Myself When I Am Laughing . . . And Then Again When I Am Looking Mean and Impressive: A Zora Neale Hurston Reader*, 152–55. Feminist Press at CUNY, 1979.

Hutchinson, Edward P. *Legislative History of American Immigration Policy, 1798–1965*. University of Pennsylvania Press, 1981.

Hutton, Mercedes. "Domestic Workers' Rights Advocates Call on Hong Kong Gov't to Mandate Monthly 'Living Wage' of HK$6,300." *Hong Kong Free Press*, August 2, 2024. https://hongkongfp.com/2024/08/02/domestic-workers-rights-advocates-call-on-hong-kong-govt-to-mandate-monthly-living-wage-of-hk6300/.

Iber, Patrick. "The Spy Who Funded Me: Revisiting the Congress for Cultural Freedom." *Los Angeles Review of Books*, June 11, 2017. https://lareviewofbooks.org/article/the-spy-who-funded-me-revisiting-the-congress-for-cultural-freedom/.

Isaac, Allan Punzalan. *American Tropics: Articulating Filipino America*. University of Minnesota Press, 2006.

Islam, Najnin, Kaneesha Cherelle Parsard, and Neelofer Qadir. "Indenture, Iteration: Race and the Aesthetics of Contract Labor." *Verge: Studies in Global Asias* 10, no. 1 (2024): 1–24.

Jameson, Fredric. "Dirty Little Secret." In *MFA vs NYC: The Two Cultures of American Fiction*, edited by Chad Harbach, 206–20. Farrar, Straus and Giroux, 2014.

Johansson, Perry. "White Skin, Large Breasts: Chinese Beauty Product Advertising as Cultural Discourse." *China Information* 13, no. 2–3 (1998): 59–84.

Johnson, Rian, dir. *Knives Out*. Lionsgate Films, 2019.

Jung, Moon-Ho. "Coolie." In *Keywords for American Cultural Studies*, edited by Bruce Burgett and Glenn Handler, 64–66. New York University Press, 2007. https://keywords.nyupress.org/american-cultural-studies/essay/coolie/.

Jung, Moon-Ho. *Menace to Empire: Anticolonial Solidarities and the Transpacific Origins of the US Security State*. University of California Press, 2022.

Juvaini, Ata-Malik. *Genghis Khan: The History of the World Conqueror*. Translated and edited by J. A. Boyle. Manchester University Press, 1958.

Kahakauwila, Kristiana. *This Is Paradise: Stories*. Hogarth, 2013.

Kamola, Isaac A. *Making the World Global: U.S. Universities and the Production of the Global Imaginary*. Duke University Press, 2019.

Kang, Laura Hyun Yi. *Traffic in Asian Women*. Duke University Press, 2020.

Kaplan, Caren. *Aerial Aftermaths*. Duke University Press, 2017.

Kearney, Douglas. "Sharpened Visions: A Poetry Workshop." *Coursera*, CalArts, 2021. https://www.coursera.org/learn/poetry-workshop.

Keevak, Michael. *Becoming Yellow: A Short History of Racial Thinking*. Princeton University Press, 2011.

Kim, Elaine H. "Korean American Literature." In *An Interethnic Companion to Asian American Literature*, edited by King-Kok Cheung, 156–91. Cambridge University Press, 1997.

Kingston, Maxine Hong. *The Woman Warrior: Memoirs of a Girlhood Among Ghosts.* Alfred A. Knopf, 1976.

Kondo, Dorinne. *Worldmaking: Race, Performance, and the Work of Creativity.* Duke University Press, 2018.

Korhonen, Pekka. "Common Culture: Asia Rhetoric in the Beginning of the 20th Century." *InterAsia Cultural Studies* 9, no. 3 (2008): 395–417.

Kramer, Paul Alexander. *The Blood of Government: Race, Empire, the United States, and the Philippines.* University of North Carolina Press, 2006.

Kramer, Paul Alexander. "Race-Making and Colonial Violence in the US Empire: The Philippine-American War as Race War." *Diplomatic History* 30, no. 2 (2006): 169–210.

Labrador, Roderick N. *Building Filipino Hawai'i.* University of Illinois Press, 2015.

Lam, Jeffie. "Regina Ip Accused of Racism over Tales of Filipino Maids Bedding Expat Bosses." *South China Morning Post,* April 17, 2015. http://www.scmp.com/news/hong-kong/education-community/article/1769002/regina-ip-accused-racism-over-tales-filipino.

Law, Wing Sang. *Collaborative Colonial Power: The Making of the Hong Kong Chinese.* Hong Kong University Press, 2009.

Lee and Low Books. "Where Is the Diversity in Publishing? The 2019 Diversity Baseline Survey Results." *Open Book Blog,* Lee and Low Books, January 28, 2020. https://www.leeandlow.com/about/diversity-baseline-survey/dbs2/.

Letman, John. "Micronesians in Hawaii Face Uncertain Future: COFA Agreements Provide US Regional Control in Exchange for Limited Access to America." *Al Jazeera,* October 3, 2013. http://www.aljazeera.com/humanrights/2013/10/micronesians-hawaii-face-uncertain-future-201310191535637288.html.

Lewis, Bernard. *Islam in History: Ideas, People, and Events in the Middle East.* Rev. ed. Open Court, 1993.

Lewis, Sydney Fonteyn. "Looking Forward to the Past: Black Women's Sexual Agency in 'Neo' Cultural Productions." PhD diss., University of Washington, 2012. https://digital.lib.washington.edu/server/api/core/bitstreams/a823bf5f-9425-4319-bbd4-443d4f6b2713/content.

Lien, Marianne Elisabeth, Heather Anne Swanson, and Gro B. Ween. "Introduction: Naming the Beast—Exploring the Otherwise." In *Domestication Gone Wild: Politics and Practices of Multispecies Relations,* edited by Heather Anne Swanson, Marianne Elisabeth Lien, and Gro B. Ween, 1–30. Duke University Press, 2018.

Lim, Eng-Beng. *Brown Boys and Rice Queens: Spellbinding Performance in the Asias.* New York University Press, 2014.

Lim, Song Hwee. "Is the Trans- in Transnational the Trans- in Transgender?" *New Cinemas: Journal of Contemporary Film* 5, no. 1 (2007): 39–52.

Liu, Petrus. *Queer Marxism in Two Chinas.* Duke University Press, 2015.

Liu, Yi-hung. "The World Comes to Iowa in the Cold War: International Writing Program and the Translation of Mao Zedong." *American Quarterly* 69, no. 3 (2017): 611–31.

Lo, Kwai-Cheung. *Chinese Face/Off: The Transnational Popular Culture of Hong Kong.* University of Illinois Press, 2005.

London, Jack. *Revolution, and Other Essays*. Macmillan, 1910.

Lorde, Audre. *Sister Outsider: Essays and Speeches*. Crossing, 2012.

Lovely, Di'. "Paseo Di' Lovely." Filipina burlesque, performed October 27, 2013, at the Hubba Hubba Revue Broadway Studios, San Francisco, CA. YouTube, posted by Miss-DiLovely, November 2, 2017. https://www.youtube.com/watch?v=-LS8soSNF5A.

Lowe, Lisa. *The Intimacies of Four Continents*. Duke University Press, 2015.

Lubbock, Percy. *The Craft of Fiction*. No. 5. C. Scribner's Sons, 1921.

Luis, Diego Javier. *The First Asians in the Americas: A Transpacific History*. Harvard University Press, 2023.

Luk, Thomas YT. "Hong Kong as City/Imaginary in *The World of Suzie Wong, Love Is a Many Splendored Thing*, and *Chinese Box*." *New Asian Academic Bulletin* 18 (2002): 73–82.

Mabalon, Dawn Bohulano. *Little Manila Is in the Heart: The Making of the Filipina/o American Community in Stockton, California*. Duke University Press, 2013.

Maich, Katherine Eva. "Domesticated Democracy? Labor Rights at Home in Lima and New York City." PhD diss., University of California, Berkeley, 2017. https://escholarship.org/content/qt3kc758f9/qt3kc758f9.pdf.

Man, Simeon. *Soldiering Through Empire: Race and the Making of the Decolonizing Pacific*. University of California Press, 2018.

Manalansan, Martin F., IV. *Global Divas: Filipino Gay Men in the Diaspora*. Duke University Press, 2003.

Manalansan, Martin F., IV. "Messy Mismeasures: Exploring the Wilderness of Queer Migrant Lives." *South Atlantic Quarterly* 117, no. 3 (2018): 491–506.

Manalansan, Martin F., IV. "Queer Worldings: The Messy Art of Being Global in Manila and New York." *Antipode* 47, no. 3 (2015): 566–79.

Manuud, Antonio G., ed. *Brown Heritage: Essays on Philippine Cultural Tradition and Literature*. Ateneo de Manila University Press, 1967.

Marple, Allan D. "The Philippine Scouts: A Case Study in the Use of Indigenous Soldiers, Northern Luzon, the Philippine Islands, 1899." Master's thesis, US Army Command and General Staff College, 1983.

Mazza, Eugene A. "The American Prisoners of War Rescued After the Sinking of the Japanese Transport, Shinyō Maru, by the USS Paddle, SS 263, on 7 September 1944." SubmarineSailor.com, February 15, 2004. http://www.submarinesailor.com/history/pow/paddlesinksshinyomaru/.

McElya, Micki. "The Faithful Slave: How Alex Tizon's Essay Echoes a Trope with Deep Roots in American History." *Atlantic*, May 31, 2017. https://www.theatlantic.com/business/archive/2017/05/the-faithful-slave/528630/.

McGurl, Mark. *The Program Era: Postwar Fiction and the Rise of Creative Writing*. Harvard University Press, 2009.

McLagan, Meg, and Yates McKee. *Sensible Politics: The Visual Culture of Nongovernmental Activism*. Zone Books, 2012.

McLynn, Frank. "The Brutal Brilliance of Genghis Khan." History Extra, February 22, 2019. https://www.historyextra.com/period/medieval/the-brutal-brilliance-of-genghis-khan/.

McNeill, William H. *Plagues and Peoples*. Anchor Press / Doubleday, 1976.

Melamed, Jodi. "Racial Capitalism." *Critical Ethnic Studies* 1, no. 1 (2015): 76–85.

Melamed, Jodi. "The Spirit of Neoliberalism: From Racial Liberalism to Neoliberal Multiculturalism." *Social Text* 24, no. 4 (2006): 1–24.

Mendoza, Victor. *Metroimperial Intimacies: Fantasy, Racial-Sexual Governance, and the Philippines in U.S. Imperialism, 1899–1913*. Duke University Press, 2016.

Michel, Serge. "When China Met Africa." *Foreign Policy*, no. 166 (2008): 38–46.

Miller, Tom. *China's Asian Dream: Empire Building Along the New Silk Road*. Zed Books, 2017.

Miller-Young, Mireille. *A Taste for Brown Sugar: Black Women in Pornography*. Duke University Press, 2014.

Morefield, Jeanne. *Empires Without Imperialism: Anglo-American Decline and the Politics of Deflection*. Oxford University Press, 2014.

Morgan, David. *The Mongols*. Blackwell, 1986.

Morozova, Irina Y. *Socialist Revolutions in Asia: The Social History of Mongolia in the 20th Century*. Routledge, 2009.

Morrison, Toni, and Fran Lebowitz. "Toni Morrison in Conversation with Fran Lebowitz." Live from the New York Public Library, November 12, 2008. https://www.nypl .org/audiovideo/toni-morrison-conversation-fran-lebowitz.

Moten, Fred, and Stefano Harney. "The University and the Undercommons: Seven Theses." *Social Text* 22, no. 2 (2004): 101–15.

Moyo, Sam. "Perspectives on South-South Relations: China's Presence in Africa." *Inter-Asia Cultural Studies* 17, no. 1 (2016): 58–67.

Muñoz, José Esteban. *Cruising Utopia: The Then and There of Queer Futurity*. New York University Press, 2009.

Muñoz, José Esteban. "Ephemera as Evidence: Introductory Notes to Queer Acts." *Women and Performance: A Journal of Feminist Theory* 8, no. 2 (1996): 5–16.

Muñoz, José Esteban. "Race, Sex, and the Incommensurate: Gary Fisher with Eve Kosofsky Sedgwick." In *Queer Futures: Reconsidering Ethics, Activism, and the Political*, edited by Elahe Haschemi Yekani, Eveline Kilian, and Beatrice Michaelis, 103–16. Routledge, 2013.

Muñoz, José Esteban. *The Sense of Brown*. Duke University Press, 2020.

Muñoz, José Esteban. "The Wildness of the Punk Rock Commons." *South Atlantic Quarterly* 117, no. 3 (2018): 653–58.

Musser, Amber Jamilla. *Sensual Excess: Queer Femininity and Brown Jouissance*. New York University Press, 2018.

Myadar, Orhon. "The Rebirth of Chinggis Khaan: State Appropriation of Chinggis Khaan in Post-Socialist Mongolia." *Nationalities Papers* 45, no. 5 (2017): 840–55.

Nadal, Paul. "Cold War Remittance Economy: US Creative Writing and the Importation of New Criticism into the Philippines." *American Quarterly* 73, no. 3 (2021): 557–95.

Nadiminti, Kalyan. "The Global Program Era: Contemporary International Fiction in the American Creative Economy." *Novel* 51, no. 3 (2018): 375–98.

Nadurata, Edward. "Who Cares? Ability and the Elderly Question in Filipinx American Studies." In *Filipinx American Studies: Reckoning, Reclamation, Transformation*, edited by Rick Bonus and Antonio T. Tiongson Jr., 343–51. Fordham University Press, 2022.

Nakamura, Lisa. "Race in/for Cyberspace: Identity Tourism and Racial Passing on the Internet." *Works and Days* 13, no. 1–2 (1995): 181–93.

Nast, Heidi J. "D Is for Dog." In *Animalia: An Anti-Imperial Bestiary for Our Times*, edited by Antoinette Burton and Renisa Mawani, 45–62. Duke University Press, 2020.

New York Times. "E-Book Nonfiction." October 12, 2014. https://www.nytimes.com /books/best-sellers/2014/10/12/e-book-nonfiction.

Nguyen, Mimi Thi. "Getting Over Ourselves." *Journal of Asian American Studies* 25, no. 2 (2022): 343–50.

Nguyen, Minh TN, Roberta Zavoretti, and Joan Tronto. "Beyond the Global Care Chain: Boundaries, Institutions and Ethics of Care." *Ethics and Social Welfare* 11, no. 3 (2017): 199–212.

Nguyen, Viet Thanh. "Dislocation Is My Location." *PMLA* 133, no. 2 (2018): 428–36.

Nguyen, Vinh, and Thy Phu. "Critical Refugee Studies in Canada: An Introduction." In *Refugee States: Critical Refugee Studies in Canada*, edited by Vinh Nguyen and Thy Phu, 1–22. University of Toronto Press, 2021.

Nicolle, David. *The Mongol Warlords: Genghis Khan, Kublai Khan, Hhuelchu Tamerlane*. Firebird Books, 1990.

Oates, Joyce Carol. *I Lock My Door upon Myself*. Ecco, 1990.

Orwell, George. "Shooting an Elephant." In *Shooting an Elephant and Other Essays*, 31–43. Penguin, 1970.

Padios, Jan M. "Mining the Mind: Emotional Extraction, Productivity, and Predictability in the Twenty-First Century." *Cultural Studies* 31, no. 2–3 (2017): 205–31.

Parreñas, Rhacel. *Unfree: Migrant Domestic Workers in Arab States*. Stanford University Press, 2021.

Patterson, Christopher B. "Brown Theory: A Storied Manifest of Our World." *positions: asia critique* 31, no. 1 (2023): 91–116.

Patterson, Christopher B. "How to Drown: Bilingual Creative Writers in a Sea of Meanings." *TEXT* 21, Special 47 (2017): 1–11.

Patterson, Christopher B. "Matronly Maids and Willful Women." In *The Subject(s) of Human Rights: Crises, Violations, and Asian/American Critique*, edited by Cathy J. Schlund-Vials, Guy Beauregard, and Hsiu-Chuan Lee, 109–26. Temple University Press, 2019.

Patterson, Christopher B. *Open World Empire: Race, Erotics, and the Global Rise of Video Games*. New York University Press, 2020.

Patterson, Christopher B. "The Programmatic, the Problematic, and the Radical Racial Tradition (or, On Being Stamped)." In *Creative Writing Scholars on the Publishing Trade*, edited by Marshall Moore, 127–39. Routledge, 2021.

Patterson, Christopher B. "Queer, Brown, Migrant: Documenting the Hong Kong 'Helper.'" *Cultural Studies* 33, no. 6 (2019): 1008–28.

Patterson, Christopher B. *Transitive Cultures: Anglophone Literature of the Transpacific*. Rutgers University Press, 2018.

Patterson, Christopher B., and Tara Fickle, eds. *Made in Asia/America: Why Video Games Were Never (Really) About Us*. Duke University Press, 2024.

Patterson, Christopher B., and Y-Dang Troeung. "Organic and Inorganic Chinas: Desire and Fatigue in Global Hong Kong." *Amerasia Journal* 45, no. 3 (2019): 280–98.

Peers, Chris. *Genghis Khan and the Mongol War Machine*. Pen and Sword, 2015.

Pérez, Hiram. *A Taste for Brown Bodies: Gay Modernity and Cosmopolitan Desire*. New York University Press, 2015.

Perez, Ma. Socorro Q. "Ilocano Immigrants' Renegotiation of Space in GUMIL Hawaii Fiction (Circa 80s)." *Kritika Kultura*, no. 10 (2008): 80–112.

Perez, Ma. Socorro Q. "Translation Politics in Ilocano-Hawaiian Writing." *Kritika Kultura*, no. 24 (2015): 206–61.

Phruksachart, Melissa. "The Literature of White Liberalism." *Boston Review*, August 21 2020. https://www.bostonreview.net/articles/melissa-phruksachart-literature-white -liberalism/.

Pillai, Daksha. "United States v. Bhagat Singh Thind: Dual Legacies of a Forgotten Supreme Court Case." The Gilder Lehrman Institute of American History, 2021. https://www.gilderlehrman.org/sites/default/files/file_media/38_Pillai.pdf.

Polo, Marco. *The Travels of Marco Polo*. Wordsworth Editions, 1997.

Ponce, Danilo E. Foreword to *Out of This Struggle*, by Luis V. Teodoro, xi–xiii. University of Hawai'i Press, 2019.

Ponce, Martin Joseph. *Beyond the Nation: Diasporic Filipino Literature and Queer Reading*. New York University Press, 2012.

Popescu, Monica. *At Penpoint: African Literatures, Postcolonial Studies, and the Cold War*. Duke University Press, 2020.

Pratt, Geraldine. "Circulating Sadness: Witnessing Filipina Mothers' Stories of Family Separation." *Gender, Place and Culture* 16, no. 1 (2009): 3–22.

Princess Orig. "Kayumanggi Versus Maputi: 100 Years of America's White Aesthetics in Philippine Literature." In *Mixed Blessing: The Impact of the American Colonial Experience on Politics and Society in the Philippines*, edited by Hazel M. McFerson, 99–131. Greenwood, 2002.

Puar, Jasbir K. *The Right to Maim*. Duke University Press, 2017.

Rafael, Vicente L. "Lola's Resistant Dignity: Reading 'My Family's Slave' in the Context of Philippine History." *Atlantic*, May 31, 2017. https://www.theatlantic.com/business /archive/2017/05/lola-unconquered/527964/.

Rafael, Vicente L. *White Love and Other Events in Filipino History*. Duke University Press, 2000.

Rangan, Pooja. *Immediations: The Humanitarian Impulse in Documentary*. Duke University Press, 2017.

Rangan, Pooja. "In Defense of Voicelessness: The Matter of the Voice and the Films of Leslie Thornton." *Feminist Media Histories* 1, no. 3 (2015): 95–126.

Reddy, Chandan. *Freedom with Violence: Race, Sexuality, and the US State*. Duke University Press, 2011.

Reid, Anthony, ed. *Sojourners and Settlers: Histories of Southeast Asia and the Chinese*. With the assistance of Kristine Alilunas Rodgers. University of Hawai'i Press, 2001.

Reyes, Therese. "Filipinos Are Defending Alex Tizon from Western Backlash to His Story 'My Family's Slave.'" *Quartz*, May 17, 2017. https://qz.com/985614/the

-atlantics-my-familys-slavecover-story-filipinos-defend-alex-tizon-from-western
-backlash.

Rice, Carla, Eliza Chandler, Jen Rinaldi, et al. "Imagining Disability Futurities." *Hypatia*
32, no. 2 (2017): 213–29.

Ricoeur, Paul. *Lectures on Imagination*. University of Chicago Press, 2024.

Rizal, Jose. *Noli Me Tángere*. 1887.

Rodriguez, Amardo. "A Case Against Colonialism." *Postcolonial Studies* 21, no. 2 (2018):
254–59.

Rodriguez, Dylan. "Not Classifiable as Orientals or Caucasians or Negroes." In *Filipino
Studies: Palimpsests of Nation and Diaspora*, edited by Martin F. Manalansan and
Augusto Fauni Espiritu, 151–78. New York University Press, 2016.

Rodriguez, Robyn Magalit. *Migrants for Export: How the Philippine State Brokers Labour
to the World*. University of Minnesota Press, 2010.

Rodriguez, Robyn Magalit. "Toward a Critical Filipino Studies Approach to Philippine Migration." In *Filipino Studies: Palimpsests of Nation and Diaspora*, edited by
Martin F. Manalansan and Augusto Fauni Espiritu, 33–55. New York University Press,
2016.

Rosenberg, Jordy. *Confessions of the Fox*. One World, 2019.

Ross, Becki. *Burlesque West: Showgirls, Sex, and Sin in Postwar Vancouver*. University of
Toronto Press, 2009.

Rossabi, Morris. *The Mongols: A Very Short Introduction*. Oxford University Press,
2012.

Roy, Arundhati. *Power Politics*. South End, 2001.

Ruiz, Sandra. *Left Turns in Brown Study*. Duke University Press, 2024.

Ruiz, Sandra, and Hypatia Vourloumis. *Formless Formation: Vignettes for the End of This
World*. Minor Compositions/Autonomedia, 2021.

Said, Edward W. *Culture and Imperialism*. Vintage, 2012.

Said, Edward W. *Reflections on Exile and Other Essays*. Harvard University Press,
2000.

Said, Edward W. *Representations of the Intellectual*. Vintage, 2012.

Saldívar, Ramón. "The Second Elevation of the Novel: Race, Form, and the Postrace
Aesthetic in Contemporary Narrative." *Narrative* 21, no. 1 (2013): 1–18.

Saraf, Aanchal. "'We'd Rather Eat Rocks': Contesting the Thirty Meter Telescope." *Journal of Transnational American Studies* 11, no. 1 (2020): 151–75.

Saranillio, Dean Itsuji. "Colonial Amnesia: Rethinking Filipino 'American' Settler
Empowerment in the U.S. Colony of Hawai'i." In *Asian Settler Colonialism*, edited
by Jonathan Y. Okamura and Candace Fujikane, 256–78. University of Hawai'i Press,
2018.

Saranillio, Dean Itsuji. *Unsustainable Empire: Alternative Histories of Hawai'i Statehood*.
Duke University Press, 2018.

Sartre, Jean-Paul. *"What Is Literature?" and Other Essays*. Harvard University Press,
1988.

Saunders, J. J. *The History of the Mongol Conquests*. University of Pennsylvania Press,
1971.

Schwyzer, Hugo. "The Real-World Consequences of the Manic Pixie Dream Girl Cliché." *Atlantic*, July 9, 2013. https://www.theatlantic.com/sexes/archive/2013/07/the-real-world-consequences-of-the-manic-pixie-dream-girl-clich-233/277645/.

Scott, James C. *The Art of Not Being Governed: An Anarchist History of Upland Southeast Asia*. Yale University Press, 2009.

Secret History of the Mongols: The Origin of Chingis Khan. Translated by Paul Khan and Francis Woodman Cleaves. Expanded ed. Cheng and Tsui Company, 1998.

Sedgwick, Eve Kosofsky. *Touching Feeling: Affect, Pedagogy, Performativity*. Duke University Press, 2003.

See, Sarita Echavez. "Language Run Amok." In *Filipinx American Studies: Reckoning, Reclamation, Transformation*, edited by Rick Bonus and Antonio T. Tiongson Jr., 370–78. Fordham University Press, 2022.

Shah, Vidya. "Brown Identities, Complicities, and Complexities: Towards Brown-Black Solidarities." *Journal of Critical Race Inquiry* 10, no. 1 (2023): 1–26.

Sharma, Nitasha Tamar. "Brown." In *Keywords for Asian American Studies*, edited by Cathy J. Schlund-Vials, Linda Trinh Võ, and K. Scott Wong, 18–20. New York University Press, 2015.

Shi, Shumei. *Visuality and Identity: Sinophone Articulations Across the Pacific*. University of California Press, 2007.

Shields, David. *Reality Hunger: A Manifesto*. Alfred A. Knopf, 2010.

Silva, Noenoe K. *Aloha Betrayed: Native Hawaiian Resistance to American Colonialism*. Duke University Press, 2004.

Sim, Amy S. C. "The Sexual Economy of Desire: Girlfriends, Boyfriends and Babies Among Indonesian Women Migrants in Hong Kong." Research Programme Consortium on Women's Empowerment in Muslim Contexts, UK Aid, 2009. https://assets.publishing.service.gov.uk/media/57a08b7240f0b652dd000ca6/Sim_Sexual_Economy_of_Desire.pdf.

Singh, Nikhil Pal. *Race and America's Long War*. University of California Press, 2017.

Sit, Tsui, and Tak Hing Wong. "Rural China: From Modernization to Reconstruction." *Asian Studies: Journal of Critical Perspectives on Asia* 49, no. 1 (2013): 43–68.

Smilges, J. Logan. *Crip Negativity*. University of Minnesota Press, 2023.

So, Richard Jean. *Redlining Culture: A Data History of Racial Inequality and Postwar Fiction*. Columbia University Press, 2020.

Sochan, Dan. "Interview: *Sleeping Dogs*' Dan Sochan, Producer at United Front Games." Interview by Colm Ahern. *God Is a Geek*, July 10, 2012. http://www.godisageek.com/2012/07/interview-sleeping-dogs-dan-sochan-producer-united-front-games/.

Spillers, Hortense J. "Mama's Baby, Papa's Maybe: An American Grammar Book." *Diacritics* 17, no. 2 (1987): 65–81.

Square Enix. *Sleeping Dogs*. Square Enix, 2012.

Stockett, Kathryn. *The Help*. Penguin, 2009.

Stretten, Amy. "Beautiful Brown Women of Today's Burlesque." *Splinter News*, October 2013. https://splinternews.com/beautiful-brown-women-of-todays-burlesque-1793839846.

Sullivan, Louis Robert. *Racial Types in the Philippine Islands.* Anthropological Papers in the American Museum of Natural History, 21. American Museum of Natural History, 1919.

Sullivan, Steve. *Va Va Voom! Bombshells, Pin-Ups, Sexpots and Glamour Girls.* General Publishing Group, 1995.

Suzuki, Yu, Sega Enterprises, and Microsoft Corporation. *Shenmue.* Sega, 1999.

Suzuki, Yu, Sega Enterprises, and Microsoft Corporation. *Shenmue II.* Sega, 2002.

Tadiar, Neferti X. M. "Challenges for Cultural Studies Under the Rule of Global War." In *Filipino Studies: Palimpsests of Nation and Diaspora,* edited by Martin F. Manalansan and Augusto Fauni Espiritu, 15–32. New York University Press, 2016.

Tadiar, Neferti X. M. "Himala (Miracle): The Heretical Potential of Nora Aunor's Star Power." *Signs: Journal of Women in Culture and Society* 23, no. 3 (2002): 703–41.

Tadiar, Neferti X. M. *Remaindered Life.* Duke University Press, 2022.

Táíwò, Olúfẹ́mi O. "Being-in-the-Room Privilege: Elite Capture and Epistemic Deference." *Philosopher* 108, no. 4 (2020): 61–70.

Táíwò, Olúfẹ́mi O. "Olúfẹ́mi Táíwò: 'Oppression Is Not a Prep School.'" Interview by Daniel Denvir. *Jacobin,* August 25, 2022. https://jacobin.com/2022/08/deference -standpoint-epistemology-activism-identity.

Tan, Amy. *The Joy Luck Club.* G. P. Putnam's Sons, 1989.

Tan, Charles, and Mia Tijam, eds. *The Philippine Speculative Fiction Sampler.* Accessed February 12, 2024. https://philippinespeculativefiction.com.

Taylor, Diana. *The Archive and the Repertoire: Performing Cultural Memory in the Americas.* Duke University Press, 2003.

Teaiwa, Teresia K. "bikinis and other s/pacific n/oceans." *Contemporary Pacific* 6, no. 1 (1994): 87–109.

Teodoro, Luis V., ed. *Out of This Struggle.* University of Hawaiʻi Press, 2019.

Thammavongsa, Souvankham. *Cluster.* McClelland and Stewart, 2019.

Theroux, Paul. *Kowloon Tong: A Novel.* Mariner Books, 1997.

Thomas, Megan C. "Isabelo de Los Reyes and the Philippine Contemporaries of La Solidaridad." *Philippine Studies* 54, no. 3 (2006): 381–411. http://www.jstor.org/stable /42633878.

Tizon, Alex. "My Family's Slave." *Atlantic,* June 2017. https://www.theatlantic.com /magazine/archive/2017/06/lolas-story/524490/.

Trask, Haunani-Kay. "Settlers of Color and 'Immigrant' Hegemony: 'Locals' in Hawaiʻi." *Amerasia Journal* 26, no. 2 (2000): 1–24.

Troeung, Y-Dang. "Between Forced Confession and Ethnic Autobiography." In *Research Methodologies for Auto/biography Studies,* edited by Kate Douglas and Ashley Barnwell, 220–27. Routledge, 2019.

Troeung, Y-Dang. *Landbridge [life in fragments].* Knopf Canada, 2023.

Tsing, Anna Lowenhaupt. "Nine Provocations for the Study of Domestication." In *Domestication Gone Wild: Politics and Practices of Multispecies Relations,* edited by Heather Anne Swanson, Marianne Elisabeth Lien, and Gro B. Ween, 231–51. Duke University Press, 2018.

Tu, Thuy Linh Nguyen. *Experiments in Skin: Race and Beauty in the Shadows of Vietnam.* Duke University Press, 2021.

TV Tropes. "Instant Book Deal." May 4, 2019. https://tvtropes.org/pmwiki/pmwiki.php/Main/InstantBookDeal.

UNLV Media Relations, "U.S. News & World Report: UNLV Most Diverse Campus in the Nation." University of Nevada, Las Vegas, News Center, September 12, 2017. https://www.unlv.edu/news/release/us-news-world-report-unlv-most-diverse-campus-nation.

US Census Bureau. "Las Vegas City, Nevada." QuickFacts, July 2022. https://www.census.gov/quickfacts/lasvegascitynevada.

Vancouver Art Gallery. "Scott Eaton." *The Imitation Game: Visual Culture in the Age of Artificial Intelligence*, 2022. https://imitationgameexhibition.ca/Scott-Eaton.

Vang, Ma. *History on the Run: Secrecy, Fugitivity, and Hmong Refugee Epistemologies*. Duke University Press, 2020.

Villarama, Baby Ruth, dir. *Sunday Beauty Queen*. Voyage Studios, 2016.

Vuong, Ocean. "A Letter to My Mother That She Will Never Read." *New Yorker*, May 13, 2017. https://www.newyorker.com/culture/personal-history/a-letter-to-my-mother-that-she-will-never-read.

Vuong, Ocean. *On Earth We're Briefly Gorgeous: A Novel*. Penguin, 2019.

Wang, Georgette, and Emilie Yueh-yu Yeh. "Globalization and Hybridization in Cultural Products: The Cases of *Mulan* and *Crouching Tiger, Hidden Dragon*." *International Journal of Cultural Studies* 8, no. 1 (2005): 175–93.

Wang, Wayne, dir. *Chinese Box*. Trimark Home Video, 1998.

Wang Xiaoming. "A Manifesto for Cultural Studies." In *One China, Many Paths*, edited by Chaohua Wang, 274–91. Verso, 2003.

Ward, Jesmyn. *Men We Reaped: A Memoir*. Bloomsbury, 2013.

Ward, Jesmyn. *Salvage the Bones*. Bloomsbury, 2011.

Watkins, James. "Genghis Khan—the Father of Globalization?" *OZY*, November 29, 2016. Accessed May 4, 2023. https://www.ozy.com/true-and-stories/genghis-khan-the-father-of-globalization/71997/.

Weatherford, Jack. *Genghis Khan and the Making of the Modern World*. Three Rivers, 2012.

Weatherford, Jack. *Genghis Khan and the Quest for God: How the World's Greatest Conqueror Gave Us Religious Freedom*. Viking, 2016.

Weatherford, Jack. "Jack Weatherford Says Genghis Khan Wouldn't Have Made the Mistakes We've Made in the Middle East." *History News Network*, October 10, 2016. https://www.historynewsnetwork.org/article/jack-weatherford-says-genghis-khan-wouldnt-have-ma.

Weatherford, Jack. *The Secret History of the Mongol Queens: How the Daughters of Genghis Khan Rescued His Empire*. Crown, 2010.

Weheliye, Alexander G. *Habeas Viscus: Racializing Assemblages, Biopolitics, and Black Feminist Theories of the Human*. Duke University Press, 2014.

Weil, Simone. *Selected Essays, 1934–1943*. Wipf and Stock, 2015.

Weinbaum, Alys Eve. *Wayward Reproductions: Genealogies of Race and Nation in Transatlantic Modern Thought*. Duke University Press, 2004.

West, Cornel. "Ta-Nehisi Coates Is the Neoliberal Face of the Black Freedom Struggle." *Guardian*, December 17, 2017. https://www.theguardian.com/commentisfree/2017/dec/17/ta-nehisi-coates-neoliberal-black-struggle-cornel-west.

Willcox, Gloria. "The Feeling Wheel: A Tool for Expanding Awareness of Emotions and Increasing Spontaneity and Intimacy." *Transactional Analysis Journal* 12, no. 4 (1982): 274–76.

Winchester, Simon. "Empire of Tolerance." *New York Times Book Review*, December 9, 2016. https://www.nytimes.com/2016/12/09/books/review/genghis-khan-quest-for-god-jack-weatherford.html.

Wink, Andre. "Post-Nomadic Empires: From the Mongols to the Mughals." In *Tributary Empires in Global History*, edited by Peter F. Bang and Christopher A. Bayly, 120–31. Palgrave Macmillan, 2011.

Winkelmann, Tessa. *Dangerous Intercourse: Gender and Interracial Relations in the American Colonial Philippines, 1898–1946*. Cornell University Press, 2023.

Wolfe, Patrick. *Traces of History: Elementary Structures of Race*. Verso, 2016.

Wong, Ali. *Ali Wong: Baby Cobra* (stand-up special). Directed by Jaime Eliezer Karas. Netflix, 2016.

Wong, Danielle. "Inorganic Asian North American Lives: Virtual Dismemberments, Copies and Wellbeing." PhD diss., McMaster University, 2017.

Wong, Erebus, Lau Kin Chi, Sit Tsui, and Wen Tiejun. "One Belt, One Road." *Monthly Review*, January 1, 2017. https://monthlyreview.org/2017/01/01/one-belt-one-road/.

Wong, Kevin. "What *Sleeping Dogs* Gets So Right About Being an Asian American." *Kotaku*, October 10, 2014. http://kotaku.com/what-sleeping-dogs-gets-so-right-about-being-an-asian-a-1644011008.

Wong, Lily. *Transpacific Attachments: Sex Work, Media Networks, and Affective Histories of Chineseness*. Columbia University Press, 2018.

Woolf, Virginia. *Orlando: A Biography*. Harcourt, Brace, 1928.

Woolf, Virginia. *A Room of One's Own and Three Guineas*. Oxford University Press, 2015.

Wu, Yuwen. "Tea? Reining in Dissent the Chinese Way." *BBC News*, January 17, 2013. https://www.bbc.com/news/world-asia-china-21027416.

Wynter, Sylvia, and Greg Thomas. "ProudFlesh Inter/Views Sylvia Wynter." *Proud Flesh: A New Afrikan Journal of Culture, Politics and Consciousness*, no. 4 (2006): 1–36.

Xenos, Peter. "The Ilocos Coast Since 1800: Population Pressure, the Ilocano Diaspora and Multiphasic Response." In *Population and History: The Demographic Origins of the Modern Philippines*, edited by Daniel F. Doeppers and Peter Xenos, 39–70. University of Wisconsin Press, 1998.

Yao, Xine. "Black-Asian Counterintimacies: Reading Sui Sin Far in Jamaica." *J19: The Journal of Nineteenth-Century Americanists* 6, no. 1 (2018): 197–204.

Yapp, Hentyle. *Minor China: Method, Materialisms, and the Aesthetic*. Duke University Press, 2021.

Yeung, Jessie, and Xyza Cruz Bacani. "When Love Is Not Enough." *CNN*, November 2020. https://www.cnn.com/interactive/2020/11/asia/hong-kong-filipino-helpers-dst/.

Zalloua, Zahi Anbra. *Continental Philosophy and the Palestinian Question: Beyond the Jew and the Greek*. Bloomsbury, 2017.

Zeiler, Thomas W. "Basepaths to Empire: Race and the Spalding World Baseball Tour." *Journal of the Gilded Age and Progressive Era* 6, no. 2 (2007): 179–207.

Zhang, Ge. "The Stroller in the City: Spatial Practice of Hong Kong Players in *Sleeping Dogs*." *Game*, no. 3 (2014): 23–36.

Zimanyi, Eszter. "*Human Flow*: Thinking with and Through Ai Weiwei's Defamiliarizing Gaze." *Visual Anthropology* 32, no. 3–4 (2019): 377–79.

Index

belonging, 4, 7–8, 10, 25; imperial, 40–41; national, 8, 22, 75, 93, 99, 133

Benedicto, Bobby, 129

Bennett, Eric, 204

bikini, 138–39

Bikini Atoll, 138

Binalonan, Philippines, 80

Black Death, 50, 55

Black Lives Matter movement, 209

Black mammy genre, 108–10

Blackness, 6–11

Black Power, 12

Blanco, Jody, 80

Blumenbach, Johann Friedrich, 2, 45, 46

Blumentritt, Ferdinand, 82

body, brown: brown embodiment, xiii, xvi, 4–5, 15, 24; "brown jouissance," 23–24; empire imprinted on, 120; race as fantasies of, 45

bodymind, colonial, 15, 24

Bonifacio, Andres, 70

Borderlands (Anzaldúa), 199

borders and borderlands, 6, 15, 22, 48, 141–42, 172, 217

Bowers, Joanna, 124, 125

British colonialism, 1–2, 12, 65, 122, 160, 163, 169–73; and 1851 fire in Sheung Wan, 178; social engineering of Chineseness, 170–71. *See also* Hong Kong

Britton, Dennis Austin, 44

Broken Earth series (Jemisin), 204

Brown, Adrienne Maree, 211

"Brown" (Guzmán), 13

brown craft, xviii, 209–13; and brown power, 200, 211–12, 218–23, 231; brown works seen as response to exceptional crisis, xix–xx, 198–99, 201; "creative brown triptych," 211–13; crossing genres, 220–21; domestication of, 208; evasion of imperial domestication, 202; flexible writing styles, 218; and forms of imperial complicity, 221–23; forms of survival, 149, 201–2, 207; repertoires, 212; romanticizations of brown creativity, 199–200; and shades of brown, 201–2, 215–16, 225, 229–30, 237, 239–40. *See also* craft

Brown Heritage: Essays on Philippine Cultural Tradition and Literature, 3

brown mass, xviii, 14–20, 103, 120; domestication of, 21–26; future of, 21–23; images of, 15–20, *18, 19, 21,* 31; as infrastructure, 14–15; large-scale tactics in response to, 17, 26; as outside history, 20; as political force, 148; queerness of, 130, 142–43; spectacle of statistics, 15–16; as uncontainable threat, 15, 112; as untraceable, 25. *See also* Chinese brownness; wildness

brown mass / domesticating brown \ shades of brown, as term, 14, 31

brown movement, xv–xvi, 191, 216–18; and brown theory, 11, 32, 47, 148–51, 191, 223, 236; and history of Mongols, 37, 42–44; motility, xviii, 77–78, 104; movement of brown movements, 223; and multiple names for author, 217; spiral, xx–xxi, 31, 75, 121, 150, 243–44; in talk-story, 76–78, 93; toward acts of creative expression, 201; transpacific, 5–6, 78

brownness: as already the way of the world, 30, 237; associated with "free" contract/indentured labor, 73, 89, 163–64; as being-in-process, 22, 32; within colonial gaze, 1–2; as "commons," 27, 30; cross-racial (Indian/Chinese) form of, 163; "ethno-visual" marker of, 2; as hybrid racial form, 9–10; in-betweenness of, 3, 78; as interactive praxis, 77; and local identity, xiii, 28–29, 108; as means of inclusion into whiteness, xix, 3, 13; as means of revealing racial relations, 76; and Mongol conquest, 42–44, 47; mycelial threads of, 243; of non-Mongolian Asians, 41; overlap with yellowness, 161–62, 191; peoples who cannot be conquered, 6, 61; as possibilities, 76; racialization of *Hakka,* 163; as racialized labor category, 2, 4; as recursive, 23, 245; as "rising up" to contrast with yellowness, 45; "sense of brown," 5, 21, 120, 130, 236; sexuality negotiated through, 144–45; shaped by colonial encounter, 4, 10, 12, 161, 172; as site for domestication, 3, 6, 7, 61; as term of endearment, 11; tragic figure of in Maria Clara figure, 147–48; transpacific geographies of, 3, 6–13; universalization of, 3–4, 6; Vietnamese, 12–13. *See also* Chinese brownness; shades of brown; slippery formations of brownness

"brown peril," 2

brown power, 200, 211–12, 218, 222–23, 231

Brown Power and Brown Berets movements, 12
brown sugar, as term, 145
brown theory, 28, 121; as antitheory and autotheory, 32; autotheory, 32, 113–14, 151, 239;
and caring, 238; and gaze of the author(ity),
32; of Hong Kong, 179; movement of, 11, 32,
47, 148–51, 191, 223, 236; narratives, brown
contexts of, 75; *Out of This Struggle* as, 70;
personal as theoretical, 239; queer theorists
of color, 27; shades of brown in, 30–32;
"theory of the flesh," 239. *See also* "Crossing
the Caucasus" (Patterson); triptych, brown
"Brown Theory: A Storied Articulation of
Ideas" (Patterson), 223–30
Bulosan, Carlos, 80, 83
burlesque, 142–48; brownness as erotic code,
143–44, *144*; shame addressed through,
146–47. *See also* Las Vegas
Burlesque Hall of Fame Museum (Las Vegas
Arts District), 143–45
Burlesque West (Ross), 143

Cacho, Lisa Marie, 27
Campomanes, Oscar, 120
Canaan, Andrea, 4–5, 148, 207
capitalism, 43, 56; East India companies said
to be origin of, 62–63; free-market, Mongol
Empire compared to, 39, 40, 41, 62; global,
167, 171. *See also* racial capitalism
care: as form of labor, 129, 139–40; healing
power, commodification of, 119
Carlin, Dan, 48
Caronan, Faye, 4
"Case for Colonialism, The" (Gilley), 48–49, 51
cease, practice of, 241–42
Central Intelligence Agency (CIA), 12, 204–5
Chakrabarty, Dipesh, 189
Cheah, Pheng, 164, 169, 183
Chen, Mel, 47, 212
Chen, Tina, xvii
Cheng, Anne Anlin, 15
Cheung, King-Kok, 73
Cheung, Maggie, 179
Chicago World's Columbian Exposition
(1893), 10, 11
Chicano movements, 12
China: borders, 59–60; brown Chinas, 158–62;
Cultural Revolution, 170, 191; economic

impact of Mongol conquest on, 56; as
emerging empire, 156; as ghastly other, 168;
"Greater China," 159, 188, 192; heavenly
mandate, 36; "internal colonialism," 188–89;
labor camps, 20; mainland imagined as
inorganic force, 164; propaganda, 40, 156;
protest and resistance on mainland, 167;
seen as space of trauma and patriarchy,
170–71; tea, being invited to (hē cha, 喝茶),
157–58; "three *T*s" policy (Tiananmen
Square, Tibet, and Taiwan), 156–57. *See also*
Hong Kong; inorganic/organic binary; Singapore; Taiwan; two Chinas, imaginary of
Chinatowns, 168, 183
Chinese Box (film), 164, 169–70, 172–77, *174*,
176, 178; global fatigue in, 177–80; transnational collaborations, 179; white savior
myth in, 175–77, *176*
Chinese brownness, xviii, 32, 163, 165; racial
imaginaries of, 160–61. *See also* Chineseness;
Hong Kong; inorganic/organic binary
Chinese Exclusion Act (1882), 79, 89, 95
Chineseness: domestication of, 168; mainland
versus Hong Kong, 171; outside of inor-
ganic/organic binary, 189; and shades of
brown, 158, 160–61, 165, 180, 185, 190; social
engineering of, 170–71. *See also* Chinese
brownness; inorganic/organic binary
chinos, 162–63, 191
Chuh, Kandice, xvii
Chun, Wendy Hui Kyong, 25, 99
cities, 168, 179; and peripheral peoples, 190; re-
designed in open-space games, 181; "sexually
progressive" and "brown," 110–11. *See also*
Hong Kong; Kowloon Walled City (Hong
Kong); Singapore
City University of Hong Kong, 165
Clark, Naomi, *227*
Clean (film), 179
Cleaves, Francis Woodman, 52
Clifford, Hugh, 1, 2, 7
Clutario, Genevieve, 115, 128
Coates, Ta-Nehisi, 229
Cold War, 49; "China-versus-the-West" myth,
167; MFA programs encouraged during,
204; New Cold War rhetoric, 165, 170, 192;
racial imaginaries, 53, 170; two Chinas rhe-
toric, 163–64, 169–70

Cole, Teju, 200

Coles, Kimberly Anne, 44

colonialism, xvii–xviii; brownness tied to logics of, 6, 7, 22; China in Africa, 58–59; colonial gaze, 1–2; covered over by bikini-clad figure, 138–39; divide-and-conquer tactics, 82, 95; educational regimes, 51, 116; historical revision of, 48–56; "internal," 188–89; violent legacies of, 243. *See also* British colonialism; Spanish colonialism; United States

color theory, 240–41

commodities, violence linked with, 222

"commons," brownness as, 27, 30

Communist Party, 156

Compact of Free Association (1986), 135–36

Compoc, Kim, 100

Confessions of the Fox (Rosenberg), 226

Congress for Cultural Freedom, 204–5

"consentacle" (Clark), *227*

Constable, Nicole, 118, 122

Contreras, Kristian, 108, 149

Cook, James, 100

"cooked" and "uncooked" peoples, 43, 54, 60–61, 168

coolie, 76, 163–64

Coráñez Bolton, Sony, 10, 15, 24, 30, 76–77, 81, 84, 162, 199

craft, 202–8; changes in notions of, 202, *203*; as collaboration, 231; lack of emphasis on social consciousness, 204–5; minimalist aesthetic, 204, 217, 219; race erased from discussions of writing, 213; ship imaginary of, 200–201, 205, 210–13, 229. *See also* brown craft; literature

Craft of Fiction, The (Lubbock), 203–4

creativity, theory of, 199

Cronenberg, David, 179

"Crossing the Caucasus" (Patterson), xviii, 35, 38, 40, 47–48, 52, 59, 63–66

Crouching Tiger, Hidden Dragon (film), 180

Crusaders, 61–62

Cruz, Conchitina, 205, 219

Cruz, Denise, 116, 147

Cuarón, Alfonso, 25

Dayuan people, 36

dazzle, 13

death: bereavement, 241; of domestication, 242–43; domestication of the dead, 239–40; large-scale, depiction of, 17–20. *See also* mourning

decay, xvi, 16, 33, 233, 240–41, 243

Delano grape strike (1965–70), 12

De Leon, Adrian, 80

Deleuze, Gilles, 13

de los Reyes, Isabelo, 81–83

diasporas, 7, 39, 74–75, 84, 123; Chinese, 156, 158–60, 170–72, 179–83; *Hakka* (客家 Kejiā), 163; video game players and developers, 182. *See also* migrants

diasporas, Filipino, 70, 76, 80, 93, 112, 116, 128. *See also* Filipina domestic workers; Ilocanos

Diaz, Josen, 112

Díaz, Junot, 205, 209, 213

disappearance, cultural politics of, 177

disgust, affect of, 16–17, 24

DNA tests, 79, 92–93, *94*

Doctor Ginger Snapz (Sydney Lewis), 146–47

documentary films: docudrama techniques in films, 177; "giving voice to the voiceless," trope of, 125–26, 127, 175; notions of "shared humanity" in, 126, 128; sedimentation of gender and racial hierarchies in, 127–29; voice-overs, 127, 129–30. *See also* films; *Helper, The* (documentary); *Sunday Beauty Queen* (documentary)

domestication: of academic work, 248–43; animality, logic of, 22–23, 36–37; of brown craft, 208; brownness as site for, 3, 6, 7, 61; in Chinese and US empires, 158–59; of Chineseness, 168; as "chosen," 29; as colonial logic, 22, 26; completion of as always deferred, 22–23, 25; of the dead, 239–40; death of, 242–43; domesticating brown, concept of, 21–26, 31, 120, 201; *domus*, as term, 26; within family narratives, 73, 109; family networks, exploitation of, 88; fear of, 241–43; historical revision as, 45; of history by imperialism, 64–66; of horses, 36–37, 60, 65; invisibility of brown labor, xiv, 110, 139; as mutual process, 37, 65; through professionalization, 231; of self-governing peoples, 168–69; as teleological framing, 72–63; tutelage of brown subjects, 24–26. *See also* domestic work; domestic workers; Filipina domestic workers; imperialism domestic work: as form of modern slavery, 117; global domestic servitude, 110; hotel work/housekeeping, 96, 131, 135, 137, 142; live-in rules, 120, 122, 126; rescue narrative of, 118–19, 121, 132; and shades of brown, 108, 109, 111, 114, 120–21, 135, 139, 145–49, 151

domestic workers: academic representations of, 32, 110–14, 117, 148–51; author/reader affective desires displaced onto, 111–12; Black housekeepers, 108–9; brown employers, 25, 108–15, 121–22, 130, 135, 140–41, 148–51; failure of research to change circumstances, 111–12; family and culture secured by, 118; as global, moralistic, and brown, 110; and global sense of brown, 115–22; heroism narrative applied to, 112, 117, 129, 132; human rights abuses directed at, 119–20; immobility of, 133–34; Micronesian, 135–40; pageantry of, 129; policing of, 116–18, 134, 142; popularity of in literature, 136–37; queering of, 122–23; as self-sacrificing, 116, 119. *See also* Filipina domestic workers; matronliness

Domestic Workers of the World Unite! (Fish), 115

Du Bois, W. E. B., 11

Dunne, John Gregory, 12

East India companies, 62–63

Eaton, Edith Maude/Sui Sin Far, 2, 31

Eaton, Scott, 16–17, *18*, *19*

Edelman, Lee, 123

Ehrenreich, Ben, 164

El folk-lore filipino (de los Reyes), 82

"emotional intelligence," 240–41

empire: Americanization process, 100–101; brown racializations, 158; Chinese, 158–59; imprinted on brown bodies, 120; race in video games, 220; recognizing reach of, 217–18; reimagining larger picture of, 41; revisionist history of, 50–56; "submit or die" mentality, 65; "without imperialism," 39. *See also* imperialism

"emplowered" (employed and empowered), 117

employers, brown, 25, 108–15, 121–22, 130, 135, 140–41, 148–51

Engelmann, Jane, *124*, 124–26

Entangled II (Eaton), 16–17, *18*, 31

Erni, John, 192

Espiritu, Evyn Lê, 75

Espiritu, Yến Lê, 12

ethnic autobiography, 209–10, 225

ethno-state narratives, 74, 192

eugenics, 11, 46

Eurasian Steppes, 36

exiles, nomads contrasted with, 78, 100

exilic sensibilities, 41, 75, 216

"Fashion in Fiction" conference, 243

fatigue, global. *See* global fatigue

fear, 239–43

feeling stamped, 211–18, 231, 239; anger processed through travel, 215–16

Fickle, Tara, 182

Fijn, Natasha, 36

Filipina domestic workers, xviii, 108–10; family reunification versus exploitation, 110; heroism attributed to, 112, 117, 129, 132; *katulong, helpers*, 131–34; matronly image converted into labor source, 115–16; in public spaces, 125; servitude as a form of religious self-sacrifice, 116, 132; as symbol of national pride, 131–32; unmaking of figure of, 112–13; work ethic attributed to, 100, 117. *See also* domestication; domestic work; domestic workers; matronliness

Filipina women: attempts to police identity of, 116–17; ideal, construction of, 115; upper-class, 131–34. *See also* Filipina domestic workers; matronliness

Filipinos: as agri-industrial proletariat, 88; as American colonial subjects, 40–41; American identity as only known option for, 101; as "brown brothers," 10–11, 12; Filipino Malayness, 7–8; mass exportation of to United States, 116; redefined by de los Reyes, 82; as still-in-process identity, 79. *See also* Hawai'i; Ilocanos

Filipinos in Hawai'i (Gonzalves and Labrador), 99

films, xviii, xix, 25, 39, 132; critical of the PRC, 179; "manic pixie dream girl" figure, 173–74; stereotypical or inaccurate traditional practices in, 180. See also *Chinese Box* (film); documentary films; *Helper, The* (documentary); *Sunday Beauty Queen* (documentary)

Fish, Jennifer, 115

China, 169; "coolie labor," racializations of, 163; diasporic same-sex communities in, 123; domesticated brownness of, 179; domestic worker organizing in, 125–26; feminized role of, 168, 173; Filipina domestic workers in, 122–30; Fishball Revolution (2016), 170, 219; fluctuation within the inorganic/organic binary, 164–65; global fatigue of, 165, 177–80, 185; "hegemonic model of family solidarity," 192; Kowloon Walled City, 186, 187, 190; kung fu and police film traditions, 182; "manic pixie dream girl" figure, 173–74; percentage of foreign domestic workers in, 122; prejudice toward domestic workers in, 128; protests against Beijing-installed government (2019), 164, 219; Queen's Road, 177–78, 178; "slow integration" of into the PRC, 192; social realist representation of, 184; as space of collapse, 185; as special administration region (SAR), 169; as subempire of America and Britain, 168, 170, 191; Umbrella Movement (2014), 166–67, 192, 219. See also British colonialism

Hong Kong Extradition Bill (2019), 167

Hong Kong Human Rights and Democracy Act (HKHRDA), 166–67

Honolulu, 110, 118, 135–40

horse, domestication of, 36–37, 60, 65

Huang, Betsy, 209

Huang, Eddie, 170

Hulagu (Genghis Khan's grandson), 57

Human Flow (Ai), 20, 21

humanitarian racial imaginaries, 117–18, 127–30, 136

Humanity (Fall of the Damned) (Eaton), 16–17, 19, 31

Human Rights Watch, 117

human trafficking, legal, 88

Hurston, Zora Neale, 11

husbandry, 23

Hwang, David Henry, 179

hybridity, romanticization of, 199–200

hybrid racial form, brownness as, 9–10

Igorot peoples, 78, 81, 100

Ilocanos, 32, 69, 75; brought to Hawai'i as semipermanent workers, 88–89, 102; diasporic identity, 93; economic impoverish-

ment of in Philippines, 80–81, 84, 87; inconsistently racialized, 98–99; Indigenous solidarities with, 70, 100; as "people of the bay," 78, 81; ratio of men to women in Hawai'i, 90; relations with Indigenous peoples, 100–101; as sakadas, 32, 78, 83. See also Filipinos

Ilocos Norte, 75, 92, 95

Ilo Ilo (film), 24, 132

ilustrados (educated leaders), 8–9, 78, 81

images of brownness, 15–20, 31; individualization of, 17, 20; refugee camps, 20, 21; trypophobic, 16–17, 20

imaginaries, brown, xvi–xvii; spatial, 169, 181, 185–86; spiral, xx–xxi, 31, 75, 121, 150, 243–44. See also racial imaginaries

imagination, 211–12

immigration: ancestral migrancy reinscribed as immigrant labor, 99–100; "captive-worker model of," 89; documentation of, 76; hardworking immigrant narrative, 90; immigrant, as term, 22, 76. See also migrants

imperialism: administration of colonized subjects, 54, 56; brown complicity with, 221–23; brownness in design of, 2; collaborators, 31–32; domestication of history by, 64–66; Mongol Empire used to justify, 49, 56; pluralist governmentality, 3–4, 6; subterranean nature of empire, 30; tolerance as pragmatic, 56–58; universalization, 4, 27, 185, 208; video games as products of, 220, 222. See also domestication; empire

inclusion, xix, 3, 13, 79, 125, 217

Indigenous peoples: Australia, 22; Ilocanos, solidarity with, 70, 100; "the Indian" entangled with wildness, 73; Southern Paiute-Shoshone, 141

individualization: and domestication, 24–26; of images of brownness, 17, 20

infrasociality, 76

"inner wars" and "outer wars," 22

inorganic/organic binary, xviii, 46, 161–62; after 1997 handover of Hong Kong, 164, 171, 177; China as space of purity and national heritage, 164, 167, 169; Chineseness as outside of, 189; divergent social reproductions, 171; false sense of security created by, 193; in films, 169–80; Hanicization of

inorganic/organic binary (*continued*)
mainland as totalizing, 191–92; Hong Kong
as organic, 164, 167–69; and masculinity,
168, 180–83; organic as burdened by excess,
167–68; organic Chineseness in *Sleeping
Dogs*, 181–84; self-governance versus state
governance, 168–69; yellow peril and orientalism reproduced by, 164, 180. See also
Shenmue II (video game)
inspiration, sources of, 223–24, 229–31,
236
In the Country (Alvar), 131–35
Ip, Regina, 128
Iraq: Mongol invasion of, 57, 62; US invasion
of 2003, 62, 65
Irons, Jeremy, 172, 179
Islam, 49, 57, 61, 65
Itneg people, 70

Jacobo, Mylyn, 128–29
Jamaica, 163
Jameson, Fredric, 205, 208
Japan, 2, 39; in *Shenmue*, 186, 189–90
Japanese migrants to Hawai'i, 87–89, 94
Jemisin, N. K., 204
Jung, Moon-Ho, 163
Junio, Kiam Marcelo, 13
Juvaini, Ata-Malik, 64

Kahakauwila, Kristiana, 135–40
Kalaimanokaho'owaha (Kana'ina), 100
Kalākaua, Kawika, King, 9–10, 100
Kalaw, Teodoro, 84
Kānaka Maoli (Hawaiian natives), 9, 28, 89,
100, 108
Kang, Laura, 112, 113
Kant, Immanuel, 45
Kaplan, Caren, 17, 20
Kearney, Douglas, 225
Keevak, Michael, 45, 46
Khan, Paul, 52
Khwarazmian Empire, 57
Kim Phuc, 17
Kingston, Maxine Hong, 73, 170, 209
Kondo, Dorinne, 211
Kowloon Tong (Theroux), 171–72
Kowloon Walled City (Hong Kong), 186,
187, 190

Ku, Ryanson Alessandro, 30
Kublai Khan, 60
Kuleana Act (Hawai'i, 1850), 87
Kurdi, Alan, 17

labor: affective, 24, 115, 118–20; care as form
of, 120, 139–40; conditional hospitality of
host country, 99; contract laws, 89, 102;
debt servitude, 88–89, 136; "free" contract
labor (indentured), 73, 89, 163–64; historical domestication of, 99–100; intimate
surplus labor, 118; laborer, as term, 99;
"life-times," extraction of, 120; Philippines
as "labor brokerage state," 87–88, 116–17,
132, 135; plantation agriculture, 78, 80–81,
87, 93, *98*, 100. See also domestic workers;
Filipina domestic workers
labor organizing, 88, 90, 94–95; Hanapepe
Massacre (1924), 95
Labrador, Roderick, 77, 88, 99
Lai, Fancisca Yuenki, 123
Landbridge [life in fragments] (Troeung), xxi,
148–49, 244; as "family memoir," 226
language, 76; encounter with voice, 130.
See also talk-story
Lapu Lapu, 100
La Solidaridad, 82
Las Vegas, 110, 118, 141–48; as borderland,
141–42; Burlesque Hall of Fame Museum,
143–45. *See also* burlesque
Law, Wing Sang, 169
Lee, Bruce, 170
"Letter to My Daughter" (Contreras), 108, 149
Lewis, Bernard, 50, 62
Lewis, Sinclair, 203
Lewis, Sydney, 145, 146
Li, Gong, 179
Lim, Eng-Beng, 2, 27
Lim, Shirley Geok-lin, 230
Lim, Song Hwee, 179–80
Linnaeus, Carl, 45, 46
literary industry: interns, 207; power dynam-
ics of, 202, 205; #publishingsowhite,
206, 210; small and independent presses,
207, 215, 219, 224; stamps, marginalized
writers as, 217; white racial demograph-
ics of, 205–7, *206*. See also literature;
scholarship

literature, 131–40; "autobiographic imperative" for Asian American writers, 209–10; CIA programs, 204–5; "cultural wars" or "canon wars," 206; English as colonial remnant of MFA workshop, 219; of exposure, desire for, 202–3, 208; first-person plural in, 132–34, 137–39, 150; "The Literature of White Liberalism," 209; memoir, 209–10, 225–26; multiple writings within same journey, 220–22, 229–30; "Program Era," 203–4; so-called ethnic literature turn, 205–7; universal aesthetics, 202, 204, 208, 209, 216, 219. *See also* craft; literary industry; master of fine arts (MFA) programs; scholarship; *specific stories and novels*

Little Egypt (dancer), 145

Liu, Ken, 218

Liu, Yi-hung, 205

Lo, Kwai-Cheung, 168, 170, 181

local identity, xiii, 28–29, 108

London, Jack, 2

Lorde, Audre, 212, 215

loss, feeling of, 102

love, 221–22, 239; "amore" of the amateur, 238; "racist," 11, 25, 43–44

Lubbock, Percy, 203–4

Luis, Diego Javier, 163

Luzon, Philippines, 81

Mabalon, Dawn, 116

Madame Butterfly (Puccini), 175

"Madonna/Whore" binary, 119

Magellan, Ferdinand, 100

Maid, The (film), 132

Malayness, 6–13; as anticolonial racial form, 8–9, 10; as not categorizable, 7–8; US colonial constructions of, 10–11

Manalansan, Martin, 129

Manama, Bahrain, 131

Manila Carnival Queen contests, 128

Marco Polo (Netflix show), 39

Marcos, Ferdinand, 96

Marcos, Imelda, 129

marginalization, 29–31; attributed to Mongols, 53, 63; of authors, 224–25; suffering presumed inherent for creativity, 198–99, 201–2

Maria Clara figure and gown, 146–48, *147*

Marshall Islands, 138

masculinity, 37, 172–73, 177, 204; China and "excess," 180–81; of diasporic Chinese martial artist, 168, 182–83; and inorganic/organic binary, 168, 180–83; nonthreatening forms of, 168; organic Chinese, 182–83

master of fine arts (MFA) programs, xviii, 208, 218; during Cold War, 204, 218; English as colonial remnant, 219; race erased from discussions, 213. *See also* literature; scholarship

matronliness, 115–20; challenges to, 133, 139–40; as collectivity, 139; as moral elderliness, 110; performance of, 127; reinforced through laws and social gazes, 119–20. *See also* domestic workers; Filipina domestic workers; Filipina women

Mauna Kea Observatories, 100

M. Butterfly (film), 179

McGurl, Mark, 203, 204, 208

Meiners, Christoph, 46

Melamed, Jodi, 27

memoir, 209–10, 225–26. See also *Nimrods: a fake-punk self-hurt anti-memoir* (Kawika Guillermo)

Men We Reaped (Ward), 210

Merv, Mongol conquest of, 64

Mesopotamian campaign (1914–19), 65

mestizaje, 8, 24, 79, 81

Mexican-American War, 141

"MFA vs. POC" (Díaz), 209

Micronesia, 108; domestic workers from, 135–40; men in US military service, 136; US nuclear testing in, 138–39

Middle Ages, 36

migrants: ancestral migrancy reinscribed as immigrant labor, 99–100; as "arrivals," 77; "at risk," 117; brown female affective laborer, 24; Chinese, 87, 89; Japanese, 87, 88, 89; male, lack of representation of, 136; migrant as term, 22; migration as motility, xviii, 77–78; precarious, 89; as term, 76. *See also* diasporas; immigration

Migrant Workers and Overseas Filipinos Act of 1995, 132

Miss Di' Lovely, 145–47, *147*

Mongol (film), 39

Mongol Empire, xviii, 31–32, 161; administration of colonized subjects, 54, 56; American academic writings on, 38–41, 44–45, 47–51; Battle of the Indus River (1221), 60; conquest seen as dual act of racial justice, 43; "cooked" and "uncooked" peoples, 43, 54, 60–61, 168; economic development arrested by, 55–56; free trade logic applied to, 38, 40, 54, 55, 62; Georgia, 1222 BCE, 42; historicized as multicultural, 43, 53, 56–57, 62, 73; imperialism justified by, 49; marginalization attributed to, 53, 63; massacre and tolerance as part of pragmatic strategy, 56–57; modern parallels to, 37, 65; neoliberal logic in characterizations of, 50, 53–55, 62, 73; Pax Mongolica, 38; protoglobalization narrative, 55; and "racist love," 43–44; revisionist views of, 38–44, 48–56; social justice narrative applied to, 54–55, 63; South and Southeast Asian resistance to, 59–61, 65; tolerance attributed to, 38, 40, 41, 44, 45, 49, 56–57. *See also* Genghis Khan

Mongolia, revisionings within, 39, 49–50

Mongolian horse (or Takhi), 36–37

Mongoloid stereotype, 43, 46–47, 53

Mongols, The (Morgan), 42

moral economies, 110–12

Morefield, Jeanne, 39

moreno (brown), 10, 78

Morgan, David, 42, 50, 56, 57

Morrison, Toni, 205–6, 211

Mount & Blade II: Bannerlord (video game), 39

mourning, xx, 17–20, 103, 139–40, 202, 241–43. *See also* death

movement: craft as about, 200–201, 205, 210–13, 229; of historical imagination, 39; "history on the run," 74; inconsistencies of migratory, 76; motility, xviii, 77–78, 104; of movements, 223; through erotic imaginaries of colonial violence, 146; travel in Asia, 214

Mulan (film), 43, 180

multiculturalist racial order, 5, 15, 23, 118

Muñoz, José Esteban, 6, 14, 27, 123; on queer possibility, 111; "sense of brown," 5, 21, 236; shame, view of, 29, 30

Musser, Amber, 23

Myadar, Orhon, 39

Myanmar, 60

"My Family's Slave" (Tizon), 109–10

"My Perceptions of the Plantation Experience" (Agsalud), 69

Nadal, Paul, 205

Nakamura, Lisa, 25, 99

Nanjing, China, 40; anti-Black/anti-African riots, 156

Nation, 164

National Memorial Cemetery of the Pacific (Honolulu), 97

nation-state, 7, 22, 26, 74–77

neoliberalism, 72; in characterizations of Mongol Empire, 50, 53–55, 62, 73; free trade logic applied to Mongol Empire, 38, 40, 54, 55, 62; responsible subject of, 117–18

New Books in Asian American Studies podcast, 158

New York Institute of Technology (Nanjing), 40, 156, 158

Nguyen, Mimi Thi, 243

Nguyen, Viet Thanh, 203, 205

Nimrods: a fake-punk self-hurt anti-memoir (Kawika Guillermo), xix, 199, 201, 223–30, *227*, 239; "Envoi" section, 226–27, *228*

Nishapur, 53

Noli Me Tángere (Rizal), 82, 146

nomadism, 7, 78, 100; *Hakka* (客家 Kejiā), 163; sakadas, 32, 78, 83

nomads and exiles, binary of, 78, 100

nostalgia, 73, 170, 183

Not-So-Hidden Histories: Performers of Color in Burlesque exhibition, 143–45

nuclear testing in Pacific, 138–39

Nyong'o, Tavia, 37

Oates, Joyce Carol, 208

Occupy movements, 167

Oceania, 2–4, 22. *See also* Hawai'i; Malayness

Ogedei (son of Genghis Khan), 65

Oken, Lorenz, 46

On Earth We're Briefly Gorgeous (Vuong), 198, 210

"On the Different Races of Man" (Kant), 45

Open World Empire: Race, Erotics, and the Global Rise of Video Games (Patterson), xix, 201, 218–23, 239

Operation Brotherhood (CIA), 12
oppressor/oppressed binary, 28
orientalism, 2, 46, 50, 122
Orlando (Woolf), 220
Orwell, George, 213, 229
"Outline of the History of Man"
(Meiners), 46
Out of This Struggle (ed. Teodoro and Ag-
salud), 69, *71*, 75, *85*, 86, *91*, *96*, *98*, 100–102;
partially written by Joshua Agsalud, 70, 93,
95, 100, 101
Ozawa v. United States, 11

Padios, Jan, 120
paranoid reading, 202, 209
Parreñas, Rhacel, 131, 133
Paseo de Iloilo traditional dance, 146–47,
147
People's Action Party (Singapore), 167
People's Republic of China (PRC), 156
Pérez, Hiram, 23
Philippines, 2, 4, 5, 6–13; American colonial project, 12; anticolonial movements
in, 95; bakla (queer) aesthetics, 119, 129;
Chinese Exclusion Act applied to, 79;
CIA-sponsored creative writing programs,
205; common origin among browned
peoples, 82; economic impoverishment of
Ilocanos, 80–81, 84, 87; Filipinos as "brown
brothers," 10–11, 12; as "labor brokerage
state," 87–88, 116–17, 132, 135; labor out-
migration encouraged by, 87–88; Maria
Clara image, 146–48; Migrant Workers
and Overseas Filipinos Act of 1995, 132;
national independence movement, 80;
nursing campaigns and matronly image,
116; pageantry and runway walking, 129;
Philippine-American War, 10, 24, 82; Philippine Independence Act, 95; Philippine
Revolution, 81, 82, 84, 101; remittances to,
87, 116, 119; tobacco exports, 80; transition from Spanish colony to US imperial
territory, 81
Phruksachart, Melissa, 209
plantation agriculture, 78, 80–81, 87, 93, *98*,
100
plasticity, 184
pleasure, 23, 221

pluralist governmentality, 3–4, 6, 14, 39–40,
216, 217
poetry, 225
Polo, Marco, 39, 60
Polynesian brownness, 9, 10
Ponce, Danilo E., 70
Ponce, Martin Joseph, 129
Popescu, Monica, 204
power: brown, 200, 211–12, 218–23, 231; imperial, enactment of onto others, 218; multiple
interlocking systems of, 73; obscured
through academic language, 242–43;
"trickle-down," 223
Pratt, Geraldine, 111–12, 114, 150
precolonial modernity, concept of, 7
presentism, 30, 45, 56
pride, 72, 73
professionalization, 231
Program Era, The (McGurl), 204, 208
protest, 221, 223; against Beijing-installed
government (2019), 164, 219; Fishball
Revolution (2016), 170, 219; multiple
genealogies of, 192; Umbrella Movement
(2014), 166–67, 192, 219; uprisings against
neoliberalism and empire, 192–93; Western
views of, 164
Protestantism, 97
Prototaxites, 243
Puar, Jasbir, 14
Puccini, Giacomo, 175
Puerto Rico, 4
Pulido, Eudocia Tomas, 109–10

Qadir, Shahid, 48
queer cultural spaces, x, 5, 26–30, 111
queerness: bakla (queer) aesthetics, 119, 129;
and brown theory, 30, 32; and burlesque,
142–48; and domestic worker community,
126–30; in *The Helper*, 123, 126; kinship of
queer resistance, 130; and publishing, 224,
226; "queer time," 123; sex work, queering
of, 119, 121–23, 129; in speculative fiction,
216, 220; in *Sunday Beauty Queen*, 126–29
queer shame, 29, 236
queer theory, 4, 27, 54, 123, 236
"Queer Theory in a Postcolonial World"
roundtable, 236
Quezon, Manuel, 84

Scott, James, 168

Secret History of the Mongols (trans. Khan and Cleaves), 52–53

Sedgwick, Eve Kosofsky, 29, 202

self-governance versus state governance, 168–69

self-indulgence, 237–39

self-making, 53–54, 133

self-oppression, 207–8

self-referencing, 211–12, 223–30, 231, 239; cross-referential verification, 229–30

Seljuk Turks, 62

Selomenio, Leo, 126, *127*

"sense of brown," 5, 21, 120, 130, 236

sexuality, brown, 23–24, 111, 139, 142; brown women's negotiation of, 144–47; challenges to matronly image, 133; colonial construction of Filipina, 115; erotic desire within imperial contexts, 221; Hong Kong victimhood contrasted with conservative mainland, 175; pathologization of brown women, 148; policed by laws in host country, 117–18, 134; protection of women from their own, 138, 142; willful woman, figure of, 137–38

sex work, 24; as affective "contribution," 118; bakla (queer) aesthetics, 119, 129; China's restrictions on, 173; in Hong Kong, 122; and improvement of class position, 133–34; in Las Vegas, 142; rescue narrative, 118–19, 121; sex tourism, 110–11

shades of brown, xvi–xviii, 5–6, 14, 26–30, 61; as axis of coalition, 28–29; and brown craft, 201–2, 215–16, 225, 229–30, 237, 239–40; in brown theory, 30–32; and Chineseness, 158, 160–61, 165, 180, 185, 190; constant reinscription of darker, 27; and domestic work, 108, 109, 111, 114, 120–21, 135, 139, 145–49, 151; in emotional advertising, 240; in hierarchies, 9–10, 25, 114, 132; and self-authorship, 239; and sexual agency, 145–47; and shame, 27–30

"Shadow Families" (Alvar), 131–37, 140

shame, brown, 27–30, 70–72, 114; and craft, 208; queer, 29; shedding through burlesque, 146–47

shards, brown, 13–14, 31, 212, 226; counterassemblage of, 121. *See also* brown mass;

domestication; shades of brown; triptych, brown

Sharma, Nitasha, 2

"shatter zones," 168

Shenmue (video game, 1999), 186

Shenmue II (video game), 164, 169–70, 181, 184–90, *188*; global fatigue in, 189–90; globality as exploitative and uneven in, 188–89; inter-Asian references in, 186; as most expensive video game ever produced, 185; as "virtual walking simulator," 184; Western players, 186

Shields, David, 210

Shinyō Maru (transport vessel), 86

"Shooting an Elephant" (Orwell), 213, 229

Sichuan earthquake (China), 20

Silang, Gabriela, 70

silences, 74–75

Silk Road, 36, 37

Sim, Amy, 123

Singapore, 132, 170, 179; People's Action Party, 167

Singh, Nikhil Pal, 22

Sit, Tsui, 188

skin color, 10, 44–46, 161–62

slavery, 62; Black replaced with "free" contract/indentured labor, 73, 89, 163; domestic work as form of, 117; modern-day domestic enslavement, 109

Sleeping Dogs (video game), 164, 170, 181–84, *182, 183*

slippery formations of brownness, xiv–xv, 3, 6, 8, 12, 13, 27, 76–77. *See also* brownness

Smilges, Logan, xvi

So, Richard, 205–7, *206*

social engineering, 167, 170–71, 192

social realist literature, 218

South Asian peoples, 2, 6; Mongol Empire, resistance to, 59–61, 65

Southern Paiute-Shoshone Indigenous peoples, 141

Spanish-American War, 2, 87

Spanish colonialism: blurring effect of galleon routes, 162–63; casta (caste) system, 163; divide-and-conquer rule, 82; Filipina sexuality constructed by, 115; Paseo de Iloilo traditional dance, 146–47, *147*

spatial imaginaries, 169, 181, 185–86

collaborations, 165, 240; on ethnic auto-biography, 210; on "family memoir," 226; scholarship in relationship, 243–44

Trump, Donald, 17, 223

trypophobic image complex, 16–17, 20

Tsing, Anna Lowenhaupt, 26

two Chinas, imaginary of, 162, 191–92; in Cold War rhetoric, 163–64, 169–70; in left discourse, 166; limitations on filmic roles, 179–80

Umbrella Movement (2014), 166–67, 192, 219

United States: American academy, rise of, 38; anti-Filipino agitation, 95; Compact of Free Association, 135–36; cross-ethnic hatreds and hierarchies emphasized by, 10–11; as "empire without imperialism," 39; expansion of anti-revolutionary capacities, 94–95; genocidal Indian Wars, 115; Hong Kong as subempire of, 168, 170, 191; imperial acquisitions, 4, 81; killings in Yemen, 223; military intrusion by, 48–49; Native Scouts and Scouts programs, 81; nuclear testing, 138–39; permanent war, 17, 49; pluralist governmentality, 6–7; sanctions against Chinese and Hong Kong officials, 166–67; transformation of Hawaiian Islands by, 87; Vietnam War, 6, 12–13, 191

universalization, 6, 118, 120; of craft-based aesthetics, 204–5; "ecliptic," 168; elided by brownness, 3–4; imperialist, 4, 27, 185, 208; of literary aesthetics, 202, 204, 208–9, 216, 219

University of the Philippines (UP) National Writers Workshop, 205

Unsung Heroes (choir of domestic workers), 124, *124*, 125

Urdaneta, Philippines, 80

value, conceptions of, 27

Vang, Ma, 74–75

Vasarely, Victor, 16

video games, xviii, xix, 39, 43; erotic playing of, 221–22; high rate of play by Asian Americans, 182; as imperial products, 220, 222; open-world, 181–84; *Shenmue II*, 164, 184–90, *188*; *Sleeping Dogs*, 164, 170, 181–84, *182*, *183*

Vietnam, 6–13, 191; militarized empire in, 12

Vietnam War, 6, 12–13, 191

Vikings, 222

Villarama, Baby Ruth, 126

violence: colonial, 10–11; commodities linked with, 222; as "necessity" for marginalized people, 53; networks of capitalist, state, and imperial, 20; revisionist histories of, 53–54; slow, domestication as, 22–23; United States, 6, 10–13

Visayans, 95

"voice," trope of, 125–26, 127, 150, 175

Vourloumis, Hypatia, xvi, 209

Vuong, Ocean, 198, 210

Waihe'e, John David, III, 101

Waipahu (Oahu Sugar Plantation town), 93

Wang, Georgette, 180

Wang, Wayne: *Chinese Box*, 164, 172–77

Wang Xiaoming, 192

Ward, Jesmyn, 210, 226

War of the Heavenly Horses, 36–37

war on terror, 5, 62, 65, 207, 223

Weatherford, Jack, 39, 50–51, 53–54, 62, 66

Weheliye, Alexander, 211

Weil, Simone, 36

Weinbaum, Alys, 24

West, Cornel, 243

whiteness: attributions of, 9–10; colonial, 4, 28; overarching standard of, 211; white liberalism, 209–10; white womanhood, sentiment toward, 25

wildness: binaries of civilized and wild, 61; of Mongolian horse (or Takhi), 36–37; racial tropes of, 3, 7, 12, 23; "running amok," 12, 73; subjects' relation to landscape on scale of, 78; used to legitimize domestication, 3, 6; of will, 37, 65. *See also* brown mass

Willcox color wheel, 240–41

"willful subjects," 137–38

Winchester, Simon, 66

Wolfe, Patrick, 22, 171

Woman Warrior, The (Kingston), 73

Wong, Ali, 61

Wong, Faye, 173

Wong, Tak Hing, 188

Woolf, Virginia, 220

Workshops of Empire (Bennett), 204

worldmaking, brown, 104, 199, 211, 239
World of Suzie Wong, The (film), 174
World War I, 94
World War II, 50, 101
"Wrath of the Khans, The," I (Carlin), 48
Wu, Emperor, 36
Wynter, Sylvia, 211

Xi Jinping, 40

Yapp, Hentyle, 20
Yeh, Emilie Yueh-yu, 180
yellowness, xviii, 6, 15, 41; as alien diasporic, 7,
    9; colonial imaginary of "depraved Orient,"
162; dualism of "yellow peril" and "model
minority," 46; inorganic, 173; overlap with
brownness, 161–62, 191; placed on cognitive
development scale, 47; of uncooked invaders, 61; yellow as imperial color, 45. *See also*
Chinese brownness; Chineseness
yellow peril discourses, 16, 189–91; and Mongol Empire, 43, 46; and organic/inorganic
binary, 164, 180
Yellow River, 45
Yemen, US killings in, 223

Zalloua, Zahi, 75–76
Zhang Yimou, 171

www.ingramcontent.com/pod-product-compliance
Lightning Source LLC
Chambersburg PA
CBHW020313290526
45785CB00007B/2781